Escape from Paradise

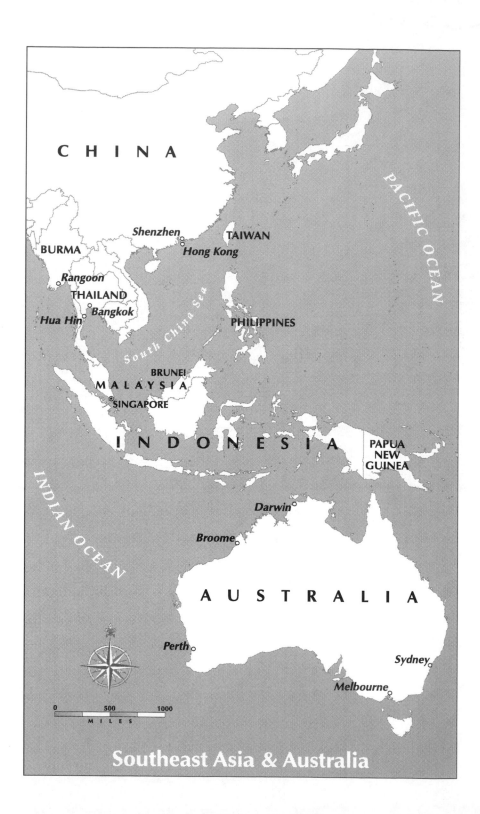

CHINA

BURMA

Shenzhen

Hong Kong

TAIWAN

Rangoon

THAILAND

Bangkok

Hua Hin

PACIFIC OCEAN

South China Sea

PHILIPPINES

BRUNEI

MALAYSIA

SINGAPORE

INDONESIA

PAPUA
NEW
GUINEA

INDIAN OCEAN

Darwin

Broome

AUSTRALIA

Perth

Sydney

Melbourne

0   500   1000

MILES

Southeast Asia & Australia

Escape from Paradise

by

John & May Chu Harding

IDKPress
#640
10645 N. Tatum Blvd., Suite 200
Phoenix, AZ 85028

www.idkpress.com

Designed by Stefano Harding

Set in Adobe Garamond Pro

Printed in the United States of America

Library of Congress Control Number: 2001091454

ISBN 0-9710929-0-7

Permissions

To my sisters-in-law, who were there as well -

Lynn Hawkins & Rosita Barlic

Contents

Authors' Note

Our thanks go to our friends, who have taken the time to read our book, and give us their advice. Mark Weiss, our lawyer, who checked the legal points, and turned out to be a master of punctuation—especially when it came to the placement of dashes. Mark's wife, Shari, provided a woman's point of view, gave suggestions on content, and helped us realize that this is largely a woman's book, even though the intrigue and political background take place in a man's world. Farley Weiss, our intellectual property lawyer, helped us through the maze of copyright law and permissions. Stefano Harding brought the photographs to life, and designed the book and its cover to his rigorous standards and elegant style. Stacey Wright of Eureka Cartography took great pains to produce a customized map of Southeast Asia and Australia to highlight the locations in the book. Finally, we are grateful to Francis Seow, the former Solicitor General of Singapore, for his invaluable advice and editorial comments.

Where important, we have converted foreign currency amounts into US Dollars. This is to avoid such frustrations as when, In Romeo and Juliet, Act V, Romeo buys his poison saying,

> *Hold, there is forty ducats: let me have*
> *A dram of poison . . .*

How much, pray tell, is "forty ducats" worth? Thirty-five cents? Fifteen bucks? The reader has a right to know, and we've done our best to oblige, even taking into account the fluctuation of currency rates over time.

SINGAPORE

S INGAPORE IS a name of a dream, an imaginary vision of the
Orient of colonial times, of leisurely lives, of verandahs, of
all the things it isn't.

There are no clouds on the horizon. Well, almost none—the CIA
claims that Singapore serves as a transit point for Golden Triangle
heroin going to the West.

Singapore is Chinese. Singapore is safe. Singapore is making money.

It's not that Singapore isn't nice. It's not a particularly interesting
or easy place, but it is nice. Singapore is slick on the surface—marble
hotel lobbies stretch sky high. It is China in paradise, with a Manhattan
skyline, where Chinese autocrats talk about preserving their core values
from the onslaught of "pseudo-Western" culture. It is materialism run
rampant—the most mercenary of environments—a Chinese dream—a
contradictory clear win for Western-style capitalism.

Today's Singapore has swept the colonialists and its history aside.
The British-favored Malays and Indians have all but disappeared. Even
the mixed-breed Eurasians—who never had much of a place—have
no place now. Singapore's population of four million is seventy-seven
percent Chinese, fourteen percent Malay, and eight percent Indian.
The remaining one percent is classified as "Others."

Located at the end of the southern tip of the Malaysian Peninsula,
less than 100 miles from the equator, Singapore is a small island, only
twenty-six miles long, and fourteen miles wide.

In 1819, with the landing of Sir Stamford Raffles on its shores,
Singapore became a ward of the British Empire. It remained so,
with the exception of the Japanese occupation from 1942 to 1945,
until England granted it self-government in 1959 with Lee Kuan
Yew becoming Prime Minister. Singapore achieved full independence
from the British by becoming a province of Malaysia in 1963. Finally,
Singapore became a sovereign nation in 1965, when it was expelled
from Malaysia over racial issues between the Malays and Chinese.

Lee Kuan Yew served as Prime Minister until 1990 and today, with the specially created position of Senior Minister, remains Singapore's undisputed ruler.

Most likely, Lee Kuan Yew will be succeeded by his number one son, Lee Hsien Loong, who retired from his position as Brigadier-General of the Singapore Armed Forces to enter politics. Lee Hsien Loong, born in 1952, was all of thirty-two years old at the time.

Singapore is moving fast. I was born there in 1957, when Singapore wasn't Singapore, the country—it was still part of Malaysia. The world I knew as a child, and as a teenager, is a long-gone distant memory.

Most Chinese arrived in Singapore as coolies during the time of British rule. They were permitted to do only the most menial of tasks and were not considered acceptable even as house servants for the British—only Indians and Malays were good enough.

Still, over time, some Singapore Chinese families grew to be wealthy—most did not.

My family arrived in Singapore by a different route. We were not coolies and did not fit any of the popular Chinese stereotypes.

We were not gloomy *Joy Luck Club* middle-class folks. We had no ancient faded family photographs of destitute peasants to gaze upon with simple pride. We were not humble. We were not obsequious. No one impressed us. No one had more than we did, or showed it off so grandly. We were flamboyant, irreverent, and loud. We came to Singapore from Burma, and arrived in style. We were already rich, very rich—we were the Tiger Balm Kings!

Our business empire grew from one simple product, an ointment called "Tiger Balm," to newspapers in Singapore, Hong Kong, Thailand, Australia, and Canada, and to banks in Singapore and Malaysia.

Our houses, the Haw Par Villa in Singapore, and the Tiger Balm Gardens in Hong Kong are now tourist attractions—free donations from our family for public pleasure and family aggrandizement.

No one had anything quite like what we had—but that was then.

IMPRISONED

IT WAS OCTOBER 1984 ...

"My husband imprisoned in Brunei?—you can't be serious!" I said to my mother-in-law, Lillian. "Hin Chew left Singapore just a couple of days ago—how can this be?"

Lillian answered in her halting English, "Everything is being taken care of, I am sure Hin Chew return shortly."

"You're lying!" I had to be out of my mind to talk to Lillian in this way. She did not answer.

"What about Jim and Lynn, they're still in Brunei, aren't they?" I said asking about Hin Chew's brother, and his brother's wife, Lynn.

"Lynn has been allowed to leave Brunei," answered Lillian.

"Will I be able to go to Brunei?"

"It's better for you to stay in Singapore. Be patient, we will see. Don't worry. There's nothing to worry about."

Lillian was unable to look me in the eye—her eyes darted all over the living room. She sat uncomfortably on the edge of her chair, not knowing whether to remain seated or to stand. This was not her way with me—after all, I was only a daughter-in-law.

"Go see Peter—he can tell you more."

"Where is, S. P.?" I asked, inquiring about my father-in-law.

Lillian managed a weak smile, "Oh not here, out of town."

Obviously, something was seriously wrong. It was not my mother-in-law's way to pay a visit to my home, especially an impromptu and unannounced visit late in the evening.

It was disturbing that she would come to my apartment, and entirely out of character for her to do so. Lillian had never been close to any of her daughters-in-law. We should go to her, not she to us. Lillian was used to summoning her daughters-in-law, not visiting them.

Still standing, I was not quite sure what to ask, and after a few minutes of fidgeting, Lillian got up to leave, "You must not telephone Hin Chew. Don't worry." With that, she left. I was not to see her again for well over a year.

"Don't worry?" I saw plenty to worry about in Lillian's voice and demeanor. I sat down, and looked around my apartment feeling totally lost. Here I was, alone in Singapore, with our two small children Marc, three, and Warren only six months old. How was I going to make it? When would my husband return? Why was he arrested? All he did was work for his father in Brunei.

It had been only nine months before that Hin Chew and I had moved back to Singapore from Brunei. The move was his father's decision and a lucky break for me, as I was Singaporean.

Brunei, for all its wealth, was a small backwater of some 200,000 souls, carved by greed from the tropical rainforest skirting the north coast of Borneo. Money poured into Brunei's coffers from its oil and natural gas resources, but there was little more to the place than that.

From the time we had moved back to Singapore, my husband, Hin Chew, S. P.'s number one son, had commuted regularly back and forth to Brunei, working to set up a Singapore office for his father, while helping out with the business in Brunei. Brunei was a short two-hour flight from Singapore, and the commute was easy. Life was easy—I was back in my hometown, into my comfort zone, and near to my parents.

Easy was coming to an end.

Jim's wife, Lynn, a resourceful strong-willed English girl, was unable to bring herself, until years later, to tell me exactly what had happened with the police in Brunei.

She and her husband, Jim, S. P.'s number two son, had been awakened during the night by a party of six plainclothesmen from the Royal Brunei Police. They were looking for Hin Chew's father, S. P. Chung. Fortunately, the wily S. P., a step ahead of the police, was safely out of Brunei.

The police searched every part of Lynn's house in Brunei, including a locked room, upstairs, where S. P. kept his "archives."

At one point, Jim, trembling with nerves, had to go to the bathroom—this he was allowed to do only with a policeman present.

After several hours of searching the house, the police left, but only after confiscating Jim's passport and informing him that he could not leave Brunei. The police carted off all the documents and papers they could find in the house.

The next morning, accompanied by a lawyer, Jim drove Lynn and their daughter, Tammy, only five months old, to the airport where he managed to get them on a flight to Singapore and freedom. Unfortunately, on that very day, Hin Chew was arriving at that same Brunei airport with no knowledge of what had happened the night before. Predictably, Hin Chew's passport was confiscated on arrival, and he too was told that he could not leave Brunei.

On reaching Singapore, Lynn went directly from the airport to the apartment of Peter, S. P.'s number three son, and his Australian wife, Rosita, an attractive brunette.

Peter was tall, slim, and the only one of S. P.'s sons able to grow a real mustache. He was considered, even by himself, to be the best looking of S. P.'s four sons.

At Peter's apartment, Lynn was surprised to find that a meeting with a third person had been arranged for her. It was someone she knew, an American named Dan Arnold.

Lynn was alarmed over the presence of this outsider, as Jim had confided to her previously that Dan Arnold was in the CIA, and that he was a business associate of the Chungs.

As though they had never met, Dan Arnold introduced himself to Lynn explaining that he was an American, and further established his credentials by saying that he was an ex-CIA employee. All this Dan Arnold conveyed in somber tones to emphasize his importance and credibility.

Lynn went along with Dan Arnold's act, pretending herself that this was their first meeting.

Dan Arnold explained to Lynn, in even tones, that everything would be all right, and that "things were being done, including the possibility of a helicopter rescue" to get her husband and Hin Chew out of Brunei.

Lynn was already unsettled by the police raid of the night before. But now, Dan Arnold, the CIA, a helicopter rescue—and why?

If Dan Arnold had been brought in to have a calming effect—it had just the opposite. Only Lynn's sense of self-preservation and fear prevented her from asking Dan Arnold any questions.

Peter and Rosita chirped in to assure Lynn that everything would be all right.

Lynn knew things were not right, being "ex-CIA" is like being "ex Mafia;" there is no "ex" about it—once you are in, you never get out.

Why would the CIA, or anyone, risk an international incident by landing a helicopter on sovereign Brunei territory to rescue the Chungs?

Why would Dan Arnold risk exposing himself to Lynn?

My take was that he did it to keep Lynn from further exposing the situation to others. Lynn was just the type to take the matter to her Member of Parliament in England, or to the tabloids to get Jim out of Brunei.

After her meeting with Dan Arnold, Lynn's plan was to return, quietly and as soon as she could, to the safety of England and her parents back home, where she would wait for Jim's safe return.

Several days after Lynn's arrival in Singapore, and Lillian's visit, Peter called to ask me over to his apartment. At that point, I had no knowledge of what had happened in Brunei, other than the arrests of Hin Chew and Jim. Still Lillian's visit was enough to unsettle me, and I was afraid—of what, I had no idea, so I decided it would be best not to go alone.

I called my long-time friend, Swee Cheong, at his office, and asked him to accompany me. Swee Cheong, always the loyal friend, and always willing to put up with my impulsive ways, and forgive my past escapades, picked me up at my apartment.

Swee Cheong and I had met years before when we were both studying law. He was taller and heavier than the average Singaporean man, quick to smile, and with a kind face. Swee Cheong had been an intelligence officer, a Captain, in the Singapore Armed Forces. Now, in his mid-forties, he had retired from the army and was pursuing business interests. He had become a good friend to my parents as well as to me. He was someone I could trust.

Peter and Rosita were waiting for us at the apartment. There was no Dan Arnold.

Peter explained to me that everything possible was being done to free Hin Chew and Jim from Brunei, and that the two captive brothers should both be returning to Singapore soon. Peter carefully avoided any mention as to why the Brunei police were after the Chungs, or what had happened—nor was there any mention of Dan Arnold or helicopters. All I knew, and all that was intended for me to know, was that there was a problem and that Hin Chew was stuck in Brunei.

I took Peter's assurances with a large grain of salt—after all, I am Asian, and had observed intrigue first hand growing up in my own family.

Rosita did not say a word during my entire visit—she dutifully kept her silence. Lynn, who was also in the apartment, appeared only briefly to give me a nod, and a quick hello, before disappearing into one of the bedrooms.

As I am Asian, I knew that my brother-in-law Peter felt he needed no "Western" stamp of approval on what I was to be told, so Dan Arnold was not present. Lynn and Rosita, my Caucasian sisters-in-law, obviously had been told more than I about what was happening. In my case, Peter had let several days pass before summoning me to his apartment to tell me absolutely nothing.

Chinese men reserve a traditional treatment for Chinese women. They don't *kowtow*, bow down, to their own as they do to Western women. It was something I knew, but didn't accept. I was Chinese because my father was Chinese and he because his father was Chinese. Only the men counted, but, if you looked at the origin of the women in my family—who didn't count—my father was part Burmese, and I had a healthy dose of Dutch from my grandmother, Dagmar Vyner. Maybe it was her genes that I had to thank for the loose cannon in me.

As Swee Cheong drove me home, I asked him what he thought about Hin Chew's incarceration. He had said barely a word at Peter's apartment. Swee Cheong, who was fifteen years older than I, was bright, but long-winded, and always careful with his words. This was due not only to his training as an intelligence officer, but it was his nature to be so. It took a lot of patience to listen to Swee Cheong.

Swee Cheong smiled. "I have no idea," he said. After a judicious pause, he continued, "You should be very careful, May Chu, and remain calm. I wouldn't discuss this with anyone. You never know."

As usual, Swee Cheong was giving me nothing. I pressed on, "Swee Cheong, what do you think the Chungs have done—what sort of trouble are they in?"

Again, there was a thoughtful pause from Swee Cheong. "You know, I have rarely spoken to any of the Chung family. I know very little about them." Swee Cheong took another pause. Finally, he spoke through a smile as Asians do when they are either embarrassed or serious. "I did speak to your father-in-law once. It was at your wedding. When I told him that I was in the military, he said that he had been a Captain in the Nationalist Chinese Army—you know, the Kuomintang."

"Swee Cheong, what does that have to do with anything?" I said. Swee Cheong could be annoying. I could easily return the favor with petulance—being petulant with Swee Cheong was a long standing habit, and a product of having known him for so long.

Swee Cheong continued as though he had heard nothing, "S. P. told me he was with the Kuomintang after the Communists had driven them from China. He was in Burma, or in the Golden Triangle Area somewhere."

"I knew S. P.'s father sent him from Brunei to some university in China, but I was never told that he was in any army," I said.

Swee Cheong smiled "Well, in the early 1950s the Kuomintang regrouped in Burma to attack the Communists from the South."

Swee Cheong seemed to be drifting into his pedantic ways—the last thing I needed, at the time, was a lesson in military history.

"Swee Cheong, what does the Kuomintang in Burma have to do with what we are talking about?"

"Nothing," smiled Swee Cheong, "but the Kuomintang financed themselves by getting into drug traffic, with the help of the CIA."

I took Swee Cheong's remark as the overactive imagination of the typical intelligence officer. I saw no connection and changed the subject. As usual, Swee Cheong seemed to have nothing to offer.

Swee Cheong dropped me off at my apartment. I was glad to be home. I needed time to think, as my head was swimming with all the news. It was time to gather my thoughts.

Aside from whatever problems existed in Brunei, there were other problems, problems at home with Hin Chew. I had to admit to myself that I was actually relieved that my husband was not coming back so soon. I felt guilty over the thought, but that's how I felt.

Thinking back, I realize that it was the most natural feeling any person in my position could have. At least Hin Chew's abuse would stop for a while. But the fear? The uncertainty? What was I going to do? My mind was racing. Maybe this could be all to the good. Maybe, when this mess was over, Hin Chew would come out of it a changed man, and we could live our lives happily. Maybe he would love and appreciate his wife and children, as a normal husband and father would.

I wondered how Lynn felt. She had the same problem with Jim. The brothers were very much alike, and she had taken a lot from Jim. Lynn and I shared some serious problems.

That very evening, I received a phone call from Rosita. She said curtly, "Come to our apartment immediately. We have something important to discuss with you, and not over the telephone. Come alone this time!"

Unlike Lynn, Rosita had never been much of a diplomat. Her parents had immigrated to Australia from Croatia when Rosita was a child, and she bore the scars of a difficult life—common to those from that part of the world.

I went immediately to Peter's apartment. It was now Rosita's turn to talk, while Peter kept silent. She was in a stern mood, "How dare you bring anyone to our apartment without our permission?"

I could feel my face redden. My immediate inclination was to tell Rosita to go to hell. I was the wife of the eldest son. Peter was only the number three son. I outranked Rosita. My family was a far more prominent family than the Chungs could ever hope to be. As for Rosita's Croatian family ... I caught myself, realizing that none of my snooty thoughts counted for anything—I was in the Chung family now, and my own position seemed very insecure. Restraining myself, I explained simply, "I was afraid. I am sorry."

Having received my admonition from Rosita, the new Queen Bee of the Chung family, there was nothing left for me to do but to leave meekly. This was not my day.

At the time, I did not understand Rosita's concern. To show up at her apartment with a friend, especially an old family friend was not unusual. I took Rosita's tirade to be her way of initiating me to the fact that she and Peter were one-up on me in the hierarchy, as my husband was, for now, defunct. This was a normal ceremony of the passing of the guard in a Chinese family. Only much later did I realize that Swee Cheong's position in military intelligence could have been the problem—had Dan Arnold been hiding behind the curtain during my first visit?

I drove straight home from Peter's apartment—glad to be alone. It was late at night, only dim streetlights, and no traffic. My thoughts were no longer on my problems with Hin Chew. My thoughts were deeper, and more selfish, but selfish in the right way. The welfare of my children was at stake. I had given up all my goals to be a wife and a mother.

From my father's family, I had learned ambition, determination, and optimism. I had also learned about power, intrigue, and money. My character had been formed in the presence of my own family's exuberance, flamboyance, and flaunting of convention. I learned both Chinese ways, and the diametrically opposed ways of the West. I learned when to choose which way to go. I was Chinese, and I was Western—it all depended what I wanted.

Unfortunately, since I was a female, my family saw no need to prepare me to make it on my own in the world. They had condemned me to be dependent on others—to cater to others—initially to my own family, and then to my husband and his family. Now it was to Peter and Rosita. How had I sunk so low? How had I reached this point? I was determined to escape from my confinement—I would do it.

This is my story.

THE TIGER BALM KINGS

MY GREAT-GRANDFATHER was a pharmacist in Rangoon, Burma. His name was Aw Boon Par, and he was Chinese. In the Chinese way, his last name, Aw, came first. Boon Par, his given name, meant "Gentle Leopard." Boon Par had an unruly elder brother, Aw Boon Haw, Boon Haw meaning "Gentle Tiger."

Boon Haw was anything but gentle. As a boy, on a dare, he reached into a tiger's cage to snatch its meat away. He was rewarded with a deep scratch, which left a scar on his shoulder for the rest of his life.

Boon Haw was sent to live for a while with relatives in China—maybe he would learn to behave.

My great-grandfather, Boon Par, was more conservative by nature. He attended an English-speaking school in Rangoon. As a result, Boon Par's side of the family became westernized, while Boon Haw and his descendants tended to be more Chinese in speech and outlook.

Boon Par was as diligent and methodical as his brother was driven and outgoing. Together, they made a perfect Mister Inside and Mister Outside, and together they parlayed a pain relieving ointment developed by Boon Par into the greatest fortune of its time in Asia. They named their product "Tiger Balm." It is still sold throughout the world in the original packaging developed by the two brothers.

Of course, their story is not as simple as that—business acumen played the lead role. When faced with lower priced competition, the brothers concocted "Deer Balm," a product that matched the competition on price but beat them on quality, since it was nothing but repackaged Tiger Balm.

When pressed for a stronger version of their white-colored Tiger Balm, the brothers simply introduced a reddish-brown coloring into the product to produce the sought after "stronger" version. Cleverly, they set the same price for both versions of Tiger Balm—leaving it for the buyer to choose. Little things like that can make a big difference.

The brothers became rich and famous. They developed flamboyant lifestyles. Nevertheless, they never lost sight of reality, and used their fame and flamboyancy to promote the family business.

Boon Haw had four wives, while the more conservative Boon Par limited himself to three. The first wives of the brothers were sisters. The brothers' wives all lived in luxury, and in harmony, if not with themselves, at least with their husbands. Our treasured family photos show the wives all posing happily together with the brothers.

Of course, there was fun on the side for the brothers; there were mistresses, but there was never, ever, a single divorce.

Barely a decade after the brothers started to manufacture and sell Tiger Balm from their mother's kitchen in Rangoon, they had already amassed a string of pharmaceutical companies stretching from Burma to Thailand, Malaysia, Singapore, the East Indies, Hong Kong and China. By the eve of the Sino-Japanese war in 1937, the Aw brothers had built a business empire with 10,000 workers toiling in the Tiger Balm factories.

The brothers originally named their company after the humble shop of their father—Eng Aun Tong, the Hall of Everlasting Peace. Each brother owned an equal share in the company. Unlike most Chinese siblings, the two brothers always lived in complete harmony, and shared their wealth equally.

The Roaring Twenties were high times for Boon Haw and Boon Par. Business was booming, profits were soaring, and cash was pouring in. The brothers were rich by any standard—of course, that's when things can begin to get interesting.

Just when everything was going so great, a squad of policemen showed up at the brothers' house to serve them with an arrest warrant. Boon Par and Boon Haw were charged with illicit trafficking in opium, and counterfeiting.

The brothers were either innocent, or way ahead of their time. Sudden wealth does raise questions, especially in Asia.

The British Chief Inspector of Police, Cyril Taylor, put the brothers under house arrest with a constable standing guard at the front door. Over the course of the next week, the brothers' house was searched several times, but Chief Inspector Taylor was unable to pin anything on the brothers.

There was also some alleged minor involvement of the brothers with the Ho Seng and Kian Teck gangs, or tongs, as they are popularly known. This involvement with the tongs also did not lead to any charges against the brothers. In Asia only fools toy with the tongs, but if you cooperate they can do a lot for your business.

How humiliating! What a devastating loss of face for the brothers to be placed under house arrest. Boon Haw decided then and there to leave Burma. He would pick up and move to Singapore. The headquarters for the Tiger Balm empire would be Singapore.

Boon Par was against the move to Singapore. He had a secret wife in Rangoon, and she did not want to move to Singapore. She was called Daw Saw.

Despite his happy life with Daw Saw and his two official wives, Boon Par suddenly contracted a debilitating illness, unflatteringly termed, "women's disease." This was something even Tiger Balm couldn't cure.

Having little confidence in the local doctors, Boon Par embarked for England to seek a cure. When he returned to Burma, he was still in bad condition, unable to make it up the stairs to his bedroom. A weakened man, Boon Par realized how much he missed Boon Haw, and needed his support. He would move to Singapore to be near to his brother.

Before moving, however, Boon Par confessed to his brother that he had a second wife, Daw Saw, and that she had borne him three children, a boy, and two girls. Boon Haw, ever outgoing and generous, was thrilled and happy over the news, and suggested that Daw Saw and her children also move to Singapore.

Boon Par's number one wife, Piah Lan, had already decided to remain in Burma, which was not a problem as she was a nag, and, more importantly, had failed to give Boon Par any children. Daw Saw, now officially wife number two, also elected to remain in Burma. Since Boon Par had recently taken a third wife, he could easily leave the other two wives behind, but the children?

With the help of Boon Haw, the master negotiator, a deal was struck with Daw Saw. She could stay in Burma and keep the two younger children, the girl, Cheng Sim, six, and the boy, Cheng

Chye, who was only three, but the eldest daughter would move to Singapore.

And so it was that Boon Par moved to Singapore with his third wife, Hong Yin, and his thirteen-year-old eldest daughter.

The daughter's name was Cheng Hu, but she was known as Emma.

She would someday be my grandmother, and Daw Saw my great-grandmother.

In Singapore, Boon Par first took up residence in a house his brother had built on Tanglin Road. This house, like everything Boon Haw touched, was special.

Boon Haw had been so impressed by the design of the American White House that he commissioned an American architect to design the house on Tanglin Road. Boon Haw would have his own White House in Singapore, and specified that the house was to be both traditional and modern, but "not Oriental."

This house eventually became known as the "Jade House," as it contained the largest private collection of jade in the world.

On his arrival in Singapore, and after a short stay at the Jade House, Boon Par moved to an enormous walled beachfront mansion seven miles from the center of town on Pasir Panjang Road. The road from the front gate to the house was nearly a mile long, and was flanked by green lawns. The mansion was of modern Malibu-style design. Nothing stodgy for the Aws.

Singapore proved to be a good base of operations for the Aw brothers. From Singapore, their business expanded beyond Tiger Balm to spawn a banking empire and a newspaper empire.

Hong Kong had become the second largest production facility for Tiger Balm, and Boon Haw was making many trips to the city, taking his second and favorite wife, Kyi Kyi, whom he had married when she was only thirteen.

Kyi Kyi liked Hong Kong, and, in 1935, Boon Haw built a mansion for her there at a cost of US$3 million (a lot in those days).

Around his extravagant new Hong Kong mansion Boon Haw built the Tiger Balm Gardens—eight acres, crammed with statues, grottoes, winding paths, and pavilions. The gardens were not grown, but built of concrete, right down to the flowers. The purpose of the gardens was not only to make Kyi Kyi happy, but to promote Tiger Balm. Where possible, the gardens were done in colors in keeping with Tiger Balm packaging—red, orange, blue and green. Only the animals in the zoo were real.

On March 15, 1935, Tiger Balm Gardens were open to the public. Vendors were allowed into the gardens to sell refreshments, and Tiger Balm. Over the next twenty years, Boon Haw would pour in another US$40 million to get the gardens right.

Even today, the Tiger Balm Gardens are open to tourists, except for the 165-foot seven-story Tiger Pagoda, which had become a popular lovers' leap where unrequited love could find solace in suicide. The real animals in the zoo have been replaced with painted concrete replicas, reinforced with bones of steel—a more practical solution.

Having completed the Tiger Balm Gardens, Boon Haw decided that his beloved brother, Boon Par, should have an equally opulent residence in Singapore. For this, Boon Haw selected a site close to Boon Par's beachfront mansion on Pasir Panjang Road. There he built for Boon Par a futuristic art deco house, with a roof of seven saucer-like domes. Surrounding the house, named Haw Par Villa, the grounds contained twenty acres of grotesque statues, figurines, and gardens, done in the same style as the Tiger Balm Gardens.

The Haw Par Villa statues depicted subjects ranging from innocent animals to guilty people—dragons, turtles, enormous spiders, more dragons, grottoes and pagodas, plants and flowers, all fashioned from concrete.

Again, the brothers were all business, and the gardens of Haw Par Villa were opened to the public, with much fanfare and publicity in March of 1937.

Boon Par was to live at Haw Par Villa for only three and a half years. In 1941, shortly before the Japanese invasion of Singapore, Boon Par fled to the safety of Burma, where he died in September of 1944, never to return to Haw Par Villa. On his deathbed, Boon Par whispered, "My dear brother will survive me by ten years." This apparently well-intended remark, was reinterpreted later as an inadvertent curse by the family when Boon Haw dropped dead ten years later in Honolulu in September of 1954.

Boon Par's futuristic art deco house was torn down after the war. The Haw Par Villa gardens remain, however, and are still open to the public.

Happily, Boon Par's original beachfront mansion on Pasir Panjang road survived the war. There, as a young girl, my grandmother had played on the same beach that would mean so much to me as a child. Sharing that beach, and over a dividing wall was another imposing mansion of similar design and size.

That would be the house where I was to live my life as a child.

THE HOUSE ON PASIR PANJANG ROAD

A S FAR BACK as my memory can take me, to a time that now seems almost mythical, I recall my life as a child in the big house on the beach at 178 Pasir Panjang Road.

I was taken there soon after my birth on November 28, 1957 at Singapore's Youngberg Memorial Hospital. It was a perfect time to go to the beach; it was summer.

In Singapore it's always summer.

The family I had been born into reeked of wealth, opulence, grandeur and flamboyance, a lifestyle created primarily by the outgoing Boon Haw.

Boon Haw's outrageous pizzazz colored the life and affected the behavior of every member of our family—we knew no other way, and I was no exception. It wasn't our fault.

I didn't know Boon Haw personally, as he died three years before I was born. Even so, everybody still talked about him.

Boon Haw wore tiger shirts, tiger ties, and, something I never tired hearing about, had a Tiger Balm army—men in tiger suits, parading through Singapore on horseback. Boon Haw also had an enormous tiger's head crafted for the front of his automobile, a German NSU convertible. The tiger's head had bouncing wire whiskers, and its eyes were special high-wattage red lights, which pierced the darkness as Boon Haw sped through the night.

Stories about Boon Haw and Boon Par were a frequent topic of conversation at the dinner table. I liked the stories. We all did.

At seven o'clock sharp every evening, the large gong was sounded in the dining room. It was time for the family to get together for dinner. My parents and I were not alone in the big house. We were only one part of a large traditional Chinese extended family, which included my paternal grandparents, two grandaunts, my uncle and his wife, and my brother, Sam, two years my junior.

All of us were always on time for dinner. We had to be.

On entering the dining room, you could not help but be struck by the size of the dining room table. It was round, a perfect circle, crafted to a geomancer's explicit specifications, and large enough for a party of twenty. The table was made of heavy teakwood, atop rested a large, very large, lazy Susan of matching teak. The whole thing had to weigh a ton. When they first moved the table into the dining room, the row of windows along the far wall looking out onto the gardens had to be removed.

On one side of the room was a long teak display case with glass windows, which were laden with Burmese silver. We had a maid only to shine the silver—it was her full-time job.

The display case was flanked by two huge elephant tusks, guardians of the silver.

There were always two servants present during dinner, with others going and coming from our two kitchens. Yes, there were two kitchens. The big kitchen was located some distance from the main house, in the cook's house. There, everything was cooked over charcoal—Chinese food tastes better that way. The second kitchen was on the first floor of the house, which was half underground. To get to the dining room from the second kitchen, you had to go down a long hallway, and then up a flight of stairs to the ground floor, with another fifty feet to the dining room. No matter that the kitchens were so far away from the dining room—that was the servants' problem, not ours.

My grandfather's place at the dining table was directly in front of the sideboard. My grandmother sat directly opposite, nearly twenty feet away.

We lived by Confucianist rules. My grandfather was the undisputed and unchallengeable head of the house. Beneath him, the family members had extremely small parts. They did as they were told, and behaved as he expected. They could only wait and watch, hoping for their chance to move up in the hierarchy.

My grandfather's name was Lee Chee Shan, but I called him "Kong Kong," Cantonese for grandfather. My grandmother, Emma, was "Mamak," literally, "great mother." Formally, my grandfather was known as *Dato* Lee Chee Shan, and my grandmother, *Datin*. *Dato* and *Datin* are Malaysian titles originally bestowed on tribal chiefs and their wives, but now reserved for the rich—especially the Chinese rich. Of course, at the time, I knew nothing of such things.

I was very proud of Kong Kong. He was the President of the family's bank, the Chung Khiaw Bank, which he had made a success, setting up many branches in Singapore and Malaysia.

My grandfather was nothing like the rest of us, which was good!

Kong Kong had not been born with a silver spoon in his mouth. He came from a small village in Burma, where his father ran a modest grocery store from the first floor of a two-story shophouse. The family lived upstairs. The shophouse tradition is time-honored in the Orient, and still exists today.

My grandfather had the good luck to be a distant relative of the Aw brothers. They needed people from Burma; people they understood and could trust, especially relatives.

Kong Kong got his start in Singapore with the job of filling, by hand, small Tiger Balm jars with the magic ointment. Quickly, he rose to the position of junior cashier, and then to assistant manager. That was in 1929, the year of America's stock-market crash, and the beginning of the Great Depression. For Tiger Balm, however, business continued to boom—there was no depression for the Aw brothers.

Impressed with my grandfather's abilities, and true to the Chinese tradition of marrying within the family, the Aw brothers decided that young Chee Shan would be the ideal husband for Emma, and so the marriage was arranged.

My grandparents were married on the 15th day of the 8th month, in the year 1931, a very auspicious day, the day of the Chinese Moon Festival. Kong Kong was twenty-two, and Mamak sweet sixteen.

Chee Shan and Emma made a striking couple. He was traditional, dignified, and yet charming. Robust and commanding at over six feet tall, Kong Kong, in his youth, was said to have been a great ballroom dancer. Emma, who had been something of a tomboy in her childhood, was short, vivacious, outgoing and, of course, flamboyant.

Sitting at the dining table, on either side of Kong Kong, were his unmarried sisters, Aye Kim and Aye Tin. I called them the "Bookends."

They loved Kong Kong dearly and, never marrying, had devoted their lives to him. Kong Kong had suffered a stroke some years before, now walked with the help of a cane and no longer spoke with strength and clarity. On the rare occasions that he did speak at dinner, the sisters would bend to listen to his words, and then repeat for all to hear what had been said.

When dessert came, always fresh fruit, one sister would peel an orange, while another worked on the grapes, carefully peeling them, removing the seeds, and finally giving each grape a careful half-slice before laying it neatly on a plate for her beloved brother.

At the end of the meal, one sister would squeeze a lemon into Kong Kong's hand-decorated Burmese silver finger bowl. The utmost care was taken to ensure that no stray squirt of lemon found its way to the beloved brother.

The other sister would take the small moist white towel, scented with 4711 Eau De Cologne Splash (well, that's what he liked) from a silver tray. She would wait patiently to wipe his fingers as they emerged dripping from the silver bowl.

No one seemed to like the Bookends, except for Kong Kong.

So much deference was shown to Kong Kong by Mamak, that you would never guess that she was the one with all the money.

This did not mean that Mamak was subdued, or mousy. Not at all. While Kong Kong usually ate in silence, Mamak did all the talking. She was very animated, gesturing as she talked. She enjoyed herself and laughed easily. She was truly Boon Par's daughter.

Still, out of respect for her husband, Mamak always dressed as he wished—colorfully, in traditional Chinese *cheongsams*, always with matching red lipstick and nail polish. Each *cheongsam* had its own matching set of jewelry—nothing subdued ever, not even during the day.

Mamak made Kong Kong very happy. Everybody made Kong Kong very happy, and even at the bank, all the ladies wore *cheongsams*—they had to.

Mamak made me very happy as well—she was everybody's chief spoiler. Of the spoiled, and one step down the hierarchy from Kong Kong was number one son, my father, Jackie Lee.

At the table, he sat in the position of honor to Kong Kong's right—well, to the right of one of the Bookends, which was as close as anyone could get.

My father was stocky, with the physique and looks of a budding sumo wrestler, or hefty Samoan. In his younger days, he wore his hair in a neat buzz, accentuating the chubbiness of his face, giving him the menacing air of a thug, which he was.

As a boy, my father was unruly, independent, and talked back—qualities not cherished in a Chinese household. Because of his behavior, as a child, he was banished by Kong Kong to eat alone in the basement kitchen.

Even after my father's marriage, we, his family, were relegated to living in the basement, with windows near the ceiling to let in the light.

So long as Kong Kong was around, my father could only be a minor player. Still, at dinner, my father got his kicks, by spinning the big lazy Susan just recklessly enough to get on Kong Kong's nerves.

My father's younger brother, Jimmy, the good brother, as good as he was, still had to sit to Kong Kong's left. Jimmy was on a very slightly lower rung of the hierarchy than my father.

While my father had been sent to local Chinese schools, and failed, Uncle Jimmy had been sent off to elite boarding schools in England and failed, as well. Somehow, the family shoehorned Uncle Jimmy into Gordonstoun School in Scotland, the Alma Mater of Prince Charles.

It was a complete waste of time. As part of his act, Uncle Jimmy became quite practiced in the King's English. This was in contrast to my father who spoke mainly "Singlish," the English slang of Singapore. Singlish, with its colorful expressions, enabled my father to be far more expressive than the King's English could ever be.

At the bottom of the hierarchy were the women—my mother, Uncle Jimmy's wife, Judy, and myself.

My mother's name was Mabel, but she was "Mummy" to me. Half white, and half Chinese, she was the most beautiful woman I had ever seen. To me she looked like Elizabeth Taylor, only without the violet eyes. The contrast with my father was such that my parents earned the nickname, "the Beauty and the Beast."

My parents met when my mother was only fourteen, and she was determined to marry into the richest family in Asia. That didn't happen until she was nineteen, and still a virgin. My father never proposed to her. Kong Kong, who liked my mother very, much did the proposing.

My mother's beauty and virginity won her a hard-earned place at the dinner table.

Jimmy's wife, Aunt Judy, was Chinese and from Malaysia. My mother nicknamed her, "Betty Boop," as Aunt Judy had both the face and voice for it. Like Betty Boop, Aunt Judy also had a great body, and big boobs—ample assets to earn her a place at the table.

My brother, Sam? He was still too young to eat with the grownups.

It was a big family, but the house had plenty of room for all of us. You could say it was three stories tall, since the basement was livable, being only partially sunk into the ground.

In addition to our living quarters, the basement was also where my father had his darkroom, which except on one occasion, I found always to be locked. He carefully developed his own black and white film, the end product usually being eight by ten glossies of nude women, his conquests.

Above the basement, the main floor contained two living rooms, the dining room, a mah-jongg room, sleeping quarters for good brother Jimmy and squeeze Judy, and for the Bookends.

My grandparents had their quarters on the top floor. Their bedroom opened onto a large circular tiled veranda, with fuchsia-pink bougainvilleas framing a beautiful view of the sea.

And where did the cooks, drivers, *kabuns* or gardeners, gatekeepers, bodyguards, and assorted help stay? With us, of course, but not in the main house.

Their quarters were on the property, but comfortably set off from the main house. Nothing squalid, mind you—we took care of our people. The staff was allowed to have their families with them, including their children. Their quarters were by no means small, much better than they could have hoped for living on their own.

Only certain servants, mainly maids, were allowed to live in the main house with the family. How else could we have them on call twenty-four hours a day? Mah-jongg can take you into the early hours of the morning.

Our security was attended to by a pack of twenty-odd German Shepherd guard dogs, uncaged every evening at sundown to patrol the grounds.

For companionship, I would take my favorite six dogs for long walks along the beach. Those were happy and carefree days for me.

They are gone, but I remember them.

Home Alone

I saw little of my parents, or of my brother, Sam. Sam and I each had our own maid.

My maid was called Ah Ngoh (ang-awe). Her only task was to take care of me.

My brother's maid, Ah Yok, hated Ah Ngoh. Ah Yok considered herself superior. She was called a "black and white" amah, or maid, for the traditional white tunic and the black pajama pants she wore. The "black and white" amahs were committed to a cloistered life entirely dedicated to their masters or mistresses—they never married. Their garb never varied, and their hair was always braided into a long pigtail going down the back.

Ah Ngoh was not a "black and white," although she wore essentially the same outfit, but with a more colorful tunic. Ah Ngoh was free to live the life she chose, something of which Ah Yok did not approve. The effect of the dislike between the two women was that my brother and I saw very little of each other.

Ah Ngoh slept in the same room with me. She had no bed, and slept on a small couch with her feet dangling over the end. My brother slept in the same room, as well, but for some reason, Ah Yok slept in the bed with him—she was lucky.

Ah Ngoh was both my confidante and mother confessor. She would regale me with the goings-on of the various members of the household. She also did her best to teach the things that she considered important, including Cantonese, a good choice as it is the most widely spoken dialect outside of China.

Ah Ngoh also taught me what she knew of Chinese tradition and culture. In this, she was assisted by the small black and white television set in our room. Ah Ngoh preferred the Chinese channels, and together we watched an endless series of Chinese dramas, most of which dealt with tales of misfortune and misery. I could never understand why the mother would bite her finger to draw blood to write a suicide note, or slice off a piece of her own flesh to give one last meal for her starving child. Gruesome stuff.

With Ah Ngoh and Ah Yok taking care of us, Sam and I saw little of our parents. Our poor maids never had a single day off, so my parents never had the chore, or the opportunity, to care for either one of us.

In a way that was good, as being my maid there was no way Ah Ngoh could discipline me. Consequently, I grew up as a wild child, with Ah Ngoh as my principal victim.

I would say to Ah Ngoh, "Talk to me, I want you to talk to me." If she didn't comply, I would hit her.

"Please don't hit me Chu Chu!" That's what everyone called me, "Chu Chu."

"Ah Ngoh, if you don't talk to me, I will hit you again."

When the hitting didn't work, I would bite Ah Ngoh. That worked. Ah Ngoh's arms usually bore the evidence of this, and one day she said, "Look, Chu Chu, look at all the bite marks on my arm. I'm going to tell your mother."

With my most stern and threatening face, I said, "You do that Ah Ngoh, and you'll be sorry. I'll really bite you, really hard." Ah Ngoh kept her silence.

The worst thing I ever did to poor Ah Ngoh was inspired by an episode of Lassie on television, where Lassie was warmly welcomed home with tears of joy after wandering off, getting lost, and then being found.

As soon as I got up the next morning, I decided to be Lassie. I hid myself behind some trunks stored under my bed, a place where no one could find me.

From my hiding place, I could hear my mother screaming at Ah Ngoh, "Ah Ngoh, where is Chu Chu? She could be drowned!"

This was great, my mother was worried about me. Finally!

I could hear voices of others searching for me. I was the center of attention! There was pandemonium! Just wait—everyone would be thrilled to see me when I finally emerged.

I stuck it out until 6:00 P.M. I had not eaten all day, and hunger was getting the better of me, so I emerged.

My return to my loved ones was nothing at all like Lassie's.

Once my mother saw that I was alive and well, she gave me the caning of my life.

Unlike my brother, I was the mischievous one—the live wire. It was easy for me to misbehave, but never in a bad or impudent way. Happy and impulsive, I frequently acted without thinking, and my childhood transgressions were always punished by my mother, and usually by caning—a good old Singapore tradition and still in use today.

And that was OK, any attention was better than no attention, and the frequent canings by my mother formed the basis of our relationship.

Life was never dull. I always worked with what I had. If I did not have a friend to play with, I created my own imaginary friend.

Then there was Ah Ngoh who was with me constantly from my birth through my teenage years. Ah Ngoh had a lasting effect on me.

I still miss having her by my side.

When I was six years old, Kong Kong sent my father to London for training at one of the English banks. My mother was determined to join him, and wasn't about to be left behind. She knew what he would be up to, alone in London. Unfortunately, she had no money for the trip.

It may seem strange, even then, that a wife in a wealthy family would be totally without funds of her own. As far as my father was concerned, her wants and needs were well taken care of—she had food, clothing, a small monthly allowance, and chauffeured transportation. Why would she possibly need any real money of her own?

Times haven't changed much today in Asia, and later in life, I was to find myself in pretty much the same position as my mother.

My mother begged Kong Kong for money for a ticket to London. He refused. She wisely turned to Mamak, the soft touch, and Mamak came through with the ticket. Happily, my mother was off to London to join her wayward husband. She would be gone for nine months. She never told me about the trip; I woke up one day and she was gone, and I was on my own with Ah Ngoh.

One day while out kite flying, the wind suddenly died down and my kite crashed into Aunt Judy's flowerpots, breaking some of her prized orchids.

I knew that Aunt Judy had a nasty temper, and would never try to understand my mistake. I was prepared for anything. Ah Ngoh had seen what happened, and hustled me off into the basement.

Aunt Judy quickly discovered her broken orchids, and knowing it had to be me, found me in my parents' bedroom, where I was hiding under their bed. She ranted and raved like a crazy woman for the longest time.

I was afraid, and did not make a sound or move until Aunt Judy had finished.

The accident really hadn't been my fault, and, seeking justice, I ran to report what had happened to Mamak. She smiled at me, but did nothing. That was Mamak, and that was how she kept the peace—for herself.

Being unprotected at such a young age made me aware of the dangers that lurked around me. I was not going to allow myself to be careless ever again.

Although my worry was about Aunt Judy, there were far more serious matters going on in Singapore—dangers I knew nothing about.

Several days after the incident with Aunt Judy, Mamak summoned the household staff, the people who worked inside the house, into the living room.

I was in the living room myself at the time, and still remember what Mamak said. She was in a serious mood. I had not seen her quite like that before.

When all were assembled, she gave the instruction, "No one is to leave the premises. I want you all to lock up the whole house. There are riots in town, but if you stay here, you will be quite safe."

A week later, Mamak was off on a trip of her own. She and Kong Kong were off to Las Vegas, where they would renew their vows, and get married for a second time.

After my grandparents left, the house became very quiet. At 6:00 every evening, one of the maids would lock up the large grilled doors protecting the front entrance, and do the same for the windows.

Except for Ah Ngoh, my brother, his amah, some maids, and me, the huge Pasir Panjang house was deserted. Everyone was away, my parents, grandparents, Aunt Judy, Uncle Jimmy, and even the Bookends—they were all gone.

I remember spending the evenings then with Ah Ngoh watching Cantonese movies on my grandparents' big black and white television set in the living room. I was very happy about this, as normally, I was not allowed to watch television in the living room—that was for the adults. Sometimes the movie would disappear, maybe for an hour or so. The screen would turn to snow, and the only sounds in the house were from occasional barks from the pack of German Shepherds, outside.

At the time, I didn't think much about what Mamak had said to the staff, or why everyone was away. It was not until many years later, that I realized they had all fled the riots in Singapore.

Singapore, then, was still a part of Malaysia, but racial tensions were mounting between the two, finally causing riots between the Malay and Chinese communities in Singapore.

My grandparents, being well connected, saw what was coming, and got out of Singapore fast. This was a well-timed move on their part, as the tensions exploded into Singapore's bloody racial riots of July and August of 1964.

The riots led eventually to the expulsion of Singapore from Malaysia, and on August 9, 1965, Singapore became a sovereign nation. The Chinese had won.

Lee Kuan Yew, Singapore's leader then, and now, said, "What has happened has happened. Everybody will have a place in Singapore."

Especially if you're Chinese, that is.

The most momentous events in Singapore's political history were taking place during those happy years of my childhood at Pasir Panjang when I was six and seven.

I was too young then to know or care about what was happening.

Why were my brother and I left behind, and in danger, while my parents and grandparents fled to the good (and safe) life in London and Las Vegas, respectively?

I still ask myself that question.

VISITORS AND NEIGHBORS

KONG KONG sent my father's younger sister to study in England. This proved to be a disaster, as she did the worst thing possible—she returned to Singapore, married to a white man. She was very proud of her catch—a six foot four blue-eyed Viking God from Iceland, named Jon Sigurdsson. In addition to marrying a white, she now called herself "Esja," some sort of weird Icelandic name that Kong Kong could barely pronounce. The family had managed to cover up my mother's being half-white, but now this!

My father, who could have cared less, and several younger family members delighted in calling Sigurdsson the "White Monkey"—even to his face, but only in Chinese or Burmese, of course.

Fortunately, Esja and Sigurdsson had decided to live in Iceland, where no one would ever see them. They came to Singapore only for holidays, and when they did, they stayed with us at the Pasir Panjang house.

Sigurdsson kept his distance from Kong Kong. Either Sigurdsson could not take Kong Kong's piercing stare, or he realized he didn't quite fit in.

Kong Kong figured that Sigurdsson was in it for the money, and Mamak's decision to finance Sigurdsson's studies in Iceland had to be very painful proof of this fact to poor Kong Kong.

Sigurdsson was not the only unwelcome white person to visit Pasir Panjang—there was my mother's own mother, Dagmar Vyner, whom I called "Granny."

To me, Granny was a sweet old lady, and on the few occasions when she came to spend the night, I slept in her bed, as she was afraid.

Nobody at the house had anything to do with Granny, or even spoke to her. Eventually her rare visits to Pasir Panjang ceased.

I missed her, and didn't mind at all that she was white.

On the other side of our wall in Boon Par's former residence lived his son Cheng Chye, Mamak's brother, the little boy who had remained in Burma with his mother Daw Saw. Cheng Chye was married, and lived there with his family.

Everybody liked Cheng Chye. He was a very personable fellow, which did much to overcome the family's jealousy for being chosen by his uncle Boon Haw to be his successor, the next Tiger Balm King. In Cheng Chye, Boon Haw saw the virtual reincarnation of his beloved brother, Boon Par. Who better to take over the family business?

Boon Par's younger daughter, Cheng Sim, Mamak's sister, who also stayed back in Burma with Cheng Chye, had married a Chinese man from Thailand, and lived in Bangkok. The family had not forgotten Cheng Sim, they gave her Thailand's major Chinese-language newspaper.

On one of their visits to Singapore, Cheng Sim and her husband, a Mr. Lee, took me to a small carnival in town. There, I spotted my very favorite album, *The Sound of Music*, and asked Cheng Sim if she would buy it for me. She shook her head with a terse "No!" Later, Mr. Lee quietly purchased the album for me, a kindness I shall never forget.

I hated to go to Haw Par Villa, the gardens of Boon Par's old house, just up the road from the Pasir Panjang house.

One of the scariest parts was the Eighth Court of Hell, where the victim is undergoing a bloody disembowelment for lack of filial piety.

The purpose of this horror show was to extol the virtues of Chinese tradition, and, of course, to promote Tiger Balm.

When Cheng Chye took over the affairs of the family, he carried on Boon Haw's task by adding to Haw Par Villa works inspired by his travels, most notable being a replica of the Statue of Liberty. Strange? Is Freedom a traditional Chinese virtue?

Haw Par Villa has been called a monument to bad taste—well, by Western standards, sure. The family eventually gave the place to the Singapore government, who converted it into an amusement park, complete with rides, billing the place as "the only Chinese mythological theme park in the world."

All that remains at Haw Par Villa of the Tiger Balm Kings today are the tombs of Boon Par and Boon Haw, marked by enormous monuments rising to the sky.

On Chinese New Year, as a special concession to our family, Haw Par Villa gives our family free tickets to pay homage to our ancestors.

Haw Par Villa gave me nightmares.

SCHOOLDAYS

A T THE AGE of five, it was decided that I would go to a private English school named Dean's School.

In preparation for this, my mother conjured up an English name for me. She was a great admirer of Jacqueline Kennedy, so, after improving the name with the ornate ending of "lyn," I was stuck with "Jacquelyn," a name that meant absolutely nothing to me.

In no time, I became known by the nickname of "Jackie," exactly the same as my father. This was a vexing and unforeseen consequence to my mother, who rarely thought ahead. Later, in my teens, she corrected the error, and "for numerological reasons," rechristened me "Monicka." Again, the trick spelling.

My mother's renaming me was nothing unusual, as Singaporean Chinese dote on fancy Western names, few of which appear in their birth certificates. There's General "Winston" Choo, a lawyer known as "Jupiter" Kong Choon, and a banker named "Finian" Bong. There's also "Picasso" Tan, and, of course, "Charley Chan." Ladies include "Caberline" Koek, "Pryscilla" Shaw, and "Jannie" Tay—all top dogs. Who else would dare?

And so it was that little Jackie Lee, whoever that was, went off to Dean's school.

All of the children at the school, except for me, were English, most of them blonde, blue-eyed, and fair.

Dean's School had a profound effect on me. English was my first language, but being among native English-speaking students perfected my speech and left me with a lasting British accent that to this day belies my origins.

Dean's School had no interest in churning out Anglophiles, and, unlike Chinese schools, chauvinistic racial and national pride had no place in the curriculum. Still, as if by osmosis, I did absorb the Western ways, which became very much a part of me. I actually learned to begin thinking for myself—something not encouraged by

Chinese culture—not even today. Unquestioning obedience was no longer a virtue to me, which was OK as I was by nature a rebel.

The difference between my classmates and me had narrowed to the point of being nearly imperceptible, and it made no difference to anybody that I was the only Chinese child in the school.

Of course, I could still be Chinese when I needed, or wanted to be.

I began, however, to notice a difference between my classmates and myself, which had nothing to do with race. When I visited my school friends at their homes, I saw, although very young, the disparity between their lifestyles and mine. Only at this point did I begin to understand that I had been born into a very wealthy family. I had naturally assumed that everyone, but the staff of course, had our lifestyle.

As time went on this economic fact became ever more obvious. I had become like my classmates, but I was not like them. Having Ah Ngoh with me at the school was enough to set me apart. Still, I had many good friends and my days at Dean's School were the happiest days of my life.

Unfortunately, my parents allowed me to stay at Dean's school for only two years. Maybe they had noticed something, but I doubt it. Most likely, they wanted to save on the expense of sending a girl to a private school. I desperately wanted to stay at Dean's School—it could have taken me all the way up to my university education. I did not want to leave my classmates.

I pleaded with my parents, but my wishes meant nothing to them. I would enter the Singapore Chinese Girls' School, a public Singapore-run school—a one hundred percent pure Chinese school.

My mother arranged everything for my first day at the new school. As usual, she did a real number on me.

For starters, she dressed me in a hideous looking frock. It was the wrong shade of red, full of frills, and had appliqué roses on the front. The skirt was supported by a crinoline can-can style petticoat, a requisite at the time for such getups. My white socks were trimmed with lace to offset my black patent leather Mary Janes. I had a China-doll haircut, bobbed at the neck. A sight to behold!

My mother, perfect as always, was impeccably dressed in a tight-fitting *cheongsam*. Ah Ngoh, yes she still attended school with me, was neatly attired in her usual flowered tunic with black pants, all perfectly ironed.

It gets worse—my entourage included both a chauffer and a bodyguard. The Indian Muslim chauffer, Karim, was resplendent in his immaculate white safari suit, complete with gold buttons, black dress boots, and black velveteen fez-type hat called a *songkok* in Malay. To qualify for a white *songkok*, Karim would have had to perform the rites of the Hajj, the pilgrimage to Mecca. Then there was the bodyguard, dressed exactly like Karim.

Our vehicle was a four door light turquoise Cadillac—the only Cadillac in Singapore. We were ready, and I was about to die!

Our bodyguard smartly opened the rear door—that was his job—Karim did not open car doors for people. My mother, I, and Ah Ngoh, in that order, entered the rear of the car. The musical comedy had begun.

Upon my arrival at the Singapore Chinese Girls School, I saw that all the other girls were dressed in neat blue uniforms—nothing fancy.

We entered my classroom where I stood mortified in my red frock. Behind me were my mother, and Ah Ngoh. My mother's hands were on my shoulders, as if to restrain any escape attempt on my part. Slightly to the rear of Ah Ngoh and my mother stood the resplendent Karim. Fortunately, the bodyguard remained outside to guard the Cadillac.

With serious anticipation, my eyes slowly surveyed my classmates, my new friends. Their stunned expressions confirmed that we were a sight to behold.

A great launch into a new school! Thanks mother! I looked like an over-grown red rose. All that was lacking was some background music from a comic opera.

The embarrassment! Even at the age of seven, I knew that the first instant of the first day in a new school was the make or break moment of a lifetime with my new classmates.

My mother dominated the conversation with the teacher, who I could tell was just biding her time to get at me. Meanwhile, my new classmates continued to gawk in silence at the strange beings that had come into their midst. A lion's den of uniformed girls, all waiting to get at me. Their decision seemed clear—"We hate her!"

This was not like Dean's School, where I was readily accepted for who I was. I can understand the thinking of my new classmates. It wasn't my fault, and it wasn't their fault either. They lived for conformity, and I was different.

Each day I was driven to school in the Cadillac by Karim. Ah Ngoh sat in the back with me.

At lunch, when it came time for the other girls to fall into line at the cafeteria, I did not join them. Ah Ngoh had already set a place for me with my lunch already on the plate, and was standing in attendance.

How could anyone be my friend?

GOODBYE TO PASIR PANJANG

In 1969, after spending twelve years of her life living in the basement of the Pasir Panjang house, my mother received the good news that she, my father, my brother, and I would be moving to a new house.

She now had something to live for—a house of her own, and a life away from the control of her in-laws. I have never seen my mother happier than when she told me the good news. I cried.

Good-bye, number 178 Pasir Panjang Road. I will miss you forever. I will miss the sea, the dogs, the trees, the house itself with its beautiful gardens, and I will miss living with my grandparents. There will never be another Pasir Panjang.

Sadly, the Pasir Panjang house suffered the fate of all the beautiful old beach houses in Singapore. It was torn down and replaced by an apartment building. The beachfront land, where I had spent many happy days, was confiscated by the government and incorporated into a public park, called West Coast Park—a picnic ground for visitors who may have visited the amusement park down the road—a place called Haw Par Villa.

In preparation for our move, Kong Kong built twin houses at 69 Holland Road, one for my father, and one for Uncle Jimmy. To show no favoritism, each house was an exact mirror image of the other. Although the houses were joined at the middle, there was no passageway between them. Good for that! The houses were extravagantly designed and flamboyant, all in keeping with family tradition.

Each house was large. Built on a slope the houses were two stories tall in front, but four in back. The houses were crowned by a Chinese pagoda-style green tile roofs, turned up at the corners. The green tiles were in the form of bamboo trees, which, representing a place to hide, was a symbol of safety for the Chinese.

For me, the only attraction in the area was a crocodile farm across the street. Something to visit, but nothing like Pasir Panjang and the sea.

This was a major change. We were no longer going to live with my grandparents, our relatives, and their retinue. No more extended family—it would be just us—my parents, my brother, myself, and Ah Ngoh. There was no room for our Malay chauffeur, Jolly, so he lived on his own somewhere.

Instead of German Shepherds, we had only a few smaller dogs, lap dogs for my mother, and several larger ones for my father, and that was it.

As a carryover from Pasir Panjang, my grandparents continued to pay all expenses for my parents, and for Uncle Jimmy. This included utilities, servants, drivers, everything, and jobs at Kong Kong's bank. Poor fellows, how else could my father and Uncle Jimmy get a decent job without university degrees? Even in those days, education was important in Singapore.

Shortly after we moved to the new house, my mother told me that a very wonderful thing was going to happen—Granny would be coming to live with us. I was thrilled!

Granny had been living with her other daughter, Zena, in a small apartment on River Valley Road. Zena had never darkened the door of the Pasir Panjang house, and I had met her only once or twice, on visits to Granny. After the first time I met Zena, I asked my mother, "Mummy, why is Aunt Zena so dark?"

My question was answered with a severe caning.

Since I hardly ever saw her, I never thought much about Aunt Zena. Now that I was twelve, my mother decided that I was ready to hear about Zena and the shocking truth about Granny—dear, sweet little old white-haired Granny.

My mother took me into her dressing room and closed the door. Expecting a caning, I was relieved to hear her say, "Sit down, child, I have something to tell you."

We both sat down.

As my mother told it, in halting sentences, Granny had five children by three men, and over a very short span of time. With my questions and her embarrassment, it took over an hour for my mother to get the entire story out.

It goes like this -

Granny started off in Singapore as the wife of a Mr. Rufus, a Portuguese Eurasian, by whom she had three children, a boy, and two girls.

For reasons not explained to me, Granny, and her three children, left Mr. Rufus. Shortly thereafter, Mr. Rufus came around and took the three children away from Granny—an easy thing for a man to do back then.

Granny was not alone for long as she took up with a Mr. Atterley, a very dark Sri Lankan, by whom she had Aunt Zena. No, Granny and Atterley were not married.

"So that explains Aunt Zena's color, huh?" I asked.

"What did you say, Chu Chu?" asked my mother, distracted by the pain of her confession.

"Nothing."

Well, then, hot on Atterley's heels came a Mr. Wee, and, less than a year after the birth of Zena, out popped my mother. This was fast work even by today's standards. No, Granny and Wee were not married, either.

From this point on, the worst being over, my mother gained a bit of confidence, as the rest of the story redeemed poor Granny, somewhat.

During the Japanese occupation of Singapore, Granny lived as a single parent with her two young daughters. These were difficult times—the three survived on stolen chickens, cheap rice, and whatever else they could scrounge. They did what they could to survive.

Times were tougher than we can imagine today. Even Singapore's founding hero Lee Kuan Yew was reduced to working for Japanese intelligence, the *Hodobu*, while engaging in black market activities on the side.

Aside from a close brush with a sword-carrying Japanese soldier, during which Granny was saved by the kindness of a Malay village elder, who vouched falsely that Granny was not white, but Malay, I have heard very little of the three women's experiences during the Japanese occupation. People don't like to talk about such things. I do know, however, that the trauma of living under the Japanese had a permanent effect on them.

After the war, Granny, and her two daughters wound up living in a rented garage. Humble origins. When, at the age of fourteen, my mother met my father at a party, she seized upon the opportunity, and the rest is history.

Beyond that, Granny's origins are shrouded in mystery. Her Rufus relatives, whom I have met, are moot on the subject. All I know is that Granny had been born in Sarawak. I always romanticized that there might have been some sort of connection between Granny, Dagmar Vyner, and the last White Rajah of Sarawak, Vyner Brooke. A long shot.

There were no more men in Granny's life. She had become disillusioned with her Anglican upbringing—maybe thanks to the men—and became a Jehovah's Witness.

As my mother put it, "Granny was never lucky with men."

To me Granny was exactly what a grandmother should be. She was a kindly old white-haired lady, absorbed with her study of religion. Out of repentance, I guess.

My mother was totally spent after her long confessional.

But there was more—there had to be more—what happened to "Wee," my mother's own father—my very own grandfather?

"Was Wee killed by the Japanese?" I asked.

My mother sank back in her chair. She might as well get it over with now.

I sat fascinated.

My mother reached for a Kleenex, blew her nose, and then continued …

My mother's father, forever known to me only by his last name of "Wee," was a tall slim good-looking Chinese fellow. He was also a drunk and a compulsive gambler—difficult accomplishments for the schoolteacher that he was.

When my parents were to be married, Wee presented a bureaucratic problem. He had never married Granny, so my mother was, she paused, blew her nose again and blurted out—"illegitimate!"

I sat up straight.

Well, in those days, there was no way you could get married if you, "didn't have a father," said my mother avoiding the I-word.

The only way my parent's marriage could ever take place, would be to get Wee's signature legitimizing my mother.

"So the Japanese didn't kill him."

Fortunately not, so my future parents, bringing along Uncle Jimmy, of all people, for moral support, went to Johor Bahru, a town just over the causeway in Malaysia, to visit Wee and get him to sign, which he did.

Wee's resurrection began and ended with his attendance at my parents' wedding. They had to invite him for what would the bride be without a father? My mother said Wee was very good looking, and resembled Gary Cooper—no mean feat for a Chinaman. It was always my mother's habit to associate a person's good looks, especially hers, with a movie star. She, herself, was at various times portraying her screen idols Lana Turner, Elizabeth Taylor, Gina Lolobridgida, and Virna Lisi. For me, my mother was, and still is, better than any of them.

I have never seen nor met Wee. He appeared to me only in the form of one lone photograph, long since lost, which was taken at the wedding. In the photograph, which I remember well, Wee stands tall, with chiseled features. He was dressed in a white suit, and did indeed look a bit like Gary Cooper.

My mother's dressing room was getting dark as I got up to leave. She remained in her chair with her thoughts. She had given me a lot to think about too.

Being unfamiliar with our new house, my brother Sam took a very nasty fall in the bathroom one night, injuring his head. Being so well behaved, he never once mentioned the incident to my parents. I did, but my parents said nothing and did nothing. This seemingly minor accident marked the beginning of the end for my brother, for shortly after, he had his first epileptic seizure, a malady which would affect him for the remainder of his short and unhappy life.

The biggest change about leaving Pasir Panjang was not the new house, nor the return of Granny, or the exorcism of Wee, but the emergence of two new personalities.

My parents changed, and without the restraint of Kong Kong and

Mamak, they became themselves.

My mother's change was fairly innocent, at least in the beginning. She no longer limited herself to wearing traditional *cheongsams* as Kong Kong required, but took on a more trendy look with miniskirts, tight fitting body-knit tops with plunging necklines, boots, an array of turbans, and a toreador hat. Driving her new white Alfa Romeo with leather racing gloves, she was quite an eyeful. Did she look silly? Not at all. Believe me, she had the looks to pull it off.

More upsetting and shocking, especially to me, was the change in my father—a change which was sudden and frightening.

Out, from the subdued son of a traditional father, sprang a veritable Mr. Hyde! Away from Kong Kong, my father was a free man.

I was shocked the first time I heard my father say, "fuck." My shock wore off quickly as the word became a much-used part of my father's limited English vocabulary—and it would only get worse.

He took pleasure in pronouncing his new motto in life, "One wife and a million sweethearts."

My life at the old house at Pasir Panjang was stable and orderly. But now, the quiet respectful family dinners with Kong Kong and Mamak at Pasir Panjang were replaced by weekly parties, drunken carousing, and talk that was shameful to a girl of my age. I missed Pasir Panjang. I even missed the Bookends.

The upheaval, the change in my life, was complicated by the fact that I was entering puberty. Things were not looking good.

I had finally met my father.

THE CURSE OF AW BOON HAW

MY GRANDPARENTS had also moved out of the Pasir Panjang house, and now lived not far from us in a modern two-story bungalow on Ford Avenue.

Their new place, christened Casa Emma for my grandmother, was not on such a grand scale as the house on the beach—not that luxuries didn't abound. Kong Kong's new white Daimler, dolled up with its red leather upholstery, which was usually parked in front of Casa Emma gave a hint of what lay inside.

My grandparents had the house built in the family tradition of garish ostentation. The front door, guarded by two outsized marble lions, had the shape of a semicircle to match the shape of the two enormous elephant tusks inside.

Beyond the tusks, everything from the larger Pasir Panjang house had been crammed into Casa Emma—exquisite Chinese antiques, 13th century Yuan Dynasty oxblood vases, Ching Dynasty rosewood screens, jade sculptures, statues, giant vases, trinkets, and *objets d'art* galore. The dining room was laden with the Burmese silverware from the Pasir Panjang house, but the old dining room table had been replaced by one much smaller.

Even the master bedroom made a statement. It contained both his and hers television sets to create a telebabel of entertainment.

The resulting décor was an incoherent hodgepodge of extravagant excess, filled with the aging memories and clutter, typical of the elderly.

Despite this comfort and luxury, problems lay ahead for Kong Kong and his beloved bank. It all had to do with Cheng Chye, the personable fellow that everybody liked so much.

Cheng Chye was as astute in business as Boon Haw had predicted, but only over the short term, and only for his own interests. In contrast to his sunny personality, Cheng Chye showed the ability to plot, scheme, seduce, and destroy anyone in his way, including Kong Kong.

Cheng Chye was a smiling tiger.

Shortly after our move from Pasir Panjang, Cheng Chye decided to take the family business public, listing it on the Singapore stock exchange as Haw Par Brothers International Ltd.

Kong Kong was vehemently opposed to the idea. He could not understand Cheng Chye's reasoning. There was plenty of cash, the family had no need of money from a public offering, and the business would be far better off without any interference from public stockholders.

Most important, however, were the last wishes of Boon Haw, who shortly before his death had decreed that the company should never pass from the family's hands. To allow outsiders into the family business would be a curse.

The disagreement between Kong Kong and Cheng Chye over going public resulted in a major two-hour argument between the two over the matter, right next door to our Holland Road house, in Uncle Jimmy's bedroom.

The unlikely coincidence of Kong Kong's running into Cheng Chye at Uncle Jimmy's was explained by the fact that Uncle Jimmy and Aunt Judy, who both worked at the bank, were lobbying Cheng Chye to remove Kong Kong, and put Uncle Jimmy in charge. Even though Aunt Judy was Cheng Chye's deep throat, she and Uncle Jimmy would be played out by Cheng Chye in the end.

Regardless of Kong Kong's opinions, Cheng Chye had control over the business and could do as he pleased, and it was his pleasure to go public.

No one could deter Cheng Chye—not even the curse of Aw Boon Haw.

To make the public offering more attractive, Cheng Chye swept most of the family's assets into the new company, including the family's Singapore newspaper, Sin Chew Jit Poh, and as much as he could of Chung Khiaw Bank.

Cheng Chye's goal was to merge all of Chung Khiaw Bank into Haw Par Brothers International, but he did not control enough shares to do so. Fortunately for Kong Kong, the bank remained independent and he was able to continue as President. Even without swallowing the bank, Haw Par Brothers International, Ltd., due to its name, was well received by the Singapore investors, and had a very successful public offering.

Cheng Chye had pulled it off.

Cheng Chye's next move was a perplexing act of generosity. He gave my father and Uncle Jimmy two large blocks of stock in Chung Khiaw Bank, 50,000 shares each. How nice! Was this a peace offering to my grandfather?

Kong Kong was very upset over Cheng Chye's apparent generosity. The shares were worth millions, and my grandfather did not want his sons to be independently wealthy at such a young age, or so he said.

Cheng Chye apologized. He had truly meant well. He explained that a block of 100,000 shares had become available on the open market, and he purchased them for Kong Kong's sons to keep the shares from falling into the wrong hands.

What a clever snake. By giving the shares to my father and Uncle Jimmy, Cheng Chye concealed his true intention, which was to keep the shares out of Kong Kong's hands.

And why? Generous Uncle Cheng Chye was scheming to take the bank away from Kong Kong. All that remained, between Cheng Chye and control of the bank were Kong Kong's shares.

Cheng Chye's next act of generosity was a golden parachute for Kong Kong.

The directors of the bank, which included Cheng Chye and Mamak, but not Kong Kong, proposed that Kong Kong be rewarded with a new contract increasing his salary to S$35,000 a month, and including expenses for a car, driver, bodyguard, and domestic staff. The agreement would be good for five years, and was renewable. If Kong Kong decided to retire, the bank would pay him a pension of S$230,000 per year for life, tax-free.

In return for the new contract, Kong Kong would have to sell his 16,000 shares in the bank, but at the generous price of S$116 a share, to Haw Par Brothers International, Ltd. giving the public company 51 percent interest in the bank.

Not such a terrible deal for a poor relative, several million up front, plenty of perks, and a lavish income for life. For Kong Kong who had never had anything of his own, it was a lot of money, but for Cheng Chye it was chump change, and he knew he would get it all back.

Kong Kong dazzled by the deal, took the bait, and when he signed his new contract on May 31, 1971, he was a very happy man.

Only four days later, Cheng Chye sold his interest in Haw Par Brothers International Ltd. to a British company, Slater Walker, a corporate raider. What had been the family business was now under the control of foreigners, including the fate of Chung Khiaw Bank, and Kong Kong.

Two weeks after the sell-out to Slater Walker, Cheng Chye paid a courtesy visit to Kong Kong at Casa Emma, bringing with him a small round-faced young man by the name of Wee Cho Yaw.

Kong Kong knew Wee Cho Yaw as a very timid and quiet person whose father owned a small bank operating only in Singapore, the United Overseas Bank.

Kong Kong, walking with his cane, led the two young men into the mah-jongg room where the three could talk in privacy.

Only then did Cheng Chye break the news to Kong Kong. Slater Walker was selling Haw Par Brothers International's controlling interest in Chung Khiaw Bank for S$22 million to United Overseas Bank. The courtesy part of Cheng Chye's visit was to give my grandfather advance notice—the sale would not take place until tomorrow. Kong Kong was out of a job. The old man had outlived his usefulness.

Kong Kong was shocked! United Overseas Bank was small; it had only a single branch and was only a fraction the size of Chung Khiaw Bank. Wee and his father were nobodies, only minor players in the banking world.

In a flash, Kong Kong understood that this had been part of Cheng Chye's strategy for Slater Walker's buyout of Haw Par Brothers International. Cheng Chye's purpose all along had been to cash out. His interest was in the good life, not the family business.

Kong Kong's voice roared through the house. He raised his cane and struck Cheng Chye—a small satisfaction, however, as Kong Kong's career was now at an end.

Cheng Chye's moves seemed brilliant at the time—first taking Haw Par Brothers International, Ltd. public, and then convincing Slater Walker to buy the company contingent upon its acquiring and selling off Chung Khiaw Bank for cash. What ever happened to Wee Cho Yaw? He's now a billionaire with his name listed in Forbes "The World's Richest People."

Cheng Chye blew it for all of us. Well, not for me, as I was only a girl. I had nothing and expected nothing. The effects of Cheng Chye's actions on the family were both immediate and everlasting.

To save face, Kong Kong was allowed to purchase two of Chung Khiaw Bank's subsidiaries back from United Overseas Bank. The companies, Public Insurance, and Public Life Assurance, although small, provided a place where Kong Kong had an office and could pretend that he was still a player.

To avoid the humiliation of working for Wee Cho Yaw, Uncle Jimmy left Chung Khiaw Bank, but my father stayed on—not as a player, but as a playboy.

My mother said that it was all to the good, as it ended the fighting between my father and Uncle Jimmy as to who was going to take over the bank from Kong Kong.

Cheng Chye fell into disgrace when Singapore attempted to extradite the Slater Walker Chairman, Jim Slater, over "irregularities" in the Haw Par affair. Singapore's extradition failed, probably because the other half of the Slater Walker team, Peter Walker, was a member of the British government—he still is, now as Lord Walker.

The stink led to Jim Slater's replacement at Slater Walker by another cagey fellow, James Goldsmith.

And Cheng Chye? After cashing himself out of the family business, he was free to do anything he pleased for the rest of his life.

That wouldn't last long, as two short months after selling the bank, on August 22, 1971, Cheng Chye, only forty-eight years old, and in the prime of life and money, dropped dead in Santiago, Chile.

I thought Santiago was a strange place for Cheng Chye to be, and I thought it even stranger, when at his wake at his Pasir Panjang house, which I attended, his coffin was closed.

They said Cheng Chye died of a stroke, but we knew better.

It was the Curse of Aw Boon Haw.

SODOM AND GOMORRAH

OUR HOUSE at 69 Holland Road had become a playground for frequent parties, given at a relentless pace of at least one a week.

A fun-loving new circle of friends had gravitated to my parents. These consisted mainly of my father's business associates, mostly bankers, and not only from Chinese banks, as less inhibited foreigners were more to my father's liking. There were Americans, French, and Italians! There were exciting and exotic names like Cesare, Jean-Pierre, and Alessandro!

In spite of having few talents as a useful human being, my father was skilled in the art of party giving. He always managed to assemble just the right group of people, usually a mixed bag of diverse and unrelated revelers. He also knew how to energize a party with the best looking girls, some were from his office, where he hired only on the basis of looks, and others from parts unknown.

In celebration of my mother's thirty-sixth birthday, my parents decided to throw a special party, a surprise party for her. This, of course, would be a surprise to no one.

In preparation for the event, my mother consulted an astrologer. What color of dress should she wear? Since she had been born under the sign of the Scorpio, the answer came back that she must wear the scorpion's color. The scorpion's color? What color was that? Somehow, it was divined that the scorpion-color would be a fuchsia-red—a color almost impossible to find.

That settled, my father decided that the male guests should all be dressed in matching fuchsia-red shirts, with black ties, black slacks, black socks and black shoes. My father would wear the same, except that his shirt would have a mandarin collar, with no tie, and not be tucked in. Well, shouldn't the host be a little less formal than his guests?

The women could wear whatever they wished, but all reds, fuchsia or not, had to be avoided.

Finally, the guests were given a choice. They could either send flowers in advance, or bring a present. It was up to them.

On the day of the party, my mother's ritual of preparation began, as usual, with a two-hour visit to the hairdresser. On her return home, she had a beauty nap, taking care to lie on her back with her neck supported by a firm pillow. No harm must come to the frozen coiffure.

At 5:00 P.M. sharp, my mother got up. It was time to put on her make-up and to get dressed—a process that would take a full two and one-half hours. Seated in front of her mirror, the backstage type, bordered with light bulbs, she began, as always, with the makeup. I loved to sit on the floor behind her and watch the transformation—she was really good at it. If I watched, someday maybe I could be like my mother. I kept very quiet, for if she noticed me, I risked being sent off, "What are you doing there, child. Go watch some television."

Of course, I knew I could never be as beautiful as my mother. She told me so many times.

She pointed out that I did not have her delicate porcelain skin, and repeated more than once, "Why is your skin not like mine, Chu? Why are you so dark? You look like a fisherman. Only peasants wading through rice paddies are so dark."

My mother and Mamak both had the luck to be born fair. My father was much darker, and I was somewhere in between, which was not as fair as a fair lady should be, at least in the eyes of my mother.

Fair skin is still worth its weight in gold in Asia. Even today, in Singapore, Ponds advertises their "Skin Lightening Moisturizer" using words which would be politically incorrect in America: "Beautifully translucent skin has been valued throughout history by diverse cultures. A considerable number of women across Asia desire lighter skin."

I would have to work with what I had.

My concentration on my mother's art of makeup magic was broken when Ah Ngoh appeared to tell me that Joan had arrived.

Joan was a Chinese-Indonesian girl, three years older than I, from a very good family, and my very best friend. The evening was so special that I was allowed to invite her over—on condition, however, that Joan and I would not attend the party at all. I was full of fun and best kept away from the party. My brother, Sam, never perceived to be a problem, would also remain upstairs.

Granny too was not a problem—she wasn't around. My mother had recently sent her back to Zena's on the pretext that Granny was a Jehovah's Witness. My mother, then a Buddhist, said there was no way the two religions could co-exist under one roof—especially since Jehovah's Witnesses were illegal in Singapore.

Minutes before 7:00 P.M., the appointed hour, my father stood at the entrance ready for the guests. Reeking of Brut, and in his getup of fuchsia-red and black, my thug-like father had all the appearance of your local nightclub bouncer. The only thing that gave him away was his diamond-studded Patek Philippe watch.

By 7:00 P.M. sharp, nearly all the guests were at the door, everyone knew that my father had this thing about punctuality.

As my father herded the guests into the living room, my mother was still in her dressing room. Her preparations nearly complete, she was standing fully dressed in front of the full-length mirror. She was resplendent. The fuchsia-red scorpion-lady dress had a plunging neckline to display her alabaster skin and her ample boobs. The dress was barely knee-length—why hide the best legs in town?

Her three-inch open-toed sling-back fuchsia-red high heels gave further thrust to the beauty of her legs and body. Her long and natural fingernails, the envy of the best acrylics, were painted pearl-white, as were her perfectly manicured toenails.

Then there was the jewelry. She wore teardrop diamond earrings, a diamond bracelet on one wrist, *her* diamond-studded Patek Philippe, matching my father's, on the other, and several large diamond rings. The jewelry sparkled as she moved. She wore no necklace. It would only detract from the boobs. The scent of Joy filled the room.

Her long hair was held in place movie-star style by a wide black headband.

As my mother batted her false eyelashes and struck poses in front of the mirror, my father entered the room. He was excited, "The guests are here. Are you ready to come down, ah?"

Still fidgeting in front of the mirror, making the final small adjustments to her dress and hair, my mother answered curtly, "Yes, yes, almost—in a minute or so, Jackie."

My father rushed back downstairs to the waiting guests.

My father loved to play up to my mother's entrances. After all, she was a prize possession and he was very proud of her looks.

Finally, the moment arrived. I ran to my spot where I could peek from behind the banister, Joan, who was both more sensible and mature, stayed back in my room.

My mother appeared at the top of the stairs, a white handkerchief in one hand, a fluttering sandalwood fan in the other. It was showtime!

Her descent down the long stairway onto the landing above the living room was taken with dainty steps, marked by brief pauses of mock surprise, as she recognized first one lucky guest, and then another. She would open her arms wide to welcome them, shaking her head with disbelief while flashing an incredulous and incredible smile.

When she reached the landing, she stopped. In mock surprise, placing her hands gingerly on her cheeks, being careful not to spoil the makeup, my mother squealed, "Oh my, the room is filled with flowers, for ... for me?"

Led by my father, the applause then started. He stood at the foot of the stairs—enraptured. My mother was playing Norma Desmond to my father's Eric von Stroheim. It was just that loony.

After a perfectly timed pause on the landing, my mother continued her descent down the remaining steps and into the living room where she was happily engulfed by her enthusiastic fans.

Whatever the guests may have thought of my parents, they all enjoyed the party. Jolly, our Malay chauffeur, tended bar, and others were brought in to help, waiters and maids. Tables were set under colorful lanterns in the back garden, and if you knew where to look, up in the tree, you could see a stick with a red chili and two red onions, a Chinese talisman placed there by my mother to keep the rain away.

Inside, discreetly hidden behind the living room, was a disco, complete with colored lights and the latest hi-fi driven dance music—the selections chosen carefully by my father.

I loved the party and, creeping down the stairs, decided to become a part of it, after all, I was nearly sixteen and coming into my own. My mother too was coming into her own. I saw her dancing in the disco, grindingly close, with a friend of ours, an American, named Geoff. He was tall, Harvard-educated, and an investment banker, stationed, with his wife, in Singapore.

Unfortunately, my mother spotted me as I watched her dance. As usual, she sent me straight upstairs.

Strangely, I wasn't upset over my mother's dancing with Geoff. I was totally in awe of her, and didn't think my father deserved her—not at all.

Upstairs, poor Joan was stuck in front of the black and white television set in my room, so it didn't take much to convince her to sneak downstairs to the party. We would have to stay away from the disco and my mother, I warned.

My father seldom danced at his parties. He had better things to do—downstairs. There, like at Pasir Panjang, my father had his darkroom. His hobby of photography continued to be a perfect compliment to his main hobby of sex.

Still photography has its limits; downstairs, was my father's very own private projection room.

As my father led some of the men, and a couple of the women, downstairs to the projection room, Joan and I followed.

Once in the projection room, the guests took their seats. Joan and I stood respectfully in the rear. The 8 mm projector was already threaded with film and ready.

My father smiled at Joan as he lowered the lights. Great, he didn't mind that we were there—we could stay!

Carefully turning on the projector, my father said simply, "This was taken by my driver in the Philippines."

The film was in black and white, and since it was shaky it was several moments before I could fully grasp what we were being shown. I saw a small waterfall. Naked girls were bathing under its cascade! Then there were men—naked men, splashing and cavorting! I took a longer look—it was like staring at a traffic accident—the reality of what I was seeing took time to register, my eyes were frozen on the screen—one of the naked men on the screen was my father! I couldn't have been more embarrassed, or disgusted. I took Joan by the arm, and we left.

Joan and I returned to the safety of my room until it was time for her to go home. It was late, and the party was breaking up. Downstairs, we looked for my mother, so Joan could say goodbye. My mother was nowhere to be found.

On our way out, we found my father in the living room holding a lady friend, Theresa, on his lap. She was squirming, trying to get off. My father was laughing. He had mixed his drinks, which was always his excuse for bad behavior.

Theresa continued to struggle as my father fondled her breasts. Suddenly, exasperated by her lack of cooperation, my father threw her off his lap.

Joan and I took this as our chance to get by my father, but he was too fast. Quickly, he grabbed Joan and pulled her to his lap placing one arm around her waist, and giving her the same treatment, fondling her breasts with his free hand.

"Mr. Lee, what are you doing? Let me go!" My father laughed and freed her. Joan left quickly. I was mortified. Did I still have a best friend? With a family like this, did I deserve to have any friends at all?

Just about everyone knew about my father, and his apartment on River Valley Road. They knew about the madam, or mama-san, who would call him at the office, to tell him of new girls, so he could pile his friends into his car to go sample the latest arrivals for lunch.

My father made no secret of such things. At parties he would brag, "I tell mama-san, get two more for the driver and his best friend."

None of this was a mystery to my mother. She said to me, "Stupid Judy thinks Jimmy is such a saint, just because he comes home for dinner." I threw it back at her, "What about my father?" My mother replied, with no emotion, "I don't care."

I understood, but still, the deteriorating behavior of my parents was disturbing. It was not a good environment for a girl in her teens.

I was disgusted with my parents.

LADY MACBETH

A T THE END of 1973, I graduated from the Singapore Chinese Girls School. By some miracle, at the age of sweet sixteen, with nobody's help but my own, I gained admission to the revered Raffles Institution, the top school in Singapore. Raffles Institution took only the best students, and boasted a long line of prominent graduates, the most prominent of all being Prime Minister Lee Kuan Yew.

I owed much of my scholastic success to the bad influence of my parents. They had given me proof that they could not be trusted, and that I had to rely on myself. I saw education as the key to freedom, got my act together, and concentrated on my schoolwork. Raffles was the result. With luck, I would graduate from Raffles in two years with a Baccalaureate Degree, the equivalent of making it through the first year of university.

Raffles Institution was founded by Sir Stamford Raffles, the "discoverer" of Singapore. Upon laying the foundation stone, Sir Stamford decreed that the school would be "a means of civilizing." Really?

Raffles was nothing like an American high school. Instead of cheerleaders, jocks, proms, sports, PTA meetings, counseling, and gunslingers, Raffles could boast only of nerds, grinds, wimps, bookworms, and virgins (mostly).

Eventually, Raffles got rid of the distraction of girls, and it is now an all-male institution in keeping with the official and ancient Confucianist traditions of modern-day Singapore.

At Raffles, it was now my turn to become one of the lesser lights. Gone were the days of the turquoise Cadillac, Karim, the magnificent chauffeur, and Ah Ngoh waiting in attendance. Like many others, I took the public bus to school, which, on my allowance of ten dollars a week, I could barely afford.

Unlike many of the girls who had their Raffles uniforms hand-tailored, mine were ill-fitting and off the rack from the school store.

I would complain to Ah Ngoh, "How can my parents spend a fortune on parties, catered food, liquor, and give me only ten dollars a week for allowance." Money is very important to Chinese—very important. Ah Ngoh never answered, it was not her place to answer, but at least she was there to listen.

My brother Sam, being a boy, should have fared better, but didn't. Sam wasn't my father's type, and *hell* was about to break loose for my brother.

I was studying in my bedroom when, all of a sudden, there was a ruckus coming from my father's room. Sam and my father were fighting! It was over a small matter, Sam's allowance. Sam was only fifteen, slender, and no match for a two hundred and fifty pound thug. It was one of the most horrible sights I could ever see.

Surprisingly, my mother stepped in and broke up the fight; apparently there were still some maternal instincts left.

The fight was over, but my father was not through with Sam. Screaming at the top of his lungs, he threw Sam out of the house, shouting one final word—"Epileptic!"

I thought that later, or the next day, Sam would return home, and that everything would be forgotten.

That did not happen.

Sam would never spend another night at home. He was on his own in the world, with no money and no place to live. Welfare and Child Protective Services do not exist in Singapore. There wasn't even a way for Sam to stay in school. Singapore public schools are not free; you have to pay. In Singapore, school is something you must be able to afford, a luxury. For those who cannot pay, it is not a problem. School has never been compulsory in Singapore, as it is in America.

The only person who could save Sam was Mamak, and so she did, paying for a small rented room for Sam, and covering his few living expenses. The family had a reputation to maintain.

While at Raffles, I took up with my first boyfriend, a law student attending the National University of Singapore, Peter Koh. Unhappily for my parents, he was from the Hainanese dialect group.

The Hainanese are best known for their chicken rice, a greasy dish featuring the yellow juicy skin of the chicken's thigh, a favorite menu item in Singapore.

Aside from their chicken rice, the Hainanese are considered to be at the bottom of the pile socially, occupying the lowest rung in the hierarchy of Chinese dialect groups—at least according to my father. I apologize for this, but such is the way of the Chinese. We have ancient traditions.

Peter first approached me on the pretext of writing an article about my family. At first glance, I was not exactly bowled over by Peter. He was not much to look at, a bit shorter than I, with slicked down hair, thick glasses, a pipe, and a cowboy shirt. It turned out that Peter loved cowboy movies.

Peter was, however, bright, and ambitious and I admired him for getting into the university, which was not a slam-dunk in Singapore.

Peter lived in a modest apartment with his parents, two sisters, and his grandmother. I visited him there only a few times. The apartment was filled with clutter, as are most Chinese dwellings. His mother was always home, and would give me her best smile with flashing gold teeth. A chicken, being fattened for the next festive occasion, roamed about the kitchen. Peter's grandmother, a tiny gray haired old lady, was also usually in the kitchen, chained by her ankle to an open pipe. Nothing unusual—in Singapore, even today, you won't see many old people out and around. We take care of our elderly.

What drew me to Peter was not his intellect, but the fact that he was poor and Hainanese, making him totally unacceptable to my parents. It was my way of rebelling against them—girls can be like that.

Under the circumstances, most parents, normal parents, might grumble a bit, say a word or two, and sulk. My father was more direct.

Peter and I were in the living room of my house. My father, smiling, walked into the room, as if to join us. Peter, always on edge with my father, stood up an offered his hand. My father, much larger, suddenly seized Peter by the throat with one hand and backed him up against the wall. Peter's toes were barely touching the floor.

"Are you a man or a mouse?" roared my father. Peter made no answer, nor did he have the courage to struggle. My father increased the pressure on Peter's throat. Peter was turning red, and actually made a mouselike squeal. "Are you a man or a mouse?" my father repeated, shouting at the top of his lungs. Peter had no choice and managed to utter weakly, "A mouse."

"Good," said my father, smiling and releasing his grip, "So you are a mouse, ah?" I doubt that Peter heard these last words, as, clasping his throat, he ran out of the house. This was not the end of Peter for me—only the beginning of the end.

I was no longer a little girl. I had let my hair grow down beyond my shoulders, and discarded my glasses for contact lenses. All this, and more, had been taken in by my father's practiced eye.

I had become a promising and marketable commodity and nothing should spoil that. My parents realized that it was time for *the talk*.

As with most parents, it was too late to close the barn door—still, my parents tried.

With my mother nodding in grave agreement, my father instructed me on the "don'ts" of dating. He didn't know or care about the "dos."

The main "don't" was don't be seen in the presence of "Whites, Indians, or Eurasians." If I were seen going out with them, no worthy Chinaman would want me.

So, did I follow my father's advice? Not really.

Had my parents understood me, they would have had no fears of my going off the deep end. They would have known that I had learned the virtues of seriousness and determination from Kong Kong, and that my boisterous and frivolous side, taken from Mamak, would never lead me astray.

Unfortunately, appearances count, and for some physical reason, I have always looked like a bad girl. My mother pointed that out to me many times, and said I looked evil, as well.

I had been typecast by my parents.

I guess it was due to Peter's influence that I had decided to study law. Since Singapore law is founded on British law, I reasoned that, once I graduated from Raffles, that England would be the best place for my university work. I would study in England, like my father's sister.

My father saw it differently. A Chinese girl going to study overseas? "No way, ah," my father said. "What you want? Your own White Monkey to bring back? No, lah!"

There was no way my parents were going pay for a mere girl to study overseas. My father was keeping his money for better things, for better girls, speedboats, and fast cars.

I approached Mamak. She would back me. She had paid for Sigurdsson's education. Unfortunately, my father had beaten me to her door. Mamak was not going to interfere. As always, she would keep the peace.

In spite of this discouragement, I still hoped that, somehow, I would be able to continue my education beyond Raffles. I wasn't about to be deterred from my ambition to be a lawyer.

But, just in case, I had to have an alternative.

Young people have many goals, as their aspirations have not yet been killed off by life. One of my many goals in life was to write. I had done some free-lancing for a Singapore construction magazine, and had seen what it took to put a magazine to bed. I understood the process. Why not start my very own construction magazine? I could do it, and begin to save on my own for an education. I called my magazine *Development and Construction*.

The magazine was a serious venture and a difficult undertaking as I had no capital, and little spare time, as my final examinations were just ahead.

Fortunately, I was blessed with the foolish optimism and infinite energy of a teenager.

I decided to approach one of our family companies, Tiger Press, to see if they would do the printing on credit. I could pay once the advertising revenue came in. This must have seemed an out and out gift by the company, but, I was in the family, which counted for something, and Tiger Press could afford to lose the money, so they agreed.

While studying for my final examinations, I wrote my new magazine's articles, solicited the advertising, sold or gave away subscriptions, set up the page layouts, checked the proofs, and delivered the finished product to Tiger Press.

One week before the end of the school year, The Tiger Press truck pulled up in front of 69 Holland Road with the finished copies of Volume 1, Number 1 of *Development and Construction*. I lugged the magazines up to my room, where I stuck on the mailing labels, and stuffed the envelopes. Peter helped me load it all into his small Fiat for the trip to the post office.

I was a one-girl gang.

To make things busier, I got the part of Lady Macbeth in our year-end school play.

This would be no easy amateur event. Raffles had its standards. There were endless rehearsals to get things just right.

Finally, a full-scale production of the play ran for three consecutive nights at Singapore's Victoria Theatre. I remembered my lines and hit my marks. It was the high point for me at Raffles, and a needed boost for my confidence.

Most important of all was the good news that I passed my examinations with good grades, good enough to continue on to university.

CUPID

IN JANUARY 1976, I was no longer in school. It was sad to be out of the system, especially since most of my friends had gone on to university, and were on their way to better things. I was a working girl, but it was not all bad.

In January, *Development and Construction* hit the streets. The front cover carried a full color rendering of the new International Plaza Building rising into the sky above. I charged the developer of the building S$2,000 for that.

The issue contained the Publisher's Message (that was me) stating, "Our editorial contents are especially designed to cater for the reading needs of professional people connected with the development and construction industry, real estate developers and business executives." Sounds grownup doesn't it? I thought so too, at the time.

The magazine started off with a bang. It was a success! I sold full-page advertisements to the Mandarin Hotel, and to Overseas Union Bank.

The magazine's first edition lead article was entitled *The Systems Approach to Construction Management*, written by Chow Kok Fong, a well-known civil engineer in Singapore.

My first issue raked in a gross of S$25,000, of which S$20,000 (US$9,600) was pure profit. Finally, I could buy some decent clothes!

No one could have been more surprised than Tiger Press, when I proudly paid them in full.

My father was not impressed at all. His only reaction was, "You know, ah, you are only going to get us all into a big peck of trouble. The law, ah. You know, ah, no way you can run a business from home. This is no good, lah." Still, for some reason, he did not stop me.

My mother? I doubt that she noticed.

Connections help—they always do. Before the sale of Chung Khiaw Bank, Kong Kong had brought the famous architect, I. M. Pei, to Singapore to design a new headquarters building for the bank. Since then, I had gotten to know I. M. Pei pretty well. Even though his young fun-loving assistant, Pershing Wong, attended a number of my father's parties, I. M. Pei had the good sense to stay away.

When I heard that I. M. Pei was visiting Singapore for the design of the Raffles International Centre, I used my connections to arrange an interview for my magazine.

The great man remembered me well, was very friendly, and insisted that I call him by his name, Ieoh Ming.

The interview with Ieoh Ming resulted in an article in the August 1976 edition of *Development and Construction* entitled, *Aspects of Modern Architecture.*

Ieoh Ming was very easy to talk to, very open, and responded to my questions graciously. I have the highest regard for Ieoh Ming; his EQ was as great as his IQ.

I asked, "There is an architectural statement saying that 'Forms follow Functions.' Does this apply to all your designs?"

"No," was Ieoh Ming's simple answer. Like all innovators, he was not bound by the rules. I liked that.

"We understand that you are the best in the design of concrete technology. Tell us your reason for not applying this material to the OCBC building. In a way, it might promote the image 'as solid as a rock.'"

Ieoh Ming responded, "That is a very good question. In fact, I wanted to build it out of concrete. We explored the use of concrete when we first came here, eight or nine years ago when your grandfather, Dato Lee Chee Shan, sent for us. We discovered that there is a problem with the use of concrete in Singapore because of your climatic conditions." Ieoh Ming went on to say that if he lived in Singapore, he would "solve the problem."

I hesitated. Most of Singapore was built of concrete, including the large public apartment houses in which 86 percent of Singapore lives. What did Ieoh Ming think about that? Better not to ask.

The magazine had been a success initially, but market dynamics were catching up with me. By 1977, construction was leveling off, and the market for the magazine had been fragmented by a number of new competitors.

I faced the painful reality that for my magazine to survive, I had to head out to the various countries of the region to expand its scope.

Singapore was no longer enough to fill my magazine.

To compensate for the lack of material, I made the magazine into a tri-monthly publication, and my next issue covered the three-month period of April, May, and June of 1977. To expand the magazine's horizon beyond Singapore, the magazine's cover featured the design model of the Tête de La Défense, in Paris.

For that issue, I sold the inside front cover to Libby Owens Ford Company. I also accepted a full-page advertisement for Singapore Airlines in exchange for a first class return ticket to Hong Kong, where I hoped to drum up business.

Since this was my first trip to Hong Kong, my family urged me to pay my respects to my illustrious relative, Sally Aw, the Hong Kong newspaper magnate. In 1954, at the age of only twenty-three, lucky Sally had inherited the main part of the Aw brothers' newspaper empire, Hong Kong's Sing Tao Group.

Sally was the adopted daughter of Boon Haw and his favorite wife, Kyi Kyi.

At the time of my visit, Kyi Kyi and the adopted Sally, a spinster, were still ensconced in their mansion in the Tiger Balm Gardens.

To prepare me for my visit, Mamak instructed me to address Kyi Kyi as "Oh Glorious Aunt." It seemed like a load of crap to me—even then children were not what they used to be.

Dutifully, I called on the two grand ladies in Sally's office at her newspaper. The office was impressive, with a spectacular view of Hong Kong's harbor. Kyi Kyi, a mousy lady, was seated comfortably on a couch. She was adorned with diamonds and a spectacular jade set of matching earrings, necklace, bracelet and ring. A miniature white poodle was clutched to her breast protectively.

Sally was positioned behind a large teakwood desk. She was dressed in a pantsuit, and wore glasses, presenting a Mao-like figure. Her face was graced with a lucky mole. The two ladies remained seated as I entered.

I greeted my "Oh Glorious Aunt" as instructed. Kyi Kyi responded with studied politeness, "You are the granddaughter of Cheng Hu, Boon Par's favorite daughter," Cheng Hu being my grandmother's first name. My uneasiness was reduced by Kyi Kyi's acknowledgement that, as a relative, I qualified for an audience. I took a seat in one of two straight-back wooden chairs facing Sally's desk.

Now it was Sally's turn to speak.

In impeccable English, she greeted me saying, "Who would have thought you were a relative of mine? If I saw you on the street, I wouldn't even recognize you."

Did I look wrong, somehow? Not Chinese enough? Had I made a mistake by sitting down? Should I be kneeling?

I didn't know, or really care. After some initial pleasantries, Sally did me the favor of giving me the heave-ho saying, "Convey our best wishes to Cheng Hu. I hope you have a good time in Hong Kong. Goodbye."

That was it—my audience was over and I didn't even get a free lunch.

In 1992, Sally reached her zenith, when she and Kyi Kyi, were welcomed to Beijing by Communist Party Chief, Jiang Zemin, and Premier Li Peng. The Chinese government put Sally and Kyi Kyi up in the Diaoyutai state guesthouse, reserved for only the most important foreign visitors, and hosted a dinner in their honor. Sally was a powerful woman and was publishing newspapers in Hong Kong, the United States, Canada, Europe, and Australia.

In Hong Kong, however, Sally had a reputation of being a miserly penny pinching recluse, a micro-manager who insisted on signing every company check. She was close only to her mother, and her widowed sister-in-law. The trio became known at the newspaper as The Three Blind Mice.

These qualities do not make, or even preserve a fortune. Sally's luck was to be the adopted daughter of Aw Boon Haw, born of his "poor distant relatives," or so the official story goes. Her resemblance to her father, however, would suggest an even more humble and curious origin.

Sally finally managed to squander the vast fortune, which luck had dumped in her lap, and reached the brink of bankruptcy. In 1998, she was arrested for falsely inflating the circulation figures of the Hong Kong Standard, her English-language Hong Kong newspaper. Even the U.S. State Department protested when Sally got off the hook, citing her "close ties to Beijing."

There is a Chinese proverb that wealth in a family lasts for only three generations. Sally managed to make it in two. Mercifully, Kyi Kyi was dead by the time, and not around to see Sally's final disgrace.

In December 1998, her dwindling finances forced Sally to sell the Tiger Balm Gardens Haw Par Mansion and the Aw Boon Haw Gardens to Hong Kong's leading billionaire, Li Ka Shing, for US$13 million. In April 1999, to avert bankruptcy, Sally sold the Sing Tao Group for US$70 million.

And that was the end of the empire of the Tiger Balm Kings.

The end for my magazine came much sooner.

Unfortunately, bartering advertising space for airline tickets is not the way to make money with a magazine, and, unfortunately, I came up empty handed in Hong Kong.

In the end, the construction downturn in Singapore, increased competition, and going tri-monthly with fewer issues, had reduced my revenue to the point where the magazine was barely profitable.

I couldn't carry on with the magazine, as I didn't have the money to wait out the bad times. I had hung on for as long as possible. So, my magazine, for which I had such high hopes, closed shop.

The magazine had rewarded me, not only financially, but by giving me self-confidence, and the satisfaction of being productive at a time when I felt very lost and left behind by my contemporaries who had gone off to university.

Next, I got rid of Peter, his pipe, cowboy shirts, and all, for the very good reason that I had grown and changed.

Education had always been my first priority, so without funding from my parents to study in England, I enrolled in an external law course, a form of distance learning, given by the University of London. The courses were conducted informally by professors and practicing lawyers in Singapore.

Also attending the law course was an older and very pleasant fellow, named Lim Swee Cheong. He became a lifelong friend.

Swee Cheong was then a Captain in the Singapore Armed Forces. He was engaging, intelligent, fun, and unassuming, and young at heart.

Judging by my family's lifestyle, and by the house in which I lived, anyone would have thought that I too had money, and plenty of it. True I had free room and board, but disposable cash—never. With my magazine gone, I needed a source of income, something to pay for my law studies, and for my clothes.

I decided to become a model. It seemed easy enough. I was tall, I was thin, so why not? Even though my father loved models, he was extremely unhappy about my becoming one.

Did I care?

Singapore is very academic, and nearly everything requires a course of some sort. This follows the time-honored Chinese tradition that you can do only what you have been taught by others to do, and, equally important, you do it in the way you are taught. Innovation or figuring something out for yourself are not options.

If you tell a Singaporean that you play the piano, the immediate question is, "What grade are you?" In Singapore, piano students must pass a national examination at the end of each year. Pianowise, I had achieved grade ten, thanks to Mamak, who paid.

So it was with modeling. To become a model you had to go to modeling school, otherwise how would you know how to walk? Who would ever hire you?

Modeling school was a rip-off, since the school doubled as a modeling agency, licensed, of course. They got you coming and going.

I modeled on a part-time basis, which I guess all models do, more or less. In Singapore, a model's pay was low, and very difficult to collect. Nevertheless, modeling gave me the income I needed, and unexpectedly provided me with a new group of friends.

It was not part of the plan, but I was entering the best period of my life.

Shortly after dumping Peter, I took up with an even less acceptable candidate in the eyes of my father—a forbidden white man—an American by the all-American name of John, "Call me Glenn, with a double-n, that's my middle name," Hawkins.

Glenn was a big step up in age for me. He was thirty-eight years old at the time to my twenty.

After bringing Glenn around to the house, my father said, "Why

you want an old man like that? The bugger's white, you know, Chu?"
Yes, I had noticed.

"No one will want you. Why so stupid? Why you become so like that? I say man."

I knew exactly what I was doing, and I was in control, whatever my father may have thought.

I was very taken by Glenn. I had never really known an American before. He was from an exotic place called Chattanooga, Tennessee, and had twinkling blue eyes. I had never seen blue eyes up close before. I thought he looked like a combination of John Denver and Dennis Weaver. He wore a baseball cap, and had a basketball hoop above his garage. He was so American!

Glenn was great fun. We went on double dates with Joan and her boyfriend, and checked out the baseball games at the Singapore American School, just like they do in America.

Glenn was very personable and self-assured. Unlike Peter, the mouse, when Glenn came to the house he made an effort to say hello to my father, man-to-man. To my great surprise, my father seemed to take to Glenn, shake hands with him, and smile. My father was being much too friendly.

Finally, it reached the point, where during the handshake-smile routine, my father turned to me and smiled, "Chu, I really like this bugger, why you never invite him to our parties?" Before I could answer, my father turned to Glenn, "You come next Friday, ah?"

I don't think Glenn had seen anything like my father's parties. He was dazzled, especially when my father introduced him to Bridget, a Singapore Airlines flight attendant, one of my father's young beauties.

Glenn and Bridget hit it off immediately, and, not long thereafter, got married, but not for happily ever after. I didn't see Glenn again, but I heard that he and Bridget eventually got divorced.

Bill was my next old flame, and I can't even remember his name, his last name, that is. Bill was also a white man, an overweight, bearded fellow, more in my age bracket, somewhere in his mid-twenties. He was the Second Secretary of the Canadian High Commission in Singapore. He drove a small vintage red sports convertible, and, of course, wore a baseball cap. Bill was a bright fellow.

On first seeing Bill, my father exclaimed, "Why you do like that to Papa? This one not only white, the bugger has a *jungut*, cannot even see the face." My father loved to spice up his Singlish with local terms, "jungut" meaning bearded in Malay.

After that, Bill was referred to by my father as the "jungut." My father loved to ask, "Where your *jungut*, today, Chu?" It made him laugh.

Again, my father's arrow struck through the heart. Like Glenn, before him, Bill was invited by my father to the family parties. Like Glenn, he fell victim to one of my father's endless supply of beauties. Did they marry? I no longer cared to know.

Then came Dennis. He was twenty-eight at the time, a forbidden Eurasian.

The term Eurasian, a combination of "European" and "Asian," denotes a person of European and Asian descent. Until recently, the European half was invariably the man, my mother being a notable exception for her time.

Consequently, most Eurasians bear European surnames. In fact, The Eurasian Association of Singapore requires that one's last name be European to qualify for membership as Eurasian. That wouldn't wash in America.

Eurasians count for only about one percent of Singapore's population. Still, they are a well-established community with roots going back to the earliest days of our history.

Dennis D'Cotta's father was a Singapore Supreme Court Judge, a Eurasian of Portuguese origin. Dennis's mother was Irish, and Dennis had the good looks to show for it. He was tall, fair, and had greenish eyes. He was also worldly-wise and intelligent. Despite his father's speaking perfect English, when Dennis opened his mouth, out came pure Singlish.

The D'Cotta's bungalow, a luxury in Singapore, was beautifully kept, and had a friendly and relaxed atmosphere, which was something new for me. I found it a pleasure to visit their house, no chained-up grandmothers, or chickens running around at the D'Cotta's.

Notwithstanding Judge D'Cotta's prominent position in Singapore, Dennis, being Eurasian, was off bounds for me.

Unfortunately for my father, Dennis was over six feet tall, which presented a problem as it ruled out any form of strangulation, à la the diminutive Peter Koh.

A girl from my father's office? No, my father realized that Dennis, with his good looks could get pretty much anyone he wanted. There must be another way.

My father befriended Dennis, engaging him in earnest conversation, finding out his likes and dislikes, probing for a weakness.

I could see what my father was doing, but I knew Dennis would be different. Unlike Americans, and Canadians, who were easy prey, Dennis was used to the alluring temptations of Singapore, and would not succumb.

And so it came to pass that my father did a very generous thing. He invited Dennis to come along with him on a trip to Bangkok, Thailand, all expenses paid.

I was suspicious of my father's uncharacteristic offer. Dennis, perhaps aspiring to become my father's future son-in-law, saw the trip as a chance to bond. And bond they did!

The day my father returned home, he didn't appear until dinner. When he finally sat down at the dining table, he seemed extremely happy. He was casually dressed in his usual outfit for family dinners, a Hanes white sleeveless undershirt, blue short pants, sandals, and a diamond-studded gold Rolex watch. In Singapore, this is said to be the dress code of Chinese millionaires.

My mother and I sat in silence. I was unable to bring myself to ask my father what had happened in Bangkok, I couldn't bring myself to speak.

My father wasted no time in opening up the conversation. He addressed his remarks to my mother, as though I were not present, "Wah, that Dennis bugger, he's quite a guy."

My mother sat silently, seemingly preoccupied with whatever was on the plate before her.

"Wah, that Dennis bugger, I took him to a place—full of women—told him he could take his pick." My father broke out in laughter, wiping his mouth with his fingers. He then made his third pass at the subject, "Chu, ah, you know, ah, he likes the old ... Took an old one, ah." My father fixed his smiling eyes on me.

Finally I spoke, "What are you saying Papa? What exactly are you trying to say?"

"Nothing, just your boyfriend, Dennis, he likes to fuck old women. Chu, why you keep a bugger like that?"

As my father was often not to be believed, I gave Dennis his last chance.

The next day, we were alone in my room. Dennis seemed distant. Something was wrong. Dennis showed no interest in me, which was quite unusual.

"What's wrong?" I asked.

Dennis confessed, "I can't be alone with you. Not just yet."

"What do you mean," I asked, eyes wide open. "Well, your father took me to a place ... There were women."

"Women!" I was bug-eyed.

"Yes, and as he was taking one, he offered one to me."

"And?" I held my breath.

"Well, I was with her," was all Dennis could bring himself to say.

Some bonding! Some father! That was the end of Dennis.

After Dennis, I cooled it with the boyfriends. It had nothing to do with my father, I just didn't run into the right person. That doesn't mean I was a stay-at-home.

I continued to see people, going to parties, making the rounds with my best friend Joan and having a good time.

So long as I was not involved with anyone, my father seemed quite happy.

My mother, however, took up where my father left off. "Now that you have been out with whites and a Eurasian, won't you be taking up with some Indian, soon, Chu?" She once caught me with Joan and said, "Since the two of you like to go out so much, you may as well get paid for it. Why don't you become social escorts?" I was embarrassed, Joan was mortified, and my mother was laughing.

Friends can be dangerous to a marriage. My mother could not have been happy with my father's bad behavior, which he proudly flaunted. His tiresome repetition of "One wife and a million sweethearts," had become more than a stupid motto.

It was not unusual for my father to show up at home long after midnight with a lady or two in tow. His purpose was to show off the house. It was in and out, and then off to his "secret" apartment with his sweetheart(s).

I had no respect for my father, and hoped that my mother would leave him. She was still in her prime, at the peak of her beauty. Any man would have noticed her. It was her time to make a move.

My mother had her chances. She was not a complete fool, and she was very savvy with men, and there were men. Under the conditions, why not? Did my father care?

She was about to find out.

My mother was madly in love with Geoff, the man I had seen her dancing with at our party several years before. Associating everyone with a movie star, she thought he was the "Bradford Dillman type."

Geoff's wife finally realized what was going on between Geoff and my mother, and charged, one day, into my father's office, threatening to make the entire affair known.

I doubt he cared about the affair, but, in Asia, everyone cares about face. From his quiver of beautiful women, my father drew his next arrow, a Chinese girl named Connie. He would invite her to his next party.

It all ended happily—for my father—Geoff dumped both my mother and his American wife for Connie.

The last I heard was that Geoff and Connie got married, were living in Hong Kong, and had a lovely little daughter.

My mother was devastated. She didn't make her move, and her time passed, forever.

Glenn and Bridget, Bill and the beauty, Dennis and the old whore, Geoff and Connie. They owed it all to my father—their unlikely, unsavory, unprincipled, uncouth Cupid.

PRINCE CHARMING

I MET MY future husband, Hin Chew, in October 1978, at a nightclub called My Place.

A group of friends, and I, were out for the evening. The group was headed by C. T. Lim, a construction project manager whom I had met while doing a piece for my magazine.

Everybody liked C. T. He was a fun-loving, party person, already well oiled for a great evening as we invaded My Place. I still remember what I was wearing—a white dress with spaghetti straps, and a plunging neckline with matching strappy high heels. My hair, parted in the center, cascaded down below my shoulders. I was looking good.

C. T., ever alert, spotted someone through the darkness, and led the way to a table where two men were seated. "Goh Boon Kok, is that you? How are you." said C. T., pulling me by the arm. "Hey, I want you to meet one of my friends ... this is the Tiger Balm Princess! Meet the Tiger Balm Princess!"

This was not how I preferred to be introduced, but C. T. was doing it all in fun.

Goh Boon Kok, his eyes brightening, stood up to shake my hand, "Oh yes, very nice to meet you, yes very nice." Goh Boon Kok turned quickly to the other man who had remained seated, "And I would like you to meet my friend, Hin Chew. Hin Chew, this is, ah ...?" I stretched out my hand and said, "I'm May Chu."

Hin Chew, much younger than Goh Boon Kok, sported a Beatles haircut, and an outfit to match—white pants, dark shirt, shoes, but no socks. He made no effort to rise, but reached out his hand to me, and after a brief shake, leaned back in his chair, cigar in his right hand, an outsized snifter in the other. Goh Boon Kok motioned enthusiastically for me to sit next to his friend.

Hin Chew came across to me as a spoiled jerk, a typical rich kid, with the qualities of dated hip, a debonair wannabe, and an attitude.

There's something about first impressions—they are usually right. Hin Chew was fair, on the stocky side, and not too tall. He had strong features, a high-bridged nose, almond eyes, and thin lips, which gave him the appearance of being Korean or Japanese rather than Chinese.

For starters, I didn't like him, and engaged him in a battle of wits.

"So, where do you come from?" I asked haughtily.

Taken aback by my attitude, but recovering quickly, he responded, "I just finished my Masters Degree from MIT. You do know where MIT is, don't you?"

I said, "Of course! It's in Boston. So, what did you study?"

"Ocean Engineering."

"Oceanography," I answered, being intelligent.

"No, Ocean Engineering and Oceanography are totally different," he sniffed.

Continuing, I said, "Do you know what MIT stands for in Singapore?"

"What?" taking a puff on his cigar.

"It stands for Made in Taiwan."

He didn't laugh. Now I was the stupid one.

Hin Chew went on to say he was the eldest of four sons. It was very important to be the eldest. How old was he? Five years older than I.

What was he doing in Singapore? "Oh, nothing, just visiting, staying at the Shangri-La."

Expensive, I thought, "Are you working here in Singapore?"

"I work for my father's company in Brunei."

Goh Boon Kok who had been listening intently, chirped in, "Yes, Hin Chew's father, S. P. Chung, owns a very large company in Brunei."

"Oh," was all I could say.

Goh Boon Kok interrupted, "I work for his father here, in Singapore, as his chief auditor."

Politely bringing Goh Boon Kok into the conversation, I asked, "You're a friend of C. T.'s?"

"C. T. is my brother-in-law."

C. T. perked up, and, from the far end of the table, pointed at me, raised his glass, and slurred, "The Tiger Balm Princess!"

That's how Fate works. If I hadn't lost hope of going on to

university, if I hadn't started the magazine, and not met C. T. Lim, I would not have been there talking to Hin Chew.

Had my father, Cupid, saved me for this?

At the end of the evening, Hin Chew asked me for my phone number, which I gave him, not expecting to hear from him again.

The next morning, Hin Chew called to ask me out for that evening. Unfortunately, I was busy, my architect friend, Ieoh Ming was in town, and I was having dinner with him. Hin Chew asked if I could meet him after dinner. Well, maybe, I told him I would call once dinner was over, if it wasn't too late.

That afternoon, a beautiful basket of the speckled tiger orchids arrived. The first to pounce on the card was my mother.

"Chu! They are for you! Chu! These are the most expensive orchids you can buy!"

I reached for the card, but my mother pulled back. "It says, 'I hope you can make it tonight - Hin Chew.'"

My mother looked up at me beaming, "Who is Hin Chew? Who is this, Chu?"

"Just someone I met, no one special," but I got the connection, tiger orchids for the Tiger Balm Princess, clever.

"Nothing special! Tiger orchids cost a fortune, child. Let me put them in the living room." My mother ran off with the tiger orchids; they were hers now.

That evening, after dinner, Ieoh Ming decided he wanted to go dancing. We went to a nightspot called The Library at the Mandarin Hotel. Ieoh Ming is fascinating, a real genius, and I always hung on to every word he said. Nevertheless, I took a powder-room break to call Hin Chew at the Shangri-La Hotel to thank him for the beautiful flowers, and give him my regrets for the evening.

Hearing the music in the background, Hin Chew asked whom I was with. "A family friend, I. M. Pei, he's an architect."

"You don't have to tell me that I. M. Pei is an architect, he's famous." Hin Chew answered. I was impressed. Maybe there was more to Hin Chew than that ocean stuff. We made a date for dinner the next day.

As promised, the following evening, a taxi pulled up in front of 69 Holland Road. Hin Chew stepped out, passed through the gates of our driveway, walked to the house and rang the doorbell.

Ready and waiting, I greeted him at the door, telling him to wait while I went to tell my parents I would be out. Hin Chew said fine, and went back to hold the taxi.

Upstairs, I found my parents in an exaggerated state of agitation. My mother, dressed in a kimono, was dancing around. My father, dressed one hundred percent in Hanes—white undershirt, white underpants—was smiling and very happy. They had both been peering trough a tiny slit of a window upstairs, looking down at Hin Chew.

"Chu! That's the bugger that sent the flowers?" my father exclaimed. I nodded.

"He's so fair! Jackie, did you see how fair his arms are? This is a high-class looking guy, Jackie, and he's Chinese. I can see an expensive watch!" said my mother, breathlessly.

"This bugger's the one, Chu. He's the one!" laughed my father.

I knew exactly where my father was going with this, but I wasn't ready to get serious about anyone. I hardly knew the guy.

Hin Chew turned out to be more fun than I thought. We wound up going out nearly every day. He was charming and had a sense of humor. I guess first impressions can be deceiving, after all.

Although it had been only a month that Hin Chew and I had been dating, my father summoned me, and said, with a big grin, "Chu, it is time for us to meet this young man. Please tell him to join us for dinner at the Brasserie on Friday."

There was nothing I could do; I had to comply, otherwise my father, himself, would track Hin Chew down to invite him.

At the dinner, Hin Chew was extremely polite, and made a great first impression on my parents. My father was, unbelievably, on his best behavior. I had rarely been on the receiving end of my father's bounty, but now the Dom Perignon flowed, even for me. At the end of the dinner, Hin Chew lit up a huge cigar, a Davidoff, to show my father that he, too, was a connoisseur of the finer things in life. My mother beamed—my father and Hin Chew liked each other. My father looked at me and smiled, finally I had done something right.

But where was this all going?

Hin Chew's mother, Lillian, was flying in from Brunei, and Hin

Chew invited me to come along to the airport to pick her up.

As soon as Lillian saw me, she looked surprised, but greeted me cordially.

Lillian was short, a bit on the heavy side, and conservatively dressed. She was not unattractive, but big-boned, with a big head, like her son. Her floor-scrubber knees betrayed a hard life, but the gold Rolex on her wrist showed a happy ending.

As we walked out of the airport, Lillian explained her surprise upon seeing me. Her soothsayer had prophesized that her eldest son would marry a Chinese girl, with very big eyes. Thanks to Granny, my eyes were large by Chinese standards, but was I that girl?

Several days later, I met Hin Chew's father. He called himself "S. P.," short for his full name, Chung Shih Ping.

As soon as he saw me, S. P. grinned widely and threw open his arms and said, "Ah, you must be May Chu," giving me a hug. Very expansive for Asia.

S. P. was of medium height, a bit taller than Hin Chew, and looked fit and healthy. He had a round and pleasant face, and his full head of black hair, parted on one side, helped him to appear much younger than his age. S. P. was meticulously well groomed and possessed a charisma, punctuated by the warm gestures that seemed to come so naturally to him. He had winning ways. Why couldn't I have had a father like that?

Once I had met Hin Chew's parents, my father lost no time, and quickly made his move. He invited the Chungs out for dinner. S. P. and Lillian wasted no time to reciprocate. The champagne flowed; it was thrust and parry as my father and S. P. matched each other as hosts.

It was all great fun, and I loved the attention. I cared for Hin Chew and he appeared to be a great catch. His parents were very nice, every bit as nice as mine were nuts, but things were moving so fast that I felt like an observer, standing on the outside.

Two and a half months after Hin Chew and I had met, our parents organized a dinner at the Shang Palace in the Shangri-La Hotel. It was in a private room, with a table for ten, in attendance were also Goh Boon Kok and his wife.

S. P. wore a dove-gray Lanvin suit. Lillian was in Nina Ricci, with a strand of white South Sea pearls.

My mother, who was all in a tizzy, had on a floor-length bubble-gum pink dress, set off by a white ostrich stole. If you could get past the ostrich feathers and the pink dress, you might notice her diamond earrings, and matching diamond necklace. My mother was dressed to kill, like some kind of alien empress. It was awful!

My father was in a very good mood, as the dinner was on S. P., and the Shang Palace was the most expensive restaurant that money could buy. My father liked that, as most Chinese would. If it's expensive, it's good. That's Asia.

My father was wearing a jacket, very unusual for him. It looked like something was going down.

Hin Chew and I sat next to each other between our two sets of parents and remained silent.

There was no mention of anything other than the superficial during dinner. It would have been impolite of the hosts.

Dinner over, it was into the lobby for after-dinner drinks. We settled down on some sofas in the center of the lobby, while Goh Boon Kok and his wife excused themselves.

Once seated, my father wasted no time. Switching gears to humble, he leaned forward, and said, "You know, ah, S. P., my daughter is getting older, twenty-one, and it is now time for her to marry."

I was listening, and so was Hin Chew. What else could we do?

S. P. responded, "Yes, Jackie, Hin Chew is twenty-six, it is his time to marry, too."

My father nodded seriously, Lillian leaned back in her chair with a benevolent smile, my mother leaned forward, transfixed, her mouth open, poised for a smile. Hin Chew and I sat in stunned silence—we had never said a word to each other about marriage.

S. P. continued, "We have had much unhappiness. This year, my number two son, and number three son, both marry. But they both marry white girls, very good girls, but not like us ... not Chinese, you know ..."

My father furrowed his brow with an I-hear-you-buddy nod of sympathy; this he followed by a lightning glance my way—then he pounced, "Good then, it is agreed, your son will marry my daughter."

S. P. began to nod, but my father still had one piece of unfinished business. Eyes downcast, switching to meek, my father said, "And, S. P., if you want, I can pay half of the expenses for the wedding."

Skewered! It was a beautiful move by my father.

S. P. answered immediately, "No, Jackie, no, no, no, I will take care of all the expenses. You just tell us who you want to invite, how many tables you will need. Where to give the wedding. I leave everything up to you."

It was a complete and total victory for my father. He would be in charge, and S. P. would pay!

And what about the prospective bride and groom? They had no say in the matter, at all. I knew what I thought, but whatever Hin Chew was thinking, he did not say.

My father wanted to get me out of the house to cut the expense, as he had done with my brother, Sam.

And S. P.'s agenda? I would find out about that some years later.

The deal sealed, Goh Boon Kok and the minions were summoned from their table.

It was time to organize the wedding.

THE WEDDING

THE WEDDING was set for Sunday, March 18, 1979. It would be topped off with a wedding dinner for one thousand at the Mandarin Hotel. It was to be the wedding of the year; one that Singapore had never seen.

Sparing no expense, S. P. put his very best people on the job, headed by Goh Boon Kok. An event of this magnitude needed planning and organization, and S. P. put the wheels of money and industry in motion to meet the challenge.

First, computerized lists of invitees were printed out for S. P. These were sorted by the categories of *Close Relatives, Business Associates, Shipyards & Bankers, Government Officials, S. P.'s Employees,* and *Outstation,* for those flying in from abroad.

The printouts gave full details for each guest: *Address, Company, Job Title,* and, for those flying in, *Air Ticket Issuance,* and *Hotel and Room Number.* All airfares and hotel bills would be paid for by S. P.

For the Brunei guests, S. P. chartered two Royal Brunei Airline Boeing 737s, scheduled to depart from Brunei at 6:00 P.M., the Friday before the wedding, returning the following Monday at 7:00 P.M. The guests would be put up either at the Shangri-La or Mandarin, a single hotel was not large enough.

My father too participated in organizing the wedding, making the most of his free ride. His share of the guest list consisted of cronies, lady friends, and those he wanted to make green with envy. My father had scores to settle.

In addition, my father had to do some major damage control regarding the entrance and seating of Granny and our Eurasian relatives. My mother was to make sure that they were among the last to enter, and my father had them assigned to a table at the far end of the room. Hopefully, no one would see Granny and our Eurasian relatives, or if they did, mistake them for the help.

To establish his position in the organization of the wedding, my father had Goh Boon Kok rush off a telegram to S. P., who was back in Brunei. It read:

WE WILL TRY TO GET STRING QUARTET FROM RADIO TELEVISION SINGAPORE AND MC FROM RADIO TELEVISION SINGAPORE. WE HAVE LISTENED TO THE PRESENT MUSICAL BAND PERFORMED IN MANDARIN HOTEL AND FOUND OUT IT IS NOT SUITABLE.

THE SITTING ARRANGEMENT IS BEING PREPARED WITH JACKIE LEE THIS MORNING.

MANDARIN HOTEL AGREES TO SUPPLY CORSAGE (ORCHID) FOR EACH LADY GUEST THAT NITE.

WE SHALL TRY THE MUSLIM FOOD PREPARED BY MANDARIN HOTEL TOMORROW WITH JACKIE LEE TO SEE WHETHER IT IS OK.

RGDS GOH BOON KOK

Not only had "Jackie Lee" taken charge of the seating arrangements, he was now an expert on Muslim food. The universal man!

Most Chinese weddings, even today, are preceded by the traditional tea ceremony, a serious ritual, which is considered legally binding, even though no official documents are produced, as tradition predates such legalities.

For the tea ceremony, I was dressed in a floor-length red *cheongsam*, with a flower behind my right ear. Hin Chew wore a beige suit.

The tea ceremony was simple. We served tea to our respective elders, in return for gifts.

To be fair, to parents and grandparents, our tea ceremony was split into three parts, beginning with my parents at 69 Holland Road.

After serving tea to my parents, Hin Chew and I knelt before them to receive the traditional red packets containing gifts. My father gave Hin Chew a Patek Philippe watch, and my mother gave me a matching set of diamond earrings.

After the short ceremony, we went with my parents to Casa Emma to pay our respects to Kong Kong and Mamak. Again, Hin Chew and

I served tea, and as with my parents, we knelt before my grandparents to receive their blessings, and our second set of red packets for the day. Mamak gave me a stunning diamond necklace, with a large diamond pendant attached. Mamak gave Hin Chew a beautiful pair of cufflinks, made of rare imperial jade.

Smiling Kong Kong handed me another red packet, and asked me to open it. I did so and was astounded to see that it contained one hundred thousand Singapore Dollars in cash. I had never seen such a large amount of money. Finally, the poor little rich girl had some cash of her own.

On leaving Casa Emma, my mother immediately pulled me aside and said, "Chu, you be sure to bring your dowry money to the tea ceremony this afternoon. Don't forget!"

The final part of our tea ceremony, which took place after lunch, was to pay our respects to S. P. and Lillian. For the occasion, S. P. had taken a private room, the Thai Room, at the Shangri-La Hotel.

As Hin Chew and I entered the hotel with my parents, my father turned to Hin Chew, and asked, with affected graciousness, "Hin Chew, ah, may I see my daughter alone? Just for a moment? Please?"

"Why, yes, of course," answered Hin Chew, fully understanding the last touching moments of a father with a daughter he was about to lose through marriage, "I'll meet you in the room."

My father walked me over to a corner of the lobby so we could be alone. "Chu, you know, all this have been very expensive for Papa."

Huh? I thought, what expense? My father wasn't paying a cent for the wedding.

"We have had to entertain the Chungs, parties, ah, and dinners, restaurants, very expensive. You know, ah?"

I said nothing. I was pretty sure where this was going, and was not about to help out.

"Chu, ah," my father smiled, "you know, Papa did all this for you. Papa arranged all this for you. I deserve my part. You give me half the money my father give you."

What was I to do? It was my upbringing. I opened my purse, pulled out Kong Kong's red packet, counted out fifty thousand dollars in crisp notes, and handed them to my father. It was very painful.

In that brief moment, my father had recouped whatever he had spent on me, not only for the wedding, but also for my entire life. He even turned a profit.

Our tea ceremony with the Chung family was the most elaborate and traditional of all, right down to the roast pig's head, resting in a basket of fruits.

Lotus seeds and red dates were placed in the tea, to help us produce children early in our marriage, and for every year thereafter. The sweetness of the tea was intended to foster equally sugary relations between my in-laws and myself.

I served the tea, passing the teacup with both hands to my parents to thank them for raising me. Thanks Papa—you got paid in full for all your efforts.

Hin Chew and I then served tea to his parents, taking care to offer the cup with both hands. To be polite in Asia, you use two hands to give something to another person.

We then knelt before S. P. and Lillian to receive their blessings. Hin Chew received a red packet containing one hundred thousand Brunei Dollars in cash, the equivalent to what I had received from Kong Kong. Lucky Hin Chew; he got to keep every cent of his gift, as no kickback to S. P. was expected. I received two jewelry ensembles—necklace, earrings, bracelet, and ring, one of diamonds, and one of jade.

The pig's head came into play at the end of the tea ceremony. It is the custom for the bride's family to return the head and tail of the pig to the groom's family to symbolize a good beginning and end of the wedding. My parents did not bother.

The schedule for the Wedding Dinner was printed in gold letters on a double-folded shiny red card:

7.00 pm	Standby for wedding dinner ceremony
7.00 pm – 8.00 pm	Arrival of guests
8.00 pm	All guests be seated
8.00 pm	Arrival of top Govt Officials from Brunei. Arrival of the President.
8.10 pm – 8.30 pm	Announcement of Bride and Groom
8.30 pm	Dinner be served
9.10 pm	Toasting Ceremony – After 4th course of dinner. (a) Cake Cutting (b) Speeches by M.C. (c) Toasting

At 7:00 P.M. sharp, Hin Chew and I, our parents, Hin Chew's three brothers, Jim, Peter, and Paul, and my two sisters-in-law were standing at the entrance of the banquet hall ready to receive the guests, all one thousand of them.

S. P. had done his calculations and instructed us, "We have only one hour to get everyone in. Keep them moving, you'll have only four seconds per guest, but that should be plenty."

For the reception, I was dressed in a long white wedding dress, with a diamond tiara, borrowed from Mamak. I wore the diamond earrings my mother had given me that day, along with Mamak's tea ceremony gift of the diamond necklace. I glittered!

Hin Chew, S. P., and my father were wearing tuxedos with white jackets to set them apart from Hin Chew's brothers who were in black.

S. P.'s parents, in from Brunei, my grandparents, and Mamak's mother, Daw Saw, were spared the reception line, and, out of respect, were seated in advance. It seemed incredible that my great-grandmother, Daw Saw, Boon Par's wife was present. She was from another era.

The guests proceeded on their long march down the reception line, and on into the banquet hall. First came Johnny Chung, the brother that S. P. detested, now a necktie salesman living in Canada.

Next, a good three dozen Chung Khiaw bank managers, friends of

Kong Kong and my father marched by. Swee Cheong and his wife were there, along with my lone bridesmaid, Joan. I shook hands with Wee Cho Yaw, for me, the usurper of Kong Kong's bank. C. T. Lim, the guy who, in a way, made it all possible, gave a hug. Even my brother, Sam, was in the line, having been resurrected for the occasion. He had become a very handsome young man, six feet two, which reflected quite favorably on my father.

S. P. kept to his four-seconds rule, and many of our closest, dearest, most cherished, and respected friends were cut off in mid-sentence, and given a virtual bum's rush into the cavernous banquet hall.

Since my father-in-law, in his white tuxedo jacket, could not be distinguished from the groom, many of the guests congratulated the wrong man, which even S. P. thought was funny. As for my father, the ogre in him dispelled any question about his being the bridegroom.

The movie kings, Runme Shaw, Shaw Vee Meng, Shaw Vee King, and Harold Shaw were all there; the White Monkey, always good for a chuckle, and Esja whisked by.

All of a sudden, I saw my father break out in a sweat.

From down the line, a dark cloud was approaching, it was Granny and our Eurasian relatives. My father, try as he might, could find no way to have them slither by unnoticed.

On meeting Granny, Zena, and my Eurasian relatives, the Chungs were shocked. Wasn't I Chinese? What was I anyway? Glances came my way. What the hell was going on? Who were these people? The Chungs were embarrassed, but I had no problem with my mother's side of the family.

The ever-suave S. P. came completely unglued. He ran his hand through his hair, undoing its perfection, and leaving his forehead with disheveled locks which turned into bangs. My father smiled meekly, and hustled Granny, Zena, and their group past as quickly as possible.

Then, came another blow—approaching us were the parents of Dennis D'Cotta! I maintained my composure, greeting them cordially, looking over their shoulders for their son. Fortunately, I did not see him.

As planned by S. P., the last to enter were government officials, members of Malaysian Royalty, the Brunei State Secretary, Dato Haji Abdul Rahman Taib, and Pehin Isa, Special Advisor, and henchman to the Sultan of Brunei.

The last two guests to arrive, as protocol dictated, were the President of Singapore, Benjamin Sheares, and his First Lady, both very good friends of Mamak and Kong Kong.

President Sheares was a very handsome fair Eurasian. As I shook his hand with studied respect, I could not help but think of the kinky affair he had been having with Mamak. For years, they had been exchanging blankets, happily dozing off in each other's smell! I don't know if it went beyond exchanging blankets, and maybe "affair" was too harsh a term, but it certainly was kinky. The President and the First Lady glided on to their table.

During dinner, still afraid of seeing Dennis, I asked my father, "How on earth did the D'Cotta's get invited?"

My father smiled, "Those buggers, I invited them to show that you are too good for their son. Papa teach those buggers a lesson!"

"Well," I said, "At least you didn't invite Dennis."

"But I did! The bugger was just too embarrassed to show his face. He dare not mention to his father about the old woman in Bangkok. So shameful! See what Papa do for you?"

The wedding ran according to S. P.'s schedule. The guests arrived on time and left after the last dish was taken away. It all was over in two hours, very perfunctory. Eat and run, which is typical of Chinese weddings.

For S. P., it was mission accomplished. He had splurged for all to see. Naturally, there was press coverage. Singapore's Her World Magazine wrote:

A total of one thousand guests were invited to a Chinese dinner at the Mandarin Hotel. The list of eminent businessman, bankers, government officials, diplomats and royal guests read like a who's who of Singapore and Brunei society. In fact, two planes from Royal Brunei Airways were chartered to fly the family and friends from Brunei to Singapore for the event. May Chu was a vision in her wedding gown and the diamond studded tiara crown which doting grandma Datin Lee Chee Shan had specially made to complement her diamond accessories.

The Chinese have their own reason for generosity. It's their way of showing off wealth and power. Generosity is for others to see and envy. It is not intended to bring happiness; it is the polite way of achieving exactly the opposite. We Chinese are very polite.

And so it was with S. P. Chung. For him, the wedding was neither for Hin Chew nor for me—it was for S. P. It was his opportunity to put on a great act of generosity, and gain a foothold in Singapore.

THE HONEYMOONERS

THE FAIRYTALE wedding would be followed by an equally extravagant wedding present from S. P., a three-month round-the-world, all expenses paid, honeymoon.

I was ecstatic as we went over the plans for the trip, as I had never been to Australia, the United States, or Europe.

Our air tickets were all first class, with a routing of Sydney, Melbourne, Honolulu, San Francisco, Orlando, New York, Boston, London, Amsterdam, Copenhagen, Vienna, Milan, Rome, Singapore, and finally back to my new home in Brunei. By that time, Hin Chew and I should know each other pretty well.

With the exceptions of Melbourne, where Hin Chew owned an apartment, and London, where there was an apartment belonging to Jim, S. P. had made reservations for us in all the top hotels.

Three days after the wedding, Hin Chew and I touched down in Sydney, the first stop on our honeymoon.

Sydney is one of the most beautiful cities in the world. It is vibrant, and active, and the ideal beginning for what promised to be the perfect honeymoon.

Aside from the usual sightseeing, and the excitement of being in Australia, I was enjoying my new surname and status as Mrs. Chung. I was full of exuberance and happiness. My doubts about rushing into the marriage were totally dispelled.

After Sydney, we flew due south to Melbourne, where Hin Chew had attended Monash University.

His apartment was on Toorak Road, in Melbourne's trendy South Yarra district, home of up-market shops, restaurants, cafes, and boutiques.

S. P had given the two-bedroom apartment to Hin Chew when he was only 18 years old. Even I, who had seen the extravagances of the Tiger Balm fortune, was impressed by S. P.'s indulgence. It didn't stop with Hin Chew. S. P. had also given the London apartment, in the posh Kensington district, to his number two son, Jim, and another, on the Gold Coast, Australia's holiday playground, to number three son, Peter. Little Paul, the number four son, was only a child and perhaps too young for a place of his own.

When we entered Hin Chew's Toorak apartment, for the first time in my life, I felt at home. Hin Chew and I could have lived there forever.

In Melbourne, Hin Chew was in his element, and gave me a tour of the city and of Monash University, where he had so many fond memories. We rented a car and took the short sixty-mile drive to the sleepy seaside town of Geelong to visit Geelong College, Hin Chew's boarding school. I drove.

Geelong College was an impressive place with staid ivy-covered brick buildings, tastefully laid out on a large and ample grassy campus. The students, boys and girls, walked to and from the buildings in smart blue and green uniforms, accompanied by an occasional dowdy faculty member. Geelong was the very model of an upper-class English public school, "public," meaning "private" for schools in England and Australia.

I wondered how S. P. Chung ever managed to discover such a school for his sons?

Geelong College had a lasting effect on Hin Chew, introducing him to the world of Anglo-Saxon ways, school ties, cricket, fistfights, football, chapel on Sunday, and future "old boy" connections.

Driving back to Melbourne, Hin Chew told me of the hard times that his family had during his childhood, before his days at Geelong. As a young child, he was fed mainly on potato curry, all S. P. and Lillian could afford at the time. This, he explained, was the reason why he was so much shorter than his brothers.

This was a surprise to me. Somehow, I had assumed that Hin Chew's childhood had been as easy as mine, economically at least. There was nothing in S. P.'s manner that suggested humble origins; his easy bearing and pleasant self-assurance reeked of money from day one. Of course Lillian did have those floor-scrubber knees.

It dawned on me that I knew very little about Hin Chew, or his parents. With all the hoopla and buildup to the wedding, we had never really talked. I had taken Hin Chew and his family at face value, and at face value, they looked super, but did I really know who they were?

Hin Chew continued: His parents, depressed by poverty, took it out on him. He was beaten frequently, and locked up in the small bathroom of their house. As a result, he built up a great deal of resentment toward his father.

"I can't see your parents, especially your father, behaving like that."

"You know nothing about my father. You have no idea what he's really like," Hin Chew answered sharply.

We drove on in silence. Finally, I asked, "Where did your father get all his money?"

After a long pause, Hin Chew told me, for the first time, the story of his father. It was a story he would tell me over and over, with many overtones, with pride, with anger, with hatred, and with jealousy. Hin Chew's ambition was to outdo his father.

This is the story Hin Chew told: S. P. was born in 1927, the Year of the Rabbit, the sign of the obliging, pleasant, cautious, and conservative. Being the eldest son, his father sent him to China to complete his university studies, which, apparently, he did. On returning to Brunei, in his early twenties, S. P. married Lillian, who was four years younger.

S. P. took a job as a schoolteacher, earning the modest salary of two hundred Brunei Dollars per month, the equivalent of only two dollars a day in today's greenbacks. This was not how S. P. would make his fortune.

When he was in his thirties, in the early 1960s, S. P., the struggling schoolteacher, with four young sons and a wife to support, approached his father about taking over his father's small labor supply business. S. P.'s father liked the idea, and sold the business to S. P. for twenty thousand Brunei Dollars (US$6,600), the equivalent of eight years of S. P.'s salary as a schoolteacher.

Lillian pawned what jewelry she had for a good faith payment, and S. P.'s father let him pay off the remainder over time, with interest.

With that, S. P. took over his father's labor supply business, and, by the time S. P. was thirty-eight, he was a rich man. He had done it in less than five years.

Although I wondered how S. P. had gone from virtual rags to riches so quickly, I didn't care about the story, what was important was that

Hin Chew was sharing his past with me; after all, I was now his wife. By the time we returned to the apartment, it was dark.

The next day, I was following Hin Chew down a busy Melbourne street. He had set a torrid pace, and, not having the shoes for it, I could barely keep up. He was ahead of me, and gaining. Suddenly, he disappeared into the crowd, and was gone!

I was upset and afraid. What was going on? Had I been walking too slowly for Hin Chew? As soon as he noticed he had lost me, I was sure he would return.

Like a loyal dog, I remained at the spot where Hin Chew had left me. It was right next to a lamppost, which I used as a buoy, waiting to be rescued.

For more than an hour, I stood by the lamppost, pretending to take an interest in the passing trams—Melbourne is full of trams. It was embarrassing, and I was getting worried.

Finally, Hin Chew returned, seemingly upset to find me still waiting.

Without a word, he motioned me to follow. At first, I kept up with his brisk pace, but my shoes were killing me.

"I have blisters on my feet. I can't walk this fast," I said.

Without slowing the pace, Hin Chew turned, and spat out, "You are bloody useless, you obviously know nothing about bush walking … fuck you!"

I was shocked.

As we neared the Toorak apartment, Hin Chew was far ahead of me, and I was doing my best to hold back the tears. Back in the apartment, he locked himself away in the second bedroom, which he used as a study. Finally, I could hold back no longer, and burst out crying. I wondered what I had gotten myself into.

In bed alone that night, I was still crying. I hoped that this incident was not like the sudden and traumatic emergence of my father's true character when we moved to 69 Holland Road. Was I now meeting the real Hin Chew?

The next morning Hin Chew awakened me. He bounced happily on the bed, as though nothing had happened. "Chu, you have a letter from your mother," he said with a smile.

Relieved that the storm had passed, I smiled and sat up. I scanned the letter quickly, reading aloud parts of it to Hin Chew. My mother wrote that she, "had gone out three times since you left with Swee Cheong and Joan," and not to "worry about the opals" she had asked me to buy. Long lost Singapore! I was happy to hear even the most trivial gossip from my mother.

Rice is extremely important to Asians, and it was only fitting that it was the subject of our first real argument.

Hin Chew had asked me to boil rice for dinner. I knew how to use a rice cooker, but, as bad luck would have it, there was no rice cooker in the apartment.

I was in a hell of a fix. I picked up a saucepan, and stared blankly into the thing. I said loudly, "I don't know how to boil rice in a saucepan, Honey."

Honey burst into the kitchen, looked at me, the uncooked rice, the saucepan in my hand, and yelled, "What the fucking hell did I marry you for? You are so fucking useless. You don't even know how to boil rice!"

The tension within me uncoiled. I screamed back, "Fuck you, who do you think I am, your fucking servant girl? You can damn well boil your own fucking rice! And who the fuck do you think you are, leaving me in the middle of the street!"

For a brief moment, it was Hin Chew's turn to be shocked. His face reddened, his nostrils flared, he took a deep breath, and then, SMACK! He gave me a tight slap in the face.

I stood there, the saucepan my hand, my eyes welling with tears, in shock. I threw the saucepan against the wall, and ran to the bedroom.

The good that came out of this was that I learned how to boil rice with a saucepan.

Where was the Hin Chew who had courted me with flowers and love letters? Only weeks into our marriage, I was seeing an alarming change in the person I thought I had known before the wedding.

If Hin Chew was haunted by some ghosts of his college days in Melbourne, or by his father's success, it was no excuse for his abusive behavior. Even in comparison to the low standard set by my father, Hin Chew was coming off second best. My father was no Angel, but I had never seen him treat my mother the way Hin Chew was treating me.

The Australian leg of our honeymoon, which had lasted three long weeks, mercifully ended as we departed for Hawaii. I was never to set foot in the Toorak apartment again. The effect of Hin Chew's temper tantrums was lasting and indelible.

We'll always have Australia.

We stayed at the Hilton Hawaiian Village on Waikiki's beautiful white sand beach. The hotel was a paradise filled with tropical plants, flowers, and cascading waterfalls.

Arguments? None. I was learning very fast how to live with Hin Chew, which was to avoid anything that might set him off, like talking.

After Hawaii, we spent a week in San Francisco, where Hin Chew had some dealings with Citibank. Then, it was Disney World in Orlando for three days, followed by a couple of days in New York City.

I was taking it all in. I loved America, and admired the openness of the people—people who seemed unafraid to speak their mind, so unlike Asia.

On a personal level, the trip was going well. I managed to keep my place, and, in return, Hin Chew was controlling his temper. We were finally having a good time, more or less.

After New York City, it was Boston and MIT, another place, which I feared, could be populated by ghosts of Hin Chew's past. Fortunately, it was just the opposite, Hin Chew told me how wonderful life was in Boston, how he had aspired to become a professor, to teach in Boston, to live there, but grumbled that he had been forced by his father to return to the family business in Brunei.

After a few nostalgic days in Boston, we took off for England. I would finally see the country where I had wanted so much to study law.

In London, we stayed, as planned, in the Kensington apartment of Hin Chew's brother, Jim.

Waiting for me was another lighthearted letter from my mother, "Mrs. SP leaves for Hong Kong on 13 May '79, to join SP. SP & Mrs

SP will be back from HK, on 18 May 1979, as SP has booked five tables for a charity dinner 19 May at the Shangri-La, in aid of the Singapore Anti-Narcotics Association. Each table costs S$2,000, and S. P. has been kind enough to invite us."

It was comforting to hear more of the goings-on in Singapore. The letter ended with, "Kong Kong's leg in bad shape." Poor Kong Kong, he had developed diabetes, and it was taking its toll.

How much I missed home, and Singapore.

I was flattered by my mother's letters. She had never paid so much attention to me. Maybe she missed me; maybe she had no one to talk to. I had been her sounding board, the child who sat on the floor watching quietly, as she applied her makeup. Now I was gone.

After London, it was on to Amsterdam, Copenhagen, Vienna, Milan, and Venice—smooth sailing, all the way.

After Venice, we flew to Rome, where we stayed in the Hassler Villa Medici, a great hotel, beautifully situated at the top of the Spanish Steps, with a view of the Piazza di Spagna, below.

I was getting to know Hin Chew. I knew he loved to wallow in reveries of the many injustices, few glories, and angry railings of his father. What had been an enjoyable sharing of his past was now becoming a soliloquy. Hin Chew's laments, however, were punctuated by long silences, during which he spent his time reading books, magazines, newspapers, and even comic books. My place was to keep quiet.

We had now been on our honeymoon one week shy of three months, and finally we were going home. It had been great seeing the world, but if this was a honeymoon, what was a marriage?

Brunei Days

THE HONEYMOON was over. I was both excited and apprehensive as our flight touched down at Brunei International Airport, outside of Bandar Seri Begawan, Brunei's capital. Brunei was new to me, an Islamic country ruled by a Sultan, said to be the richest man in the world by virtue of Brunei's oil.

That was it for the excitement. Aside from the glitz of the Sultan and his oil, there was nothing to be said for the place. Brunei is a small enclave, its borders artificially carved out of Eastern Malaysia by greed and British oil interests.

At the airport, S. P.'s driver was waiting to pick us up in a Mercedes—a good beginning, I hoped.

The Chungs did not live in Brunei's capital. Their home and business were near the oilfields, seventy-five miles west from the airport on the north coast road.

During the drive from the airport, we rode in silence, as we passed fields of long grass, buffalo, and more fields of long grass.

It got worse and worse.

After an hour and a half, we arrived at our destination, a town called Mumong, which was every bit as drab and depressing as its name.

We turned off the main highway onto a narrow dirt road, bordered on either side by weeds, and drove up to one of two large plain white houses, looking like unadorned concrete blocks. The houses, which were attached—shades of Holland Road—had been recently rented by S. P. in preparation, not only for our arrival, but also for Hin Chew's brothers and their families. The entire family was converging on Mumong.

The Chung boys would all be working for S. P. It would be one big happy extended family; something I knew a lot about.

S. P. came outside to welcome us. Gone were the Lanvin suits, and immaculately tailored appearance. S. P.'s shoes were brown and scuffed. His khaki pants were held up by a cracked leather belt that had seen years of use. His undershirt showed through his cheap white short-sleeved shirt. This was not the S. P. that I had known in Singapore.

After hugs, S. P. lead us into one of his houses, apologizing as we entered for the mess, as he and Lillian were still moving in. Lillian, who was unpacking boxes in the living room stood up and greeted us cheerfully.

Glancing about the room, I noticed the furnishings were bare and spartan, matching the drab look of the twin houses. After S. P.'s extravagances in Singapore, I was surprised by the simplicity of the Chungs' Brunei lifestyle.

We spent our next few days settling into the second of the two houses. We took the upstairs; Hin Chew's brother, Jim, and his wife, Lynn, were living downstairs. Jim and Lynn had been little more than a blur to me at the wedding, now I was getting my first good look.

Jim, at six feet two, was a good head taller than Hin Chew. You could see right off that he was also a kinder soul, not driven, but a beta-wolf. Lynn was ideal for him. She was blonde, diplomatic, cautious, and strong.

Peter and Rosita were still in Singapore, at S. P.'s Westwood apartment, as Rosita had just given birth to a baby boy, Bobby.

Paul, the youngest brother, was off to boarding school.

Once we were comfortably installed in our house, it was time for S. P. and Lillian to set down the rules. They did it after dinner, with S. P. doing the talking.

First off, Lynn and I could now address S. P. and Lillian as "Pa," and "Ma," a privilege, S. P. pointed out, heretofore reserved only for their sons. Lillian nodded.

Collectively, Ma and Pa would be addressed as "Parents," and, in the third person, we would refer to them as "Father," or "Mother," as the case would be. Lillian nodded.

Lynn and I exchanged glances.

You could see the schoolteacher in S. P., as he continued. We could not associate with Brunei Shell people, or with other subcontractors. We had to keep Mother company. We had to keep to ourselves, maintaining a low profile. We could not go to Mumong's lone movie theater, but we could rent videotapes, and were free to watch Brunei's single television channel. Finally, we should never go to the beach, which was just a short walk across the street from our house, but where "Malay men are always on the prowl." Lillian gave a final nod.

"Oh yes, one more thing," said S. P., rising from his chair, "we eat all our meals together, lunch and dinner." S. P., now "Father," smiled, and with "Mother," left the room.

The rules set, our daily routine began. At 7:00 each morning, Hin Chew, Jim, and S. P. went off to work.

With the men away, Lynn and I would spend the day with Lillian, as was our duty. Lillian would do most of the talking, as was her right.

She loved to tell us how hard her life had been, how poor she had been, how terrible her own mother-in-law had been, and in the face of all this, how she, herself, had been so stoic, and been such a good wife. There was a message there for both of us, including, possibly, the part about the terrible mother-in-law.

Most mornings, we had to accompany Mother to the market, not a supermarket, but a large collection of individually owned outdoor stalls. The food had to be fresh.

Like two chicks following mother hen, shopping baskets in hand, we would follow Mother, several respectful steps behind.

Mother did the cooking for lunch, straight from the wok, with no interference from the inept brides. We were, nevertheless, expected to carry the bowls of food to the table.

At high noon in Mumong, when the men returned home for lunch, we would be ready and waiting in attendance.

We ate only Chinese food. For Lynn, this was a problem. She would fumble with her chopsticks, while yearning for fish and chips, shepherd's pie, or some such British thing. Lynn complained to me a lot about the food. She was losing weight, while poor Jim, bored with work, was piling it on.

At the table, all conversation was limited to the men, who spoke exclusively in Hakka, the Chung's dialect. Lynn and I had no chance of understanding a single word, which was, of course, the intention. My knowledge of Cantonese, Hokkien, and Mandarin were of little help with Hakka, but I would listen, learn, and try to crack the code.

Unlike Lynn, I was used to eating in silence while my "betters" did the talking. Family dinners with the Chungs were like those at Pasir Panjang, but a poor man's version. True, S. P. had put on a fabulous show with my wedding, but in Brunei, he put on just the opposite, a show of humble and modest circumstances.

Will the real S. P. please stand up?

At 1:00 P.M., the men returned to work, while Lynn and I cleaned up the kitchen. Lillian gave us a free hand with that.

Afternoons in Mumong were long. Mercifully, Lillian would eventually disappear into her room, after which we were free to do as we pleased, within the rules, of course.

At 6:30 P.M., the men returned home from work. The dinner ritual was a repetition of lunch, but with some shots of whiskey thrown in. It was time to relax, but only for the men, of course.

With Hin Chew, the evenings were no better than the days—they were worse. After dinner, back at our house, he would usually wander off into a small study room to spend the evening with his first-generation Apple computer, of which he was enormously proud. The computer widow was little known in those days, but I was one of that unhappy group's earliest pioneers.

When Hin Chew tired of his Apple, he would come to bed with a book. To initiate a conversation with Hin Chew was to invite trouble, so I would remain silent, hoping that each turn of a page would be the last, and some attention would come my way.

Around midnight, it was lights out.

Soon after my arrival, it was time to pay my respects to S. P.'s parents. They lived only a short distance away, right by the market place, in a modest two-story shophouse, much as the Aw brothers had done in their early days in Burma.

S. P.'s father, Chung Pah Hing, a thin-faced man with gray hair gelled straight back, wearing glasses, welcomed us into his shop. He was cleanly dressed in a crisp white shirt, and black pants, the model of a trustworthy shopkeeper. Behind him, was, a tiny smiling old lady, introduced only as "Ah Por," or grandmother.

S. P.'s father ushered his son and grandsons into a small windowed office at the back of the shop, while Ah Por, gave us a brief tour of the house. The front room was where S. P.'s father ran his small shop, selling jewelry, watches, and, oddly, typewriters. The family dining area, and kitchen, with its charcoal stove, was on the first floor, behind the store. There I saw the infamous bathroom where Hin Chew spent many lonely hours locked up in growing bitterness. On the second floor, were three bedrooms, very simple.

After the brief tour, we returned to the shop, where Ah Por, motioned for us to sit on the floor. The old lady spoke only in Hakka, so Lynn and I could communicate only with nodding smiles.

Later, Hin Chew told me that his father's meetings with the old grandfather were always the same. S. P. would brag about how well he was doing, never failing to show how much better off he was than his hated and mediocre brother, Johnny Chung, in Canada. Chung Pah Hing, a captive audience, and father to both, would listen stoically.

Happily, the visit didn't last long, for having made his point, S. P. gave a brief hug to the old man, and came out, whisking us all into the car for the drive back to dreary Mumong.

On the way home, S. P. told us the story of his parents' first meeting, a story I was to hear more than once.

S. P.'s father was from China. There, as a young man, he came upon a man carrying two small girls balanced at either end of a long pole in rattan baskets. The man was on his way to the market to sell the girls to the highest bidder. Chung Pah Hing, ready for marriage, stopped the man, flipped a coin, and picked his wife.

"My mother was very lucky," said S. P., ending the story. Lillian nodded and smiled, and Lynn said diplomatically, "How delightful, lucky Ah Por!"

I had observed that every word, every gesture, coming from S. P., had its purpose. I got the point of this grim fairy tale, which was to inform us of the status of women's rights in the Chung household.

That'll work in China, but what kind of a life was it for us? I hadn't been plucked from any basket, and neither had Lynn.

How could the Chungs be so daft as to think that Lynn and I could swallow this crap? We were not in Ancient China, at least I wasn't. Sooner or later, someone had to get real.

Happily, we never had to return to the shophouse. Shortly after our visit, we were awakened in the middle of the night to hear that the shophouse had burned to the ground.

S. P. and Lillian were away at the time, in Singapore, where S. P. had been setting up a corporation named SPCO Shipyard Pte Ltd.

Hin Chew, Jim, Lynn, and I rushed out to find the grandparents. Fortunately, no one was hurt, but Ah Por was in tears, this had been her home; it was far better than a basket.

"Wouldn't you know that the fucking Gutless Wonder would be away," growled Hin Chew. "Gutless Wonder" was Hin Chew's favorite term for his father.

To complete the lucky ending of the shophouse fire, insurance covered the loss. It was perfect timing for S. P., as he had recently bought an apartment for his parents in one of Singapore's best buildings, Cairnhill Plaza. S. P. had it ready and waiting for them, so Chung Pah Hing and Ah Por took the "opportunity" to move to Singapore, never to return to Brunei.

I remember thinking that the whole thing seemed strange. Why would S. P. want to have his parents so far away from Brunei in Singapore? Was the shophouse burned down on purpose? Well, I don't think so, but you never know.

Our next family visit was to S. P.'s uncle, his mother's brother. The uncle lived about thirty miles away from Mumong on a deserted road in a small dwelling—dwelling being the politest word for it. Lynn and I were briefly introduced to Sook Kong, Hakka for great-uncle, and his wife, Sook Por, great-aunt. S. P., Jim and Hin Chew disappeared into the humble abode, leaving the womenfolk to wander about outside, admiring Sook Kong's collection of pigs, chickens, ducks, and cabbage.

On the drive back home, we heard the love story of S. P. and Lillian, as told by S. P. It went like this:

Lillian was not from China, not even from Brunei, she was from Sarawak across the border from Brunei, and was born while the White Rajahs were still in power.

When the time came for S. P. to marry, Ah Por sought out a matchmaker, who advised her that there were good brides to be found, just across the border from Brunei in the town of Miri, in Sarawak. Ah Por traveled to Miri, where she was shown an array of prospective brides. She watched them cook, sew, and took stock of their bones, hips and teeth. Ah Por needed an obedient girl, a hard worker who could take care of S. P., and who would be of good breeding stock. Finally, Ah Por chose the very best candidate of all, a Miss Yeoh Noy Heok—now known as Lillian.

Voilà! This was lesson number two for us, teaching us the wifely virtues of cooking, sewing, and good hips, that the bride does not choose—she is chosen, and that Lillian was the cream of the crop!

Lillian looked at me, and I returned her brief expressionless stare. The selection of Lillian, as though she were a barnyard animal, sounded more like something from the distant past, and was nothing S. P. should brag about.

So far as I was concerned, S. P. and Lillian were on another planet, with Hin Chew orbiting somewhere in between.

Unlike Hin Chew, Jim was supportive of his wife. Of course, this was due in large part to the undeniable fact that Chinese men reserve far better treatment for western women, than for their own kind. Western women haven't been conditioned to put up with the nonsense that goes with Chinese tradition, and Chinese men know it.

Western women expect to be treated as equals—we don't.

Therefore, Jim did make an effort to understand Lynn, and did what he could to relieve the boredom of Mumong, taking her for frequent drives and outings. Of course, there was no place to go, but out of the house was good enough.

Still, Lynn was very unhappy, and missed her life and freedom in England, especially their posh Kensington apartment, not far from Princess Diana's Kensington Palace. Lynn explained to me that she was not like me. Since I was Chinese, I could easily endure life with the Chungs. She was only half right, I could endure it, but not easily, and I was far from happy.

Living in Mumong, the mentality of S. P. and Lillian, their relatives, the isolation, none of which would have mattered to me if Hin Chew had remained as he was when we first met in Singapore. I still could not understand the reason for his behavior, maybe it was my fault; maybe I was to blame. With youthful optimism, I resolved to do better, even though I had no idea of what "better" was.

Yes, I would try.

Hari Raya Haji is the Muslim holiday marking the end of the fasting month of *Ramadhan*. It's a time to celebrate, and to pay visits of respect to wish friends "*selamat Hari Raya aidilfitri,*" "good *Hari Raya.Haji.*"

It was a major holiday, and was something I had been looking forward to because we were off to see the Sultan.

We bundled into the Mercedes, and another car, Parents, Jim, Lynn, Hin Chew, and I, and headed off to Bandar Seri Begawan, home of the Sultan, no wandering amongst the pigs, chickens, ducks, and cabbage on this trip. The Sultan, Hassanal Bolkiah, had not yet built his new palace. He was still in the process of tooling up, and things were a bit simpler in those days. S. P., Hin Chew, and Jim wore suits; we womenfolk were very conservatively dressed from knee to neck, with arms fully covered. Any show of skin would certainly offend His Majesty's sensibilities.

Naturally, we weren't the only visitors to the Royal Palace, but we were among the few who would receive the honor of shaking hands with the richest man on earth.

Once in the palace, we took our place in line in a corridor. I could see the Sultan standing, dressed traditionally in the national dress, the *baju melayu*, with a black velvet cap or *songkok*, on his head. He was flanked on either side by three or four men, similarly dressed. It was all quite informal and relaxed.

When it came my turn to shake the Sultan's hand, I bowed my head slightly as I had observed others doing. The Sultan was very polite and unaffected. As I took my hand away, I heard him say "*siapa ini?*" or "who is this?" to the man on his left, who answered something about, "Chung Pah Hing."

Further down the corridor, was a large room where the ladies were paying their respects to the Sultan's jewel-encrusted wife; he had only one then, the Raja Isteri, who was with her ladies-in-waiting. I saw as dazzling a display of jewelry as could be imagined. No men allowed.

I was not to see His Majesty again, as this was the last year that women would be permitted to attend the affair.

After the Sultan, we paid a visit to a very useful, and powerful friend of S. P.'s, Pehin Isa. I had already met Pehin Isa at my wedding, and remembered that he was the Sultan's Special Advisor, and number two man in the Brunei government. The "Pehin" part of his name was a title conferred by the Sultan.

Pehin Isa, a tall, handsome, and friendly man, dressed traditionally, welcomed us into his immense house with a graciousness that belied his exalted position. Like the Sultan, and most Malays, he was polite, cordial, and friendly.

Pehin Isa's wife, Datin Rosna, was Chinese, and from Singapore, where she had served on the police force, of all things. She spoke Teochew, Lillian's original dialect, which created a common bond between the two women. When together, they would spend happy hours chatting in Teochew.

We were led into a very large living room, furnished lavishly with two rows of chairs on opposing walls, in the style of an Arab *majlis*. Tea was served as we sat down. Only Pehin Isa and S. P.'s spoke, their words echoing through the room. Their conversation was very friendly and relaxed, consisting of polite small talk and inquiries into the well being of each other's families. This took some time, as both Pehin Isa and the very respectful S. P. had large families. The initial pleasantries over, Lillian and Datin Rosna remained behind, as Pehin Isa took the rest of us upstairs to show off his prize three-foot long golden koi fish with long whiskers. With great deference, a manservant handed Pehin Isa a glass jar containing live cockroaches for the koi. Pehin Isa carefully unscrewed the lid, and gingerly picked out a cockroach, which he dropped into the tank. The happy koi immediately gobbled it up.

The koi, a giant cousin of the goldfish, brings good luck, but at a price, a top specimen can easily cost ten thousand dollars, and this was the best I had ever seen.

Pehin Isa loved that fish.

This was not the last we would see of Pehin Isa. Somehow, behind the scenes, he was involved in S. P.'s affairs, and S. P. spared no effort or expense to keep the contact alive.

Several years later, when Pehin Isa was ill and hospitalized in Singapore, S. P. took the entire family with him to Singapore to pay Pehin Isa a bedside visit. While the rest of us waited respectfully in the living room of Pehin Isa's hospital suite, S. P. was the only one allowed into Pehin Isa's room.

Who would have thought that, in time, S. P. would suspect his good friend, Pehin Isa, of betraying him with a "set-up," as Hin Chew would later put it.

Our last *Hari Raya* visit in Brunei that day was a quick in-and-out pit stop to the house of Freddie and Nora Chong. Freddie was an officer in the Royal Brunei Police Force. Being Chinese, a major disadvantage in Brunei, Freddie set his career right by converting to Islam, and marrying a local Malay girl, Nora, who was also a police officer.

Compared to what we had seen earlier that day, Freddie and Nora's house wasn't much, but they were a nice, smiling, fawning couple.

S. P. named his company "Chung Pah Hing," out of respect for his father. Everybody called it "CPH" for short. Nearly all of S. P.'s business was with Brunei Shell Petroleum, "BSP," a joint venture of Shell Oil, and the Brunei government.

CPH's main line activity was the supplying of labor to BSP. It was that simple. CPH provided the welders, painters, blasters who worked with cranes, forging jackets, pipes, and barges for BSP's twenty-eight acre marine fabrication yard in Kuala Belait, a couple of miles from Mumong.

The yard's purpose was to build and maintain offshore oil platforms. Beyond that, the details were unimportant. I was more interested in the personalities, and the finances.

Hin Chew and Jim held top management positions in S. P.'s company, and were ranked second only to their father, even though they knew nothing of business.

This premature exposure to responsibility, along with S. P.'s gifts of apartments and outright cash had turned his sons into spoiled self-centered dilettantes.

To me, the parallels were clear. S. P. was at the level of the Aw brothers, and his sons were the Cheng Chyes, Jimmy, and Jackie Lees of the dynasty.

In another family, in another country, a similar history to the Aw and Lee families was repeating itself with the Chungs. And where did that leave me? In the same position as my mother?

No, I had learned, and refused to be condemned to repeat history.

I was making great strides learning Hakka. At the table, the discussions, always in Hakka, consisted solely of shoptalk, led by S. P. in a business-like and tough manner. There was never any laughter or kidding around.

S. P. referred to most of the BSP officials as "fat cats." Some of the "fat cats" were allies. There was the Dutchman, Rudy Michels, who, according to Hin Chew was always most cooperative, and a great help to CPH. Ken Walsh, an Englishman, and Peter Tapper, a senior director, also worked "closely" with the Chungs. At the top of the BSP pile were Peter Everett and Ron Timmerman both "good friends" of the Chungs.

Directly under his sons in the company, S. P. cleverly placed some white faces, "Judas goats," as he called them, men with good clean white friendly names like Jim Bell, Ted Collins, and Neil Birkbeck. This was done to keep the "fat cats" at BSP happy. The key back office areas of administration and accounting, however, were trusted only to a Chinese team, headed by everybody's good friend Goh Boon Kok, who kept the books in far-off Singapore.

I was mesmerized the first time I saw S. P. in action with one of the top white BSP officials. S. P. was going to Peter Tapper's huge house in the BSP compound to pay him a courtesy visit. As usual, S. P. brought his entire family along.

For the visit, S. P. dressed in his usual outfit of a cheap shirt, cheap khaki pants, and well-worn shoes. He avoided using his Mercedes, driving, instead, his small Mitsubishi Colt, while the rest of us followed in a convoy of cheap Japanese cars. Arriving at the BSP compound, we pulled up in front of the Tapper's sumptuous home.

Paupers at the door!

Once inside, after Peter and Anne Tapper had made sure we were all comfortably seated, S. P. went into an act I had not seen before. He groveled beautifully.

"I am nothing more than a stupid Chinaman, with no education. You see, my English is so bad," said S. P. to the Tappers.

Then, bowing slightly, and folding his hands, he continued, "I send all my sons overseas, to learn proper education, and speak proper English."

Mrs. Tapper silently placed a drink, with a small napkin under it, on the side table next to S. P.

His head bowed still lower, and peering over his tinted glasses, S. P. continued, "I have to work, to feed my family. My wife, Lillian, she is the boss and in charge of the house." S. P. took a sip of his drink, inviting the Tappers to do the same.

"Oh S. P.," laughed Peter Tapper, "I'm sure you're doing quite well, quite well, indeed."

"Thank you, Mr. Tapper, you are most kind," replied S. P., nursing his drink.

"Please, S. P., you must call me Peter," said Tapper, with his broadest British accent.

Bowing his head again, with a toothy smile, S. P. answered, "Yes, Mr. Tapper, yes, Mr. Tapper."

Then, putting down his glass, S. P. apologetically steered the conversation to matters of business.

Just about everyone took an immediate liking to this "humble" Chinaman. He made the Tappers smile, and realize how well off they were, in comparison to S. P.

Hell, S. P. could buy and sell the Tappers.

I had seen S. P. in many forms, in Brunei as the humble Chinaman, in Singapore as the sophisticated tycoon, at my first meeting with him as the warm father-in-law to be, with Pehin Isa as the respectful friend, and, at the dining table in Mumong, as the stern tyrant.

S. P. was whoever he needed to be, and whoever you wanted him to be. S. P. was a chameleon.

My mother continued to write cheerful letters, keeping me up-to-date on happenings in Singapore.

She wrote, "Joan's friend, Roger, is only 33 and not in love with his wife. At the West End Nightclub is where the trouble started. I was very nice to Roger, and Papa got kind of jealous, so the evening didn't end very nicely. I don't know what is wrong with Papa now, but in his old age he is beginning to get more possessive. He has told me to stop calling people darling, honey, sweetheart, etc & also to stop kissing men. Well, so much for that."

Kissing men? That was my mother.

Unfortunately, neither my mother's letters, nor our little family outings could make up for a thankless life in servitude to Hin Chew and his parents.

Lynn was also unhappy, and talked to me about it all the time. She said, in her British accent, "Chu, I don't know how much longer I can take this life with Ma and Pa. Pa is always on Jim's back, and Jim has put on so much weight. This life that we are having under Ma and Pa's rule is putting so much stress on my marriage. I want to have a baby, but we never seem to have the time, as Jim is always tired and grumpy when he comes back from work. This is no life."

I had no life either, but her problems were not my problems, and her husband was not Hin Chew.

One evening, as Hin Chew and I were driving back home after renting videotapes, I asked, "Could you drive a bit slower?"

This prompted an immediate screaming harangue, and, instead of going slower, Hin Chew went still faster.

For the first time in our arguments, I was not reduced to tears, and after the storm had passed, I risked it again with Hin Chew by asking calmly, "Why do you use such foul language?"

Hin Chew spat back, "I'm educated in the States, and everyone there talks like that!" This was to become his oft-repeated excuse for the filth that spewed out of him nearly every time he spoke. It was awful.

Finally, one afternoon, I telephoned my mother, and told her that I wanted to come back home to Singapore, as I couldn't take it any longer with Hin Chew. I pleaded, "Mummy, can I please, please come home?"

"Come home to what? You are married now, and you belong to your husband's family. You are a Chung and no longer a Lee," my mother answered, resting her case on Chinese traditionalism.

I continued to beg, but to no avail. My own family had turned me down.

In her next letter, my mother responded more positively to my plea, "I know what you must be going through, but for your own sake and your husband's please bear up. Both Aunt Zena & I had a discussion & we both feel that you should bear up & wait until '82"

So, my mother was not totally against the idea of my leaving Hin Chew, but why 1982? Under Singapore law, you have to be married for three years before filing for divorce.

Shortly after receiving my mother's letter, my unhappiness received a strong vote of validation. Jim and Lynn came out with the announcement that they were going to leave Brunei, and return to England. Their official reason was that Jim wanted to make his own way in life and had decided resume his study of architecture, while Lynn would go back to her job as a nurse. I was very sad that Lynn would be leaving. We had shared our problems, and had become friends.

Within a week, they were gone.

I discovered that S. P. was intercepting my mail.

My mother addressed her letters to me in care of CPH, the family company, the only address we had. Several of her letters did not get through to me.

My mother wrote, "I'm really quite worried about you not receiving my letter as it was really quite confidential. I sincerely hope Madam Du Barry didn't intercept it. I guess you know whom I mean!" Of course I did. My mother gave nicknames to almost everyone, and Lillian's influence over S. P. was akin to Madame Du Barry's over Louis XV.

I immediately went to the post office and got my own private post office box.

Every day, I would go to check the box, saying "Just going out for a bit, Ma," as I needed her permission to leave the house.

My mother's next letter arrived safe and secure, and was waiting for me in the box. She wrote, "I am happy now that you have your own PO Box, so now I can write without any worries, as I am certain my letters won't be intercepted."

She continued, "That bitch next door, it seems has a Spanish type house in Double Bay, in Australia."

Judy and Uncle Jimmy had decided to move from Singapore to Double Bay, the upscale part of Sydney, also known as "Double Pay," for its steep property prices. They would, however, keep the Singapore house, staffed with a maid, for their visits home.

My mother ended her letter with, "I hope you & Hin Chew are hitting it OK as I was worried about you & was very sad to hear that you had trouble with Hin Chew. Don't talk too much to him unless he talks to you ... I understand how miserable you must be & I sympathize with you."

My mother was giving me good advice, speak only when spoken to.

My mother's next letter was a racy one, it read:

Dear Chu Chu:

Su Lan and I went to the Hilton downstairs bar. The music was swinging and we had a beer each. Finally we met an old, about 50 years old, English man who is the Vice President of some computer firm. We went with him to the Library – finally I got to go there, just the three of us. One Australian fellow danced with Su Lan. He was quite interested in her. All the time she got propositions, but you know her. Nothing came of it.

So, I'm going to take it easy after a very successful week – if you know what I mean. Sunday, PaPa will be back like a Saint, and there'll be another Saint at home to keep him company.

Well, my darling child, so much for that. I'll be back in the cage again, starting Sunday.

Love, Mummy

Refreshing, shameless, and great entertainment for one so alone in Brunei. Su Lan? Oh, Su Lan was my mother's maid.

Fun letters were still not enough for me, and I continued begging my mother to take me back. For her part, she tried to be sympathetic, writing, "I was upset to hear about your bad week & hope to God that you will not go through it again."

I think S. P. knew that I was not happy, so he started bringing Hin Chew and me on some of his trips with Lillian, at a pace of about one a month. Hong Kong and Singapore were the destinations, as S. P. was setting up companies in both cities.

He was on the move, and why?

CPH had lost money for three years running, something that I had been surprised to learn. In 1979, S. P. had managed to turn things around, making a profit of US$2.5 million on sales of US$15 million.

That was surprising also, not the profit, but the US$15 million gross sales. I had thought that S. P.'s operation was much larger. The final disturbing fact was that S. P. was negotiating to sell half of CPH to Global Engineering, a small company that Hin Chew had worked for as a student apprentice back in 1974.

Based on those facts, S. P. really didn't look much like a tycoon, even though, outside of Brunei, he certainly acted like one.

Lynn kept in touch with me from England. I enjoyed her letters, and she seemed happy.

She wrote, "Glad to hear that Parents are going to Singapore quite often. Jim applied for a design job but didn't get it."

"No bother," she continued, "Jim is organizing a recruiting operation for S. P. in England on behalf of the family business."

So much for the independent life, I thought. I could see that Jim and Lynn were on a moonwalk back from independence.

S. P. had also bought them a £58,000 house, mortgage free, in Kenilworth, just southeast of Birmingham, Lynn's hometown, and she was very happy to return to her home turf and be near to her family.

The trips away from Brunei were a diversion, but they were not the solution to my problems with Hin Chew. Like many optimistic and inexperienced young wives, I thought our marriage could be saved by having a baby.

This was easier said than done, as the Apple was tough competition, but finally, late in 1980, my home pregnancy test gave me the good news. I was expecting a child.

I waited in anticipation and happiness for Hin Chew to return home for lunch, I couldn't wait to give him the wonderful news! I was so proud of myself and happy!

As soon as Hin Chew entered the house, I said, "I'm pregnant! I'm pregnant!"

Hin Chew's reaction was immediate. He screamed, "How the fuck do I know it's my kid? If it doesn't come out the right color, I'll tell Parents, that I'm not the father."

I was stunned, "Well who do you think did it, the gardener? How can you talk like this? I thought you would be happy."

Hin Chew replied curtly, "Well, I'm not!"

Hin Chew never showed any happiness about the pregnancy. Naturally, he put on a good act when he told his parents, and they, thrilled at the prospect of a second grandchild, began to treat me slightly better. Hin Chew, however, made no such concession to my happy condition.

Soon after I announced my pregnancy, it was temporarily forgotten when Lillian was rushed to Singapore to undergo a hysterectomy. The entire Chung family was totally unprepared for this. A hysterectomy was an entirely new and unknown thing for them. Ah Por never had one. How to deal with it? What would Lillian be like after the operation?

She was fine, and my parents visited the hospital to pay their respects. For her own devilish reasons, my mother brought Su Lan along. My parents and Su Lan, the infamous maid, found S. P. at Lillian's bedside.

In her letter to me, my mother described the scene beautifully:

Dear Chu Chu

We went to see MaMa Chung yesterday. This time PaPa Chung didn't kiss me, and MaMa Chung was really happy about it! She was very nice to me. Your father was getting unduly worried as PaPa Chung was really interrogating Su Lan. The old boy asking how old she was, and what not.

After we left, PaPa said to me 'Now you see what you have done! You've got Chu Chu into trouble. You better get in touch with her and keep her informed.' Well, I had introduced Su Lan as a niece, and he must have thought – Oh! What a good match for my son Paul, since she is also Hakka. Oh Boy! What a joke that'll be!

If that were so, she will really be the lucky one, especially since her mother is a full time gravedigger and a part-time waitress. Su Lan gambles, drinks, smokes and is a thief to boot. Don't think I'm being mean, we get on well, and it's hard to get help these days. Your father has gone off to the cinema. God only knows with whom. Ah, I've given up worrying about him – you just have to accept him for what he is.

Love, Mummy

My mother could accept my father for what he was, because, with all his shortcomings, he was never abusive or cruel to her.

With Hin Chew, the situation was different. There was something wrong with Hin Chew, some lack of empathy, or a missing gene, that made him cruel and unfeeling. I was not about to accept Hin Chew for what he was. I had thought that having a child would make the difference. Now I knew better, and now that I was expecting a child, my whole outlook on life was changing.

For me to escape from the marriage, or even to survive in it, I had to weaken Hin Chew and the Chung family that supported him. I would do whatever I could to protect myself, and my child.

I would pay close attention to what S. P., his sons, and their associates were up to in their business dealings.

I knew something was amiss.

It gave me strength, purpose, and hope to find out whatever fact, or document, I could to weaken the Chungs. It was my only option to armor myself and my child against their onslaught of abuse.

TOP The Tiger Balm Kings, from left Aw Boon Par & Aw Boon Haw.

RIGHT Aw Boon Haw's Tiger Car.

"The tiger's head had bouncing wire whiskers, and its eyes were special high-wattage red lights, which pierced the darkness as Boon Haw sped on through the night."

BOTTOM Aw Boon Par's house. Haw Par Villa had been the private gardens of Boon Par's futuristic art deco house, which had been built for him by beloved brother Aw Boon Haw.

ABOVE Jackie Lee, with his girlfriend, Mabel, my mother to be.
BELOW Jackie and Mabel get married.

*"Half white, and half Chinese, she was the most beautiful woman I had
ever seen. To me she looked like Elizabeth Taylor, only without the violet
eyes. The contrast with my father was such that my parents earned the
nickname, 'the Beauty and the Beast.'"*

TOP LEFT Here I am, in
1959, with my father.
TOP RIGHT Behaving myself
at the Pasir Panjang beach
house with Ah Ngoh, and
my maiden grandaunt, Aye
Kim.
RIGHT My grandmother,
Dagmar Vyner, Aye Kim,
my brother, Sam, and I are
enjoying a party.
BELOW RIGHT My father's
look-alike younger brother,
Jimmy Lee at the dining
table in the house on
Pasir Panjang Road.

*"My father's younger brother,
Jimmy, the good brother, as
good as he was, still had to
sit to Kong Kong's left. Jimmy
was on a very slightly lower
rung of the hierarchy than my
father."*

ABOVE A Chung Khiaw bank lunch. From left: Uncle Jimmy, his wife, my Aunt Judy ("Betty Boop"), my father's sister, Esja, her husband, Jon Sigurdsson ("blue-eyed Viking God from Iceland"), four Chung Khiaw bank employees, and my parents.

"In addition to marrying a white, she now called herself 'Esja,' some sort of weird Icelandic name that Kong Kong could barely pronounce."

BELOW Me at sweet sixteen.

TOP I play Lady Macbeth
in the Raffles Institution year-
end school production at
Singapore's Victoria Theater
in 1974.
RIGHT I. M. (Ieoh Ming)
Pei being interviewed by me
in 1976 for my magazine,
Development & Construction.
MIDDLE RIGHT Candlelight and
drinks with my future husband,
Hin Chew Chung in 1978.
BOTTOM RIGHT Hin Chew and
I getting serious.

*"Hin Chew called to ask me out
for that evening. Unfortunately,
I was busy, my architect friend,
Ieoh Ming was in town, and I
was having dinner with him."*

TOP LEFT Hin Chew and I, at the Registry of Marriages, with my best friend and bridesmaid, Joan Lai in the foreground.

TOP RIGHT My new family, the Chungs. From left, standing, Paul, Peter, his wife, Rosita, my mother-in-law, Lillian, the bride and groom, my father-in-law, S. P. Chung, Lynn, and her husband Jim. Seated in front are my father-in-law's parents.

ABOVE LEFT Hin Chew and I, at the end of the wedding ceremony, as my mother, Hin Chew's mother, and my father watch the happy event.

LEFT I cut the king-sized wedding cake, as my adoring husband looks on.

BOTTOM LEFT Hin Chew and I at our tea ceremony with my father-in-law (the flower behind the ear was my idea).

"The sweetness of the tea was intended to foster equally sugary relations between my in-laws and myself."

TOP LEFT The house in Mumong, Brunei, where Hin Chew and I began our married life in 1979.
TOP RIGHT Hin Chew and Captain Lim Swee Cheong, Singapore Armed Forces intelligence officer.

RIGHT Hin Chew and I at Peter and Rosita's house in Mumong on Christmas Day, 1980. I was expecting our number one son, Marc, at the time.

"We were surprised to see a fully decorated real live Christmas tree in their living room. Rosita had insisted on a proper Christmas tree, something virtually impossible to find in an Islamic country, also not known for its pine forests. Peter came up with the solution; he had the tree flown in from Singapore."

TOP LEFT Dato and Datin Lee Chee Shan, my grandparents, celebrate 50 years of marriage at their golden wedding anniversary in 1981. My grandmother wore her crown of diamonds, which was topped by an emerald measuring nearly two inches high by an inch and a half wide.

"It was a lavish affair, like the old days. Friends and relatives from all parts of the world attended the affair, more than a few of them receiving air tickets and having their hotel bills picked up by my grandparents."

MIDDLE LEFT Richard Anderson of The Six Million Dollar Man, flanked by Lillian and my mother, at a charity gala in Singapore in 1982.

BOTTOM LEFT At the same party, my mother takes up with Cliff Robertson.

NUMBER ONE SON

NOT LONG after Jim and Lynn had left for England, Peter, Rosita, and their son, Bobby, arrived in Brunei. Instead of sharing the house with us, S. P. rented a place for them not far away, a strange little house, elevated on stilts over a carport.

Rosita was direct, dominating, fearless, and foolish, nothing like Lynn. Her in-your-face attitude would not serve her well in a Chinese household, and Lillian couldn't stand her. Rosita's chain smoking, seemingly a small thing, annoyed both S. P. and Lillian, especially since Peter had taken up the habit, as well.

It was fortunate for Rosita that she had given the Chungs a grandson. That gave her a bit of status in the family. She was OK for now, but, if I too had a son, the first born of the first born, I would replace her as the family's prized cow. My fingers were crossed, and I'm sure hers were, as well.

Rosita was three years older than Peter, being twenty-one to his eighteen when they met at Monash University. Back then, she had a voluptuous figure, and a heart-shaped face, offset by almond eyes, and framed by long cascading brown hair. Unfortunately, with the birth of Bobby, Rosita had put on a lot of weight, and no longer looked like the same person.

After meeting Rosita at Monash University, Peter grew a mustache to make himself look older, more her age. Unwisely for Peter, they married while still in college; she graduated, he didn't.

Being older, Rosita was one-up on Peter from the start. She would boss him around, not hesitating to call at the office to give him an errand to run, or to give him a list of what to buy at the market on his way home.

Rosita and I got on fine, as long as we were not together too much. She lived in her own house, and paid little attention to the family's rules, avoiding the Chung family dinners, and making friends with the ladies at Brunei Shell.

For Peter, things had come easy. He was nearly as tall as Jim, and Parents doted on his good looks. He was clearly Lillian's favorite. S. P.'s favorite varied from day to day.

Peter was the best of the brothers when it came to speaking and writing English, which made him appear to be the brightest of the four sons, which maybe he was. He was also the laziest. It was less painful for him to *kowtow* to Rosita, than knock heads with her. With S. P., Peter would bend with the slightest breeze. It was the easiest way, and should pay off in the end.

Where it was easy for Hin Chew to boss Jim around, "I can destroy Jim," Hin Chew liked to say; clever, lazy Peter was more of a problem. Peter knew he was the favorite, and had no problem standing up to Hin Chew.

The eldest brother ran on hate, and was openly out to destroy not only his brothers, but also the "the Gutless Wonder," his father.

For his part, S. P. mercilessly played his sons off against each other. If he were looking for a successor, he might not find one, as the fittest survivor, and the last and only man standing might well turn out to be S. P., himself.

Maybe that was what he wanted.

Hin Chew and I spent Christmas of 1980 with Peter and Rosita at their house on stilts. On arrival, we were surprised to see a fully decorated real live Christmas tree in their living room. Rosita had insisted on a proper Christmas tree, something virtually impossible to find in an Islamic country, also not known for its pine forests. Peter came up with the solution; he had the tree flown in from Singapore.

That same Christmas, my mother wrote, "We are also having guests over for 25th Dec. All your father's good for nothing friends. Dinner will be simple, turkey, spaghetti, sausages, some vegs and Christmas pudding."

Well, she almost got the menu right.

In the same letter, she wrote, "I spotted PaPa Chung and Goh Boon Kok at Orchard Towers – God only knows what he was doing there, probably buying something expensive from Larry Jewelers for his beautiful wife. Papa Chung also went to see Kong Kong."

She ended her letter with, "Please be happy – as you know a

'Happy mother to be is a Happy baby to come.'"

S. P. was traveling a lot, especially to Singapore. There seemed to be a trend in this. Happily, I too was going to spend more time in Singapore, as well, as it had been decided that I would have the baby there.

In March 1981, seven months pregnant, I left for Singapore, where I would be staying with my parents. Now that I was expecting, it was safe for my parents to let me back into their house, as my mother knew there would be no more pleas from me to return home; it was too late for that.

It was great to be back in my old room at 69 Holland Road. Ah Ngoh was there to take care of me, sleeping on the couch in my room. It was nice, and for the first time in a long time, I felt secure and comfortable.

Little had changed in Singapore. My parents were still giving their usual parties, and going out for leisurely dinners around town, their current favorite being the Churchill Room at the Tanglin Club, a private club formed by the British back in 1866, great food in a traditional colonial atmosphere.

My son was born on May 23, 1981. On that day, Hin Chew was in England, visiting Jim and Lynn. However, S. P. and Lillian were present, and visited me at the hospital, as did my parents.

I named my son Marc, but that was only a nickname, as S. P. was in charge of the official name that would appear on the birth certificate.

S. P. claimed that the names always came to him while sitting on the toilet. Once he knew the name, he would then take his calligrapher's brush to create an original Chinese character representing the child's first name. Chinese first names consist of two words, or characters, which S. P. would combine, with a third modifying character to form a complex, and esthetically pleasing character for the child's first name.

S. P. had given Rosita's son, Bobby, the name "DaLun," meaning "big wheel." Marc, he named "YiWen," for "great knowledge."

S. P.'s naming of the children was more than just a linguistic exercise.

The preservation of Chinese calligraphy and language was the way to follow our tradition of keeping the past alive. For Chinese tradition, the present can never be as good as the past. We must look to the past for our standards, and the past must live in the present.

This blurring of time is facilitated by the Chinese language, which has no past tense. Our ancient tales are told, therefore, in the present tense as though they were happening today, erasing the distance of time.

I called my son Marc.

Hin Chew managed to return to Singapore shortly after our son's birth, and we took up temporary residence in Singapore at the Chung's Westwood apartment.

Raising the baby was tough, as I had been unprepared for such a task. Hin Chew would come and go as his father's business dictated. I had no maid, and little help from anybody. Ah Ngoh would come by when she could, bringing me food which she had prepared at my parents' house.

I had always been independent, and I would do my best to raise Marc on my own. Happily, I set about buying the necessary diapers, bibs, pajamas, waterproof pants, clothes, blankets, and a bonnet. I bathed Marc, changed him, talked to him, exposed him to alphabet blocks, and sat him in front of the television set to watch Sesame Street. I was determined that Marc should become a good student, and receive the education that I had been denied.

In time, I began to go out, and see old friends, like Joan and Swee Cheong. Even though I was living alone at the Westwood apartment, I was happy to be away from the Chungs and Mumong.

I would try to stay in Singapore as long as possible.

In September 1981, while I was still in Singapore, my grandparents celebrated their fiftieth wedding anniversary. Nearly one thousand guests were invited to attend a banquet in their honor at the Island Ballroom of the Shangri La Hotel. It was a lavish affair, like the old days. Friends and relatives from all parts of the world attended the affair, more than a few of them receiving air tickets and having their hotel bills picked up by my grandparents, à la S. P. Chung. The President of Singapore, Benjamin Sheares, Mamak's blanket-buddy, and his first lady, were there, along with a raft of Singapore Government Ministers.

I was slim again, and looking good in a sequined pink chiffon ball gown, but no one could outshine Mamak, in a golden *cheongsam* with real threads of gold woven in, and a crown of diamonds, which was topped by an emerald measuring nearly two inches high by an inch and a half wide. The banquet marked the last of many high points in my grandparent's fortunate lives.

Shortly after the banquet, in October 1981, Swee Cheong received the terrible news that he had nasopharyngeal cancer, a disease more common in Asia than in the West. On delivering the diagnosis, Swee Cheong's doctor had said simply, "Ten weeks."

Swee Cheong was, by avocation, a student of Chinese herbs, and alternate therapies, things I did not hold much stock in at the time. He was against western medicine, and, a few weeks into treatment, cut off all chemotherapy and radiation treatments, setting out to cure himself with herbs.

Miraculously, Swee Cheong survived. He did so without the benefit of chemotherapy, radiation, or surgery, and came out of it with minimal damage.

After five months in the Westwood apartment, the Chungs told me it was time to return, so Hin Chew and I flew with Marc to Brunei. Marc was now the most precious thing in my life, and I would do everything to protect him.

Emotionally, I hoped that Marc would be a new bond for Hin Chew and me, and our marriage might now be different. This could be a new beginning, and a new life.

That was my hope, but, on a conscious level, I was no fool, and would continue to keep my eye on the Chungs.

THAILAND

BACK IN BRUNEI, my life focused on raising Marc, which kept me very busy, and gave me all the incentive I needed to carry on.

The Chungs were traveling more than ever, and they always traveled well. Flights were first-class, and the hotels were always the best. Whenever I went along, I made it a point to take Marc. I would not allow his progress to stop. This kid was going to be raised by a parent!

S. P.'s business horizons were expanding to Singapore and Hong Kong, so these became our main travel destinations.

The trips could be pleasant, but only if Hin Chew's parents were with us, as he always behaved well in their presence. In addition, and unlike Hin Chew, S. P. had his lighter side, and was an entertaining traveling companion.

We were all in Hong Kong for Chinese New Year in 1982, and everybody was in high spirits, except of course Hin Chew.

S. P., Lillian, Hin Chew, and I were seated at our table in the Chinese restaurant of the Hong Kong Shangri-La Hotel. We were waiting for Rosita and Peter to come down from their room to join us for the traditional Chinese New Year lunch. It was usual for Rosita to keep us waiting. With a rare bit of humor, Lillian said to S. P. in Hakka, so I would not understand, or so she thought, "Ah, Ping. Get your Manitowoc crane and lift that fat sow off the hotel room bed. Maybe that's the only way to get her downstairs on time."

S. P. replied laughing, "*moi kong, moi kong,*" don't talk, don't talk.

Rosita, a beauty in her day, now carried a hefty 250 pounds on her five foot four frame.

I managed to keep from smiling, but glanced at Hin Chew. He didn't notice. He was staring down at his plate, expressionless, probably thinking of how to outdo his father, the "Gutless Wonder."

Fun and games aside, Chung family politics continued. Lynn and Jim were not included in the group for Chinese New Year celebrations, as they had become estranged from S. P. and Lillian, not having spoken or written to them for over a year.

When we were back in Mumong, it was the same old story for me, not just with Hin Chew, but, increasingly, with Lillian.

I didn't have an easy time of it with my own parents, but at least I felt I belonged. With the Chungs, I never had the feeling that I was a true family member.

Part of the problem was a contrast in personalities. I am, by nature, enthusiastic, fun loving, and outgoing, and always ready to see the bright side of things. It was not so with the Chungs. Theirs was a life of doom and gloom, intrigue and wealth. My own family had the intrigue and wealth part of that equation, but no doom, no gloom. My family's failings, if they can be called that, were those of flamboyance, extravagance, and, yes, a bit of bad taste, but pleasant failings, so to speak.

The doom and gloom side of S. P. and Lillian was limited to their life at home. Outside, and especially in Singapore, the face they presented was far different.

At that time, the Celebrity Tennis Gala was the biggest social event in Singapore. The top Hollywood stars, and entertainment celebrities of the day were featured guests, including such luminaries of the time as Cliff Robertson, Jonathan Winters, Connie Stevens, Barbara McNair, Ed Ames, and Peter Graves.

The culmination of the gala was the charity dinner, where, for an extra S$10,000, you could have your very own movie star sit at your table.

All of Singapore top people were at the dinner, including Mamak and Kong Kong, my parents, and the new President of Singapore, Devan Nair. Mamak's old friend, President Sheares, had passed away several months before.

S. P. and Lillian were also present.

In the name of charity, various items belonging to the stars were auctioned off. Dina Merrill's rhinestone earrings went for S$1,200. The cowboy hat that was worn by Jock Ewing in the TV series, Dallas, was snapped up for S$1,500, and, of all people, by Lillian. She plopped it on S. P.'s head, and he stood up, beaming to the applause—Jock Chung!

After the auction, as my mother glommed on to Cliff Robertson, came the entertainment, Jonathan Winters, Ed Ames, and others putting on their acts. However, as a Singapore magazine put it, "A local 'star' outshone the visiting ones, as a very sporting Datin Lee Chee Shan sang a song at the request of the Brunei tycoon, S. P. Chung, who happily parted with S$10,000 after being serenaded by her."

S. P. was dishing out the cash, and turning on the charm.

Whatever happened to that shabby little Chinaman from Mumong?

By the end of 1982, Jim and Lynn had given up their dream of living in England, made peace with S. P. and Lillian, and returned to Brunei. They could not make it on their own, at least not in the style to which they had become accustomed. For me, this was good. Misery invites company, and Lynn was always good company.

Unfortunately, S. P. and Lillian were not always off living the highlife in Singapore. They were still spending some time in Mumong.

One afternoon, Lillian was in the kitchen, where she had brewed a cup of hot ginseng tea for Hin Chew. Being a Buddhist, she was big on herbal drinks, amulets, charms, countercharms, spells, and such.

I was in the kitchen at the time, and Lillian told me to take the ginseng tea to Hin Chew, with the instruction that he had to drink it hot, right away.

It was Sunday, and Hin Chew and Jim were transfixed watching a videotape of "Superman - The Movie." Superman was one of Hin Chew's favorite characters, he had already seen the movie more than once, and had a large collection of Superman comics.

Even though Hin Chew never could stand interruptions when watching a movie, I had my instructions from Lillian. Holding out the cup, I said, "Mother says you should drink this, while it's still hot."

"What the fuck! Just leave it on the TV," Hin Chew said, with a menacing glance. Jim, the younger brother, remained silent.

Stopping the videotape, he said, "See what you've done? We have to rewind to see what we missed!" Hin Chew did not want to miss a single word of Superman.

I bravely repeated, "Mother wants you to drink this right away."

Shooed away again, I put the drink down on the table next to Hin Chew, and left the room.

The next day, Mother came over to our house, and casually asked

Hin Chew if he had taken the tea.

He answered, "No."

The next thing I knew, and without any warning, Lillian was screaming at me, "You bitch, can't you do anything right? You only married my
son because he's educated. You married him for his money, didn't you?
You're good for nothing! My son should never have married you!"

In a total state of shock, I said nothing, and neither did Hin Chew.

"I demand that you beg me for forgiveness!" screamed Lillian.

I could feel my face redden with anger, and fighting back the tears,
said, "I'm so sorry Ma, it will not happen again."

"That's not good enough!" Lillian shouted, "you will beg for my
forgiveness on your knees!"

I hesitated.

"On your knees!" she screamed, pointing at the floor.

To my eternal shame, I got down on my knees, and, with Hin Chew
watching in silence, said, "Ma, please forgive me, it was all my fault."

I rose, but Lillian resumed her screaming harangue, directing her
remarks to Hin Chew. "She married you only for the money. We
spent good money to send you to MIT, but your wife is totally
unworthy, all she wants is your money, our money."

Neither Hin Chew nor I uttered a word. After Lillian had finished,
she turned her back on us, and stomped out of the house.

What a nightmare! I had done nothing, and said nothing for Lillian
to behave in this way. Getting down on my knees to beg for forgiveness!
No one should ever have to endure such crap! How dare she treat me
like that! How dare Hin Chew stand by and do absolutely nothing!

I was filled with rage and anger, but wise enough to keep it in, as I
was on the Chungs' home turf, for now.

The story of my humiliation in front of Lillian was too hot not to
leak. That evening Rosita called saying, with a touch of arrogance, "If
Ma ever yelled at me, I would have packed my bags and left."

I replied, "How can you say this to me? I am not going to put
myself, or even my husband, in such a position."

"Oh well, we all have our opinions," Rosita said, as she hung up.

At least someone was happy.

In 1983, I went on a short trip to Singapore. Lynn and Jim would be going as well, as they were once again back on the team.

S. P. had organized a lunch in a private room of the Pine Court Restaurant at the Mandarin Hotel, and I was summoned to attend. I was dressed in a black and white peplum top with a black skirt. I always remember my outfits, and when I wore them.

We met up in the lobby of the hotel, and I was happy to see that Jim and Lynn, who were in Singapore at the time, were there. Lynn and I could keep each other company.

Before entering the restaurant, S. P., who knew my frivolous good humor, pulled me aside, and said, "Chu, my American friend, Dan Arnold, will be joining us. Do not talk to Dan, or make any jokes, because Mr. Arnold don't like all this, you know." I nodded in agreement, even though I couldn't have cared less. I had no interest in the lunch affair, but knew it was S. P.'s habit to bring family members with him for business affairs.

I was not impressed by Dan Arnold. He was the typical poorly dressed American you find all over Asia. He was middle-aged, and short, a good deal shorter than I was that day, in my high heels. He wore dreadful square-shaped rimmed glasses, which added to his stern unsmiling appearance. As is the habit with older American men, his polyester long-rise slacks were well secured above his stomach. To me, he looked like a younger version of Milton Berle, but without the smile, or the charm.

Before lunch was served, Dan Arnold and S. P. moved away from the table to a corner of the room, and huddled together in serious conversation. Dan Arnold did most of the talking, while S. P., his arms folded, nodded seriously, frowning and biting his lower lip as he gazed mainly at the floor. I had never seen S. P. being so attentive. Usually, S. P. did all the talking, especially when he was paying the bill. Now, however, S. P. was very deferential, as Dan Arnold did all the talking while S. P. listened. This was no humble Chinaman put-on by S. P.; he was being sincere.

The atmosphere throughout the lunch was strained. Dan Arnold was very uneasy. He said barely a word, except for "Pass the salt," and with no "please."

The subject of conversation was limited to the food before us.

When not busy eating, Dan Arnold kept his arms folded protectively and remained silent. It was my bad luck to be sitting next to him, and my only amusement was to play haughty to his sullen.

After lunch, I asked Lynn, "Who was that boring creep, Dan Arnold? Lynn whispered, "He's a good friend of Pa's. He's in the CIA."

On my way out from the lunch with Dan Arnold, I noticed a brown manila envelope left on one of the chairs in the private room. It was one of three such envelopes that I had seen at lunch. I hesitated, as the others left the room, then quickly picked it up, and stuffed it in my bag.

As soon as I was back in my hotel room, I opened the envelope.

Inside was a document bound with an ochre-yellow cover. Crudely affixed to the cover was a bold half-inch red strip of DYMO label tape warning, "STRICTLY CONFIDENTIAL."

The title page of the business plan read:

CHUNGCO GROUP DEVELOPMENT
A PROPOSED BUSINESS PLAN
(1ST JANUARY 1983)

According to the plan, S. P. would move his headquarters to Singapore, with the establishment of a shipyard, a real estate development company, and the acquisition of a public company, all in Singapore. An IBM mainframe would be purchased in Singapore to monitor the rapidly growing empire.

The Brunei business would continue, but at a reduced level. "Maintain a low profile during the transition period," S. P.'s plan cautioned, and make an effort to "revive CPH's name."

Hong Kong would be S. P.'s financial center. There, S. P. would enter into the banking and finance business, and acquire yet a second public company. In addition, market surveys were to be undertaken "ASAP" as a first step in the establishment of a flourmill and biscuit company in Hong Kong. S. P.'s finger would be in every pie.

Offshore marine services would be developed in Thailand for the oil and gas industry, and "opportunities" would be explored for the establishment of a car and motor cycle industry there—Chungmobiles!

In Taiwan, S. P. would set up a design and engineering office, with another office to be opened in Darwin, Australia by 1984.

Each country's new Chungco offices would be budgeted at several million dollars. Additional millions would be allocated to various miscellaneous projects, including the purchase and conversion of two oil tankers for offshore drilling.

If that were not enough, the plan called for S. P.'s empire to explore and identify opportunities in "Malaysia, the Philippines, Australia, India, Indonesia, and Sri Lanka."

Regarding management, S. P. wrote, "I shall be in overall charge." Next in line, and reporting directly to S. P., were three "Executive Directors," Jim, Peter, and Hin Chew—Huey, Dewey, and Louie, I thought.

Jim would be in charge of Brunei, and would move from dreary Mumong to the capital, Bandar Seri Begawan, as befitted his new position. Peter would be in charge of Singapore, and Hin Chew would be in charge of Hong Kong and Thailand.

S. P. was well off, but did he have this much disposable cash? S. P.'s plan was wildly ambitious by any standards, and especially considering that CPH's sales for 1982 had grown slightly to US$26 million, the company's profits were down, and a loss was developing for 1983.

Where was all the money coming from? Was this a business proposal for Dan Arnold? Was Dan Arnold a backer, a boss?

After going through the document, I stuffed it into my suitcase.

I was to see Dan Arnold only one more time. About a year later, in 1984, Hin Chew and I were entering the Shangri-La Hotel, when I spotted Dan Arnold standing with S. P. in the lobby. As Hin Chew ushered me quickly past them, I said, "Hello there, Mr. Arnold! Hi Pa!"

Soon after our lunch at the Mandarin Hotel with Dan Arnold, S. P. announced that our next trip would be to Thailand. S. P. would be taking everybody, sons, daughters-in-law, and grandchildren.

It was a business trip, but had every appearance of a happy holiday group of benevolent grandparents, harmonious siblings, well-behaved wives, and excited grandchildren. S. P. was using us to create the image.

On our arrival in Thailand, S. P. checked the whole group into the Oriental Hotel, Bangkok's best.

S. P. and his sons, the Executive Directors, would now get down to business, while the women and children embarked on a carefully planned itinerary, including elephant rides, tours, and the obligatory for-tourists-only folk dances, something to keep us busy.

On our final Saturday in Thailand, S. P. took us on a drive out of Bangkok, to where, we were not told. Lynn, sitting next to me, said, "Isn't this just so typical of Pa, he never bothers to tell us anything. Everything looks so desolate here. Do you have any idea where we are going, Chu?"

Thailand had its reputation, drugs, prostitution, and money laundering.

Having Marc with me, I was a bit apprehensive, and wondered to myself, "What is Pa up to now?"

After a three-hour drive south along the coast from Bangkok, we pulled up to a large beachside villa, where a pleasant Thai fellow with a mustache welcomed us. We were not far from the resort town of Hua Hin, and less than fifty miles east of the Burmese border.

There was nothing for the women and children to do, but sit around and wait, as the men disappeared for the whole day.

As I sat, waiting with the ladies waiting for the men to return, I could imagine human "mules" plodding down secret jungle trails in nearby Burma, carrying their lethal cargo of drugs, opium, and its derivative, heroin.

Downstream, some of these drugs would be transferred to other mules, taking flights for the United States, Europe, or Australia. Some mules would take flights, which passed, in transit, through Singapore's Changi Airport. In transit, the mules felt safe, as they were not really entering Singapore, or so they believed.

Sniffer dogs, profiling, and informer's tips, enable Singapore's police to harvest a continuous supply of these unsuspecting mules, as they wait in the Changi Airport transit lounge.

In Singapore, a mere 15 grams of heroin, 500 grams of cannabis, 30 grams of cocaine, or 250 grams of methamphetamine will get you the hangman's noose.

There are no jury trials in Singapore, as juries had been abolished by Lee Kuan Yew. The defendant, who is not entitled to a public trial, faces a lone judge, a government appointee, who hands down his sentence quickly. The system is very efficient, no waiting around for an appeal, no hanging out on death row for years.

Singapore does everything with excellence, and the pre-dawn Friday morning hangings are no exception.

Mercifully, our high tech gallows use the "long drop," so, the prisoner, hooded, and with arms and legs bound, dies instantly, in a snap. The gallows can accommodate up to seven people at a drop, a great convenience when you are hanging fifty or more people every year.

Ironically, drugs are readily available in Singapore. A favorite place for "scoring" drugs is the Newton Circus Hawker Centre, a favorite late night haunt of open-air food stalls popular with young Singaporeans and foreigners, alike.

More importantly, Singapore, boasting the world's largest port for shipping tonnage, and the most Asia-Pacific air-links, is a major transit point for drugs.

The bulk business of drug distribution is not done by small-time couriers, but by the big boys, who never touch the drugs, and are never touched by them.

They rely, instead, on shipping containers, and air cargo flights, hiding the drugs in large shipments of legitimate products, such as canned goods, or electronics.

The big boys never join the lowly mules on Singapore's high-tech gallows.

That evening, the men returned, and we were treated to a wonderful outdoor barbecue, Thai style. It was almost worth the wait.

The following day, we drove back to Bangkok, and, as S. P.'s mission was over, we immediately took a flight back to Brunei, and home to Mumong.

After the trip, in his usual fashion, S. P. wrote a thorough and painstaking analysis of his Thai business prospects.

In his report he wrote, "In making our initial venture into Thailand, we should adopt a low profile approach especially in our dealings with Thai nationals … Avoid association with locals. By proceeding cautiously and by taking time to establish contacts with the right people, we should be able to avoid getting smeared with an ugly reputation."

Humble Charlie Chan at work!

RIPPING OFF ROYALTY

AFTER OUR return to Brunei from Thailand in 1983, things were changing. S. P. and Lillian were no longer around. Peter and Rosita were off in Singapore, and no one was telling me anything.

I waited. The answers would come.

Finally, in August, someone talked, it was Hin Chew, "I want you to pack, Father has decided that we should move to Singapore."

"Why?" I asked.

"None of your business," came the answer.

"Are we coming back?"

"Just do what the fuck I tell you to do."

"For me to do what the fuck you tell me to do, I'd better know what to pack," I shot back.

"Pack whatever you need. Anything we leave behind will be shipped by Joe Curio."

"Joe Curio?" I asked.

"Joe Curio Forwarding, it's a moving company, what the fuck difference does it make? Just pack and get ready."

"And when do we leave, pray tell?"

"Day after tomorrow."

S. P.'s moving his favorite son, Peter, and now his eldest son, Hin Chew, back to Singapore was an indication that the Chungs' business in Brunei was in trouble. We were getting out of town—fast.

Only Jim, the expendable son, and Lynn would stay behind in Mumong.

On September 4, 1983, Hin Chew, Marc, and I boarded our flight in Brunei, bound for Singapore.

Once again, we took up residence in Singapore at S. P.'s Westwood apartment. I was back where I had spent my first months with Marc. I was on my own most of the time, as Hin Chew was still busy with Brunei, going back and forth, as business, and S. P. dictated.

S. P. and Lillian too were frequent travelers, and were in and out of the apartment, their comings and goings always unannounced.

Company was on the way; I was two months pregnant. This time, Hin Chew took the news in stride, primarily because he was preoccupied with problems in Brunei.

My mother wasted no time in telling me that, considering the state of my marriage, one child was enough, telling me, "Abortion, Chu, get rid of the child. Now!"

Even though I was beyond the youthful hope that babies fixed bad marriages, and appreciated my mother's advice, there was no way I would follow my mother's order.

I wanted this baby.

With our sudden departure from Brunei, a growing family, and no explanation of what was happening, I was worried, as any young mother would be. I was worried about money. S. P. and Lillian would be all right, but what about us? We didn't own anything, not even a car. Hin Chew had a salary of S$5,000 (US$2,400) a month, barely enough to cover the rent on a modest apartment with Singapore's inflated prices.

I took a chance and dared to ask Hin Chew about the state of his finances.

He didn't mind the question at all; it gave him the opportunity to brag.

I was surprised and relieved to hear that he had well over a million dollars in cash, all in time deposits, stashed in various banks in Singapore, Brunei, and London, including US$850,000 with Citibank in San Francisco.

Not bad for a guy only five years out of university on a salary of US$2,400 a month!

Where did all the money come from? Hin Chew claimed he had made it on the stock market, but I thought, "Daddy."

Having already sold one of his companies, Brunox, to QAF Brunei, an enterprise controlled by the Brunei Royal Family, maybe S. P. could dump the main company, CPH, on the Sultan's brother, Prince Jefri, who was known as a big spender and a soft touch.

It was worth a try.

Since S. P. had decided to give up CPH by mid-1984, if things didn't improve, and it didn't look like they would, what was there to lose?

As a first step, S. P. sent Hin Chew, and Michael Yap, S. P.'s "legal advisor," to meet with Prince Jefri's representative.

The meeting took place on September 14, 1983. Michael Yap took handwritten notes, which referred to the prince's representative as "C," and to the prince as the "principal."

The meeting started with Hin Chew's presenting S. P.'s letter to "C," offering Prince Jefri a half-interest in CPH, and at a very reasonable price. According to Yap's notes, "The only payment will be the $1,340 mentioned." Since the amount was in Brunei Dollars, the amount came only to about US$630.

Huh! The amount was so low that maybe "C" had misunderstood the 50 percent offer in S. P.'s letter.

What percentage of CPH would the prince receive for that, "C" asked?

"We said that it would be on a 50/50 basis throughout the whole scheme," answered Yap's notes.

Half of CPH for the price of a good suit? What a deal!

"Scheme" was the operative word here, as there was a catch.

In addition to the ordinary shares in CPH, S. P. would own non-voting redeemable preference shares in the company, which would pay 5 percent interest, on a face value of $6 million Brunei Dollars.

Financial complexities aside, the bottom line was a win-win for S. P. His preference shares would receive dividends before anything could be paid to the prince for his ordinary shares. When, eventually, S. P's dividends on the preference shares reached $3 million Brunei Dollars, (something more than the price of a good suit), the preference shares would be liquidated, and S. P. would receive 4 million bonus shares to make him an equal partner with Prince Jefri.

S. P.'s scheme for Prince Jefri of ordinary shares, preference shares, and bonus shares, with a low, low down payment, was complex and nearly impossible to understand.

The bottom line was that even though Prince Jefri might think he was buying 50 percent of CPH for only US$630, the company still would have to pay S. P. $3 million Brunei Dollars, whether or not it made any money.

Only Prince Jefri could lose—brilliant!

The prince's representative nodded, and said he would be getting back to Hin Chew.

Although only the number four son of the former Sultan, Prince Jefri was the favorite of his eldest brother, Sultan Hassanal Bolkiah. That made Prince Jefri the second most powerful man in Brunei. He was entrusted with anything that interested him, and was the appointed, but unspoken, head of BSP.

In Brunei, you were at Prince Jefri's mercy.

The only thing the Chungs had going for them in proposing such a deal to Prince Jefri, was their incredible arrogance. How out of touch could the Chungs have been? How can a commoner hope to negotiate a deal with the absolute rulers of Brunei?

The Chungs assumed that everyone was their patsy, and that extended all the way down to me.

Obviously, I wasn't on the level of the prince, but that's not the point; you had better know with whom you were dealing, at any level.

I could not understand how Prince Jefri, a man who dealt in billions, could possibly be interested in the Chungs' two-bit money-losing deal. The prince had to know that CPH was on the ropes. BSP knew it, and wasn't Prince Jefri the head of BSP?

If Hin Chew had asked my opinion, I would have told him he was way out of his league, and that he'd better back off humbly and quietly. Nothing good could come of ripping off Royalty.

I could just imagine Prince Jefri saying, "Bring him to me."

And that's exactly what happened.

Shortly after his meeting with "C," Hin Chew received notice that he would be allowed to make the prince's day on September 16, 1983 at 4:30 P.M. The audience would be at His Excellency Prince Jefri's palace.

Again, instead of going to the meeting in person, S. P. made the mistake of sending a boy to do a man's job. Once again, Michael Yap, the "legal advisor" would be going with Hin Chew

As Hin Chew and Michael Yap were ushered into the Prince's office, Hin Chew was awed by the Prince's huge TV screen, probably wondering how Superman would look on it.

Behind a large desk sat Prince Jefri, a young man with rugged good looks, and about Hin Chew's age. Notwithstanding his power, or perhaps because of it, Prince Jefri was very affable and friendly to his two guests.

Prince Jefri had been briefed on S. P.'s proposal. He began with questions concerning CPH's giving business to *bumiputra* companies, the *bumiputras* being the local Malays. The Prince, himself, was a *bumiputra*.

Hin Chew replied vacuously that business was indeed being given to *bumiputras*.

The prince nodded, and smiling, eased back into his large leather chair, a signal for Hin Chew to put forward his proposal.

Referring to S. P. as the "Managing Director," or as "MD," and Prince Jefri as "H. E.," Yap's diligent notes read, "CHC said that MD asked him to approach H. E. whether he would consent to be a shareholder."

Prince Jefri replied that neither he nor members of his immediate family could be shareholders.

Instead of backing down, Hin Chew continued to press the issue, asking Prince Jefri, " ... if he has any nominee," someone who could hold the shares for the prince.

Prince Jefri smiled; he must have been thinking how clever these Chinese were at business. No wonder they were beating out his poor *bumiputras*.

After a brief pause, according to Yap's notes, "He then agreed to accept the offer and named a nominee for us to contact. He said that he will contact the nominee, himself that night. He asked us to make it clear to his nominee that the shares are meant for H. E."

Mission accomplished! And so easy! The Chungs might not be any richer for the deal, but Hin Chew had been very clever in passing a loser on to the prince, or so he thought ...

Coincidently, one week later, BSP called for a meeting with CPH.

Hin Chew, Jim, and their lackeys, Feng, and Jim Bell were present.

According to BSP's minutes of the meeting, "BSP opened the meeting by expressing disappointment at the fact that CPH had not constructively countered the BSP proposal and that CPH had taken

2 months to respond."

The notes then recorded that CPH apologized and "revealed that the 1983 operation was showing an overall loss and, therefore, the position forced upon CPH by BSP for 1983 was not tenable for the future."

Fighting words from the arrogant Chungs!

Since the various rates at which CPH could charge for its services to BSP had been agreed upon by both CPH and BSP, "BSP expressed amazement that CPH accepted rates that meant operating at a loss."

Strong words from BSP!

After some bickering over the possible termination of CPH's contract with BSP, the meeting ended on a sour note, "BSP expressed concern that the Chung Pah Hing family seemed to be separating themselves from the negotiations."

The Chungs were running out of friends in Brunei.

Back in Singapore, I couldn't stay at S. P.'s Westwood apartment forever, especially with S. P. and Lillian showing up at odd times. Hin Chew too realized our need for privacy, and decided it was time for us to buy a place of our own.

Hin Chew was still very busy, usually off to Brunei or Indonesia, attending to S. P.'s affairs. When in Singapore, he was busy supervising the setup of a new company, Dachung, which would provide management services for CPH in Brunei.

Dachung was no small operation. In accordance with S. P.'s plan, the company had purchased an expensive IBM mainframe computer.

Since Hin Chew was busy, he delegated the search for an apartment to me. Well almost—I was required to submit a daily written report of my progress to Hin Chew, or to his office when he was out of town.

In Singapore, there are two types of apartments, private, and those built by Singapore's Housing Development Board or HDB as it's called.

The HDB apartments, which house 86 percent of Singapore's population, are tightly regulated by the government, and, being subsidized, can be purchased only by Singaporeans below a certain income level.

The HDB apartment buildings all follow the same basic design, large concrete buildings, elevated over an open ground level floor called the "void deck." The void deck is a common area, available to all residents, for playing checkers, for marriages, and even for funerals—from cradle to grave on the void deck.

Inside, the HDB apartments are utilitarian, drab, and open onto exterior walkways. You can watch your neighbors as they pass by your living room window, and they can look back at you, as well.

The HDB apartments are fundamental to the political control of Singapore. Residents who misbehave can be evicted, and once evicted, where could they afford to live?

HDB apartment buildings in a particular area are grouped into larger complexes called "estates." The racial mix of these "estates" must correspond to that of Singapore. Consequently, the Chinese dominate not only the neighborhoods, but the election districts, as well.

This permits Lee Kuan Yew's Peoples Action Party, the PAP, the winner of every election since 1965, to win all but one or two of the seats in parliament.

Notwithstanding their utilitarian nature, HDB apartments don't come cheap, and can run into several hundred thousand dollars, payable over thirty years. With the average Singaporean's low pay, an astounding 49 percent of the national take-home pay goes into mortgage payments.

By virtue of his income, Hin Chew did not qualify for an HDB apartment. If he had, his temper probably would have got us evicted in short order.

With most everyone living in HDB apartments, the supply of private apartments was limited, so my search did not take long.

After seeing several very expensive apartments, I was lucky to find one in a small building, pleasantly named Mount Rosie. Being a three-story walkup, the apartment was reasonably priced, only S$526,000 (US$247,000). I say *only*, because, even then, it was usual to pay over a million dollars for a private apartment in Singapore—a house, forget it!

Hin Chew was up to the expense, and bought the apartment with cash.

In October 1983, our shipment from Brunei arrived at the

Westwood apartment. It was time to move into an apartment of our own.

As happy as I was about Mount Rosie, the move came at a difficult time. I was pregnant, Marc was in the terrible twos, and Hin Chew was Hin Chew.

For the move, we rented a blue Mitsubishi Lancer, and, as usual, I did the driving. Although Hin Chew claimed he never felt safe with me at the wheel, he always had me do the driving. The unspoken fact was that Hin Chew was a terrible driver, having obtained his license in Brunei, by bribery.

With Hin Chew by my side, supervising from the "death seat," we began our trips to Mount Rosie, with as many boxes as we could cram into the back seat of the little car.

After many trips to Mount Rosie with both of us carrying the boxes up three floors to the apartment, we finished the move and it was time to start unpacking. That was my job.

Hin Chew dropped me off at Mount Rosie, and left for the office. I cheerfully went to work opening boxes, and organizing our new apartment.

In mid-afternoon, Hin Chew returned. I stood up, and bending back with my hands on my hips, pregnant-lady style, said happily, "See, I've made pretty good progress. It's a great apartment, plenty of space for everything."

"Have you written down an inventory?" Hin Chew asked.

"Yes, I checked off the list of the boxes, and they're all here," I answered proudly.

Hin Chew smiled sweetly, "Yes, but have you taken a stock check of everything *inside* the boxes?"

"Well no, why would I need to do that?

Hin Chew's false smile changed into a wide-eyed stare, he screamed, "What the fuck are you doing unpacking the boxes without taking a stock check?"

I answered, "I've only been unpacking kitchen stuff, cheap pots and pans, what's the point in taking stock of that?"

"Come, let's go, I'm in a hurry," said Hin Chew, motioning me to the door.

As I followed him down the stairs, his yelling echoed through the stairway, "How could you unpack the boxes without taking a fucking stock check? How can you be so fucking stupid?"

I rushed into the car, and once Hin Chew was in, I started to drive out of the Mount Rosie parking lot. Hin Chew raged on, reaching such a volume that, even with the windows closed, a crew of Indian laborers, working in front of the building, could hear.

They stopped their work, and turned to look at us. Hin Chew was frothing at the mouth. With Hin Chew, "frothing at the mouth," is not just literary license, he actually did it.

There was nothing I could do, but put on my sunglasses to hide my face, and tears. What a monster!

It would be another ten years before I would find out another reason for Hin Chew's abuse.

There was another woman. She had the alluring name of "Vei Vei," and lived in Indonesia, where Hin Chew visited her on his "business" trips. Aside from her name, some love letters to Hin Chew, and a post office box address in Jakarta, I never knew who she was.

In those days, I probably would not have believed that Hin Chew had another woman, even if I caught him butt-naked with a blonde.

To me, he was anything but a lover.

Bad temper and abusive language aside, I saw him as a nerdy loner, a person who liked to laze in bed, matching wits with small electronic games, reading comics, and watching Chinese Kung-Fu movies on television.

That's how perceptive I was.

Number Two Son

THE CHINESE New Year is on the second New Moon after the Winter Solstice. This keeps the Chinese calendar pretty much in step with the Gregorian calendar. In 1984, Chinese New Year fell on February 2, the first day of the Year of the Rat, one of the animals in the recurring twelve-year Chinese calendar cycle.

Hin Chew was a Dragon, the sign of those said to be intelligent, perfectionists, but unduly demanding on others. I was a Rooster which made me one who speaks my mind, a flashy dresser, and extravagant.

Not bad, the Chinese calendar.

Every Chinese New Year, all Lee family members present in Singapore had to pay their respects to my grandparents.

Hin Chew was in Singapore at the time, so he came with me to Casa Emma. Naturally, my parents were there, along with Uncle Jimmy and Aunt Judy.

Aunt Esja and her husband Jon, I refused to call him the "White Monkey," were also in attendance as they had moved back to Singapore, after spending twenty-five years in Reykjavik, Iceland.

Jon's marriage to Esja had raised suspicions in Kong Kong's mind, suspicions of money-grubbing. It was bad enough that Jon was not Chinese, but worse, he was not rich, nor being a mere teacher, would he ever become rich.

With Esja's return to Singapore, Kong Kong had become doubly suspicious, and in a rare moment of candor with my father, said, "Tell your mother to watch out for Esja. Her own daughter will take her for every penny, if she can."

Naturally, my father passed this remark on to my mother, who agreed with Kong Kong's assessment of Esja, and for good reason.

For twenty years, it had been my mother's privilege to manicure Kong Kong's nails. However, since Esja's return, this had come to a halt, and a professional manicurist had taken over the job, obviously, Esja's doing. In my mother's eyes, Esja had been greatly weakened by Kong Kong's remark to my father, and a weakened animal invites attack.

The Chinese New Year's ceremony never varied. My grandparents' two favorite armchairs, unoccupied, were placed next to each other in the main living room of Casa Emma. The minor personae, which included my parents, Uncle Jimmy and his wife, the Bookends, and now Jon and Esja, would assemble, standing, in front of the empty armchairs. It was nearly showtime.

After a well-timed interval, my grandparents would enter, and, once they were comfortably seated in the favorite armchairs, the group would sink to their knees.

The children, the only audience permitted to attend, would watch silently from the side. For me, it was incredible to see my father, the reigning bully of his own house, on his knees before his parents.

It gets better. After sinking to their knees, the supplicants all bowed in unison—three times.

Now came the reward, the traditional *ang pows*, small red packets containing two crisp banknotes, as custom dictated. Each supplicant would strain forward, still kneeling, to receive the *ang pow* with two hands as Chinese etiquette dictates. In the past, there had also been manila envelopes containing shares of stock, but those days were gone. Still everybody was very happy, and after the last *ang pow* had been passed out, the supplicants arose and hugs of joy were exchanged all around.

The formalities were over and it was on to the next event, Mamak's coin throwing ceremony.

This event was not only for family members, but also for everybody present including children, friends, drivers, gardeners, all of whom had been waiting eagerly, outside on the large cement driveway.

Being eight months pregnant, and knowing what was to come, I stayed inside with Hin Chew. Most of the women stayed inside, as well, including my mother and Esja.

An elaborately carved wooden chair, resembling a throne, was placed in front of the entrance of the house for Mamak. Viewed from the driveway, as she took her seat, Mamak was appropriately framed by the two large marble lions, which flanked the front door.

Next, two servants, clad in traditional black pants and waist-length white tunics, emerged bearing a large and ornately sculptured Burmese cauldron made of solid silver. The servants, each taking a handle at opposite sides of the cauldron walked unsteadily, bent over by the weight of their burden. The cauldron brimmed with gleaming new coins of ten, twenty and fifty cents.

The tension and excitement grew, as those assembled on the driveway jostled for position.

Slowly, and carefully, the servants placed the heavily laden cauldron at Mamak's feet.

Smiling, she reached down into the coins and, with a sudden and unsuspected burst of energy, screaming, she began throwing fistfuls of coins to the anxious throng. There was a mad scramble for the coins, as Mamak continued to shower them on the participants.

My father and Uncle Jimmy, ever the bumpkins, loved the competition.

At an easy two hundred and fifty pounds each, they were built for the sport, and had years of experience behind them. The brothers threw their weight around with merciless abandon, enjoying any excuse to step on hands, to push, and to shove, to be themselves, and to do whatever it took to win the prized coins, as Mamak screamed with laughter and delight over the prowess of her two lumbering boys.

The scene brought back vivid childhood memories of my receiving an elbow from Uncle Jimmy, and winding up with skinned arms and knees, from playing the game. Blood was shed at these events; people were injured—Chinese gladiators on the rampage for money!

The excitement over the coins ran high, but had any of the scrambling contestants lifted their eyes to glance though the window of the mah-jongg room, they would have seen an even more dangerous "game" taking place.

In the mah-jongg room, my mother had taken a twelve-inch carving knife from the turkey, and was chasing the screaming Esja with it. Hin Chew and I heard Esja's screams, and arrived at the mah-jongg room just in time to see Esja come bounding out with amazing speed.

Fortunately, Kong Kong's nurse had already jumped in and taken the knife from my mother.

I was mortified! I didn't give a damn about Esja, but there was the matter of face, so many people were present and this was Chinese New Year, the very day that would set the tone and luck for the entire year. So shameful!

Immediately after the incident, my mother was strangely calm. "Don't worry Chu," she said, "I wasn't really going to kill her." In her tan tailored pants, matching blouse, and olive-green turban, my mother looked cool and composed, nothing like a killer.

Everyone feared Kong Kong's reaction. What would the patriarch do under such circumstances? Esja ran to report to Kong Kong, "Mabel attacked me! She tried to stab me with a knife, the knife from the turkey!"

Kong Kong simply smiled, and said nothing. My mother had been socially incorrect, but, what was more important, she had been politically correct.

My mother's position as manicurist to Kong Kong was immediately restored.

The next month, on March 20, 1984, I was pregnant and alone in our Mount Rosie apartment. Marc was attending a Montessori school, as you can never start school too soon in Singapore's competitive academic environment.

Around noon, I began to have some contractions, but thought nothing of it; the baby wasn't due for another two weeks. A half an hour later, as the contractions were increasing in intensity, and coming more often, I telephoned my obstetrician, Dr. Teoh.

He told me to check into Gleneagles Hospital right away, saying he would meet me there later in the afternoon.

Next, I telephoned Hin Chew, but, before I could tell him anything, Hin Chew asked, "Have you cleaned up the apartment. I don't have space to breathe there, the place is a pig-style." He meant "pigsty," but "pig-style" was one of Hin Chew's favorite expressions, and who would dare correct him?

Ignoring his question, I told him that this was it, ready or not, I was going into labor.

"I'm busy at work. Do you think you can make it to the hospital on your own?" he asked.

I was angry, any normal husband would come home right away to accompany his wife to the hospital under the circumstances.

Curtly, I answered, "Why sure, I'll drive right over there, myself. Would it be too much for you to pick Marc up from school?"

Quickly, I packed a small bag of things I would need in the hospital, locked the door, and went carefully down the flights of stairs to our new car, a red Honda Prelude.

Fortunately, the car was always home, as Hin Chew preferred to take a taxi to work, safer that way.

I drove to the hospital, and checked in.

My number two son was born at about 8:00 in the evening, an hour before Hin Chew arrived, bringing Marc with him. Well, sorry he was late, but he had to pick up Marc, take a shower, and have dinner, "these things take time," he explained.

Even my happy-go-lucky parents, the playboy and the party-girl, had beaten Hin Chew to the hospital.

So the Chungs wouldn't see them, my mother carefully coordinated the visits of Granny and Zena, as they were an embarrassment to her. She had done the same when Marc was born.

S. P. was in town, so, the day after my son's birth, when he visited me with Lillian, he was able to tell me that the baby's name was Dayong, meaning Big Warrior.

I called my baby Warren.

In no time, Warren and I were back home at Mount Rosie. Warren was a good-looking baby, and, from day one, Hin Chew's favorite. He would actually hold the baby, in fact shortly after we had brought Warren home, Hin Chew, cradling Warren in his arms, began to cry!

He looked at me, tears in his eyes, and said, "We can be a family now." For a brief moment, he looked down at the baby in his arms, and after a sniffle, continued, "We can start our life anew. With this baby, we can start all over again."

I was speechless and dumbfounded, Hin Chew in tears? Maybe miracles did happen, after all. That miracle lasted for less than a week.

In July 1984, S. P.'s father, Chung Pah Hing, died.

For the superstitious Lillian, this was a bad sign, and everything had to be done to overcome whatever was portended by this omen.

Assisted by Buddhist monks, Lillian and S. P. arranged an elaborate Buddhist funeral, a ritual to placate Fate. They arranged for Justmen's, the top tailors in Singapore, tailors to the Brunei Royal Family, to fashion black outfits for the entire family, black pants, and a black tunic top, for each of us, male and female, Viet Cong style. Lillian decreed that the women's hair had to be neatly tied back, and no makeup allowed.

S. P. held his father's wake in a special building at the Mount Vernon Crematorium. The coffin was open, and had an eternal flame burning underneath, giving it the look of an outsized chafing dish.

The family members traveled back and forth to the wake in a convoy of chauffer driven white Mercedes limousines rented by S. P., one for each family group.

Limousine-loads of Buddhist monks, working in shifts, chanted day and night. Caterers brought in Buddhist vegetarian food for everybody. Joining us at the wake were S. P.'s business associates, relatives, acquaintances, and my parents.

S. P. had a communications center set up, with four men seated at a table manning four black telephones, surely a first for a wake. Ah Por, the grieving widow, wailing, crying, howling, and fainting, as was fitting and proper, was dragged from her limousine by S. P. and Lillian.

"My fucking grandmother always has to be the center of everything," Hin Chew whispered to me. He was right, Ah Por had always craved attention, but this was not the time or place for such a remark.

"It's traditional to behave like that," I whispered back, "after all, her husband just died."

"Fucking Ah Por!" replied Hin Chew, under his breath.

Hin Chew apart, everything was being done, not only to honor his grandfather, but also to appease the gods, and free us of the karma and bad omen that Chung Pah Hing's death could bring upon us.

Rosita, Lynn, and I had to be present day and night, and were put to work by Lillian.

Our job was to squat on the floor folding the ceremonial Chinese paper money for Chung Pah Hing, so he could buy his way into heaven. Once folded, the money went into large rattan baskets to be burned at the prescribed time, sending it directly into the deceased's next life.

This went on for three full days and nights. We would go home around midnight, only to return early the next morning.

Rosita was fuming, and complained, "May Chu, this is crazy, my feet are killing me. I have bad feet, you know, and I'm dying for a cigarette." On nearly an hourly basis, Lynn would lean back and say, "I don't think I can do any more of this, Chu. Leave it to Ma to put us to work, bloody hell!"

I agreed with both Rosita and Lynn, but told them it was the Chinese tradition.

At the end of the three-day wake, S. P.'s father was not cremated, but buried. With her husband gone, Ah Por instantaneously lost her top position in the family hierarchy to Lillian. Ah Por had become a nobody. This was also the Chinese tradition.

By the summer of 1984, the Chungs had increased the scope of their business activity in Singapore, by setting up three new corporations, Chungco Trading, Chungco Investments, and Chungco Electronics. That brought their Singapore corporations to nine, so far as I knew.

Although no one told me what was going on, I did have an excellent source of information.

Hin Chew liked to drink beer, a lot of beer.

After a few beers, he would become very talkative, and a few beers happened every evening he was home. Hin Chew would then treat me to rambling tales of what S. P., the "Gutless Wonder," and Hin Chew's "useless brothers" were up to.

With the Lees and the Aws, and especially with Kong Kong's difficulties, I had experienced family intrigue first hand, long before the Chungs appeared in my life. I knew that even in the best of times, things could go terribly wrong.

In spite of Hin Chew's healthy finances, I was still worried. The equation was simple; I could see no money coming in, and a lot going out. The Brunei business continued to be in trouble, and the Chungs were spending a small fortune setting up their new corporations, the prized IBM mainframe alone, cost over a million dollars.

Hin Chew traveled to Brunei frequently, as CPH continued to face difficulties. S. P. was no longer taking an active part in the management of the Brunei business, and, to my knowledge, hadn't set foot in Brunei for over a year.

Only Jim was still living in Brunei, a token Chung to placate BSP.

It was only natural for me to wonder how long this could go on, before the money ran out.

In August 1984, Kong Kong, suffered a second and more serious stroke. He was in a coma for the first twenty-four hours, and was in the hospital for two months. Kong Kong had lost the power of speech, and, partially paralyzed, was bed-ridden. He would never be the same again.

Kong Kong's remaining days were to be spent helpless, cared for around the clock by private nurses, and his aging sisters. He lay paralyzed, and usually alone, his bed facing a television set, mercilessly left on twenty-four hours a day.

The death of Chung Pah Hing, and Kong Kong's terrible stroke were clear signs of impending bad luck.

Did I believe in such things? I'd be afraid not to.

THE FALL OF S. P. CHUNG

OCTOBER 22, 1984, was the day that Hin Chew flew from Singapore on his fateful trip to Brunei.

I was not to see him again for a year.

After Lillian's visit to the Mount Rosie apartment to tell me that Hin Chew had been arrested by the Royal Brunei Police, she disappeared, as did S. P. They were no longer at their Westwood apartment in Singapore. No goodbyes, no forwarding addresses, they were gone, and on the run.

My own family, the Lees, had problems in their day, but nothing like this. Kong Kong never had to flee from the law. Even my father with all his shenanigans had never been arrested, not yet anyway. My dear mother was never caught doing anything wrong. She was too smart for that.

The Aw brothers, before they came to Singapore had been arrested in Burma for trafficking in opium and counterfeiting. What could explain the Aw brother's rapid accumulation of wealth?

More Tiger Balm is being sold today, than sixty years ago.

Yet, the present Tiger Balm company, publicly traded Haw Par Healthcare Ltd, in the year 2000, earned under US$10 million—certainly not enough to keep the Aw brothers, their seven wives, mistresses, Tiger Balm Gardens, and Haw Par Villa going while they started banks and bought up newspapers. From 1929 through 1949, the brothers donated US$71 million to build schools and hospitals in China, Hong Kong and Thailand—and all that came from Tiger Balm?

Sudden wealth often points the finger to questionable activities, especially when the fertile opium fields of Burma are nearby. What could be more natural than the transition from opium and counterfeiting to Tiger Balm, and newspapers, the Aw brother's legitimate businesses?

But that was long ago and far away.

So far as recent history was concerned, I knew where my family was coming from ... but the Chungs, what were they really about?

In Singapore, I had no choice but to keep a very low profile, not for any covert reason, I wasn't under investigation, but out of embarrassment.

Only my family and a few close friends had any knowledge of what was happening, so I limited my social contacts mainly to my parents, Aunt Zena, Joan, and Swee Cheong.

After my unpleasant meeting with Peter and Rosita, I saw them only out of necessity.

Several days after Lillian's visit (and disappearance), Keith Wilson called on me at Mount Rosie.

Keith was from England, and I knew him on a casual basis. He was one of S. P.'s people, and had attended my wedding. Keith did odd jobs for S. P., but not as an employee, as he had a small company of his own.

Keith explained to me that Hin Chew had been detained in Brunei, as though I didn't know. He assured me that the Chungs were doing every thing they could to have Hin Chew and Jim out of Brunei by Christmas, by which time they could resolve the problem.

"What problem?" I asked, casting out a line.

"I can't say, but what I can tell you is that Hin Chew's and Jim's passports have been confiscated. They are both incarcerated in Brunei, but only under a kind of house arrest."

"Where is S. P.?" I asked.

"Out of town."

"Out of town where? In Brunei?"

"No."

"And Lillian?"

"Out of town."

I was pretty sure that Keith knew the answers, but was not in a position to say.

Keith then got to the point of his visit.

S. P. was using him as a courier to fly things in and out of Brunei. Keith, with his British passport, was the man for the job, as he was not likely to have a problem with the Brunei authorities.

If I had any letters or personal items for Hin Chew, Keith would be only too happy to take them into Brunei for me, "Just call, if you have anything for me."

As though suddenly remembering, he cautioned, "You'd better not telephone Hin Chew. His telephone is bugged, for sure."

I thanked him, and said that I would be writing to Hin Chew.

As Keith was leaving, I asked, "Who's in charge of S. P.'s business, now?"

"Peter."

When the emperor is away, the little emperor will take over.

With the absence of S. P. Chung, and with his two elder brothers out of the way, Peter was in full charge of the Chung businesses—the little emperor! Peter was having himself a gala time; there was plenty of company money to spend for entertainment, and for whatever else touched his fancy—nights on the town, pushing people around, and, inevitably, women. He kept Rosita busy and happy with an expensive and useless redecoration of their rental apartment.

To be politically correct, I decided to pay Peter a visit at the Chungs' new headquarters, located in the Overseas Chinese Banking Centre.

As I waited in the outer office, I could hear Peter's voice echoing down the hallway, as he talked to Lim Jen Howe, a Chungco employee. The discussion was about Ronnie Lee, Hin Chew's lawyer in Brunei. I heard Peter say, "That bastard is asking for an arm and a leg."

After a half-hour's wait, Peter was free to see me. I was ushered down the hallway to find him happily ensconced in S. P.'s lavish office. He was smiling, gracious, and pleasant, just like Daddy.

Peter stood up and walked toward me. With open arms, S. P.'s old gesture, Peter flashed a bright smile, gave me a warm hug, and said in his deep voice, "Hi, Sis, how are you? Hey, great to see you! How nice of you to drop by, don't be a stranger, now."

"Oh, hi Pete, of course not. I came by to say hello, and see how everything is going … I'm worried."

Peter replied, "Don't you worry, everything is under control, Hin Chew and Jim are fine … in fact, they might be coming back very soon. Keith is going to see them again."

"Uh huh."

Peter put his arm around my shoulder, "Hey, by the way, Sis, if you need anything, give Rosita a call, and we'll see what we can do for you, OK? No worries."

Peter was glowing and so happy. Why not? He was the boss, and he was clearly in charge.

Peter told me that I would be receiving S$2,000 a month for expenses, and not to worry about money. Well, we were off to a good start.

The atmosphere of the visit was completely different from that of my recent scolding by Rosita, for showing up at their apartment with Swee Cheong.

Our conversation was polite and friendly. It was only a courtesy call, a recognition of what I hoped would be only a temporary change in command.

I regarded Peter as being very intelligent, but lacking motivation for much other than good times. Peter was a great sprinter, and the best of S. P.'s sons for the current turmoil, but on a short track only.

Unfortunately for Peter, the job that Fate had given him was not going to be over very soon.

Peter had to get Hin Chew and James out of Brunei. Then, he had to deal with the legal problems the Chungs were having in Brunei, and salvage whatever he could from Brunei, including the company, CPH.

Finally, there was the rehabilitation of S. P.'s reputation.

Peter was not alone for the struggle. His camp was staffed with S. P.'s most able and trusted employees, no one was jumping ship.

Feng was there to do the bookkeeping, keeping track of the intricate accounts of the interlocking and interwoven Chung companies.

Goh Boon Kok, the ubiquitous lead auditor, was there to check on Feng.

Agnes Chua, had been hired as S. P.'s personal secretary several years before. She had become the discrete handler of all of S. P.'s affairs, both business and personal.

Michael Yap, who had moved with his family to Canada some years before, was S. P.'s most trusted employee, his advisor, hand-holder, and utility journeyman. Michael had studied law, but never managed to become a lawyer.

Still he had excellent connections.

Michael's university classmate and good friend was Andrew Ang, a senior partner at Lee & Lee, Singapore's premier law firm run by Lee Kuan Yew's wife, which was good reason for S. P. to have Michael on the payroll.

Michael was away from Singapore at the time, accompanying S. P., as he ran from continent to continent to keep ahead of the law.

John McCormack was the Managing Director of Coopers and Lybrand in Singapore, a position that earned him S. P.'s respect.

Mac, as he was called, was an active participant in many of the Chungs' dealings, and was getting more active, all the time.

Mac was a huge, barrel-chested, Englishman, with a ruddy face, and a hearty laugh. His hair, which had seen better days, had its strands gelled and slicked back. Mac was seldom without a cigar wedged between his sausage-like fingers, drawing attention to his pinkie ring. He was an immaculate dresser, cufflinks and all. Mac was always tanned and healthy, a result of his yearly skiing trips to the Pennines.

Keith Wilson, as chief mule, had more important things to do than carry my letters back and forth. He was entrusted with bringing out the Chungs' valuables from Brunei, including jewelry, gold, and cash.

Most importantly, however, he delivered letters and minutes of meetings, all with coded names, to keep Hin Chew and Jim informed, and to advise them as to what their next move should be.

This correspondence was one-way traffic only, as orders were that no correspondence was to come out of Brunei.

In Brunei, the Chungs were faced with two problems, the incarceration of Hin Chew and Jim, and the deteriorating relationship with BSP.

The more serious was the incarceration, which was putting Hin Chew and Jim in jeopardy, and threatened even S. P.

All I was told was that the Chungs were under investigation in Brunei for bribery. To me that didn't make sense. Bribery is a way of doing business in Asia. Even in Singapore, bank loan officers expect a hefty 2 percent kickback for a commercial loan.

Why would Brunei care about the supposed bribery? In Asia, bribery is easy to beat—you do it with more bribery. There had to be more to the Chungs' problem.

Second, there were the persistent difficulties with the BSP contract. CPH was not making money, and the contract for the coming year, 1985, was in doubt.

Regarding the BSP problem, Hin Chew had written in his diary, "MD feels that he was set up by BSP/PI/P Everett."

"MD" was, of course, S. P., and "PI" was S. P.'s good friend Pehin Isa. It was understandable that Peter Everett, the managing director of BSP, might set the Chungs up, but why would Pehin Isa be interested?

Whatever was causing their difficulties, the Chungs had no choice but to rush to get their assets out of Brunei.

On November 2, 1984, moving fast, Lillian sent a letter to the Hong Kong and Shanghai Bank in Brunei, where she had a fixed deposit sitting in the bank of 3.5 million Brunei Dollars (US$1.4 million). Lillian's letter gave Hin Chew the authority to use the funds to purchase shares on the Hong Kong stock exchange.

The day after Lillian's letter, Peter wrote Hin Chew and Jim, passing along S. P.'s instructions.

In the typewritten letter, revealing the cunning duplicity of S. P., the names were changed to protect the guilty:

To HC/JHC
From: Pete
3 Nov 1984

1. Following some extensive discussions with Uncle, we feel that there is a limited window in which to act plausibly. The rough time frame for this is about 10 days to 2 weeks from the above date.

2. It was agreed that a meeting with No. 4 (per orig.plan) is the most appropriate action to attempt to arrange at this stage. Regardless of whether he had foreknowledge of the matter or not, we will assume the latter for the time being. The following are some of the salient points for your consideration in your meeting with No. 4 (if it can be arranged).

    2.1. Inform him of the investigation, when it occurred & the allegations made. Be careful not to make any accusations against anyone at anytime during your discussions.

2.2.   You do not know what had caused this investigation until you were advised last Wed. 31 Oct. i.e. shown the money that was alleged to have been 'given.' You have no knowledge of the alleged matter.

2.3.   Inform him that your passports have been confiscated.

2.4.   Stress that while you have no knowledge of such matter, you are certain that it was not and could not have been company money.

2.5.   Explain that father's trip to the U.S. had been planned months ago and he was originally scheduled to leave in July of this year. Father's original travel schedule had to be postponed due to Grandfather's demise (14 July). The new schedule was to begin on 18 Oct (one day after the end of the 100 days mourning for Grandfather). The nature of his trip: business, medical as well, and to enroll PHK into a suitable univ. in the U.S.. NB : Father had heart trouble, his admission to hospitals in Singapore twice within the past six months further attests to his ill health.

2.6.   Father did not learn of this investigation until he had arrived in the U.S. and having made the high level appointments twice, he cannot return immediately. At any rate, his physical condition did not permit the long journey back and medical tests are continuing.

2.7.   You have had almost no knowledge of father's trip to the U.S. (with the exception of the points covered in item 2.5). This trip was planned by father himself and he often made such trips in recent years. There was little need for him to call back often during these trips since they were of a personal nature and had little to do with the company. In any event, you only learnt of the allegation on Wed. 31 Oct.

2.8.   It seems as though your enforced stay and this allegation had caused father's physical condition to worsen.

2.9.   You should stress your innocence and if it was a misunderstanding, you would be grateful if No.4 in his wisdom can put things right again.

3.   KEY POINTS again:

3.1.   Your lack of KNOWLEDGE of any wrong doing and innocence.

3.2.   Father's ABSENCE – long scheduled, medical checkup and business meetings, confident that he will return soon.

3.3.   COULD NOT be Company's MONEY.

3.4.   Grateful if No. 4 can ADVISE and ASSIST in amicably resolving this matter.

GOOD LUCK!

Please make own notes & destroy this note.

The letter was pure Mafia Don, a line of excuses and lies for Hin Chew to feed to Prince Jefri, including S. P.'s ill health, a death in the family, a period of mourning, misunderstandings, feigned ignorance, and, why, that couldn't have been company money! This was typical of the Chungs—no respect for the truth.

To hide the true identity of the usual suspects, Peter had conjured up such code names as, "Uncle," and "No. 4." "Uncle" was a mystery to me, but "No. 4" was Prince Jefri, the number four son of the former Sultan of Brunei.

The letter told Hin Chew to have the prince "ADVISE and ASSIST" him in resolving the matter. The Chungs were pinning their hopes on Prince Jefri.

As cautious and methodical as Hin Chew was, he did not follow Peter's handwritten postscript to "destroy the note." He saved it, and why?

In my opinion, he kept it for future leverage against his father.

Hin Chew wasn't keeping the letter for the family archives, he wasn't interested in history, only in money.

Two days later, Peter sent a second, shorter, letter to Hin Chew and Jim:

5th Nov 1984
Dear HC & JC,
I hope you are keeping your spirits up, if we can help in any way pls let me know.

1. The man is well and is in good spirits.
2. Ingersol-Rand's Brother will be collecting data and background on Donald Duck.
3. Extradition – ASEAN – HK – Treaty - ?
4. Try to get money transferred out of Citibank bit by bit also find out if they will release items in the man's deposit box these are personal.
Cheers

Some new code names, "Donald Duck," "Ingersol-Rand's Brother," and "The man" had now joined the cast of characters. "The man" was S. P., but who were the others? I was never able to find out.
"Extradition?"
No wonder S. P. was nowhere to be found.
If extradition was his fear, S. P. should have remained in Singapore, a haven from extradition.
Singapore does not enter into extradition treaties with its neighboring countries, as much of its success comes from being a haven for wealthy fugitives from the area, along with their money.
In addition to protection from extradition, Singapore offers banking secrecy, which is great for Generals from Mainland China, drug lords from Burma, and money launderers within Singapore.
When Nick Leeson, the notorious currency trader, fled Singapore in 1995, after bankrupting Baring Securities, he and his wife went first to Malaysia, where they hung out for several days. During this time, Leeson's story, and face, were featured on television and in newspapers.
From Malaysia, the Leesons flew to Brunei, where they had an eight-hour layover in transit, while waiting for a connecting flight

to Germany.

The Malaysian and Brunei authorities knew where the Leesons were all along, but made no move to arrest them for extradition back to Singapore.

It was tit for tat; you won't extradite for me, so I won't extradite for you.

When the Leesons' flight arrived in Frankfurt, Germany, the police arrested Leeson for extradition to Singapore. By catching up with Leeson in Frankfurt, Singapore wouldn't scare off any potential rich crooks from its neighboring countries. Like everything else in Singapore, this is the way Lee Kuan Yew wants it, even for himself.

It was an open secret in certain circles of the Singapore Government that Indonesian Prime Minister Suharto kept an airplane ready at Singapore's old Seletar Airbase for Lee Kuan Yew to flee Singapore, should the need arise. There was a getaway speedboat, as well. Now that Suharto is no longer around, I'm sure other arrangements have been made.

The next two meetings of the Chungs took place at S. P.'s office in Hong Kong, so "the man" could attend.

The minutes of these meetings produced a laundry list of things for Hin Chew to do in Brunei:

NOTES OF MEETINGS HELD ON THE 14 AND 15 NOV.

PRESENT: THE MAN, PHILIP AND KEVIN.

1) SELL ALL ASSETS TO NO 4
2) PAYMENT FOR THESE CAN BE MADE OVER THE NEXT 10 YEARS.
3) PUSH AHEAD WITH THE CLAIMS AGAINST B.S.P.
4) KEEP CALM AND DO NOT PUSH TOO HARD.
5) DO NOT SEND OUT ANY OF THE YARD EQUIP.
6) HAND OVER BY 1985 1ST OF JANUARY.
7) TELL JIM BELL TO KEEP QUIET AND NOT TO PUSH B.S.P.
8) TRY TO GET H.C. OUT FOR A SHORT VISIT TO SING.
9) CHECK WITH RONNIE IF ASSETS IN SIN. OR H.K. CAN BE CONFISCATED.

10) CHECK IF THE STATES HAS AN EXTRADITION TREATY WITH BRUNEI.

11) S. P. TRYING TO ARRANGE TRANSFER OF THE 5.8M FROM NEW YORK.

12) FIND OUT WHAT IS THE FEELINGS OF HARDY IN C.B.

13) AFTER FATHER READ THE BOYS LETTERS HE DID NOT SLEEP FOR THREE NIGHTS.

14) FATHER IS VERY UPSET AND WORRIED HE IS DOING ALL HE CAN TO PUT THINGS RIGHT BUT HE FEELS VERY HELPLESS.

15) TRY TO GET HARDY TO EXCHANGE THE GOLD FOR PHYSICAL GOLD IN H.K.

16) JEWELS AND GOLD COINS WILL BE TAKEN OUT TO SIN. BY K.C.W.

17) S. P. WILL ISSUE A POWER OF ATT. FOR H.C.

18) CHECK ON THE LIABILITIES OF MRS. C. WHAT LIABILITIES HAS SHE GOT.

19) GOLD IS TO BE PUT IN MADAME YEO'S NAME.

20) H.C. HAS TO KEEP FIT AND LOSE A BIT OF WEIGHT. HE IS TO STOP DRINKS.

The Chung gang was becoming professional with the use of code names. "Philip" and "Kevin" had joined the gang, code names for Peter, and Goh Boon Kok, respectively.

Could Brunei extradite S. P. from the United States?

Could they confiscate his assets in Hong Kong or Singapore?

This was beginning to sound like something more than a simple case of "bribery."

The Chungs were still hoping for "No. 4," Prince Jefri, to purchase the company, and were willing to give the prince an easy ten-year payment plan, which I doubt that Prince Jefri really needed.

Keith Wilson, aka "K.C.W.," was to smuggle out the Chungs' jewels and gold from Brunei, and Jim Bell, who didn't rate a code name, as he was doing too much blabbing, should shut up.

Madam Yeo, Lillian's maiden name, was to get the gold, which Hardy of Citibank was to deliver in gold bars to Hong Kong.

I could envision the staid Citibanker, Hardy, rowing up to a lonely

Hong Kong wharf in a small rowboat laden with gold bars, and nearly sinking under their weight.

Citibank always did a lot for the Chungs. The situation was growing desperate, and on November 16, the next day, the third meeting was called to order at 10:20 A.M. This meeting was attended by "The man," "Philip," "Eric," "Amy," and "Kevin."

More gangland style "handles" were appearing. Feng, the accountant somehow signed on as "Eric," Agnes, S. P.'s trusted secretary, joined up as "Amy." Hin Chew and Paul, S. P.'s youngest, became "Carl," and "Patrick."

The important players had to be protected, although most of the unimaginative code names were a dead giveaway.

The minutes of this meeting revealed that, "The man will take his wife to the University Land on 19 Nov., Philip will follow ASAP." Countries were also being protected by code names, "University Land," was the United States, and "Philip," who was Peter, would follow.

"All contacts with the man to be made through Eric or Amy." Only Agnes and Feng would know S. P.'s whereabouts.

"Try to arrange for Carl to go the Supply Land for a short visit. He will not return." "Supply Land" was Singapore. S. P. would try to spring Hin Chew from Brunei, but Jim would be left holding the bag. Jim was expendable.

"Ask Mac and Carl to see No. 4, if he doesn't want the company, give it to H.H., keeping only 5 to 10% for 'face.'"

"H.H." was a thinly disguised reference to His Highness Sultan Hassanal Bolkiah.

It was interesting to see that S. P. had been able to involve "Mac," in the deal. Why would John McCormack of Coopers and Lybrand want to associate with the Chungs at this point, didn't he have a lot to lose? Was there a compensating gain on the other side of the ledger for Mac?

The minutes of the November 16 meeting continued with, "Buy shares immediately with the 3.5m in H.K.S.B. to be put in a nominee company in Hong Kong under the name of Madame Yeo. They must buy shares immediately no matter what the price is. Afterwards the link with H.K.S.B. will be cut. Transfer the 225,000 in OUB to a deposit in the name of Madame Yeo in Singapore."

"Locked box in City to be taken out by Carl. The bricks are to be exchanged with Hardy then put in the name of Madame Yeo in H.K."

We all know what "bricks" are in gangster-lingo, gold bars. The money was moving fast, and the money trail was being erased.

"The office in Thailand is to be given up and closed down."

It was not a good time for S. P. to go on with his business plan, it was a time to cut losses, and to lower profiles.

"Maximum expenditure permitted in S'pore and H.K. is 2.8 to 3.5m. Meeting ended 11:45AM"

The expenditures, 2.8 to 3.5 million, were surprising to me. Again, where was all this money coming from?

At this point, S. P. and Lillian were scheduled to make their getaway to America, but suddenly the information was received that Hin Chew's life was in danger, and an emergency meeting was called.

Lillian would also attend this meeting, after all her son's life was now at stake.

This final meeting, a crucial and emotional event, took place on November 17, at 8:30 in the morning. Present were "The man, Philip, Kevin and Mrs. Man," S. P., Peter, Goh Boon Kok, and Lillian.

Goh Boon Kok was the only person, outside of the family, who would be allowed to know of the threat to Hin Chew's life.

"The man said that Carl's life is in danger if he cannot sort things out by December he will be in for a difficult two years."

Hin Chew's life in danger? Why? For bribery? It didn't make sense. There had to be more than bribery involved.

And how did the "word" get to the Chungs that Hin Chew was in danger? Who would know such a thing? Did the news that Hin Chew's life was in danger come from Inspector Freddie Chong in Brunei? Possibly, but I doubt it as he was highly placed. He didn't have advance notice that Hin Chew would be arrested at the Brunei airport, or so he claimed.

Who then? The only person I could think of was S. P.'s guardian angel, Dan Arnold, who had high-level intelligence connections dating back his days in the CIA.

If Dan Arnold felt capable of arranging a helicopter escape from Brunei for Lynn and Jim, he must have had some clout.

Hin Chew and I had our problems, but his life being in danger was the last thing I expected to hear, or wanted to hear. It was very upsetting.

S. P. was truly a "Gutless Wonder."

All his experience, his savior faire, his scholarly knowledge of Chinese traditions, the material gifts to Hin Chew, meant absolutely nothing. S. P. was despicable. How could he do this? How could he sacrifice his children? And for what?

The minutes continued, "Force BSP to arrange everything with No. 4. Use Mac's relationship with BSP to push this. Build up the claims with BSP, then give them some back. You must note these points: Control your temper, losing your temper will not solve your problems. Your position is too young to shout at the other people."

Vintage Hin Chew! There you have it, his own father knew his son was unable to control his temper. Usually Hin Chew reserved the shouting for the children and me, now he was treating others in the same way. It was his weakness.

The minutes continued, with the "Gutless Wonder" groveling, "Sounds like we are the loser, take advantage and use any chance to flee the country.

"Material things do not matter at all. Your life and safety is more important. Take my points seriously. If all the property in Brunei can buy your Freedom I am prepared to give up. I am prepared to lose everything. If you and your family are safe this is the most important. I say this as I feel this is my responsibility for creating this present situation. I am very shamed to do this to my family."

As much as S. P. deserved to be despised for having placed his son's life in danger, he also had to be pitied for this apology. For S. P., a Chinese father, to admit such shame to his child, was as humiliating as anything I could imagine.

Responding to Lillian's prodding, S. P. continued, "Your mother has given you some medicine you have to take it on Sunday and then pray to Buddha."

I could see Lillian brewing her potions, and S. P. the dutiful husband passing on her wishes.

That done, the minutes returned to business, "The best solution is for BSP to buy on behalf of No. 4 all of CPH (B) assets. Keep a little bit for Mr. Man so that they give us a bit of face."

Face, the overriding concern of Asians. Even if S. P. were to lose everything, including a son or two, some degree of face had to be preserved.

S. P. ended with, "You have to make No. 4 happy. Don't say, 'If you don't want it I will go to No. 2.' This is very stupid. Donald's uncle seriously questioned your father and asked 'why we went first to No 4 and then offered it to No 2.' he said that this is a very dangerous game and nobody can help you if you do like this way." "No. 2" was Prince Muhammed, Prince Jefri's older brother. The Chungs were playing one Brunei Prince off against another, not a very wise move.

S. P. continued, "This work and company is my 'blood' and 'tears,' I am sorry and I am very ashamed to my family that I make them lose everything 'I leave it to the God to protect you.'

"Meeting ended 10:30AM."

For the family business in Brunei, the end came quickly. On December 3, 1984, Hin Chew broke the rules by writing Peter to tell him of the final demise of CPH:

Dear Peter,

I know I am breaking the rules by writing to you directly. But it is difficult to write an impersonal report and discuss what is happening here to our family and business in Brunei. Still I must write to you and tell it to you straight on a personal basis.

Well, it has finally happened. The balloon has gone up. BSP has written back to us rather quickly (rather obscene haste) and reaffirmed their wish to terminate our contract. We have little choice left on what we can do.

I am worried on how father would have taken this news. After all the years and efforts he put into the yard, after all the sacrifices he made and then only to have it taken away from him. You must understand by now that the yard is his baby. Here in the yard, he is home, with the respect of his employees and his peers. Without the yard, he has nothing. Even if we get $100 million or $1,000 million for the yard, I feel that he would still take it badly.

I do not believe that we can now salvage our position anymore. BSP is dead set on moving us out. At the same time, they are withdrawing all the original work in our 1985 yard fabrication program. What they are doing constitute a serious breach in their contract with us.

We have no response from 4 to our last proposal. It looks like Donald Duck is actively pushing BSP's management to this impasse. We must now assume collusion between BSP and 4's representative. Whether 4 is aware or not we again must assume that he is fully informed. After all, he is the chairman of BSP.

Our choice now is rather simple. We must go to arbitration and salvage what money we can. The consequence should be rather obvious. Our future business activities in Brunei is finished.

"Perhaps if father was here, he could still salvage the contract. I hope that we are doing the right thing. If you have any thoughts on this, let me know.

Right up to the very end, the Chungs had been hoping for Prince Jefri to save them by buying their company.

It never occurred to the Chungs that Prince Jefri was not the solution, but the problem.

The Chungs never considered that the issues of incarceration and difficulties with BSP might have come from the same source, Prince Jefri.

Prince Jefri certainly had the opportunity to do whatever he wished to the Chungs. He was the Chairman of BSP, and the second most powerful person in Brunei.

Prince Jefri also had a motive, and it certainly wasn't to grab the Chung's small money-losing company. Prince Jefri was worth billions, and CPH could have only been a waste of time for him. Face, however, was extremely important to Prince Jefri, much more so than it would have been to a commoner. Instead of coming himself to meet with Prince Jefri, S. P. sent his son to do the job. This was a real slap in the face for Prince Jefri.

In Brunei, you were not Prince Jefri's equal, and if you had to crawl on your knees, you did so. Prince Jefri could destroy you with a telephone call. When Prince Jefri said that neither he nor members of his family could be shareholders in CPH, Hin Chew, at the very most, should have humbly asked the prince for any suggestions, or advice.

Instead, Hin Chew, trying to be clever, and, with a show of arrogance, pushed the issue, proposing that Prince Jefri circumvent his own laws, by purchasing CPH through a nominee. Prince Jefri, cleverer still, appeared to agree, volunteering to telephone the nominee that very evening. How cooperative!

S. P. had sent a spoiled boy to do a man's job. In one brief moment, Hin Chew had destroyed the Chungs' business in Brunei, leading to the fall of S. P. Chung.

2 + 2 = US$48 MILLION

With the loss of their business in Brunei, how much did the Chungs have left? Anything? Nothing?

It was time to total up the financial damage.

In January of 1985, while still in Brunei, Hin Chew instructed Feng to prepare a preliminary estimate of the Chungs' net worth.

Feng's brief estimate was itemized by currency and country, and given in terms of millions, and sent off to Hin Chew in Brunei:

Summary
1. London   US$ 8.1
2. USA   US$ 0.73
3. Singapore   S$ 0.48
4. Brunei   B$ 2.18
5. Hong Kong   S$ 2.31
6. Others   US$ 4.25
Company
1. Hong Kong   S$ 8.0
2. Hong Kong   US$ 3.16
CHC
As requested.
    Regards,
        Feng
        1/18/85

After having lost his company, S. P. was still sitting on piles of cash, and at the exchange rates of the day, Feng's estimate of the Chung's net worth came to a little over US$22 million.

However, this was not good enough; it counted only the cash held in the Chungs' various bank accounts.

Surely, the Chungs had other assets. What about the gold, jewelry, real estate, company shares, automobiles, and so forth? Feng had more work to do.

The Chungs were not like your average well-to-do family, who maybe had a brokerage account with Merrill Lynch, one or two bank accounts, a nice retirement plan, a home, and maybe a small time-share, all very easy to keep track of, even for the IRS.

The Chungs were different.

They had real estate sitting idle in several countries, a bunch of corporations passing money around, and their cash and valuables were stashed all over the place. This was very convenient, especially if you had problems with the law, but keeping up with it was a daunting task.

Feng set to work at a fever pitch to compile a comprehensive and detailed list of S. P.'s assets. It took a while to piece the puzzle together, but, after three months, by April 1985, Feng had completed the arduous task of counting up the Chungs' assets.

He proudly presented the results to S. P. and Lillian (wherever they were), in a formal bound twenty-three page report, innocuously titled, "A Financial Report."

The report's table of contents included sections for "MR. & MRS. CHUNG SHIH PING'S WORLDWIDE DEPOSITS, FIXED DEPOSITS, GOLD CERTIFICATES, CHUNGCO GROUP SHAREHOLDINGS, PUBLIC SHARES, PRIVATE SHARES, PROPERTIES, and MR. CHUNG SHIH PING'S VEHICLES."

According to Feng's report, Ma and Pa were not doing too badly.

Their personal bank accounts in New York, Switzerland, Singapore, and Brunei came to a cool US$16.3 million.

The Chungs' wholly owned company, SPCO Offshore Limited, had cash deposits of another US$4.4 million, plus another S$2.3 million, bringing the total to US$20.8 million, close to Feng's preliminary estimate of US$22 million.

Nothing like setting aside some cash for a rainy day!

Just in case world currencies collapsed, Ma and Pa's bank vaults contained 75 kilograms of gold and 129 thousand ounces of silver, worth another US$3.8 million. You can never be too safe!

Feng valued CPH, in Brunei, as being worth about US$4 million, assets that might prove a bit difficult to recover.

The rest of S. P.'s privately held companies, over twenty of them, mainly in Singapore and Hong Kong, including some "nominee" companies held by Citibank, and Coopers and Lybrand, fronting for the Chungs, were valued by Feng at around US$12 million—a good starter kit for S. P., should he surmount his current difficulties.

S. P.'s holdings in publicly traded stocks in Singapore, Australia, Hong Kong, and Malaysia accounted for a modest US$1.9 million, conservatively invested in twenty-six separate companies. Ma and Pa didn't want to miss any moves in the stock market, did they?

To keep a roof over their heads, Ma and Pa owned six luxury apartments, and a large house in Singapore.

To give some perspective on that, three of the apartments cost well over US$500,000, the most expensive being a penthouse at the Claymore, the best address in Singapore, which cost S$1,875,500 (US$890,000) when the Chungs bought it in 1984.

It was an apartment to die for, the very best to be found in Singapore, with views from the city to the sea.

On the single occasion that Hin Chew allowed me to visit the apartment with him, I was astonished to see that the Chungs used the apartment as a warehouse. The rooms were piled high with packing boxes, and old dilapidated furniture from Mumong.

On our way out, I said to Hin Chew, "With such a beautiful apartment like the Claymore penthouse, why are Ma and Pa using this place as a warehouse to store their junk from Mumong? Why don't they get an interior designer to fix this place up?"

Hin Chew said, "Shut the fuck up!"

Feng's report showed that Pa owned two offices in the financial district, which could keep him busy, should he ever be able to return to Singapore.

For their vacations, the lucky couple owned an apartment on the Australian Gold Coast, and there were six parcels of land in Brunei, which S. P. could probably forget about.

Feng also counted S. P.'s automobiles in Brunei, among them two Mercedes, which were now of use only to the two captives, Hin Chew and Jim.

The grand total came to US$48 million, over twice that of Feng's original estimate—good work Feng!

That was a lot of money to earn from a small labor supply company that didn't really get going until 1972.

How did S. P. do it?

For me, two plus two equaled four, but, for S. P., it equaled US$48 million!

China Resources Co & Dan Arnold Revisited

ON October 1, 1985, after Hin Chew had been detained in Brunei just short of a year, I received news that he and Jim would finally be released, and would be returning as soon as possible to Singapore. No one was sure what flight Hin Chew and Jim could get from Brunei, so I waited patiently at the apartment.

I had mixed feelings over Hin Chew. I was happy for him that he was leaving, but had to admit to myself that I was terribly unhappy that he was returning.

What would life be like with Hin Chew back in Singapore? The children and I had enjoyed one full year of absolute peace, with no shouting, no yelling, and no senseless outbursts of rage.

I had written many letters of support to Hin Chew, enclosing pictures of the boys to show him how they were growing, and progressing.

These letters were one-way. Hin Chew never sent me a letter in return—not one letter!

Shortly after I received the news of Hin Chew's release, he arrived. It was the middle of the afternoon, and the children were having their naps. Hin Chew still had his key, and I knew he was home on hearing the unlocking of the front door.

Being apart for so long gave us both a feeling of uneasiness. I put on my best face and smile, and gave my husband a hug, saying, "The Gods are with us. You are finally home—I'm so happy! Oh! I have a beer all ready for you, Honey."

I nearly choked on my own words.

Hin Chew came out of the Brunei nightmare in good physical shape. He had lost a lot of weight, and I told him so. This was the best he had ever looked.

Hin Chew walked over to the sofa, settled down with his can of beer, and immediately began to tell me about what had happened in Brunei. I could see this was something he needed to talk about, almost therapeutic, and for both of us, a good way to break the ice after our long separation.

Hin Chew smiled, and said the experience had taught him how to "Sit, wait, and plot."

As he sipped his beer straight from the can, Hin Chew told me that all the problems were brought on by Brunei Shell. That wasn't my opinion, but I listened.

He and Jim had been the "fall guys" for that "fucking Gutless Wonder," his father. In return for what they had gone through, and perjuring themselves in the investigation, S. P. had promised to pay them one million dollars each.

Hin Chew growled that while he was stuck in Brunei with Jim, his worthless brother Peter had "blown away" well over a million on entertainment expenses, fooling around in Singapore.

"Fucking Father forgave Peter for that, and just wrote it off."

Without thinking, I said, "Well, I guess Peter was under a lot of pressure, himself."

"What the fuck! He wasn't risking his butt. Jim and I were making midnight raids into the yard to shred documents. That was a helluva risk. Do we have more beer?"

"Sure, in the fridge, I've stocked up, the way you like it," I said.

Hin Chew followed, and I handed him a second can as we both sat down at the dining table. He took a long drink from the can.

"You know, I always had a bag packed, in case I had to go east through the backwaters, and cross over the border to Miri in Sarawak. I had a plan, worked it out with Freddy Chong."

Hin Chew took another sip and fell silent.

"You had plans of escape?" I chipped in. "No helicopter?" I thought to myself.

"Of course we had plans to escape, what do you expect us to do, just sit around and wait. No fucking way!" he retorted.

"Thanks to our connections with the right people, we got out without having to sit in Jerudong Prison. At least we were allowed to roam freely ..."

"Well, that was good," I said, filling the pause.

"The fucking Brunei Government and Father wasted a year of my life. It was all a setup; Prince Jefri wanted to grab the family business from us. Anyway, I have the goods on Father and Peter."

I kept quiet—best to let Hin Chew get it all out.

"My fucking gutless father is still afraid to return to Singapore, even now that he has been told that the coast is clear."

Hin Chew's mood lightened, as I handed him a third can of beer.

He smiled, "We were too fucking clever for them, we outsmarted the Brunei Government. The last time they came to fucking check the house, they found nothing. They even checked Jim's shoes, but didn't think to look in the small closet under the stairs, where we had a suitcase loaded with stuff. The fucking Malays were so stupid! They had nothing on us. We were too smart for them."

I listened, as Hin Chew rambled on. He was understandably bitter.

Finally, trying to introduce a happier note, I said, "It was nice of Keith Wilson to come by to pick up my letters for you."

Hin Chew continued to ramble on, not letting himself be sidetracked from his anger, "Nice? The fucking guy was paid, and not just for some silly letters, he was taking bags full of cash, jewelry, and other stuff out for us. The fucking guy was paid. OK?"

"Where is Father?" I asked, getting off the subject.

"He telephoned Paul, about three months ago from Paris, said Europe agrees with him, and was planning to head south to Nice, fucking Father, running around America and Europe."

"Was Mother with him?"

"No, fucking Michael Yap is with him, holding Father's hand and keeping him company."

I was getting some answers, thanks to the beer, so I pressed on, "And Mother?"

"She's in and out of Singapore, with all her fucking Buddhist monks."

How nice of her never to call me, I thought.

I continued, "So where is Paul?"

Hin Chew smiled, "Little Paul is in Colorado, going to the Colorado School of Mines, well on his way to flunking out."

"Oh? OK, so what are you and Pa going to do now?"

"We're going to sue fucking BSP, and from now onwards, don't you ever gas the car up at any Shell gas station. You hear me?"

Welcome home Hin Chew.

Over the next couple of days, I saw very little of Hin Chew, as he was wrapped up in constant meetings with Peter, Jim, Jim Bell, Keith Wilson, and others who worked for S. P.

They were working up a legal claim against Brunei Shell for damages, not only for the money involved, but to save face.

On October 28, 1985, Hin Chew received an urgent memo from Agnes. A meeting had been arranged for him the very next day, in Hong Kong, with Dan Arnold, and the now infamous China Resources (Holdings) Co., Ltd.

Hin Chew wasted no time. He left immediately—after all, it was Dan Arnold who was waiting.

Hin Chew took Peter, Jim, Feng, and Agnes with him. In Hong Kong, they stayed at the old Lee Gardens Hotel, a place that has since been torn down.

The sleeping arrangements were cozy, as everybody took rooms on the 18th floor to be near Dan Arnold who was in room 1801.

S. P., himself, came out of hiding to meet with Dan Arnold.

The coming together of S. P., Dan Arnold, and China Resources (Holdings) Co., Ltd., conjures up some interesting scenarios.

In 1985, China Resources was still a small operation, founded by the Chinese People's Republic, the PRC, having begun "business operations quietly in 1948," according to the company's promotional literature. Today, China Resources has over 500 subsidiaries, and assets of billions, including a joint venture with Chinese billionaire James Riady's infamous Indonesian-based Lippo Group.

The Chungs were way way ahead of their time.

They were out of the gate nearly a decade before James Riady's man, the bungling John Huang, arranged for China Resources's President, Shen, to visit the White House in 1993, a visit that resulted in the United States Senate's 1998 investigation into campaign finance.

The Senate's report concluded, "China Resources Holdings, Shen's company has been identified as a PRC intelligence-gathering operation; one with reported ties to the People's Liberation Army."

Strange bedfellows!

I have no idea what took place at the Hong Kong meetings, only that there were two of them.

Therefore, long before the Clinton presidency, there was a connection of Shen, and of S. P. to the Republican Party. Dan Arnold had been a campaign worker in 1979 for George Bush, who was, at that time, in 1984, Vice President of the United States.

Immediately after the meetings with China Resources and Dan Arnold, Hin Chew flew directly from Hong Kong to London.

Did he tell me where he was going?

Of course not!

Once again, less than one month after Hin Chew's release from Brunei, I was on my own in Singapore.

It was back to my usual routine, the life that I had led while Hin Chew was away, and not a bad life at all. I had a maid to help with the children, and plenty of time on my hands.

To keep myself occupied, shortly after Hin Chew's arrest, I had resumed my law studies with the London University external degree program. That, and the children, took up most of my time.

My social life was simple. My mother would pay me visits, and sometimes we would go out together. Aunt Zena was also around, and we often went out to lunch together. I rarely saw Mamak, Kong Kong, or my brother, who was still living in the rented room paid for by Mamak.

Uncle Jimmy and his family were in the process of migrating to Australia. Uncle Jimmy wanted to sell his Holland Road house, but was unable to do so, without my father's permission. It had to do with the title deed, and the fact that the houses were joined at the hip. In spite of Uncle Jimmy's pleas to sell the place, my father refused.

Peter's newfound freedom, power, and company expense account had a predictably harmful effect on his marriage. Up to this point, Rosita, being three years older than Peter, and strong-willed, had been the dominating force of their partnership.

Rosita led, and Peter followed.

But little boys do grow up to become big men, and Peter had taken up with someone new.

Her name was Elsie, and she was tough competition. She was at least 5'10", had high cheekbones, a big wide smile, thick bangs, and hair down to her ass. Elsie was a former Miss Singapore, and had taken third place in the 1984 Miss Asia Pacific beauty contest—two places ahead of the American contestant—top quality merchandise!

In no time, Peter moved out on Rosita, and took up residence in the family's luxurious (and empty) penthouse in the Leedon Heights apartment building.

Rosita didn't know about Elsie then; all she knew was that Peter had moved out, and something was wrong. In a pique, Rosita decided to return to Melbourne with her two children, and with a third one on the way.

She would have her baby in Melbourne, and was convinced that Peter would quickly run back to Australia to join her and their children.

Peter was only too happy have Rosita off in Melbourne, and, to keep her there, bought her a beautiful house with a swimming pool and sauna, plus a BMW. It's amazing what love can do.

Lynn and Jim were staying at S. P.'s Westwood apartment, with their daughter, Tammy, now one year old.

In terms of personality, Jim was the nicest of the brothers, the one to whom I was closest, and to whom I would run to for advice on coping with Hin Chew.

Jim and I could talk.

He talked more freely about what had happened in Brunei, than did Hin Chew. In Brunei, Jim wore a tracksuit to bed, and so did Hin Chew. They slept on mattresses, with their running shoes close by. That way, "if the time came," they could be up and running to the designated spot on the nearby beach where a helicopter would pick them up.

The rear door to the house was left unlocked at night, for a quick exit, Jim said, "We weren't afraid of burglars, only of the police. It was a scary experience. We had no idea what was going to happen to us, Chu. You have to be there, going through this shit, to know actual fear."

I nodded in agreement, "Thank God you had some plans of escape, Jim. Hin Chew had told me," I said.

Jim replied, "Yeah. Thanks to Pa's friend, Dan Arnold, who could arrange for a helicopter…" Jim paused.

"Yes, and how did that feel?" I prodded.

"It was a damn good feeling to know we had backup, Chu."

"Jim, I'm so glad that you are back. I know, apart from Lynn's worrying, I too was very concerned for you."

"God, Chu, it has been a life-altering experience for me. I still have nightmares," Jim shook his head.

The Hong Kong meetings? All Jim had to say on the subject was that he had been to Hong Kong and met with his father.

End of conversation.

LORD ALEXANDER IRVINE, BARON OF LAIRG

THREE WEEKS after his arrival in London from the Hong Kong meetings with Dan Arnold and China Resources, Hin Chew telephoned me with the "instruction" that the children and I were to join him in London.

Marc, Warren, and I arrived at London's Heathrow Airport on November 24, 1985. Hin Chew was waiting at the airport to pick us up, but did not seem overly pleased to see us, but then these were busy days for him.

Jim's Kensington apartment was vacant, so that was where we stayed. It suited me just fine, as the children were far better off in an apartment than in a hotel.

Hin Chew was very busy. He had the task of finding the very best lawyer—a Queen's Counsel.

The English, with their respect for hierarchy, have three levels of lawyers.

At the first level is the "solicitor," a lawyer who deals mainly with contracts, and small matters that don't require a court appearance.

The next step up is the "barrister," who deals only with more important matters which require his appearance in court.

The top dog is the Queen's Counsel, often referred to as a "QC." The QC is a senior barrister appointed by the Queen on the advice of the Lord Chancellor. Only a small percentage of English barristers ever reach this level.

A Queen's Counsel will cost you plenty.

One quiet evening, after we had been in the Kensington apartment for a little over a week, the doorbell rang. Strange, we weren't expecting anyone, at least I wasn't.

I opened the door, and there stood S. P. Chung!

He was wearing an expensive black trench coat, had a black umbrella in hand, and looked very smart.

"Pa!" I said.

"Chu," he gave me a hug.

I don't know what I expected to see—sunglasses, a slouch hat, fugitive attire, but, as S. P. took off his trench coat, I saw he was immaculately dressed. He was wearing a black three-piece suit, Savile Row style, white shirt, and tie.

I was genuinely happy to see him. He was looking very good, and seemed his old self, although a bit subdued.

Hin Chew said simply, "Hi, Pa."

We were behaving as though we had all seen each other yesterday. Polite denial.

"Pa," I said, "you look very good, so well dressed!" Inane, but the best and least inquisitive greeting I could think of at that moment.

"Yes, I buy my clothes wherever I go."

That was the extent of my conversation with S. P. The children had been staring at him, not quite sure of who he was. Hin Chew told them to say hello to their grandfather, which they did, shyly.

S. P. walked over to the sofa and sat down. Hin Chew pushed a chair next to the sofa, and the two engaged in a hushed conversation in Hakka. I did what was expected of me, and tended to the children.

Their conversation over, S. P. stood up and, in English, invited us to visit him that evening at his hotel. He was staying at the five-star Grosvenor House, on Park Lane—not bad digs for a fugitive.

That evening, as planned, Hin Chew, the children, and I met S. P. in the lobby of his hotel. It was a month before Christmas, and there was a large and beautifully decorated Christmas tree in the lobby. We had never had a Christmas tree; it's not part of our culture. Still, the children took a great interest in the tree, attracted by its bright lights.

In turn, taking an interest in the children, was the hotel staff, uneasy over the great excitement of Marc and Warren. Sensing the problem, S. P. suggested that we go up to his room, which we did.

The Grosvenor House is staidly British in taste, and S. P.'s room was exquisitely furnished. I half-expected to find Lillian in the room, but there was no trace of her or any other woman, that I could see. No explanations offered; no questions asked. To fill the void, I ventured another inanity, "What a beautiful room!"

"Yes," came S. P.'s answer, "costs me £300 a day, very expensive, and room could be bigger."

The meeting was brief, and without as much as a piece of candy for the boys or a drink for me. We were out and gone in no time.

I was not to see S. P. again until December 1986 in Hong Kong.

Man on the run!

Back in the Kensington apartment, life went on normally, while Hin Chew was out searching for a Queen's Counsel.

Even though the business side of the trip was a distraction for Hin Chew from the children, when he was in the apartment, they made him nervous. The confines of the small Kensington apartment were closing in on all of us.

Finally, the day came when Hin Chew couldn't take it any more; he put the children "on ice," literally. The apartment had a small balcony, overlooking some tennis courts. With no warning, he shoved the children outside, and locked the door. "That'll give them a chance to enjoy the snow," he said, going back to his reading.

Being from Singapore, the boys had never felt the cold, and were not used to it. They didn't even have their coats on. I protested.

"Don't you ever fucking dare undermine my discipline, understand?"

It was half an hour before Hin Chew let the boys back in from the balcony.

Why, I wondered, had we been dragged to London. The boys had hardly been noticed by their grandfather, and were barely tolerated by their father.

In the midst of our stay in London, Hin Chew had to make a brief trip to Zurich to attend to "banking affairs." What banking affairs? I dared not ask.

I also dared not ask why Hin Chew was stocking up the apartment with food. The food part became clear when he left. Hin Chew took the keys with him, locking the apartment door's deadbolt lock from the outside as he left.

It was our turn to be under solitary confinement. Unfortunately, since the apartment was little-used, it had no telephone. We were isolated from the world.

With no idea of when Hin Chew would return, being locked up in the apartment was a traumatic experience. Under such conditions, you begin to appreciate small things, and the balcony overlooking the tennis courts became our biggest luxury—fresh air and sanity.

Fortunately, the building didn't catch fire while Hin Chew was away, and, after three nights, he returned.

As was usual for his returns, he was in a very good mood, thank God, and said his work was done. He had succeeded in hiring the best Queen's Counsel that money could buy, and I'm sure that's how he did it.

Alexander Irvine was the chosen Queen's Counsel.

In the prime of his life, at forty-five, Alexander Irvine was England's top Queen's Counsel, and had a record to prove it.

Both Tony Blair and his wife, Cherie Booth, got their start by working for Irvine, or by "joining his Chambers," as the British would say, with Irvine as their "pupil master."

Later in his illustrious career, after representing the Chungs, Irvine would go on to become Right Honorable Lord Irvine Baron of Lairg, with his appointment to the British Cabinet on May 2, 1997, as Lord Chancellor of Great Britain. He was appointed to this position by his ex-pupil, Prime Minister Tony Blair.

That same year, in 1997, Irvine was to come under fire for spending over 650,000 pounds (US$1.07 million) of the taxpayer's money to re-decorate his official London apartment. This included 59,000 pounds (US$97,200) for the wallpaper, alone.

If he liked money, Irvine was going to love the Chungs.

In representing the Chungs, Irvine was assisted by Richard Field, a very good-looking fellow in his mid-thirties, and somewhat of a jock. Richard was not yet a QC, but would become one, or "take the silk," as they say, in 1987, less than two years away.

To complete the picture, Tony Blair's wife, Cherie, took the silk herself in 1995.

A foursome of QCs—the Chungs were in good company.

I may never know how the Chungs, an unknown and shady family from the boondocks of Mumong, ever got to Alexander Irvine. Maybe his name came out of the Hong Kong meeting. Even murderers can get top lawyers to defend them, and I'm sure that, for Alexander Irvine, the Chungs would see to it that the price was right.

With Irvine and Field on their team, the Chungs sued Brunei Shell for damages, $47 million Brunei Dollars (US$22 million), according to Hin Chew.

News of the lawsuit was published immediately in the Borneo Bulletin, Brunei's quaintly named, but leading newspaper.

The first step in rehabilitating the Chungs' good name had been taken.

Alexander Irvine and Richard Field were flown first class to Singapore by the Chungs to set the wheels of justice in motion. They were to make many such trips, all first class. Queen's Counsels travel only by first class, I was told. Of course, all the Chungs' men flew first class.

These were heady times for the Chung boys in Singapore. They were no longer in the backwaters of Brunei—they had emerged!

This was Singapore, they had a QC at their behest; they were wheeling and dealing, big time. The Chung money was at their disposal and whim. Goh Boon Kok, Feng, and the entire Chung staff were theirs to command. They had a free hand. Ma and Pa were still on the run.

Alexander Irvine was all that should be expected of a QC. He was serious, personable, imposing, arrogant, and oozed the all-powerful mystique of a Queen's Counsel. The Chungs put Alexander Irvine and Richard Field up at the Shangri-la Hotel, Singapore's best.

We wined and dined them, even to the extent of organizing a dinner one evening for about twenty in one of the Shangri-la's private dining rooms. The group included the Alexander Irvine, Richard Field, Hin Chew, Peter, Jim, Lynn, myself, and a small cadre of Chung employees.

We were at several tables, and I had the good fortune to be sitting next to Richard Field, a very attractive fellow, indeed. Hin Chew was at another table with Alexander Irvine.

I was dressed in a yellow jacket-suit with small red appliquéd sequined flowers near the shoulders, this I paired off with a pair of high-heeled red shoes, and a matching red handbag.

I was in my element. You have to understand, that for a frustrated law student, like myself, meeting Alexander Irvine, and the gorgeous Richard Field, was like being a groupie at a Rolling Stones concert.

I was totally mesmerized by Richard Field, who looked to me like Clark Kent. As far as I was concerned, it was a "QC-moment" for me. Richard and I chatted happily away, and … time stood still.

Twice, Hin Chew sent his personal secretary, Wai Lin, to whisper in my ear that I should circulate to some of the other tables. The first time, I whispered, "I'm busy, Wai Lin, go away." The second time, I hissed, "Buzz off!"

After dinner, most of the group decided to call it a night, including Lynn, who was now happily expecting her second child.

Hin Chew, Richard Field, Alexander Irvine, Goh Boon Kok, and I decided to have a final drink at Lost Horizon (my idea), the hotel's nightclub, just off the downstairs lobby.

Whatever thoughts I entertained about dancing with Richard Field ended when Alexander Irvine sent him to his room to do some work.

The four of us sat down at a small table at the nightclub. Hin Chew ordered his usual snifter of brandy, and lit up his Churchillian cigar. He was ready to talk business with Alexander Irvine—big business. Hin Chew's cigar was ready, but his words could barely be heard above the disco music. Goh Boon Kok smiled and nodded; for him whatever Hin Chew was saying was OK, but Alexander Irvine was straining to listen. For Hin Chew, time was money.

"Alexander, let's dance," I said to the chagrin of Hin Chew, and the shock of Goh Boon Kok.

"Wonderful! It will be my pleasure, May Chu," the great man answered, getting up, and moving my chair back as I rose.

Alexander was a wonderful dancer. He was a huge man, very tall, but he could do it all. He swept me across the dance floor, he rocked and rolled, he did the twist; he even loosened his tie.

I could see Hin Chew fuming, and Goh Boon Kok staring in wonder. Fume on! I was having a great time. Here I was, the wannabe law student, dancing with England's number one Queen's Counsel. Incongruously, the song came to mind, "I Danced with a Man who Danced with the Girl who Danced with the Prince of Wales."

Alexander and I bogeyed most of the night away, as they say. Finally, sweating, and tired, we returned to the table. Hin Chew had already paid the bill, and Goh Boon Kok was smiling with embarrassment.

Our Queen's Counsel, and his assistant, drew their services out for a good six months, and many first-class trips to Singapore.

Finally, the claim against Brunei Shell was settled by arbitration. The Chungs received only a disappointing $5 million of the $47 million Brunei Dollars they claimed.

Irvine's bill came to $2 million, the $3 million Brunei Dollars, the equivalent of US$1.4 million, was deposited into the Chungs' Overseas Chinese Banking Corporation bank account, number 1-1612 … safe in Hong Kong.

In the words of Hin Chew, "Fucking Irvine took two million of that for himself, and we got only three million—some fucking Queen's Counsel!"

THE RETURN OF S. P. CHUNG

AND WHAT about the problems with Brunei? Extradition for S. P.? For Lillian? It all fizzled out. Maybe the settlement had something to do with it, but I was never told.

In the end, the Brunei government did nothing more to the Chungs.

For me, the final curtain closed on Brunei with the visit of Freddie and Nora Chong to Singapore in June 1986. Hin Chew and I visited them in their hotel room at the Marco Polo Hotel. Hin Chew had a brief discussion with Freddie, while I made small talk with Nora.

On leaving the hotel, Hin Chew said, "That's the last we'll ever see of those fuckers." And it was. From that moment on, it was as though Brunei had never existed.

After the final closure with Brunei, my grandfather died.

Esja rushed in to fill the vacuum. With Mamak's backing, she set up an operation in Burma to produce a rival to Tiger Balm, called "Sea Horse Balm." I'm still waiting to see the first jar.

Rosita finally found out about Peter's new love, Elsie. With her children, and new baby, she quickly came running back to Singapore, where she rented a huge house. There was no way Peter was going to leave his apartment to live with Rosita and the children. However, he still had good reasons to keep her happy, and was willing to pay the price, at least for a while.

Lynn and Jim were faring much better; they had their second child, a boy named Andrew. Having a boy was a blessing for Lynn, as she was held to the Chinese standard of "no boy, no good." I was happy for Lynn. On the surface, it looked like at least one of the Chung marriages seemed to be working out.

However, Jim had come out of Brunei with a drinking problem, and when drinking, his personality changed completely, he would go out of control, becoming very abusive with Lynn and the children.

Lynn told me, in tears, that Jim got drunk at the pool of the Hyatt Hotel, and horrified everybody by holding their screaming baby, Andrew, over the edge of the pool. I told Lynn, that I was sure that, as Brunei faded into the past, Jim would get better. What else could I say?

And my marriage? Our few friends had been reduced to almost none after Brunei. I was still seeing the same people I knew before my marriage, mainly my own family, most of all, I was spending time with Zena.

She had worked for many years for First Interstate Bank of California, and it was time for her annual leave. Exposure to the corporate environment of an American bank, had given Zena more perspective on life than her sister, my mother, would ever have. Zena had been the executive secretary to a succession of the bank's Managing Directors, always Americans.

Her experience made her both more open and people-smart than are most Singaporeans. She was great company, great fun, and had a wonderful sense of humor, a rare commodity in Asia.

One Friday evening, after we had been out for dinner, I brought Zena back to the apartment for a nightcap. It was still early. Hin Chew was upstairs in the bedroom.

Earlier that day, I had purchased some shirts and pants for Hin Chew, at Melwani's, one of Singapore's best men's shops. I had left the clothes on the bed for Hin Chew, as a surprise.

Hin Chew must have heard us downstairs, as he started to yell. Leaving Zena in the living room, I rushed upstairs to see what was wrong.

Opening the bedroom door, I found Hin Chew standing, dressed in shorts and an undershirt.

"You fucking cunt! These fucking clothes don't fit. You're wasting my money, you fucking bitch!"

I backed out of the room, quickly closing the door, just in time to catch Marc and Warren coming out of their room.

I shooed the children back into their room, and ran downstairs.

Hin Chew appeared on the landing, his face red, frothing at the mouth, and still yelling.

Zena had heard of such incidents from me, but seeing one was another thing.

Hin Chew grabbed the railing of the landing, and, leaning pack with his eyes closed, howled, "Bitch!" He then stormed back into the bedroom, slamming the door.

Zena was in a state of shock.

"Zena, it's nothing. He's always been like that," I said.

Zena wasn't listening. She was taking off her high-heeled shoes, and heading for the door ... she stopped for an instant, and said, "Chu, I'm very sorry for you, but I'll never ever come to your apartment again, or call this apartment, or talk to ... him."

"You'll have to call me," she said disappearing down the stairs.

It was 1986, and I had endured seven years of marriage with Hin Chew. This was no seven-year itch; I had wanted to leave Hin Chew since the first year of our marriage.

I wanted out, but how? Hin Chew would never consent to a divorce, as there would be too much loss of face.

Divorces are extremely expensive in Singapore, and I had no money of my own. I was given credit cards, but every transaction was entered into Quicken by Hin Chew's secretary, Wai Lin.

Any cash withdrawals by me would have come to Hin Chew's immediate attention. Hin Chew loved to analyze anything that involved money. Counting money was a hobby for him. He loved to write out long tables showing the projected value of his fixed deposits, month by month, and on and on ...

His jottings were a good source of information for me.

Aside from Hin Chew's opposition to a divorce, and my lack of money, I feared a possible element of danger, especially from S. P., should I try to leave the Chungs.

The Brunei affair alone would have given anyone qualms, but there was also the Chungs' connection to Dan Arnold, and the unexplainable source of their wealth.

So long as I was one of them, one of the Chungs, everything should be all right. But what if I picked a fight with them? Then what? I was frightened.

Still, a single visit to a lawyer shouldn't hurt, and is usually free, so I decided to visit Vivien Quahe of Gracie Chan and Co., one of Singapore's few lady-owned law firms. I felt I might have a better chance talking to a woman.

To cover my visit, and to have a hand-holder, I invited my mother to come with me. She was quite willing, as there might be some interesting information in it for her, as well.

In Singapore, the idea of getting a divorce was just this side of unthinkable.

Would Vivien Quahe listen to us? Well, of course, Vivien would listen; there could be money in it for Vivien, right? We were from well-known families, right?

The truth was that my mother and I were both paupers in our own right—no better than harem girls.

Vivien was a very attractive woman in her thirties, with a pleasant but firm manner. Vivien had seen others in the same fix, and was able to give me the benefit of her experience. She advised me to lay away money, not just for legal fees, but for living expenses also, as Hin Chew would most likely cut me off financially for initiating a divorce.

As for the legalities of divorce, Vivien said there were only four grounds for divorce in Singapore—adultery, unreasonable behavior, desertion for two years, voluntary separation for three years with the other party's consent, or four years separation with no consent.

The Singapore divorce laws were archaic, and nothing like America, where no reason is required, and no fault is given.

Hin Chew was certainly not the type to commit adultery, or so I thought at the time, and there had been no separations sufficiently long to qualify as grounds for divorce. Therefore, I was left only the grounds of unreasonable behavior, something nearly impossible to prove, according to Vivien.

In Asia, where the woman is chattel, what is unreasonable?

At the end of our meeting, Vivien reached into her desk, and pulled out a small pamphlet, and handing it to me said, "Here is a copy of the 'Women's Charter,' Singapore's divorce law. You may want to read it"

"Thank you."

Vivien's parting words of advice were, "Try to reconcile your differences with your husband."

As I was driving my mother home, she said, "Child, I think that lady was right. You should try your best to get along with Hin Chew, like I do with Papa."

"Sure, Mummy", I said telling my mother what she wanted to hear. She didn't want to understand the difference between my father, a womanizer and a clown, and a cruel and abusive husband like Hin Chew.

At home, I looked at the "Women's Charter." By its title, it sounded very good, as do most things in Singapore, but the very first line of the "Women's Charter" reads: "'brothel' means any place occupied or used by any 2 or more women or girls whether at the same time or at different times for the purpose of prostitution."

That incredible and insulting one-liner, kicking off the Singapore Women's Charter with the word "brothel," was telling. It was my introduction to Singapore's strong legal bias against women.

Shouldn't brothels be a part of the *criminal* code, rather than civil divorce law? Like I said, "harem girls."

The laws of Singapore are there to protect men, especially rich men. Have money, and want to divorce your wife. Go to Singapore.

It's so easy; simply transfer your funds out of the country to a safe haven like Hong Kong, where the Singapore courts have no jurisdiction. By the time the legal process gets to the point where money is involved, the husband's funds are safely out of the country.

Walk out on your husband, without a divorce? Sure, anyone can do that, but, then what? There is no social welfare in Singapore. Asian poverty is nothing like American poverty; you don't get paid for it in Singapore.

Within easy distance from the marble hotel lobbies of Singapore's fashionable Orchard Road, just north of Kampong Java Road, off Wee Nam Road, and hidden in a spot of jungle is a small *kampong*, a Malay word for village, something tourists rarely see.

The Wee Nam Road *kampong* consists of a small group of wooden shacks, with corrugated zinc roofs, and dirt floors. Unemployed elderly, aging hookers, laborers, and drug addicts live there.

There are plenty of *kampongs*, like the one off Wee Nam Road, hidden in the remaining pockets of the tropical rain forest that once covered Singapore.

Those in the *kampongs* are one step up from Singapore's homeless, who live in cardboard boxes wherever a space can be found. Mercifully, Singapore is always warm, so no one freezes to death.

So, what would be my fate, if I took the children and walked out on Hin Chew? I could certainly do better than a cardboard box, or a *kampong*; I could find some sort of entry-level job, as a receptionist, typist, or salesperson. With no real work experience, my pay would have been in the area of S$1,000 a month, a little less than half of what Zena was earning after her many years of corporate life.

One thousand a month was not enough to afford an apartment. We would have to live in a rented room for about S$500 a month. Could we make it on the remaining S$500, the equivalent then of US$200 a month? With food, utilities, clothes, school uniforms and fees, schoolbooks, bus fare, and medical expenses, there was no way.

Finally, I would have to transfer Marc out of his top-rated school to a lesser one, attended by the have-nots, in one of the "less fortunate" parts of Singapore, where most of the children are dead at birth, so far as their chances in Singapore are concerned.

To make it in Singapore, you need the right schools, and, of course, the right connections. When you reach voting age, you'd better have the right politics, too.

Singapore is a Third World Country hiding behind the antiseptic facade of a First World Country.

Nothing like "the American Dream" exists in Singapore.

My children came first, and I was not going to compromise their future, by walking out of my marriage with nothing.

I was shaken by my visit to Vivien Quahe, but not discouraged. I was more determined than ever in my resolve to divorce Hin Chew, but in the right way.

Even in more enlightened societies the legal remedy of divorce, on its own, doesn't always work. In Singapore, against a rich Chinaman, I was convinced that going to court, and placing my trust in Singapore's legal system, in and of itself, would never work.

I knew that to escape, money, luck, planning, trickery, and guerrilla warfare would all have to play a role.

For now, I would have to endure the marriage, and do my best to shield the children from Hin Chew. I had no choice, but to wait for the right time to strike.

In December 1986, I took Marc and Zena with me for a tour of the western United States, including a brief foray into Tijuana, Mexico.

There were several reasons for the trip. First, it was a chance for Marc to see Disneyland, and have a vacation, before entering the first grade of Singapore's elementary school system. Since I needed someone to accompany me, it provided a chance for me to make up for my embarrassment with Zena over the scene with Hin Chew, by offering to bring her along.

When I proposed the trip to Hin Chew, I told him that Zena was quite willing to pay for herself, which she was, but that it would be difficult for her. I suggested we pay. We were part of a group tour, and the cost was reasonable.

"You're really putting me on the spot with this, aren't you? I'll pay for fucking Zena." was Hin Chew's response.

Our flight was on Singapore Airlines, and, by coincidence, my Eurasian cousin, Cindy Berlandier, was one of the flight attendants, or "Singapore Girls" as the airline calls them. The Singapore Girls were chosen for their looks and their weight, and Cindy, with her French origins, was a beautiful girl and qualified easily. Zena was especially happy to run into Cindy, one of her favorite relatives on the flight. Zena naturally preferred the Eurasian side of our family.

This was my first trip to the United States without Hin Chew. Now on my own, I would be able to take in more of what America had to offer.

Coming from Singapore, there was much for me to learn. I was impressed that everyone in America seemed to be able to say just about anything, and did.

Americans knew how to talk.

In Singapore, say one word against the Prime Minister, and you will find yourself in court, or worse.

In America, I found new words to learn. When I was given directions like, "It's two blocks in that direction," I was perplexed. Who knew what a "block" was? I had a lot to learn, but was learning fast.

The lessons I learned about America were valuable, more so than I realized at the time.

The trip was all I had hoped it would be. We had a great time.

On the way back to Singapore, we had a stopover in Hong Kong where, after the long twenty-hour flight from Los Angeles, the tour put us up for the night at the Excelsior Hotel. The next day, we would proceed to Singapore, and home.

As we were relaxing in our room, the phone rang. I answered very casually, thinking it must be from the front desk.

It was S. P.!

"Chu?"

I answered, "Yes."

"It's Pa, I would like to come over to see you and Marc."

S. P. sounded much more upbeat than he had been when I last saw him in London.

"What are you doing in Hong Kong, Pa? How did you know where to reach us?"

"I have your itinerary, I'll be over in about an hour to see you … Come to the lobby, and don't bring Zena."

"OK, Pa."

Zena, who is no dope, understood, and was rightfully offended. I apologized as best I could, and got Marc ready.

We went to the lobby to wait for S. P. It didn't take long for him to show up.

As usual, S. P. greeted me with a simple, "Hello, Chu," and a quick hug.

After less than half an hour of innocuous conversation, "How was America?" "Did you go to Disneyland, Marc?" "Did you like Disneyland, Marc?" "You both look fine," S. P. said it was time to go.

His parting remark was, "Why are you staying in such a cheap hotel?"

"It's part of the tour, Pa."

He nodded, and disappeared through the crowd in the lobby.

S. P. Chung had returned.

"Jock" Chung Invades Australia

With his affairs in order, and no longer a man on the run, S. P. decided to invade Australia.

In the beginning of 1987, S. P. began making frequent trips "Down Under." The prospects looked good, especially around Perth, which was only a five hour flight from Singapore, and had the advantage of being in Singapore's same time zone.

Perth is a beautiful city, situated on Australia's west coast, looking out over the Indian Ocean. Perth has a small city center, which is surrounded by low-rise residential areas. With only a million people, it is, supposedly, what Los Angeles once was.

S. P. began his conquest of Australia with the purchase of a parcel of land located outside of Perth.

His next move was to appoint Hin Chew as the head of his Australian operations. Hin Chew was ecstatic, and got to work immediately, setting up two new corporations, Chungco (Aust) Pty Ltd, and Wescorp International. S. P. always liked to have plenty of corporations around.

Another thing S. P. liked to have around was an entourage.

Even when he was on the run, fearing extradition, S. P. had Michael Yap with him, to hold his hand, and help with the luggage, a sorry one-man entourage, but not bad, considering the circumstances.

Now things were different, and, for his trips to Australia, S. P. was always accompanied by a full-blown entourage of helpers and yes-men.

The retinue included the trusty, smiling, nodding, and ever-reliable Goh Boon Kok, and, of course, Michael Yap. In addition, along for the free ride, were a select number of Coopers and Lybrand accountants, led by S. P.'s friend, John McCormack.

S. P. liked to brag, "Coopers is getting $35,000 just for this one trip." That always got a big smile out of Mac.

Agnes, S. P.'s trusted little secretary, was an indispensable member of the group, tagging right behind S. P., efficiently taking memos and instructions; Singaporeans are good at that type of thing. Details.

Then, there were the family members.

As the Chungs' rapid rehabilitation was now complete, Lillian had reappeared as though nothing had happened, and was the *grande dame* of the entourage, much in the role of a dowager empress.

Since Hin Chew was "in charge of Australia," as S. P. put it, Hin Chew, the children, and I were in on most of the trips.

Neither Peter nor Jim joined the entourage, as Australia was strictly Hin Chew's baby. Jim was spending all his time in Singapore, and Peter's work assignment involved constant trips from Singapore to Papua New Guinea.

Papua New Guinea? What could the Chungs want with a backward and impoverished country, 100 miles north of Australia, across the Torres Strait, where most of the population spoke only pidgin English, or *tok pisin* as the locals call it?

Curiously, Papua New Guinea's only world-class statistic is that it has nearly twice as many airports as does the United States on a per capita basis. The country has 500 airports for a population of about 4 million, mostly natives. Go figure.

I was glad that Hin Chew didn't get that assignment.

Wherever S. P. went, he received the full celebrity treatment from his personal entourage. Long gone were the days, only a few months ago, when S. P. was living out of suitcases in America, Europe, and safe havens in Asia, like Hong Kong.

In Australia, S. P. was flaunting himself, strutting like a peacock. While looking into the purchase of a farm that bred thoroughbred horses, he smiled into the camera, while posing in front of sleek thoroughbred racehorses. Good God! S. P. had even taken to wearing the Jock Ewing hat that he had bought years before at the Singapore charity gala.

S. P. had decided to join the landed gentry, something he knew nothing about, but something he could buy, which was all that counted. Hin Chew was well equipped to handle Australia.

His days spent among Australians, and contacts gleaned from Geelong College, and Monash University, added to his value. He quickly recruited his ex-Geelong schoolmate, and long-time friend, Andrew Hewitt, making him Corporate Secretary for the two new

Chung Australian companies.

Andrew was your all-Australian blonde, blue-eyed boy. He was tall, well built, and had a disarming smile that went with his friendly personality. Andrew was a Chartered Accountant, with the firm of Barrington Partners, of which he was also a partner. Beneath Andrew's pleasing façade, however, lurked a very cunning businessman.

In the summer of 1987, S. P. splurged for his most grandiose acquisition, with the purchase of a one million acre cattle station called "Anna Plains."

This crown jewel included 15,000 head of Brahman cattle, several hundred horses, an airplane, a helicopter, houses, and even some humans. To put things in perspective, this enormous property, of 1563 square miles, was larger than the famed King Ranch in Texas by several hundred square miles. Anna Plains was larger than the entire state of Rhode Island!

The purchase of the Anna Plains cattle station was made on the advice of S. P.'s panel of cattle experts, who were, in reverse order of expertise, Hin Chew, Goh Boon Kok, Andrew Hewitt, and Tim Coakley.

Tim, a recent addition to S. P.'s entourage, was an agricultural advisor. Tim was a tall, strawberry-blonde, rough and tough Australian farm boy, who knew the cattle business. He was a "jackaroo," which is "Strine" for "hayseed," and "Strine" is slang for Australian slang, a lingo which includes such words as "imichizit," meaning, "how much is it." Any Australian would understand.

"G'day," we all understand.

The Anna Plains cattle station was located near the small and isolated beach town of Broome, some 1,400 miles north of Perth, far up in the isolated and desolate northwest corner of Australia. The only easy access to Anna Plains was by air, except during the rainy season, when the cattle station's dirt airstrip turned to mud.

Shortly after the purchase of the cattle station, Hin Chew, S. P. and Tim planned to fly there from Perth in a small private airplane, with a bush pilot at the controls.

Three days before the flight, I had seen a huge black red-eyed crow banging on the window of our hotel room. Asians are superstitious, and I took this to be a very bad omen, but of what I did not know, so

I telephoned my mother in Singapore to see what she thought.

My mother said that any visit from a black crow is very bad luck, and in the same breath, said she had a very bad feeling that this particular omen had nothing to do with me, but concerned my brother, Sam.

I knew Sam was doing fine—not great, but fine. He still received nothing from our father, but Mamak continued to support him. Sam still lived in a rented room, and had been in and out of several jobs, like many young people his age. He had a girlfriend, and was on the way to making a place for himself in the world.

Hin Chew had overheard the telephone conversation, and said, "What a fucking load of crap, Australia is full of crows. We are living in modern times." Nevertheless, he came up with some important tasks to do which prevented his taking the flight. So much for modern times!

While the rest of the entourage, Hin Chew, and I remained in the Perth Hyatt Regency, S. P. and Tim Coakley were bound for the Anna Plains cattle station airstrip.

S. P. sat up front, next to the bush pilot; Tim was behind, in the rear seat. After they had reached cruising altitude, the door next to S. P. sprang open, and a blast of air suddenly tugged at S. P.'s natty multicolored jumpsuit, giving him a quick jolt outward. Luckily, the seatbelt held, otherwise, it was the end of an empire.

As the bush pilot quickly banked the airplane sharply to the right to relieve the pressure, S. P. hanging above the void, held only by his seatbelt, saw nothing under him but the ground, thousands of feet below. Miraculously, and with considerable risk to himself, Tim managed to hang out of the airplane far enough to be able to "grab the bloody door, and slam the damn thing shut."

When they returned to Perth, Tim could not wait to entertain the entourage with the harrowing tale of S. P.'s near-death experience.

Tim finished off his story with, "Mates, when that side door sprang open, it was the first time I've ever seen a Chinaman turn white." Tim punctuated this with a raucous belly laugh, to which Goh Boon Kok, and the other "mates" smiled with polite embarrassment. I thought it was hilarious.

S. P. had been very lucky, as always. He had left his Jock Ewing hat behind; had he been wearing it in the airplane, the hat would have been a goner.

Now that S. P. had forged the path to Anna Plains, it was time for the entourage to do the same. In addition to Lillian, the yes-men, Coopers and Lybrand, Hin Chew, the children, and me, Andrew Hewitt, Tim Coakley, and their families joined us. We took a commercial flight to Broome, where S. P. put us up at the Cable Beach Club Resort, a four-star hotel on the beach, and the best that Broome had to offer.

S. P., having once made the arduous trip, decided that only the men would be up to the rigorous overland journey to the Anna Plains cattle station. Women and children would have to stay behind, just like we did in Thailand.

Although Marc was only six at the time, S. P. decided that he qualified for the trip. Warren did not. So, Marc and the men set off for the cattle station in a caravan of four-wheel drive vehicles.

When Marc returned later the same day, he was very excited, saying that it had been like Disneyland. How many boys get to ride grandpa's horses, and fly in grandpa's helicopters? Not many.

According to Hin Chew, S. P.'s business plan for the Anna Plains cattle station was simple, "The steers will be grown to a shipping weight as determined by the market. Our objective is to produce steers for export," Hin Chew recited. Obviously, he had done his reading, probably out of something like "Cattle Stations for Dummies."

The plan of breeding cattle for export sounded simple enough. That is, if you have lived the life of a rancher, and really know its ins and outs, including such niceties, as inserting your arm up the cow's most private part, all the way to your shoulder, to feel if there is a calf inside, a bit of knowledge gleefully imparted to me by Tim.

It is easy to delegate the jobs of breeding cattle, shearing sheep, working with castrating irons, dealing with indigent aborigines, and even fighting off the cattle rustlers, which, incredibly, would later play a large part in the drama of Anna Plains.

However, to delegate the work properly, you had to have some hands-on knowledge of the business. There were problems with a cattle station that you would never encounter in an office or boardroom.

S. P. was not stupid. You don't wind up with US$48 million by being stupid. Why would he take such a long shot in a business totally new and unknown to him, and in such a remote and inaccessible part of Australia?

The Australian corporations and Anna Plains, all of which had been acquired with lightning speed, now combined to form a major enterprise.

I assumed, that, with Hin Chew's new responsibility, we would be moving to Australia. When I asked him about it, he answered, "I will leave it to Father to decide, but, most likely, I will commute." Hin Chew had his reasons for wanting to get out of the house.

And S. P. did decide. He decided that Hin Chew was no longer in charge of the Chungs' Australian operations. Instead, of Hin Chew, S. P. put Jim in control of the Australian businesses. Jim, Lynn, and their children would move to Perth.

Hin Chew was crushed. He was bitterly disappointed. He had worked very hard to set up the groundwork for the Australian businesses. He had even gone so far as to involve his school chum, Andrew Hewitt.

This was a great loss of face—the second worst fate that can befall a Chinaman—the worst being loss of money.

Hin Chew hissed, "Fucking father, I spent all my time and effort in building up Australia, and he decapitates my head, and gives it to Jim. I'll fix Jim up. Wait and see! Jim is no match for Andrew. Andrew will eat Jim alive, and spit him out! I will see to it. Jim has no killer instinct, like me. And fucking Father—I'll piss on his fucking grave."

Hin Chew was right.

Jim was the worst of the brothers to send to Australia. He was too nice a guy, and, in addition, he was drinking heavily. What had been apparently the one good marriage of the Chung boys was on very shaky ground.

For Hin Chew, the children, and me, the Australian adventure had come to an end.

Long live Jock Chung!

MICKEY MOUSE ELECTRONICS

WITH AUSTRALIA out of the way, life returned to normal in Singapore. As before, Hin Chew was traveling frequently. He was off to Hong Kong, Indonesia, Malaysia, and, occasionally to Australia.

That was perfectly OK with me.

The death of Kong Kong had removed any reason for my father to keep up his pretense of going to work, so, like Hin Chew, he too did a bit of traveling, but not for business, only for pleasure. For the most part, however, my father stayed put in Singapore. There is enough sin for anybody in Singapore.

I was back to tending to the children during the day. My evenings were punctuated with frequent dinners out with the usual suspects, my mother, Zena, Swee Cheong, or Joan. Sometimes my mother and I, the two lonely women, would put on our fanciest outfits to attend some of Singapore's mindless social events. My mother was always very good company at these affairs.

When Nicola Bulgari came to town, we were there. My mother was wearing all jade jewelry, including a beautiful jade necklace given to her by Mamak. This attracted the attention of Nicola Bulgari, himself, who came over and said, in a very suave, and Italian way, "I have never seen such lovely jade. It's beautiful. You know we sell no jade, only colored stones."

My mother can't remember what she said to Bulgari, and neither can I, but afterwards, always one for the limelight, she was thrilled. "Oh, I still have it, Chu," she whispered to me.

I was all dressed up, in a fuchsia-pink jacket, black tank top with a scoop neck, black skirt, and black stockings, with high-heel shoes to match. The occasion was lunch with two lady friends, from my law-study days, at La Tour, the French restaurant at the Shangri-La Hotel.

No sooner had we taken a seat at our table than I quickly scanned the room, and whom should I spot, seated at a corner table, at the other end of the restaurant, but S. P., and, with him, was a classic Chinese beauty, and two young children.

S. P.'s companion was fair and in her mid-thirties, her beautiful face was set off by her jet-black hair, pulled back into a chignon. She had the perfect Chinese looks, and was dressed to kill. Thank God, I too was looking my best. S. P. with a Hong Kong movie star? I had to check it out.

I excused myself from my lunch companions for a moment, and politely went to pay my respects to S. P., as I normally would.

"Hi Pa," I said sweetly, "fancy meeting you here."

With my hands behind my back, and my head tilted forward, I asked, "Aren't you going to introduce me to your friend, Pa?"

S. P., surprised to see me, bounced out of his chair, holding his napkin in front of his chest, as though for protection, stammered, "Ah, Chu, good to see you. We ... we were just having some lunch with Goh Boon Kok ... he is coming."

The beautiful Chinese lady, who never got up from her chair, flashed me a confident smile, which I returned.

S. P. continued—I had never seen him so rattled—"Yes, this is, and this is May Chu, she is my daughter-in-law, ah, and Chu, I would like you to meet, ah, ah ... my friend." No name was given.

As the "friend" and I shook hands, I scanned her at speed that only a woman can achieve, when sizing up one of her own.

She had the perfect oval face, with flawless rosebud lips. When she smiled, it was a beautiful wide, confident, smile, and she knew it, displaying a dazzling set of gleaming white teeth. Her dark eyebrows offset her large almond-shaped eyes. Her makeup and her manicured red nails were impeccable, and she was dressed in a black Chanel suit, with real Chanel buttons to prove it. This woman could do no wrong!

She oozed confidence and composure, two things that had momentarily left S. P.

As she extended her hand to mine, I took in a couple of Bulgari diamond bangles on her right wrist. After our handshake, I noticed a diamond watch glistening on her left wrist. On her ring finger was a huge diamond of at least eight carats, set in an eighteen carat gold ring, with channel set diamonds along the side. Her earrings were also made of large channel-set diamonds. I'm good at picking up details like that—most women are.

"Ah, Goh Boon Kok will be back in a minute," said S. P., interrupting the mutual inspection society.

"Of course," I answered, "Well, I'd best be getting back to my friends. So nice meeting you! Bye Pa."

Poor S. P., of all the daughters-in-law, it had to be me, the direct, Chinese daughter-in-law, devoid of the artful and duplicitous Western ways of Lynn and Rosita.

Walking back to my table, my thoughts were racing; who was this beautiful woman, and the two children with S. P.?

What really got me was that the little girl looked so much like Marc. Marc's looks go pretty well on Marc, but don't wear well at all on a girl. The little boy was younger, a nice nondescript Chinese boy. The children were about the same ages as my sons, and were clamoring around S. P., as normal children would with their father.

When I told my mother of seeing S. P. that day, she said excitedly, "Oh my God, Chu, didn't I already tell you that a man who is as well dressed and conscious of his looks as S. P., has someone? So S. P. got himself a Hong Kong movie star type of dame. Well, I'm not surprised at all. He seems the type."

My mother had her moments of wisdom, which she loved to express with piercing bitchy statements, continued, "You think your father-in-law is such a goody-goody? I guarantee you that he doesn't eat chicken rice everyday. It's your mother-in-law's fault, she has all the money in the world, but lets herself look worse than Tai Seng's wife!"

How delightfully catty my mother could be! Tai Seng was Mamak's old family cook, and his wife was a larger, warped version of Lillian.

"Child," my mother said, raising her eyebrows, "you've just seen S. P.'s other woman."

I had to admit that my mother had a point. Most men of S. P.'s wealth and position did have a mistress. I wanted to find out.

Sometime later, I took S. P.'s trusted secretary, Agnes, out for a purposeful dinner at Nutmeg's Restaurant at the Hyatt Hotel. One thing I love to do is loosen up the tight-assed, and liquor is often the key; it can do a hell of a lot for certain personalities.

And so it was, that, after consuming too much red wine, and further weakened by my understanding remark, "Oh, Agnes, we have known each other for so long, it must be difficult working for someone like S. P.," Agnes loosened up.

She began to talk, and in the course of her ramblings, she revealed to me, with a tipsy smirk, that S. P. did indeed have a mistress, and a second family.

Nevertheless, I could not be absolutely certain. After all, like any faithful and long-serving secretary, Agnes was frequently upset with her boss, and might have been taking a bit of personal revenge on S. P. Maybe Agnes, herself, aspired to the role of being S. P.'s mistress.

Several years later, I heard that poor Agnes had been fired over the mistress. It seems that she had inadvertently booked both the mistress and Lillian into the same floor of the same hotel, at the same time. A slip-up? I would have thought Agnes was too Singaporean and too careful to make such mistakes.

It took me a good two years after the lunch with Agnes, to get a better confirmation of the existence of the mistress and the second family.

This time it came from Hin Chew, who, normally, was very good at keeping me in the dark. However, one evening when he was both under the influence of his after dinner ritual of beer, and in a broody and bitter mood he blabbed.

Staring into space, Hin Chew uncharacteristically shared a thought with me, "Can you imagine, Father had his mistress, even before we were married in 1979, and their two children are the same age as ours."

What more proof did I need, a signed confession from S. P.?

Hin Chew's overriding ambition was now, more than ever, to outdo his father. which was no easy task, as he was working for S. P., who was in full control of the purse strings.

Hin Chew was a shareholder and director of virtually all of S. P.'s Singapore companies, of which there were more than ten. This gave Hin Chew a good deal of latitude as to which company he would pick to run. Being into computers, and electronic gadgets, he chose to become the Managing Director of Chungco Electronics.

Chungco Electronics' formally stated purpose of business was "the development, manufacturing and sale of computers, electronic equipment and communication related products." The company had been dormant from the time of its incorporation, which was shortly after Hin Chew's arrest in 1984.

With Chungco Electronics, Hin Chew would show his father what he could do.

Once he got Chungco Electronics set up, Hin Chew decided to show me the operation. I was interested, even though my knowledge of electronics was nil. Hin Chew told me, "We have a production line, and a warehouse area, where the goods are prepared for shipment. I really want to know what you think."

This I had to see, and agreed immediately to visit Chungco Electronics.

I drove Hin Chew to the Chungco Electronics plant, which was located in one of Singapore's light industrial parks. It wasn't General Electric, but, from the outside, I must say that I was impressed.

We entered the company through an office area, which was deserted, except for some empty desks. "Nice," I said politely.

"Nice? This is nothing; the production line is the heart of the business. Follow me," said Hin Chew, leading me down a hallway.

Hin Chew held open the door to the production area, as I entered. This, I believe, was the first time he had held the door open for me since the day of our marriage.

"See!" said Hin Chew, coming in behind me.

All I saw were five Chinese ladies, painting Mickey Mouse telephones! No conveyor belts, nothing.

"Hmmm ... this is it?" I asked, politely.

"Yes," said Hin Chew walking me over to the ladies. "See, pulse tone dialing. Not the old rotary stuff."

"Back there," said Hin Chew, pointing to a wall of boxes, "we have the finished product. All those boxes are packed for shipment. Inside are the Mickey Mouse telephones.

I stared at the boxes, and remembered that I had seen Mickey Mouse telephones during my trip to America—they were nothing new—how could Hin Chew possibly hope to make any money, and outdo his father, by selling Mickey Mouse telephones?

"And what's inside the Mickey Mouse telephones?" I asked, impulsively.

"What do you mean, what's inside the Mickey Mouse telephones," Hin Chew smiled, and, after a brief pause, said, "Electronics, wires, and stuff. Hey! We can take a Mickey Mouse telephone home with us, for the children."

"Yes, good," I answered, hoping we didn't have to put it on display in the living room.

Hin Chew brought the telephone home and it made the children very happy.

Apparently, the Mickey Mouse telephone was Chungco Electronics only product, at least the only product I was told about.

Royalties to Disney? I wouldn't know, but since I never heard of Hin Chew's selling a single Mickey Mouse telephone, maybe royalties weren't a problem.

According to its annual statement, Chungco Electronics revenue came mainly from collecting interest on fixed interest deposits. It also did a lot of transferring of funds back and forth, with other Chung companies.

Did Chungco Electronics make money? Officially, none. The company was dissolved in 1990, with the Board of Director's resolution stating, "It has been proved to the satisfaction of this Meeting that Chungco Electronics cannot by reason of its liabilities continue its business and that the Company be wound up voluntarily."

Chungco Electronics finished its existence with an accumulated loss of close to S$260,000 on gross sales of under S$30,000, for the entire period of its operation.

Strangely, at the end, Chungco Electronics owed S$1,337,789.65 (US$767,000) to Sinri Enterprises, another Chung company. So, what was Hin Chew up to with Chungo Electronics?

I have seen the audited annual financial reports of the most of the Singapore Chung companies (they are a matter of public record), but I never saw a single instance where any of them made a profit. Never! I guess that is what good business is all about.

There was nothing Mickey Mouse about the Chungs.

No Second Chances

ZENA TOOK very good care of Granny, getting up each morning at 5:00 to bathe her, and to prepare breakfast and a dish, usually curry, for lunch. By 7:00 A.M., Zena would leave for work.

In early August 1987, after Zena had left home for work, Granny began to feel very weak. She was unable to stand, but using all her strength crawled to the phone and called Zena at work. Zena came home immediately, and seeing Granny's weakened condition, took her to nearby Mount Alvernia Hospital.

There, Granny began to lose consciousness, and the doctors diagnosed her as having suffered a heart attack. They rushed her to the intensive care unit where they put her on a respirator.

Several days passed with Granny steadily slipping deeper and deeper into a coma. Finally, the doctors told Zena and my mother that Granny was not going to make it. Keeping her alive was of no use.

On August 15, 1987, the hospital took her off the respirator, and poor Granny died.

Sadly, in death, Granny received the respect that was denied her in life. All our family members, my parents, Hin Chew, and our Eurasian relatives attended her funeral. Even S. P. and Lillian were there. Others present included friends and acquaintances all the way from Swee Cheong to Andrew Hewitt.

Losing Granny was a terrible experience for me. For a brief period, she had lived in luxury with us at 69 Holland Road. After my mother moved her out, Granny was comfortable at Zena's, but Zena worked, and Granny was alone most of the time. Granny deserved better, but now there was nothing that I, or anyone, could ever do to make it right.

It took Granny's death to teach me that you don't always get a second chance.

My brother, Sam, was nearly twenty-eight. He had been living on his own ever since the age of fifteen, following his terrible fight with my father. Fortunately, Sam's basic needs were taken care of by Mamak, and he was trying to make it on his own. Sam had a series of jobs, none of which amounted to much. In Singapore, without a university degree, and without family influence behind you, you have little chance to succeed—combine that with epilepsy, and you have no chance.

More than once Sam had seizures in public. Fortunately, he survived, but several times was stripped of his wallet, and whatever small amount of cash he had. From the day he left home, Sam did all he could to get back into the family. He would show up for dinners, hoping to be asked to stay the night, only to be reminded by my mother that it was time to leave.

One of the few times I saw Sam was at an informal dinner at our parents' house. It was a chance meeting. My father stayed upstairs in his bedroom, as Sam's visits were limited to seeing our mother. After dinner, came my mother's queue for Sam to leave, "Sam, it's getting late." Standing up from the table, Sam asked if he could have some of the leftover sausages to take home.

"Those belong to your father," was my mother's curt reply.

My parents warned me many times not to have anything to do with Sam. "Be careful, or he will ask you for money. Let Mamak handle the problem," my mother would caution. Their concern, as always, was money.

Fortunately, Sam was becoming less dependent on my mother for what little emotional support she gave him. He was becoming a happier person, and with good reason. He had someone of his own, a girl with whom he was deeply in love. Apparently, the young lady felt the same about Sam. They were thinking of marriage.

Even though my father had not supported Sam for many years, he saw Sam's possible marriage as a potential threat to his wallet. "He gets married, and then what? They have children, and can't support them," grumbled my father. "Then who do they come to? They come to Papa for the money. No way in hell that I am going to pay for that useless bugger and his kids. No way, I say!"

As always, when it came to matters of the heart, my father had the solution. In this case, he avoided his usual ploy of dangling a more alluring piece of bait in front of his victim. In Sam's case, it would serve no purpose, as Sam might decide to the wed the bait.

My father needed a different approach to get rid of Sam's girl. He would telephone the girl, and tell her whatever he could to undermine Sam.

My father told her that, if she married Sam, Sam would never see a penny of the family's money. He told her that Sam was worthless, that his grandmother supported him, that he was unable to hold a job. He went so far as to tell her that Sam was mentally ill, that Sam was an epileptic, and that their children would be flawed.

My father's cruel and ruthless tactic worked. That ended it between Sam and the girl he loved.

The next day, Sam went to see Swee Cheong. Poor Sam had no one else to turn to in his desperation. He was in tears as he told Swee Cheong what my father had done. There was little that Swee Cheong could do, other than offer whatever comforting words he could.

Several days later, on October 15, 1987, exactly two months after the death of Granny, my mother received a telephone call. She picked up the receiver with annoyance, as it was shortly after midnight. No one was supposed to call at that hour.

The caller was Sam's landlord, the owner of the apartment, where Sam rented his room. Sam had not been seen for two days ... worse, there was a terrible odor coming from under the door to Sam's room.

My mother listened silently ... the landlord continued. He had entered Sam's room where he found the stench overpowering. The room was empty. The landlord went to the bathroom door. It was closed. Slowly, Sam's landlord opened it. Inside was a horrible sight—Sam had hung himself from the rungs of the grill of the bathroom window.

Sam was dead, and had been so for at least two days, his body decomposing in the hot, humid, climate of Singapore.

My mother telephoned me immediately. It was a call I shall never forget. The telephone rang at exactly 12:30 A.M. I was in bed with Hin Chew. I knew something was wrong as soon as I picked up the receiver. For the first time in my life, I heard my mother cry. I too began to cry. Through her sobs, my mother managed to tell me what had happened to Sam, and that he was dead.

"Can you meet us at Sam's apartment?" my mother asked.

"No, I can't. It would be too much for me to bear. Please don't ask me to do that, Mummy." I was in tears, I thought of poor Sam, and how we had seen so little of each other. I could have helped him …

Hin Chew, awakened by the call, and hearing my side of the conversation, understood what had happened.

He laughed, "You're crying crocodile tears. What do you expect? You all never cared for him when he was alive. Why should you care for him now, when he's dead?"

"You shouldn't say that," I said weakly.

Hin Chew continued, harshly, "What kind of family do you come from?"

I repeated, "You shouldn't say these things. Someday something like this could happen to your family, as well."

Hin Chew didn't answer. With a grunt, he turned his back to me, rolling over to return to sleep.

For me, there was no sleep and no peace that night. It was shameful that I had avoided Sam to please my parents. What had they ever done for me? But more painfully, what had I ever done for Sam?

This was the second time in two months, that I learned the bitter lesson that you don't always get a second chance. Like Granny, Sam deserved better. Again, there was nothing I could ever do to make it right. All I could make right were the lives of my children. It would be tragic, and clearly my fault, if history were to repeat itself with my children.

Since that night, I have never slept in a room with the telephone connected.

In the death of that same night, my parents were driven to Sam's place by their chauffer, Jolly.

My father took Jolly up to Sam's room. My mother could not bear to go, and waited in the car. Shortly, my father returned. He had given Jolly the task of cleaning up the grim and messy consequences of Sam's Last Act.

Aside from Jolly, none of us had ever seen the inside of Sam's room. Jolly told us that in Sam's room, on the table by his bed, on his lone dresser, and on the walls, there were many photographs—photographs of us—of my father, of my mother, and of me.

That was all he had of us.

The next morning, Jolly drove my father, mother, and me to the morgue. Sam's body had to be identified.

Entering the morgue was a terrible experience, and identifying Sam's body was more than I could do. The very thought that Sam was there was more than I could bear. My mother stayed with me in the waiting room, while my father went inside to identify Sam.

After a couple of minutes, my father reappeared. Nonchalantly he remarked, "I say; the body all decomposed a'ready."

"You want to take a look, ah?" my father asked without a trace of emotion. I declined, and so did my mother.

Sam was cremated, and his ashes remained in the funeral home. My father would not let Sam, even in the form of ashes, back into the house.

Chinese tradition dictates that parents and grandparents do not attend the funeral of their descendants.

Mamak broke with that tradition, and attended Sam's funeral. I was there, as well, as we laid his ashes to rest.

Once again, I had no second chance.

MR. CHUNG GOES TO WASHINGTON

Rosita was still living apart from Peter in her large and luxurious rented house in Singapore, but her life was becoming a series of disasters.

Her youngest son, Lucas, still a toddler, managed to stick a cotton bud into older brother Bobby's ear, piercing his eardrum. Bobby was rushed to the hospital to undergo emergency surgery.

Still recuperating from the operation, and having problems with his balance, due to the inner-ear injury, Bobby fell and broke his leg. It was off to the hospital again, and out on crutches.

Shortly thereafter, while Rosita and her children were having dinner with S. P., Lillian, and Peter, at the Chinese restaurant on the second floor of the Regent Hotel, nobody, not even Rosita's maid, noticed that Lucas had wandered off.

Suddenly there was a scream! Lucas, barely two years old, had fallen out of the second-floor dining room window, overlooking the pool at the back of the hotel. Peter, Rosita, her maid, and some of the hotel staff dashed down the stairs to the rear exit of the hotel, while S. P. and Lillian rushed to the window.

Everyone feared the worst.

By some miracle, Lucas had landed on a plastic tabletop, next to the swimming pool. A foot or so either way and he would have hit concrete. Incredibly, Lucas survived, with only some minor bruises—no hospital this time.

With these three accidents taking place over a short period, Rosita decided she needed a vacation.

Taking her children and maid, she flew to Hong Kong. Peter was still being very cooperative, and understanding, at least with his wallet.

Of all the things to do in Hong Kong, Rosita went ice-skating. A bit heavy for the sport, she slipped, fell, and broke her leg.

Rosita, her children, and the maid, had to take the earliest flight back to Singapore, with yet another visit to the hospital.

After her recovery from the broken leg, Rosita trucked on.

One evening, as luck would have it, she happened to be in the parking lot of Peter's apartment building at the same time as Peter's girlfriend, Elsie.

Rosita caught sight of Elsie, whose beautiful long ponytail bobbed as she walked. Catching her from behind, Rosita seized Elsie's from behind and gave the ponytail a vicious yank, winding up with strands of Elsie's hair in her hand.

Rosita was strong and determined. She would muscle her way back into the Chungs' lives, no matter what. She would not be discouraged. For well over two years she had been fighting tooth and nail to win Peter back.

Rosita's long siege, brought to a head by the ponytail incident, had exhausted Peter's patience.

He had had enough.

Rosita and her children all had Australian passports and were in Singapore on dependency passes, visas which permitted them to reside in Singapore, but only as Peter's dependents.

Without warning, Peter cancelled Rosita's dependency pass, and those of their children, ruthlessly giving her and his three children less than twenty-four hours to leave Singapore.

Singapore is strict, and the penalty for overstaying a visa in Singapore is jail with two strokes of the cane for men, and a fine for women.

Rosita could not believe that Peter was capable of doing such "a wicked and vile thing," but she and her children were gone in a day, on their way back to Melbourne.

Rosita and her children would not return to live in Singapore.

After losing Sam and Granny, my life returned to its normal routine, which was staying at home, caring for my children, but now mourning the loss of my brother.

Eventually, I began to go out occasionally to diversionary social events, most of which I attended without Hin Chew, as he was usually away.

Hin Chew never told me when he would be leaving, or when he would return. This was the way of the Chungs. They never divulged their comings and goings.

It wasn't until I read about it in a magazine that I learned that S. P. and Lillian had "been to a party with American President George Bush."

Did any of the Chungs tell me? Of course not!

My informant was the Singapore Tatler, a glossy society magazine published for those who love to read about themselves. In addition to the Singapore Tatler, there are other regional Tatlers, catering to local snobs wherever they are. There is a Hong Kong Tatler, a Taipei Tatler, and an Ulster Tatler. Then, of course, for England, there is The Tatler, the mother of all Tatlers.

I have to admit the truth; even I have been mentioned in the Singapore Tatler, and more than once.

In its April 1989 issue, the Singapore Tatler published an article entitled *Ranching Out*. It featured, of all people, S. P. Chung. The article wrote of S. P.'s "mind-boggling property acquisition" of an Australian cattle ranch, "11 times as big as Singapore."

The article continued, "The Chungs' Number One son, Hin Chew, is the computer expert of the family and has shown a penchant for wise investments. Incidentally, Hin Chew's wife, May Chu, the granddaughter of Datin Lee Chee Shan, and daughter of Jacky and Maybelle Lee, would rather be called by her Christian name, Monicka. She thinks it is easier to remember and less likely to be confused with her husband's name.

"Her adorable boys, aged four and six have no problems remembering her name; they simply call her Mummy."

Undaunted by the frivolity of the article, I waded on. S. P. was described as "keeping a low profile generally." How true!

Now came the kicker—"but on a recent trip to the United States, with a week in Honolulu and San Francisco before heading east, I hear he and his charming wife Lillian were lucky enough to be invited to a party with new American President, George Bush."

I was stunned! From a fugitive in disgrace, to a party with the President of the United States, George Bush, and in only four short years. What a leap!

Talk about rehabilitation! Talk about being way ahead of John Huang, James Riady, Johnny Chung, Charlie Trie and the like, except that S. P. was in with the Republicans.

How did the "fucking Gutless Wonder" do it?

Immediately I realized that the Washington connection had to be S. P.'s friend, Dan Arnold.

I connected the dots—S. P., Dan Arnold, Bush.

Far fetched?

Was the shabby little Chinaman from Mumong with US$48 million in liquid assets far fetched? Was Anna Plains, larger than the state of Rhode Island far-fetched? Hin Chew's detention in Brunei with his "life in danger." Was that far-fetched? Was Alexander Irvine a mirage? Were Dan Arnold's helicopters a fib?

For me, this was all much more than far-fetched—it was a nightmare.

Could S. P.'s connections, his world whatever it was, cause problems for me, if I tried to leave Hin Chew? Life with the Chungs was making me ever more isolated and alone, devoid of friends or allies.

How could I escape from a family like the Chungs? I saw what Peter had done to Rosita.

And what were my chances?

X-10 AT RADIO SHACK, HOME DEPOT, & AT A STORE NEAR YOU!

IN CHEW was away from Singapore more than ever, usually in Hong Kong, and spending so much time there that he had rented himself a very upscale deluxe apartment costing US$5,600 a month.

I had no idea what Hin Chew was doing in Hong Kong, but now that he had taken an apartment there, he felt he owed me an explanation, and so did I.

"The computer business is coming to an end; it's already overdeveloped," Hin Chew pronounced wisely, "and that's why I got out of Chungco Electronics. I have no interest in any of Father's companies; I want to get away from him."

I waited silently for him to continue, thinking, "Why in the hell do you need an apartment in Hong Kong? Taking up a mistress?"

Hin Chew continued, in measured tones and doing his best to sound like a reasonable human being. "I have been approached by some Americans. They have a company, called X-10, which they want to sell."

I nodded.

"It really has great potential," Hin Chew brightened. "It's in the electronics business, but not the computer business. This company makes timers to turn lights off and on, along with electronic security systems, but very advanced; their systems can communicate with light switches using ordinary electrical house wires."

"OK," I said, "is X-10 a Hong Kong company?"

"The head office is in Hong Kong, but it's really more of an American company, that's where most of the sales come from." Hin Chew was beginning to sound like a commercial.

"Have they been in business long?"

"Over ten years. They invented the home automation business."

Since Hin Chew was being so open, I asked, "Well, wouldn't it be expensive to buy a well-known American company like that?"

"That's the best part." Hin Chew was really beaming. "The

company is run by a bunch of typical *ang moh* idiots, stupid Americans, and it's on the verge of bankruptcy, actually in receivership. They have to sell at any price; I think I can pick it up for only about US three million dollars. I'll be Chairman!" he laughed.

Ang moh, meaning literally "red hair" is one of the less flattering terms that Chinese use for Caucasians.

I wondered where the three million dollars would be coming from, but my guess, which later proved right, was that S. P. would put up some of the funds. So much for independence!

"But if X-10 is bankrupt, how can it be a good buy?" I asked.

"We can turn it around, it has a lot of potential. It's already selling to top American companies like Radio Shack, Leviton, even Sears. X-10's products are on shelves all over America. It's a known brand, already in five million American homes."

Hin Chew went on to explain that, one of the original founders, George Stevenson, already lived in Hong Kong, because X-10 did its manufacturing in Shenzhen, just over the border from Hong Kong, in China, "so we can get workers at only us US$60 a month."

The other founder of X-10, Peter Lesser, ran the American subsidiary in New Jersey, and the company had a research and development facility, called Pico Electronics in Scotland.

I knew I might be risking it, but I had to interrupt Hin Chew; there was one final question, I had to ask, "Will we be moving to Hong Kong?"

"Of course not." Hin Chew said putting his hands together, shaking his head with a condescending smile, "We will live right here, like always. The children are in the best schools, so why disrupt them? I will have to make trips to Hong Kong, but everything will be just the same."

Uh-huh.

Hin Chew finished by paraphrasing a Chinese saying, "You know the Chinese saying, 'man who has no baggage, travels faster than man with albatrosses hanging on his neck.'" This, he followed with a good hearty laugh.

To kick off his X-10 venture, in June 1989, coinciding with the Tieneman Square massacre, Hin Chew decided we would take a break, with a visit to Lynn and Jim in Perth for a three-week family vacation. For this, through the good offices of Andrew Hewitt, Hin Chew rented a very nice private apartment, in South Perth facing the Swan River, for our stay.

Perth is a bright and lively city, with none of the big business atmosphere of Sydney, or the antiquated European gloom of Melbourne. It is a great vacation spot, and we were very excited about the trip.

The children, my maid, Viola, who had become a friend and confidante, and I left in advance; Hin Chew planned to follow later, but he never showed up, telling me that X-10 business in Hong Kong required his presence.

Jim had purchased a large and beautiful house, with a swimming pool, in Nedlands, one of the best parts of Perth.

In spite of the beautiful house and the surroundings of Perth, Lynn was very unhappy. Jim's drinking problem had not gone away with the move to Perth. In fact, it had gotten worse. As nice as Jim was when sober, he wasn't a pleasant drunk, and Lynn was doing what she could to protect her children from him.

Lynn, always resourceful and intelligent, was trying to get Jim proper help and counseling for his drinking problem, but with no cooperation from Jim. Her experience as a trained nurse had taught her how to deal with difficult cases, but with Jim, her efforts had been to no avail.

She told me quite openly, "I cannot see myself, or the children living our lives with this man, for the next twenty or thirty years. This drinking, and mistreatment of my children has to stop."

She continued, "I'm not like you, Chu. You're Chinese, you're Asian, and you wouldn't understand."

I nodded in agreement, even though I did understand. I could have been insulted by Lynn's remark, but I understood what she meant was that, being Asian, I could endure more than she could.

She was right.

Lynn's next remark further confirmed her opinion of my endurance, "Among the three of us, I know you have the worst husband of all, but if I don't leave Jim, and remove my children from this terrible environment, take that risk in life, I will never be at peace with myself."

Her mind was made up. Lynn's words struck home; we were

reading from the same page. Fortunately for Lynn, she and her children had British passports, plus she had the option of divorcing Jim in England, a civilized country.

Good for Lynn! She had it right. Our lives had changed from the time when we, the three daughters-in-law, were young and submissive.

I too wanted out, but I had to wait for the right moment, not only for me, but also for my children.

Seeing the condition of their marriage, I saw less of Jim and Lynn in Perth, than I had planned. Alone with the children, and without Hin Chew, we still had a wonderful time in Perth.

Several days before I was to leave Perth, Hin Chew called; he was in urgent need of two king-size duvets, or quilts, with machine-washable covers. He also needed matching pillows, pillowcases, and fitted sheets, all for his bed in the new Hong Kong apartment. This was a must-have, and the specifications were rigorous, the inner quilt of the duvet had to be as thick as possible, "real fat," Hin Chew said. "Bring the duvets with you on the airplane to Singapore, and then I want you to fly to Hong Kong with them. I really need them."

"Why don't you buy them in Hong Kong?" I asked.

"Buy the fucking duvets in Australia. They don't have the quality shit in Singapore, or Hong Kong. Just fucking do it!" he shouted.

I yelled back, "You are fucking nuts. You can buy the duvets and everything else you need at any big department store in Hong Kong. Go to Daimaru or Mitsukoshi." It was safe for me to yell, as Hin Chew was thousands of miles away.

"Are you arguing with me? I have an instruction for you, and that is to buy the duvets, and bring them here."

We both slammed down our respective telephones.

Lynn came shopping with me, to help choose the items. In the store, she said, "I cannot believe what we are doing, Chu. Hin Chew is an absolute sod to put you through all this. He must be out of his mind."

I agreed. Hin Chew would have his Australian duvets, at any cost.

Before returning to Singapore with the duvets, I said my goodbyes to Jim and Lynn.

I could see that Jim's world was deteriorating. Hin Chew was right. Jim could not handle the Australia business. His lack of experience, and low self-esteem, made him the willing pawn of Andrew Hewitt.

I thought S. P. and Lillian should have brought Jim back to Singapore, and placed him in a safe environment. Australia could do with a temporary replacement. I had suggested as much to Lillian, but she did nothing, except to reply, "Jim is a grown man, so there is nothing we can do."

Jim's plea for help, and I took his drinking to be just that, went unheeded.

As we parted, there was nothing I could do for Lynn, other than offer my moral support.

The next year, in 1990, Lynn would return to England, with her children, and sue Jim for divorce.

The five-hour flight back to Singapore was depressing.

Lynn was getting her life back. The grounds for divorce in England are the same as in Singapore, but Lynn would not come upon anything like a Confucianist Chinese judge in Singapore, and that would make all the difference. Lynn was also close to her family, her parents, her brothers, and her sister, all the components of a normal family, which would give her support.

Then there was X-10, like Lynn, Hin Chew was getting on with his life, as well.

The Chungs, the despicable Chungs, who had fled from the law, feared extradition, suffered incarceration, were invading America with S. P. at a party with President George Bush, and now Hin Chew with X-10. Hin Chew's products would be on the shelves, and in the homes of America, "already in five million American homes," as he had put it.

Meanwhile, my life, and the lives of my children were going nowhere. I was filled with rage.

Watch out America! X-10 and the Chungs would soon be at Radio Shack, Sears, Home Depot, and at a store near you!

THE WIFE OF X-10

DESPITE BEING under a lot of pressure from Hin Chew to fly immediately with the duvets to Hong Kong, my main concern was getting the children ready for school, now that their summer vacation was over. I was very serious about education. From their earliest days, I had my children playing with alphabet blocks, and decorated the walls of their bathroom with the multiplication tables, going all the way to twenty times twenty.

Warren was only four years old, but I had enrolled him in Newton Kindergarten to get an early start, and Marc was attending the Anglo-Chinese Junior School.

There were several Anglo-Chinese schools in Singapore, and they ranked second only to Raffles Institution in reputation, having been founded a bit later, in 1886, by Reverend Bishop W. Oldham. Like all good Singapore schools, there was nothing Anglo and everything Chinese about the schools.

In Singapore, in addition to school, nearly all schoolchildren are given tutoring in the evening at home. For Marc and Warren, I was lucky to find a very mature and conservative tutor, a nice elderly lady named Mrs. Chang. There was no fooling around, no laughter, and no wasted time with Mrs. Chang.

As though Mrs. Chang were not enough, I also enrolled the children into the Lorna Whiston Study Centre, a part-time school specializing in teaching English. I did this to counterbalance Singapore's strong educational bias toward Mandarin Chinese.

My first language was English, and I spoke it perfectly, which was unusual for a Singaporean. I was not going to have the children speak in the stilted, halting, English, which is so typical of even the best-educated Singaporeans. For me, English came first.

It took a full two weeks for me to get the children settled into their schools, and up to speed with the serious Mrs. Chang, who came twice a week.

It was not until the middle of July, missing Hin Chew's birthday by a week, that I took off on leg two of my trip, to haul the king-sized duvets and all, to Hong Kong.

In Hong Kong, Hin Chew had made a comfortable nest for himself.

His apartment was in a building called Victoria Apartments, an extension of the Victoria Hotel, on Connaught Road. The apartment was much nicer than I had expected, and had a beautiful view of Hong Kong harbor.

It was a perfect and luxurious bachelor pad, with no room for a family. In case I might have had any suspicions, Hin Chew carefully pointed out to me that he had placed photographs of the children and me on the dresser.

The day after my arrival, Hin Chew proudly gave me a tour of X-10's offices, which were utilitarian, including Hin Chew's office, which was behind an unmarked door. I had expected to meet some of the "stupid *ang mohs*," as Hin Chew called them, but none were around.

I stayed in Hong Kong six days, and then it was time to get back to Singapore and the children.

The pattern of our new life was set. I took care of the children in Singapore, while Hin Chew scuttled back and forth to Hong Kong, taking care of X-10. Most of the time, he was away.

During the first year, Hin Chew was away for a total of 243 days, or two-thirds of the time. I kept records of such things.

Hin Chew's reason for returning to Singapore had nothing to do with me, or the children. His stays in Hong Kong were limited to three-month visitor visas. This way Hin Chew managed to avoid becoming a Hong Kong resident, thereby avoiding Hong Kong income taxes.

The pattern of Hin Chew's arrivals back in Singapore were set in a new ritual: Hin Chew would call to tell us he was coming back to Singapore only just before boarding his flight in Hong Kong. That gave the boys and me five hours lead time before picking him up at Singapore Changi Airport, which was plenty of time to be there physically, but not nearly enough time to prepare ourselves emotionally for what was to come.

The children and I were always on time, which for me meant ahead of time. I would park the car, and we would go to the arrival lounge, where we would stand peering through the large plate glass windows, which separated us from the baggage claim area. All flights to Singapore are international flights, so passport and customs control are always necessary.

Through the glass wall of windows, we could see the baggage arrive. Singapore's Changi Airport prides itself on the fact that the luggage always arrives at the baggage claim area before the passengers.

We would watch with eager apprehension for Hin Chew to appear. Finally, a happy, beaming, good Hin Chew would emerge. He would wave; we would wave, with smiles all around.

Hin Chew would walk briskly to the baggage carrousel, with small mincing steps, his typical cork-up-the-ass walk, to pick up his luggage.

Hin Chew traveled light, usually with one small suitcase, which he would swing happily, as he passed by the customs guards. Customs in Singapore was swift and unobtrusive, unless, of course, if they stopped you—then it could be the gallows.

Upon his arrival, Hin Chew would be the picture of fatherly happiness, together again with his wife and two sons. This brief state of happiness would last as we drove from Changi Airport down the East Coast Highway, which runs along the beach, as we headed back to the center of Singapore.

For some reason, Hin Chew never sat up very high in the passenger's seat. In the car, he always appeared to be much shorter than I, even though we were the same height (without my heels). Sitting so low, Hin Chew had to bend his head back to look out over the hood of the car. There he would be, his head bent back, playing with his hair in a girlish way, looking like a small person by my side.

These are things you notice when you really begin to hate someone.

It was constant tension.

We would still be bathed in happiness, as we turned off the East Coast Highway, and headed north on Rochor Road on our way through the center of town.

As each moment passed, I waited for Hin Chew to turn his head up to me, and start to shout. Seldom did he disappoint.

Somehow, always at the same bend in the road, an uncanny Pavlovian response would be triggered in Hin Chew by some minor detail—a passing motorist, a building, a memory, or us. His happiness would disappear, to be replaced by annoyance over something, anything.

Usually, the anger did not begin with the boys or me, but that was where it would invariably end. There was no escape.

The ritual of Hin Chew's return would continue with the family's dining out at one of Singapore's best restaurants, usually Japanese. One of Hin Chew's favorites was the Shima Restaurant at the Goodwood Park Hotel, where dinner for four could easily cost US$450.

Hin Chew's dinner conversation always found its way to the fact that Marc was overweight. The waiter would bring the menu. This was Hin Chew's queue to look at Marc, and tell him that he was a fat ugly slob, and not to be a pig by ordering too much. "Look at your brother, so nice and slim, and you're so fucking fat!" Hin Chew would try to play the boys off against each other, in the same way that S. P. did with his own sons.

After a brief pause, Marc, afraid to order anything, would be reprimanded by Hin Chew for being slow to order. By then, Marc would be reduced to tears, and we would all sit in silence until the food arrived.

The boys and I could take comfort only in the thought that we would soon be returning home, where the boys could take refuge in their bedroom, and I in the living room downstairs.

In the evening, Hin Chew would get into bed with a couple of cans of Tiger Beer, some comics, his electronic bridge game, and watch television. Like seventy-one percent of the population of Singapore, Hin Chew preferred watching the Chinese-language channel. His favorites were Chinese movies, the more traditional the better, and the more violent, the better. Being partially deaf, Hin Chew would play the television at top volume, filling the bedroom with the sound and fury of martial arts and Zen masters flying through the air. When it came to scenes of violence involving women, Hin Chew would join in. "Yeah, rape the fucking bitch."

Since the children often watched the Chinese movies with Hin Chew, his vulgar remarks bothered me. Whenever I caught the children watching Chinese thrillers with their father, I would send them straight to their room.

During commercials, Hin Chew would indulge in a bit of electronic bridge, continue with his comic, or, if necessary, hustle downstairs to retrieve more beer from the refrigerator.

While Hin Chew watched television upstairs, I was watching television downstairs in the living room. For me, these were golden moments of peace.

Unfortunately, Hin Chew did not always stay upstairs. He liked to take a break by coming downstairs and sit at the dining room table to read comic books, carefully taking them out from their protective plastic wrappers. He always kept his comics in their original clear plastic wrappers.

On one such evening, tired, and a bit drunk, Hin Chew went up the stairs to bed with his comic book, leaving its plastic wrapper on the dining room table.

After midnight, after everybody had gone to bed, I was shaken awake by Hin Chew, "I can't find the fucking plastic wrapper for my comic!"

"Someone fucking threw my plastic wrapper away!"

I raised myself to my elbows, still waking up.

"You fucking wake the fucking maid up, and I want to find the wrapper right now!" Hin Chew instructed.

"Who would want to touch the wrapper?" I asked, rubbing my eyes.

"Fuck, go and look for it, and wake the fucking maid," Hin Chew yelled.

I went downstairs, and tapped on Viola's door, which was behind the kitchen.

"Viola? Quick! Please help! Sir is yelling!" I said.

Viola opened the door, "What Ma'am? Is everything all right? What happened?"

"Viola, I'm sorry to wake you. Have you seen Sir's comic book wrapper?" I asked.

"No, Ma'am."

"Sir is screaming and yelling again, Viola. C'mon, let's go through the trash."

"Ma'am, I did straighten things up on the dining room table, after Sir went upstairs," Viola said nervously, as we left the apartment, and walked downstairs into the apartment parking lot, where the trash bins were kept.

As we went through the trash, both Viola and I were in tears.

Finally, we came up with the plastic wrapper. Viola had thrown it in the trash, unaware of its importance to Hin Chew.

"Ma'am, I am so sorry," said Viola.

"At least, I can leave and get away from Sir, but you cannot," said my maid and friend, Viola.

It was tough to hear it, especially coming from my maid, but, with her simple sincerity, Viola was right.

"I wish you and the children were coming to Canada with me, Ma'am. I really do."

Viola had been with us for nearly four years, and had an opportunity to get a job in Canada, for which I had sponsored her. Soon she would be moving on. Even Viola was getting ahead in life.

Viola and I went up to the bedroom to deliver the plastic comic wrapper to Hin Chew. He looked at it, looked at us, and said, "Well, it's no fucking good; it's wrinkled and dirty. This comic will now … have no wrapper."

DISINHERITANCE 101

I T WAS IN spring of 1990, that I received an urgent telephone call from Wai Lin; she was looking for Hin Chew. She told me there had been a terrible argument between Hin Chew and S. P. "They were yelling and screaming at each other, here in the office. They were speaking in Hakka, so I couldn't understand anything, but the swear words. It was awful," said Wai Lin.

"Is there anything I can do?" I asked.

"No," answered Wai Lin, sounding a bit shaken, "It's late, I'll try to reach Hin Chew in the morning."

"I'm so sorry, Wai Lin, that you had to hear such a terrible thing. Are you sure, you're OK?" I asked.

"Yes, yes, I'm fine; it's all part of business, I suppose," she answered. We both gave a polite laugh and said our goodbyes.

S. P. had a reputation of having a terrible temper, although, I had never seen him angry, and, apparently, Hin Chew's temper had finally taken its toll with S. P.

I was worried.

I couldn't have cared less about what went on between S. P. and Hin Chew, but what would Hin Chew's mood be when he arrived home?

No sooner had the thought left my mind, than Hin Chew came though the door. He was distraught, but composed.

"I had a screaming argument with Father," Hin Chew put down his briefcase.

"I reached the breaking point with him. I will never work for Father again."

Quickly, with the urgency of an emergency room nurse, I went to the kitchen to get Hin Chew a beer.

Hin Chew sat down at the dining room table, as I returned with his can of beer.

Hin Chew popped open the can, took several gulps, and looking at the can, continued, "I'll drink 24 cans of beer and pee all over his fucking grave, the fucking Gutless Wonder. I'll be richer than he ever was. He'll see."

"Of course," I said.

"X-10 will make me rich, richer than Father." Hin Chew drained the can of beer.

There was a long pause, as I sat waiting in silence for Hin Chew to continue. Slowly, as he began to rise to his feet, with his head down, I thought I heard a sniffle. Then, as he raised his head, his face had a pitiful expression, and his eyes were red. He stood for a moment, took in a large gulp of air, and then burst into tears!

I was stunned! Who ever expected to see *this*? Before I could think of what to say, Hin Chew, sobbing, got up from his chair, ran across the dining area, and dashed up the stairs and into the bedroom.

Hin Chew and his father were no longer on speaking terms, and Hin Chew was on his way out of his father's businesses. He was a Director of at least ten Chungco companies that I knew about, and I am sure there were more. He also held shares in the companies, which were located, not only in Singapore, but in Hong Kong and Bermuda, as well.

The process of Hin Chew's disengagement from S. P.'s businesses would be involved and difficult. S. P.'s people, Goh Boon Kok, Feng, the accountants, and lawyers would take months to unravel Hin Chew from the Chungco companies.

Breaking up is hard to do.

Even though Hin Chew was on his way out with S. P.'s companies, the future didn't look too bleak, at least not to me. Suddenly, and at odd times, Hin Chew would burst into tears.

In spite all the bad things that Hin Chew had done to us, I was not heartless, and would remind him that he still had X-10, and the children, and that I would give him whatever support I could.

That only seemed to make him cry harder.

I didn't dare point out that Hin Chew also had plenty of money, how much I could only guess. So why cry?

In the hopes of bringing father and son back together I kept the lines of communication open, so that down the road there might be a reconciliation.

I did so, not out of any pity for Hin Chew, or for the family business, but for our children. Grandparents are important to children, and with my parents not fitting the mold at all, S. P. and Lillian were the best I could hope for in the way of grandparents.

Out in the cold, and without an office, Hin Chew finally roused himself, and decided that he needed an office of his own, and a company of his own, right in Singapore.

This would be his first very own company, and, for that reason Hin Chew incorporated his new baby, Zhongli Investment Company Pte Ltd, on his birthday, July 7, 1990. The name "Zhongli" was special also because it meant Chung-Lee in Pinyin, the modern Romanized form of Chinese.

Not only did my last name appear in Zhongli, Hin Chew also split the stock with me fifty-fifty, and made me a Director. Was Hin Chew becoming a human being? Naturally, S. P., Lillian, and the Chung brothers played no part in Zhongli. We were now completely "independent."

Next, Hin Chew hired his secretary, Wai Lin, away from his father. Out of defiance or nostalgia, Hin Chew rented a two-room office suite for Zhongli on the fourth floor of Sime Darby Centre, the same floor of the same building from which S. P. had recently vacated his own offices.

With me at the wheel, Hin Chew sitting next to me, and Wai Lin in the rear, we set out to buy furniture for the new office. We bought three desks for the front office, where Wai Lin, George Seow, an X-10 accountant, and I would be sitting.

A fourth, and larger desk, was purchased for the inner office, where Hin Chew would sit. A wall of filing cabinets, office chairs, a photocopier, a fax machine, and office supplies completed our purchases. No expense was spared.

We were ready for business. But what was the company going to do?

Zhongli's corporate bylaws stated that its purpose was to advise X-10 on business matters. For this, X-10 paid Zhongli a monthly "consulting fee" of S$35,400 (US$20,000). From this, Hin Chew gave himself a salary of S$9,000 (US$5,200) a month, paid Wai Lin, and the office expenses. Zhongli also paid our household expenses, and credit card bills. This was far better than Hin Chew's taking the S$35,000 as salary, as there would be no corporate profits from Zhongli, and nothing for the taxman. The only taxable income would be Hin Chew's monthly salary of S$9,000.

A pretty good setup, nothing to cry about.

Hin Chew began to refer to himself as a "businessman,"

So, what was my job at Zhongli? Hin Chew made it clear that there was little reason for me to come to the office. Wai Lin would do everything. This included the accounting, and the preparation of checks, which she could bring to the apartment for me to sign. That was my job—signing checks.

Zhongli, therefore, was nothing but a device to funnel tax-free money out of X-10, and into Hin Chew's pockets.

In addition to Chungco Electronics, the "Mickey Mouse" company, Hin Chew had been deeply involved in Dachung, the company which had been set up to manage the now defunct Brunei business, and which had purchased the prized IBM mainframe computer.

Dachung had changed its name to Chungco Technology Pte Ltd, and was getting into the sale and maintenance of personal computers.

After his rift with Hin Chew, S. P. decided to give Chungco Technology to favored son Peter, giving Peter 95 percent of the stock in the company. Hin Chew somehow managed to hang on to the remaining 5 percent, which did not mean much, but did allow him to be a lingering thorn in Peter's side.

Like all of the Chung companies, at the time of its transfer to Peter, the books of Chungco Technology looked unappealing. The company showed an accumulated loss of S$829,626 (US$475,000) for the brief time it had been in business. The accumulated loss would have been even greater, except an amount of S$1,483,199 (US$850.000), which was "due to a Director," but had been "waived." We all should have such generous "Directors."

Hin Chew was on his way out of all of S. P.'s companies.

To me, Hin Chew's loss was not that great, as the Chungco companies were losing millions. Still, the experience was a terrible blow to Hin Chew, and he was in a teary mood for months, sobbing now and then.

S. P., the master, however, had not finished with Hin Chew. He was saving his best blow for last.

It was a warm humid sunny day, just like any other day of any other month in Singapore, where neither the climate nor the length of the day ever changes. The telephone rang; it was Hin Chew. He was very pleasant on the phone. Hmmm.

"Sweetie, would you mind dropping by the Zhongli office? I need your help with something." Hmmm.

I arrived at the office to find Hin Chew a bit more like his usual bossy self, than he had been when he called me.

Wai Lin was at her desk, and gave me her usual polite hello.

"I have something for you to sign," said Hin Chew, "Here, sit at your desk."

I took my place at my seldom-used desk as Wai Lin placed a document before me. Hin Chew handed me a pen.

I was used to signing the company checks, so no big deal. What was I signing? Did I have a choice?

"First, initial some of the paragraphs and each page. Wai Lin will show you where."

I caught sight of the first page; it was an agreement between S. P. and Hin Chew

Wai Lin began to turn the pages, showing me where to put my initials. Naturally, I was expected to initial without reading. God forbid I should have asked what I was signing. Nevertheless, as Wai Lin turned the pages, and as I slowly and deliberately applied my initials, I got an inkling of what it was.

From what I could understand, the document appeared to be a separation agreement between Hin Chew and his father, by which they agreed, "to terminate the business relationship and association of the parties ..."

The first part of the agreement was simple. S. P. was selling a company called Chungco Bermuda Ltd., which owned part of X-10, to Hin Chew for US$9,000.

I was right, S. P. had been the backer of X-10, after all.

Then the agreement got a bit more involved.

In addition, Hin Chew had to pay S. P. S$2,665,848, which Chungco Bermuda owed to S. P.

For one United States dollar, Hin Chew would buy "the X-10 share" from S. P., a good deal, but he would also have to reimburse S$540,000 to S. P. for additional X-10 "set up" expenses, and replace S. P.'s million-dollar line of credit for X-10.

Finally Hin Chew owed S. P. personally another S$76,752, but then, somehow, S. P. also had a personal debt to Hin Chew of S$1,945,844.

I had never seen such a crazy thing. I owe you, you owe me, I sell, you buy, my expenses … This shell game gave a telling picture of the mindset of the Chungs. The mindset was money.

Did I memorize all those numbers on sight? Not quite, someone, and not Hin Chew, was nice enough to sneak me a copy of the agreement several days later.

The bottom line of the agreement was that, with all the debts washing out, Hin Chew had to pay his father a cash consideration of S$500,000 (US$287,000).

For this, Hin Chew would own 75 percent of Chungco Bermuda, which, in turn, owned 50 percent of X-10. I supposed, at the time, that the "X-10 share" mentioned represented the other 50 percent of X-10.

The agreement did not end there.

Hin Chew also had to resign from all the Chungco companies, and give up his shares in them, as well. He even had to give the Toorak apartment in Melbourne back to his father.

S. P. giveth and S. P. taketh away.

What did I have to do with all that? Absolutely nothing, *nada*, so far, but my role was saved for last.

At the end of the agreement, was a short paragraph entitled "WAIVER OF RIGHTS IN ESTATE OF S.P. AND WIFE." Hin Chew and I were to be disinherited by Ma and Pa!

We've all heard of prenuptial agreements. Well, the Chungs had a better solution—the postnuptial agreement.

On reaching this paragraph, I looked at Hin Chew, and said simply, "What's this?"

He explained, with his most blank and innocent face, "Father and I have decided to go our separate ways in our business affairs because our business philosophies are different."

Hin Chew paused, as I kept staring at him, silently.

He continued, "I am giving up all my interest in the family companies in return for Father giving me control of Chungco Bermuda Ltd, which owns 50 percent of X-10 Ltd."

"And, for this, I too am to give up all my rights, and the rights of our sons, to inherit anything from the family I married into?" I asked, with measured words.

Hin Chew simply stared at me. He knew I had no choice.

I looked back at the document, and signed.

With Hin Chew cleanly out of the way, S. P. decided it was time to get rid of another useless son.

After Lynn and the children had left him, Jim sold their beautiful house in Perth, and purchased a smaller house in the Bull Creek suburb of Perth, along with an apartment in South Perth. He had also treated himself to a metallic-blue Porsche, which he could no longer drive, as his license had been revoked for drunk driving.

Jim spent most of his time in the Bull Creek house, where he lived with a Chinese Singaporean girl named Margaret. He was drinking very heavily, and showing little interest in the affairs of Chungco, or anything else in life.

Since Jim had played far less of a role in the Chungco companies than Hin Chew, the agreement between Jim and S. P. wasn't nearly so complicated.

S. P. had a three-page letter prepared. It was written in legalese and in the form of a letter from Jim to S. P—a clever twist.

The letter, dated September 17, 1991, began with Jim's salutation to his father as, "Dear Sir," started with S. P.'s agreement to give Jim "gratuitously the sum of S$1,080,000," and to waive any claim on the Kensington apartment, which S. P. had purchased for Jim. The letter pointed out that the apartment had a current market value of S$500,000.

The letter also forgave a S$1,500,000 debt, which Jim somehow owed S. P.

Not bad, the total benefit for Jim from S. P. came to s$3,080,000 million, the equivalent of us$1.8 million.

For this, Jim agreed to return to S. P. any shares he held in the Chungco companies, and resigned from his sixteen Chungco directorships. Furthermore, Jim agreed not to represent himself as having anything to do with the Chung's business affairs in the future.

Finally, in the letter, Jim waived all rights of "my children and myself," to "the estate of Chung Shih Ping, and Madam Yeo Noy Heoh," should they die without leaving a will, and agreed not to challenge any will they might have.

The closing salutation of the letter read "Yours faithfully," which was followed by Jim's signature, duly witnessed by Goh Boon Kok, who, as usual, played Igor to S. P.'s Dr. Frankenstein.

In the short span of three months, S. P. had managed to disinherit two sons, two daughters-in-law, and four grandchildren.

Given the s$1.5 million (us$860,000) debt to S. P., Jim also had no choice but to sign.

If S. P. could reduce Hin Chew to tears, he could probably push Jim to the brink—and beyond.

The disinheritance of Jim and Hin Chew, Hin Chew's move to Hong Kong, and the sham of Zhongli, were all indications that the children and I were slowly being cut off. For me to go on as before would have been foolish. I had to make a life for my children and myself. I would not rest until the children and I were free of Hin Chew.

I was going to play by my own rules!

We were leading separate lives.

Each day that I spent with Hin Chew harm was being done, especially to Marc. For some reason, Hin Chew favored Warren, but my poor little overweight and serious Marc was easy pickings for his father.

The first step in getting away from Hin Chew would be to find a safe haven for Marc, where he could be away from his father, and not see my growing hostility toward Hin Chew. I had suggested several times to Hin Chew that Geelong College would be a good school for Marc, as foreign exposure would expand his experience beyond Singapore schools could offer. Now that Marc was nearly eleven, I tried again, with the concrete proposal that Marc go to Geelong for the next school year, assuming he could pass Singapore's tough sixth grade year-end examinations.

I thought that Hin Chew, a proud Geelong "old boy," would go for this, but I was wrong, he was dead set against the idea, "Marc will never go to Geelong. He doesn't have what it takes. He will be no match for the Australian boys there, and besides he doesn't have the grades. No fucking way."

Luck intervened when Paul Sheahan, the Head Master of Geelong College showed up in town, at the end of March 1992.

Paul was in his forties, had a full head of coarse salt and pepper hair, very little forehead, and a very strong chin. Not only did he have the typical Aussie looks, but he was a jock to boot, and an important one. He had played test cricket for Australia from 1967 to 1974, appearing in thirty-one international test matches. This claim to fame was more than an ample qualification for him to gain the academic position of Head Master of Geelong College. Hin Chew had met Paul at several of Geelong's "old boy" reunions, and was in awe of him.

Paul had a liking for Hin Chew, as well, since contributions to Geelong's endowment fund were always most welcome.

I knew Hin Chew gave US$5,000 a year to the MIT Alumni Fund, and I guessed that Geelong might be getting something too.

Hin Chew arranged for us to take Paul to lunch at Lei Gardens, the most expensive restaurant in Singapore. Hin Chew did the ordering, selecting only the choicest delicacies for the occasion, including sea cucumber. I felt sorry for Paul, who, I am sure, would have much preferred a steak and potatoes, washed down with a pint. Paul had powerful jaws, and did his best to chew the impossible-to-chew sea cucumber, finally, giving up, his eyes bulged as he swallowed the thing whole.

The conversation consisted of oohs and aahs about Geelong, and more oohs and aahs about Paul's cricket career. Knowing absolutely nothing about cricket, I did my best to nod and smile at the right times. I wanted to be pleasant. I was on a mission, and, while Paul was jawing a particularly large hunk of sea cucumber, I made my move.

"Paul, you know that our son Marc will be eleven in May." Paul looked my way, and nodded, his powerful jaws at work.

"Hin Chew and I have decided to send Marc to Geelong after he finishes elementary school here."

Paul, excited, forced a swallow to answer with only a slight hesitation, " ... Why, why that's wonderful, we would love to have your boy attend the College." Paul was elated; after all, his reason for coming to Singapore was to recruit students and money.

He turned to Hin Chew, who had the expression of a stunned mullet, something not on the menu, and said, "Hin Chew, you're a fair dinkum old boy, mate, that's a ripper! I knew you would be sending your boys out to Geelong. Let's all drink to that!"

Hin Chew, still stunned, managed a weak smile, as Paul instinctively reached for a pint, but looking down, realized he would have to settle for a dainty cup of Chinese green tea. Good sport that he was, he raised the small teacup for a toast. Being properly polite, Hin Chew and I lifted our teacups and clinked them with Paul. As the toast ended, I caught Hin Chew's intense stare.

Mission accomplished. Hin Chew would lose face if Marc did not go to Geelong. For me, with Hin Chew's anger, there would be a price to pay, but it was worth it.

Marc would be off to Geelong College, for the Geelong term starting February 1994. One of us would be escaping from Hin Chew.

Two to go.

ABOVE The Chungs meet the Sultan of Brunei at his palace in 1983. From left: Peter, Paul, the Sultan, Hassanal Bolkiah, Hin Chew, and S. P. Chung.

BELOW The Chungs in their new Singapore offices in 1983. From left: Hin Chew, Jim, Peter, and Paul, with their father, S. P. Chung, seated.

"When it came my turn to shake the Sultan's hand, I bowed my head slightly as I had observed others doing. The Sultan was very polite and unaffected. As I took my hand away, I heard him say 'siapa ini?' or 'who is this?'"

TOP LEFT The year, 1984, was momentous for us. It began happily, with my grandmother, at her Chinese New Year's party, energetically tossing coins to her guests. My father dutifully held the coin bowl for her.
TOP RIGHT Hin Chew, Marc, and I (pregnant with Warren) with my mother, "Mabel the Knife," who is calm and enjoying the 1984 Chinese New Year's party, after attempting to knife her sister-in-law, Esja.

The year ended with Hin Chews' October 1984 detention in Brunei. In October 1985, after being detained by the Brunei authorities for nearly a year, Hin Chew returned home, but only briefly before flying off to Hong Kong to meet with his father (who was then on the run) and ex-CIA agent Dan Arnold.

Dan Arnold (AP/Wide World Photos)

LEFT The Associated Press caption for this photograph reads:
"*Daniel Arnold, former Central Intelligence Agency station chief in Bangkok, answers questions at a news conference in Bangkok on Thursday, January 25, 1996. Arnold and two other former U.S. government officials came to the defense of a Thai politician who has been denied a visa to the U.S. because he is suspected of drug trafficking.*
(AP Photo/Sakchai Lalit)"

TOP Following the meeting, Hin Chew took off for London, and, in November 1985, had me join him with the children. Here I am in London's Trafalgar Square with Marc.

MIDDLE Alexander Irvine, then the England's top Queen's Counsel, who was hired by Hin Chew. Irvine has now become Lord Chancellor, Lord Alexander Irvine of Lairg, a member of the British Cabinet.

"I may never know how the Chungs, an unknown and shady family from the boondocks of Mumong, ever got to Alexander Irvine."

BOTTOM Richard Field, Alexander Irvine's assistant, later to become a Queen's Counsel in 1987.

ABOVE Our 1986 Chinese New Year visit to Haw Par Villa, where, each year, we are given free admission to visit the monuments of our ancestors, Aw Boon Haw and Aw Boon Par. From left: Me, my parents, my brother Sam, with Warren and Marc in front.

BELOW In December 1986, on a group tour to the United States. From left: Marc (angry), me, Aunt Zena, and by coincidence, my Eurasian cousin, Cindy Berlandier, who was one of the flight attendants, or Singapore Girls, as the airline calls them.

"The 'Singapore Girls' were chosen for their looks and their weight, and Cindy, with her French origins, was a beautiful girl and qualified easily. Zena was especially happy to run into Cindy, one of her favorite relatives on the flight—Zena naturally preferred the Eurasian side of our family."

ABOVE The return of S. P. Chung and our Australian adventure of 1987 provided a welcome change of scene. In Perth, Hin Chew, looking as though he's about to lose it, with his ex-schoolmate, and employee, Andrew Hewitt looking on in fear.

RIGHT I'm having dinner in Perth, with the fashionable and rehabilitated S. P. Chung.

BOTTOM I'm having a pint, sitting on the tailgate of an SUV, Aussie-style.

"S. P. had decided to join the landed gentry, something he knew nothing about, but something he could buy, which was all that counted."

ABOVE Marc surveys his grandfather's Anna Plains cattle station, a one million acre spread.

LEFT Marc with the ranch hands, or "Jackaroos," as they are sometimes called in Australia. These good-looking guys haven't been near a woman for months!

BOTTOM Marc stands in front of granddad's helicopter.

"To put things in perspective ... Anna Plains was larger than the entire state of Rhode Island!"

TOP RIGHT In 1988, Rosita was looking slim and glamorous, here with me in Singapore. She had returned from Melbourne in a final and futile attempt to recapture Peter's heart. RIGHT The same year, Jim and Lynn were living in Australia, where Jim only had eyes for Lynn–or did he? BELOW In January 1989, my mother (togged out as an ersatz high-fashion Mandarin Empress) and I enjoyed a moment with Nicola Bulgari in Singapore. It was one of my rare appearances on the socialite circuit. Bulgari admired my mother's jade, but she hoped there was more to it than that.

ABOVE My father and I dining out in Singapore in 1989.
BOTTOM LEFT Chinese New Year, 1990, my father with Joan—watch out Joan!
BOTTOM RIGHT Chinese New Year, 1990, my grandmother and I at her house, Casa Emma. Growing rebellious, I had entered my blonde period, with one brown eye and one green. It was fun, but only for a very short while.

AN AMERICAN IN SINGAPORE

JOHN AND I met at the American Club. For me, the evening started out innocently enough. It was a public holiday in Singapore, *Hari Raya Haji.*

Hin Chew was out of town as usual, so Joan, an old friend of hers, C. K., and I decided to meet for a drink and then go to hear some jazz at a spot called Saxophone. I was wearing a tight fitting blue elastic dress of sequined material, low cut, but with a navy blazer, for the sake of modesty. Joan was dressed in black stirrup pants, with a matching black top.

We met in the Union Bar of the American Club, a dark wood-paneled place, with pennants of various American baseball and football teams decorating the walls. It was very American, as was the loud crowd around the bar.

I'm not sure who spotted whom first, but I had noticed a person whom, by his behavior, I took to be an American. He was in his late forties, or beyond, and was getting a great deal of attention from an Asian girl, who must have still been in her teens. What a fool to be pursuing a child. Wasn't he a bit old for this nymphet? Were we witnessing a philanderer in action, or what!

My attention switched to Joan, who was sitting between C. K. and me. As Joan and I were talking, really about nothing in particular, I noticed, out of the corner of my eye, that the cradle robber, who's Lolita had vanished, was now talking to C. K. He was getting nearer.

I enjoy being provocative, not in a sexual way, but more as an agitator. I have always loved to be inquisitive, to see what makes a person tick. In the case of the approaching letch, what he deserved was some prodding and needling. I leaned over and threw a remark his way. I have no idea of what I said, but his reaction was as I expected. He immediately left C. K.'s side to move in on me. Typical!

"Sorry, I couldn't hear you from over there." Yeah, sure, I thought, observing him. He was not too tall, and not too good looking, brown hair and eyes, and not too young. I'm John," he said. "Hello, I'm Monicka." It was great protection to have a name that wasn't on any official document, and not in any telephone book.

We shook hands. Having nothing else to say, John decided to talk about tennis, an easy subject, not too taxing—after all, we were in a tennis club.

"You play tennis?" John asked.

I smiled and told him I did.

"I haven't seen you around the club. Do you play here?"

John was doing his best to keep the conversation alive, and I was doing nothing to help. I hoped he noticed the difference between me and his little floozy, the fool. After a long pause, I answered with my most saccharine smile "No, I'm not a member here. Joan is, and we are meeting up here for a quick drink. I play at the Tanglin Club, I suppose you've heard of the Tanglin Club?" I said with a bit of haughtiness as this guy needed to be put in his place.

"Yeah," was his answer.

When you first meet somebody at a bar, the usual conversation revolves around who-are-you, and who-am-I. I am very good at the who-are-you part. My technique in this is always very direct. I love to find out what someone is all about. Part of my interest is sincere; the other part is a game of cat and mouse.

No matter how casual or unimportant the acquaintance, I always make it a point to get the person's name. It makes no difference who they are, doorman, waiter, businessman, or a guy at a bar. I always start by getting their name. That is their handle, which I can use as a leash to drag them around.

Taking control of the conversation, I asked, "Do you work here in Singapore, or just visiting?"

"I work here. I've been here for a couple of years. I work for Citibank," John answered.

"Oh, Citibank, that's very good! Good for you!" I smiled. My touch of mockery seemed to pass unnoticed.

"Are you married," I asked. The directness of John's answer caught me by surprise, as he said simply, "Yes." Well, at least he was honest about that! This, however, condemned even more his shameless behavior with Lolita. Certainly *that* could not be his wife!

I pressed on, choosing my words carefully, "Who was that young girl you were talking to before."

"No one, just a girl here at the club that I know," he answered unblinkingly. I moved in for the kill, "And your wife?" John looked at the ground—I was waiting to see what sort of tale he would concoct. He looked up and said, "Well, recently my wife left me. I'm living on my own with my two teenage sons." The way John said this was not confessional, but in a natural and direct way. Given his prior performance in the bar, with the young girl, his honest answer seemed surprising.

"What are your son's names?"

"Stefano and William."

"Only boys, don't you have any daughters?"

"Yes, I have a daughter by my first wife."

"And your daughter's name is?"

"Domitilla."

"Domitilla? What sort of a name is that?"

"Italian, I was married twice to Italian ladies."

"Ladies of Italian origin, you mean."

"Well, they weren't Americans, if that's what you're getting at. They were both from Italy, from Rome."

I am good at what I do. Even though the only thing John knew about me was my name, Monicka, not really my name at all, I was able to probe into the details of his life.

Cat and mouse.

"Is your father alive?"

"Sure."

"And what does he do?"

John smiled, "He's a movie star."

I laughed, "Come on, you must be kidding, a movie star? So what's his name?"

"Same as mine," John said, in an offhand manner, "John Harding."

"John Harding? I never heard of a movie star named John Harding."

"No one did. He's not really a star. Most of his roles were walk-ons in movies his wife wrote. He was kind of like her Hitchcock."

"Your mother was a movie writer?"

"No, that was my Dad's third wife, my step-mother."

"What was her name? What did she write?"

John looked at me and said, "Her name was Isobel ... Isobel Lennart, and she wrote mainly old Hollywood musicals, way before your time."

"So what Hollywood musicals did she write?"

John took another drink, "Well she wrote Frank Sinatra's first movie, *Anchors Aweigh*, and she wrote Barbara Streisand's first movie, *Funny Girl*; wrote the play too."

"What are you drinking," I asked, pointedly.

"The usual—Diet Coke."

John didn't seem to mind my questions. My first impression was that he thought I was stupid enough to believe his bullshit. My second impression, based on my first impression, was that he was not too bright. Still John was easy to talk to, and in spite of the tall stories, seemed non-threatening, so, on impulse, I decided to invite him to join Joan, C. K., and me for the rest of the evening.

The American club was only our starting point. We had intended to go to Saxophone, but I thought my old hangout, The Club, would be more fun.

John didn't have his car, so we took mine. C. K. and Joan would meet us there.

The Club was a small, intimate nightclub located in the basement of the Marco Polo Hotel. It was a colorful spot, and one of my favorite places. It always had good disco music, and had the reputation of being a place where Singapore ladies from good families, and others, could meet Western men. The place had a truly cosmopolitan atmosphere.

That evening we were in luck, as the disco music was good. I still enjoyed going out, but I was nearing the end of my time for loud music and discos. At John's age, whatever interest he had in the disco scene had to be for an ulterior motive, I was sure. When he gave me a quick kiss on the dance floor, I was doubly sure. Still, I was having a good time, and a break from the grim world of the Chungs was very welcome. After a short time, Joan and C. K. left. John and I stayed on dancing, and engaging in mindless conversation. John was obviously having a very good time. He continued with the occasional kiss, not much of a kiss, a peck, really. A toe in the water? Still, he did not press the issue, and seemed content to have a lighthearted good time on the dance floor.

It was getting late, and it was time to end my evening of wild indiscretion. I had been very stupid. Anyone could have seen me.

What surprised me was that I didn't give a damn!

On our way out, John said he lived nearby and told me it would be easy for him to walk home. "No," I said, "I'll give you a ride."

John's apartment was on Grange Road, the same street as The Club. He lived in an older three-story walk-up building, which contained only six apartments. I pulled into the dark outdoor parking lot. John, gave me a proper thank you, and opened the car door to leave.

Who knows why, I didn't, but I said, "Why don't I come up to see your apartment?"

We walked together to the open entrance to the building, where John motioned me to go first, up the steps to his second-floor apartment.

Westerners always seem to know how to fix their places up, and John's apartment was no exception. The living room had a local flavor as John had decorated it with antiques purchased in Singapore. A huge Bokhara carpet covered most of the living room floor, and a baby grand piano rested in the corner.

I sat on the sofa at the far end of the living room, while John went to the kitchen to prepare a drink. I had asked for scotch. It felt good to be in a world that was completely foreign to the Chungs, and to be with someone who had probably had never heard of the Chungs.

John returned with the scotch, and sat next to me on the sofa.

At five o'clock in the morning, John showed me down the steps from his apartment to my car.

I woke up early, in my own bed, when the alarm went off at 8:30 A.M. What had I done?

Unfortunately, I had been sober enough to remember very well what I had done, every moment of it. It had, I told myself, been a frivolous mistake on my part.

Fortunately, there was not much time for me to dwell on the error of my ways. It was Friday, and I had to be at a rehearsal by 9:30 that morning, for a fashion show that was being given by the ladies of the Tanglin Club. I wasn't in great condition, but true to my Singaporean roots, I made the rehearsal on time.

The only lady I knew at the rehearsal was Mandy Fairfield, a tall British blonde. I had met Mandy when I was sixteen, when my mother bought a Doberman from Mandy's mother. Later, we met again at various modeling jobs, and, over the years, we ran into each other occasionally.

Mandy and I were assigned to walk the catwalk together, as we were the tallest of the group. It was good to see her, as she was another reminder that there was more to life than the Chungs.

I had lunch at the Tanglin Club with the other ladies, after our rehearsal, and felt good that I didn't regret too much what had happened the night before.

John and I had made an appointment to meet later that day, after John got off work, at the bar in the Hotel Meridien.

First, I thought I wouldn't go, then I thought I would, and after changing my mind at least a dozen times, I picked out a short brown skirt, with a Chanel-type brown jacket to wear for our meeting. This relatively conservative getup were meant to establish a serious tone for our meeting, as I intended to set some ground rules with John, who was, by the light of day, an unknown quantity, and complete stranger.

I had already parked my car in the hotel parking lot, and was sitting in the bar and on my first scotch, by the time John arrived.

We sat at a tiny round table that made me aware that my legs were overexposed. What did John think of me? I had to set him straight. My reputation, or what was left of it, was at stake.

I started by telling John that people knew who I was in Singapore. People I didn't know, and possibly some of the people seated around us, might know who I was. Without mentioning names, I told John that I came from a well-known family in Singapore, and had to be very careful.

John did not seem affected or the least impressed by what I said. Not that I was trying to impress him; I just wanted everything to be under control.

Of course, everything was going out of control!

After listening to me patiently, John answered, "Outside of work, I don't think anybody in Singapore knows who in the hell I am."

"But what about your clients at Citibank?" I asked.

"I'm not in that part of the bank. I run their computer center."

I wasn't ready to reveal anything about myself, so I kept the conversation on the subject of John.

He had come to Singapore four years before to work for the Singapore Inland Revenue Department, which is our IRS. Immediately, that put me at ease. No government anywhere is more cautious than Singapore. You have to be better than squeaky clean for them to take you on.

"What did you do for them?" I asked.

"The same thing I do for Citibank; I ran their computer center. It was interesting. Everyone but me was a Singaporean. When I first came, I would get stopped in the hallways all the time with a polite 'May I help you?'"

Being Singaporean, I asked the obvious question, "There must be plenty of Singaporeans qualified for the job, why would they hire *you*?"

"Dunno. I wrote them a letter from Saudi Arabia, where I was working before; told them what I could do; came here for an interview, and got hired."

"Why didn't you stay with Inland Revenue?"

"Well, I came on a two-year contract. They asked me to renew for a year, which I did, and after that I left for Citibank."

"Why would you ever do that?" I asked. Being Singaporean I was astounded that anyone would ever leave such a secure and respected position with the Singapore Government.

"Well, I didn't like attending the Personal Grooming and Effectiveness Workshops for Senior Management."

"Really?" I said, believing him.

"No, just kidding, I left for money."

"Was that the smart thing to do?" I asked being very direct and Chinese.

"Yes and no, actually I was the only Westerner in your civil service, and most likely, the last. An honor, I suppose ... maybe I could have stayed forever, but that's not my style."

"You just hop from job to job?"

"You could say that. I never wanted to be stuck in one place forever.

Maybe I would have done better if I had. Who knows? At least I can kid myself that I'm not a corporate lifer."

John's way was not the Singaporean way. One job, one wife, forever.

"Leaving Inland Revenue also improved my tennis game."

I just stared at him.

He continued, "Most of the people I knew at the American Club were afraid that I had some kind of connection with the IRS or CIA, which limited my choice of tennis partners. When I started with them, back in 1988, I think Inland Revenue was suspicious of me too."

"Why should that be?" I asked.

"Remember, 1987 was the year things were bad with the United States, that was after Singapore virtually banned Time magazine in 1986, limiting their sales to a couple thousand copies a week, and when Singapore expelled the first secretary of US Embassy here for alleged meddling in Singapore politics."

"What did that have to do with you?"

"Nothing except that Singapore was looking for two CIA people who were involved, a 'Mr. X,' and a 'Mr. W.,' and my boss at Inland Revenue asked me if I were one of them, but I think he was joking."

"I'm sure he wasn't joking," I said, "Singaporeans don't joke like that."

John may have not known everything about Singaporeans, but I knew even less about Americans. For me, America was a holiday place, a good place to take your children. There was Disneyland, with its Mickeys and Donalds; Universal Studios, with its theme park rides; Knotts Berry Farm, Las Vegas, Rodeo Drive, a melting pot of races, the Statue of Liberty, the Golden Gate bridge. America's list of tourist attractions was endless.

For Singaporeans, and for me, America was a place you went to either as a tourist or as a student. We Singaporeans admired America's universities, which we knew were ahead of us, at least in technology.

I checked my watch. We had been talking for a long time. "Let's roll," I said.

"Where?"

"Your place."

John's apartment looked every bit as nice the second time around. I felt very relaxed. John went to check on his sons, William and Stefano.

I dawdled in front of the piano, wondering if anyone ever played it. It was an older Yamaha baby grand, the kind Singaporeans have in their homes for show. The lid was raised, and there was some sheet music on the stand. It looked very contrived. The only thing lacking were candelabra, and a shawl draped over the lid. I took a closer look at the sheet music. I had to smile. It was a piece called *Keep A Song In Your Soul*, written by someone named "Fats Waller." Didn't this ruin the whole effect? At least have something classical to show off your piano.

John came back, "William's already asleep. Stefano's out. You'll have to meet them another time."

"Nice piano," I said.

"I bought it here, in Singapore."

"What's this piece of music, on the stand?"

"Oh that, that's a piece by Fats Waller. I thought I might be able to learn it since it looks easy, only one sharp; I never could read music very well."

John laughed when I sat down at the piano. "Sure, give it a try." The first few bars were difficult for me. These were chords I had never seen, but, by the time I made it through the introductory stanza, I got a feel for what was going on, and by the time I got to the words, I finally began to sing, not quite up to speed, but I was making it.

John was stunned. "You play?"

I stopped. "Sure, tenth grade. What grade are you?"

"What do you mean? What grade am I?"

"Don't you have grades? In Singapore, when you take lessons, at the end of each year, you take an official examination. If you pass, you get your certificate and go on to the next grade. We all know what grade we're in."

"Well, it's not quite so organized in the States."

I didn't leave John's apartment until six the next morning.

When I woke up the next day at Mount Rosie, I was back in my world. Reality. I could hear the noise from the television set coming from the boys' room. It was Saturday, and there was no school.

I went downstairs to fix myself a cup of coffee. Then, back in my bedroom, I opened the curtains, and stared out into the jungle across the street. It was a nice view, no buildings, only the remnants of Singapore's tropical rain forest.

I thought about the crazy last two days of my life.

All John knew about me was the name Monicka, and my telephone number, given in a moment of extreme weakness. The less he knew the better. Still I wondered why hadn't he asked anything about me. I didn't take his not asking for discretion, or for politeness. Chinese are not polite in that way. Obviously, John was getting what he wanted, so why shouldn't he leave well enough alone?

Hin Chew was away, so John and I saw each other every day, always winding up at his apartment.

Initially, the only thing I was willing to believe about John was that he had worked at Inland Revenue, and was now at Citibank. Those facts were so easily verified that there was no need to check them out.

Over the course of the next two weeks, I got John to tell me a lot about himself. It was fascinating to listen to him talk. He was far less guarded and free with his conversation, than I was used to, even more so than I, and he came from a world that was, for me, exotic.

According to John, his parents, John and Mary, were much less conventional than their names might imply. Mary was from a small town in Illinois. Her father was a judge, and Mary was the youngest and most spoiled of his three daughters. In the 1930's, she looked exactly like a 1930's movie star should look, and went off to New York to become an actress.

John's father, a handsome cad, was the blackest of black sheep from a fine old Boston family, with fine old Boston money.

John and Mary met on an improbable stage, as acting students at the American Academy of Dramatic Arts in New York City. John and Mary eventually ran off to get married by a justice of the peace. Since then each of them had divorced and remarried several times.

Fortunately for John, at the age of only six months, his parents were not getting along, and he was sent to live with his grandparents in the small Illinois town of Lebanon.

There he lived with his grandfather, Earl Chamberlin, the judge, and his grandmother, Ruth, the Methodist. Nothing strange about these people except perhaps for the fact that Ruth had graduated from college in 1899, with a degree in mathematics, explained, perhaps, by the fact that her father had a reputation about town for being a calculating genius, no matter how drunk he got.

In Singapore, what we call "core values" are very important and, I thought, a good thing. Singapore's official stance is that no nation has better core values than Singapore, and no nation has worse core values than America; you can't call them worse, because there just weren't any.

You can read about it every day in the Singapore newspapers.

Notwithstanding my current situation with John, I was as proud of my core values as was anyone in Singapore.

John knew Singapore and its lingo. When I mentioned "core values," he quickly said, "My core values were instilled in me by my grandparents. I always regarded them as my true parents."

An American with core values?

As a teenager, John wound up living in Malibu with his father, and his father's third wife, Isobel. His solid midwestern core values were about to be tinged with a bit of Hollywood glitz.

Against my better judgment, I was beginning to believe John's stories. He no longer had any reason to feed me a line.

Spending so much time at John's apartment, I got to know his sons very well.

William, the younger boy, was fifteen at the time. He was a very polite boy, with brown hair, and a cherubic face to match his calm disposition. The older boy, Stefano, was something else. He was eighteen, with beautiful wavy long titian-red shoulder-length hair, and a temperament to match.

I learned that Stefano had only recently returned to live at home. He had been away. "At boarding school?" I asked. No, it turned out that he had been living with his girlfriend, a beautiful fourteen-year-old blonde, and her mother, right here in Singapore.

I was shocked on hearing this, and more so by the fact that the mother, a European, was a doctor working at Singapore's National University Hospital. Upon the return of the girlfriend's father from some sort of treatment, Stefano had to return home.

Talk about core values? Shocking!

I am a very serious person. I may not look it, and I may not always act it, but I really am, at least I think I am. Therefore, to a strict Singaporean like me, John's bizarre stories, whether true or false, were a bit off-putting.

I was not a very trusting person when I met John. I had been through so much with the Chungs, that my inborn good will, and hopes for a happy future had dissolved into a cloud of bitterness and mistrust.

My acquired suspicious nature spilled over to my relationship with John, and I frequently thought of breaking off with him. However, I was having a good time with John, and was enjoying a world that was very different from mine.

For a change, there was no hierarchy, no screaming, no tragedies, and, above all, no Hin Chew. I would stick it out with John, for now.

"By the way, John, your daughter, Domitilla ... where is she?"

"Married, lives in London."

"How old is she?"

"About your age."

"What does her husband do?" I asked, as would any money-faced Asian.

"Investments."

"Well, what kind of investments? Does he have a name?" I asked.

"Family investments. His name is Mark Getty."

"You mean one of the real Gettys?"

"I guess; he's the brother of the guy who was kidnapped and got his ear cut off in Italy."

"How did you manage to arrange that marriage for your daughter?" I was impressed.

"It had nothing to do with me. I was only breeding stock. My first wife came from an old Italian noble family, Dukes, two popes, and forty-eight cardinals. She had all the contacts."

Could this be believed?

FAREWELL TO HONG KONG

IN THE FIRST week of July 1992, it was the third anniversary of X-10, or rather its third anniversary under the reign of Hin Chew.

As the wife of the distinguished Chairman of X-10, my presence at the party was suggested, requested, and finally demanded by Hin Chew. I was to be in Hong Kong on July 1.

My boys had their school to contend with, so I couldn't take them, and would be on my own in Hong Kong—unprotected.

When I arrived in Hong Kong, Hin Chew was there to pick me up at Kai-Tak Airport, and was in his lovey-dovey airport-greeting mood. Since the children were not with me, I stayed in the apartment with Hin Chew.

The X-10 party would be held the very evening of my arrival at Gaddi's, a fancy French restaurant with elegant European décor.

Gaddi's had the reputation of being the best restaurant in Hong Kong, and was in the best hotel in Hong Kong, the Peninsula Hotel, the hotel that maintains a signature fleet of green Rolls-Royces, for the convenience of its guests.

For the occasion, I wore a new black spandex dress, which I bought from La Perla boutique in Singapore. Very comfortable. Very revealing.

Hin Chew took one look at my dress, and freaked out. He said, "You look like a slut in that."

"Fuck you, this is the best I've ever looked, and you should be proud. I look great in this dress; it's very elegant and tasteful," I shot back.

Hin Chew had on a brand-new gray suit made of shantung silk, and very shiny. When I saw him in the suit, I said, "You look like some kind of a metallic robot in that. It looks awful," and it did.

The party guests included only the top X-10 guys. Original X-10 founder, George Stevenson, was there with his date, a Chinese lady named May. It was good to see that he was becoming acclimatized to Hong Kong. David Miller, a nondescript Englishman, and X-10's

Managing Director, was present with his Hong Kong Chinese wife. Finally, there was George Seow, who worked in Hong Kong as X-10's accountant. George also had the unused desk next to my unused desk at the Zhongli office in Singapore.

Everyone seemed to enjoy the party. Gaddi's has great food, and there was live music, drinking, and dancing. I had only one dance, with George Stevenson, my second heaviest dancing partner of all time, the first being the Right Honorable Alexander Irvine. What George lacked on the dance floor he made up with personality.

George was the friendly Western face that X-10 showed to America.

He handled the sales with Leviton, and dealt directly with the President of Radio Shack. Hin Chew said that George was great; he would go to America begging for orders, hat in hand. George was OK for an *ang moh*.

Peter Lesser, whom I had met briefly in Singapore, and, with George, the other X-10 founder, was not at the party. Peter ran the X-10 offices in New Jersey, and was not one of Hin Chew's favorite people, as he was "difficult to control, and doesn't listen to my instructions."

After the party, Mr. Lovey-Dovey turned back into the persona of Hin Chew. Leaving Gaddi's, he took his usual position, at least six paces ahead of me. Had I been knocked cold by one of the doors swinging behind him, Hin Chew would not have noticed, at least not for a while.

There is plenty to do in Hong Kong. It's a vibrant city, with not a spot of boredom to be found anywhere. Squalor yes, and plenty of it, but boredom, never. The shopping is great, and everyone agrees that the food is the best in Asia, maybe the best in the world. Everyone loves Hong Kong, but, with Hin Chew around, it was tough duty.

I lasted four days in Hong Kong, which made it look good for Hin Chew, and made it look good for me as well.

This would be my last trip to visit Hin Chew in Hong Kong.

An Evening out With Jim

B ACK IN Singapore, I once again picked up the routine of my new life. I played early morning tennis at 7:30 with the ladies at the Tanglin Club, did my shopping chores, saw that my boys were doing their schoolwork, and continued to see John.

I was surprised how much John knew about Singapore. Much of his knowledge came by way of working for Inland Revenue, and getting to know the people in government. Not many foreigners have that opportunity.

Since John had worked for the government, they knew everything about him, including the fact that he spoke Italian fluently, and could get along in Spanish. This led to his receiving occasional calls from the Singapore police to help in their interrogations, which was interesting work. I was impressed by Singapore's show of faith in John.

"No, it's nothing, the police call me in to translate for them, now and then. Hey, in this country, everyone wants to help the police."

I agreed with that, but asked, "What kind of interrogations do you do for the police?"

"Criminal. Small stuff. Once they called me in the middle of the night, and asked politely if I could come down to the police station to help them talk to a Peruvian man who spoke only Spanish."

I listened.

"When they brought the poor guy from his cell, he was dressed only in a shirt, underpants, and shoes with the shoelaces removed. He couldn't have been more than five-four, and looked completely harmless. He had been arrested in the lobby of the Cockpit Hotel, charged with—get this—the crime of loitering with the *intent* of committing a felony! They had me give him the charges in Spanish," John laughed.

"So?" I said.

"The poor guy said that he was sitting in the lobby, waiting for a friend. He had no weapon, nothing. How could the police know he was dreaming up some felony?"

"So what happened?"

"The guy complained to me in Spanish that he had been beaten up by the police. I translated this, and the police inspector said 'Tell him that if he complains of being beaten, we will have the police doctor check him out to show he is OK, and then we can charge him with a second crime, as it is now, he will have to serve only six months.' I repeated this to the prisoner in Spanish, and told him to shut up, otherwise it would only get worse."

"Then what?" I asked.

"The inspector asked if I had explained the charges. I said yes, and they took him away. Who would ever believe there was such a crime as loitering with the intent of committing a felony? What felony? Are the police mind readers, and the guy, a tourist, gets six months?"

"I'm sure the police knew what they were doing," I replied defensively.

"Yeah, sure they did. He was a bit too dark to be sitting in the lobby. His crime was something like 'driving while black,' back in the States."

I didn't understand, then, what John meant by "driving while black," so I let it drop.

As I said, John knew a lot about Singapore.

I had thought, as do most Asians, that all Americans were one homogeneous product, loud, brash, and not very polite.

On the plus side, Asians admired Americans for their ability to talk. Americans could find something to say about anything, and could do a great job talking about absolutely nothing, while Asians were better at smiling. I thought about Americans as stereotypes, pretty much the same way they do about us.

So, John, as an American, was not what I had expected. True, he was a good talker, but there was more to him than that.

I discovered, also, that we had lot in common. John's family had been better off than the average. His paternal grandfather had been a very successful businessman, same as mine. His father was also a womanizer, and not too responsible, very much like mine.

His mother, a beauty, was apparently very bright, and had written two books about Italy, under her maiden name of Mary Chamberlin, One was entitled *Dear Friends and Darling Romans*, and, the other, *The Palazzo*. Both books were published by Lippincott and had received excellent reviews. However, John's mother did not persist with her literary career, and, was content to live in Rome, watching over John's daughter, Domitilla.

Finally, John had a younger half-brother who had died tragically, drowning in the surf at Malibu, at about the same age as my brother.

John and I enjoyed each other's company. If he got away from the office at a decent hour, we would meet up to go for dinner. It was dangerous for me to be seen alone with him, and, for many of my outings with John, Joan, ever my bridesmaid, would come along as our cover. If we were seen, obviously John was with Joan, after all, I was married, wasn't I?

Naturally, these shenanigans were put on hold (somewhat) with Hin Chew's arrival from Hong Kong, the first week in August.

Out of loneliness, and out of a need for help, unrealized or not, Jim made frequent visits to Singapore from Perth.

On the day of Hin Chew's arrival, August 5, 1992, Jim, too, arrived in Singapore coming from Perth. Joan picked him up at Changi airport to drive him to his hotel. On their way, Joan noticed Jim had bruises on his arms. He caught her glance, and explained that he had been drinking in Perth, only several days before, and had gotten into a fight.

Jim stayed at the Marco Polo Hotel, one short block from S. P.'s apartment. On his visits to Singapore, Jim still visited his parents, but S. P. had little to say to him, and Lillian would limit herself to helping Jim through the teachings of Buddha, giving him knotted strings, and other Buddhist paraphernalia. She would say, "This will be of help. You know, the power of the string is in the knot."

Jim had been paid off, and disinherited, but like the horse that runs back to the burning barn, he kept running back to Ma and Pa.

After I heard about Jim's bruises from Joan, I phoned him at his hotel and did what his parents should have done.

I set up an appointment for Jim with Dr. Vargas, the Chungco company doctor, to look at the bruises and at Jim's general condition.

Jim was in good spirits, when I picked him up at the Marco Polo Hotel to drive him to Dr. Vargas's office.

In the doctor's waiting room, Jim showed me the bruises on his arms, and unbuttoned his shirt, to show me more on his chest. To me they looked more like black and blue welts than bruises. I wondered how you could come out of a fight with such a badly bruised chest. I had never seen such a thing.

Jim's examination by Dr. Vargas was over quickly, and, as Jim emerged from his office, I could hear Dr. Vargas say, "And don't get into any more fights." Apparently, Jim was in good shape. Still, it seemed strange to me that there were so many bruises. Jim must have taken a terrible beating.

To cheer Jim up, I decided that we would take him to one of my favorite restaurants, Nutmeg's, on the second floor of the Hyatt Hotel. We went there often, and were always treated very well.

To make it an even foursome, I had invited Joan to come along. She was free that evening and said she would meet us directly at the restaurant. I was looking forward to a pleasant, quiet evening, and, to keep Hin Chew happy, I put on a conservative red jacket suit.

Jim took a taxi from the Marco Polo Hotel to the Mount Rosie apartment. He was all dressed up for the evening in a dark blue suit. He was more subdued than usual, and it was obvious that he had been drinking, not heavily, but enough to put him in a very relaxed mood.

"Jim, you know you've lost a bit of weight, but you're looking good," I said. Actually, he looked drawn and fragile.

"Yes, it must be the suit," he smiled, holding out his arm for me to feel the material.

"It's my favorite suit—Hugo Boss."

Our pleasantries were interrupted by the arrival of Hin Chew, coming down the stairs from the bedroom. He was wearing a short-sleeved linen shirt with black pants, and took his usual place, sitting on the bottom steps of the stairs to go through the usual ritual of putting on his shoes.

"Hi Jim," Hin Chew said casually.

"Good to be here," answered Jim.

"How are things in Australia?"

"OK."

"How are Andrew Hewitt, and Tim Coakley?"

"All right, I guess."

"All right? I'll bet they're all right; they ran wild with our Australian business."

Jim didn't answer.

I could see where this was leading.

True, Jim had been unable to handle the Australian business, but why beat him up. He had paid some heavy dues, and I thought the ordeal of being detained in Brunei, for a year, had taken its toll on Jim.

Unlike Hin Chew, Jim never complained, or spoke to me of the difficulty of that period. He never revealed anything about what went on in Brunei. Jim's revelations about the CIA, Dan Arnold, and of a possible helicopter escape, from the nearby beach in Brunei, were made only to Lynn, out of necessity, and, in confidence, to me.

Jim may not have been the great businessman, but he did keep the faith with his father. That is more than I can say for Hin Chew, who squirreled away documents on his father, just in case he might need them.

His shoes on, the laces patiently and carefully tied, Hin Chew rose to his feet, and, changing the subject, said, "Jim, how would you like to do the driving to the restaurant. You can try my new car. It's a BMW 730iL, maroon, special plates, cost over S$250,000."

"Sure," Jim answered.

In the car, Hin Chew took his usual position in the front passenger's seat while I sat in the back. Jim, being quite tall, looked impressive in the driver's seat. Next to him, big brother Hin Chew's head barely cleared the back of the seat. From behind, Hin Chew's floppy hair, which he was playing with, gave him the aspect of a young matron. He could have been someone's ugly Aunt.

How many times had I seen Hin Chew dish out crap and abuse from that same passenger's seat. Well, I was about to see it again. This time Jim would be the victim.

Once we were underway, Hin Chew returned to the painful topic of Australia. His attack, which had been oblique, at least by Hin Chew's standards, now became painfully direct.

"You couldn't fucking handle Andrew Hewitt. He was too much for you. You let him get away with everything. Tim Coakley, too."

Jim said nothing.

Hin Chew continued in this vein until we reached the indoor parking lot of the Hyatt Hotel, where Jim steered the car into a parking space.

"Jim, you fucking could have done a better job parking the car. Wait while I get outside and check."

I got out along with Hin Chew. As he had done so many times with me, Hin Chew gestured, waved, and winced, as Jim struggled to park the car, just so, to meet Hin Chew's nit-picking tolerances. I stood some distance away, and watched, which was all I could do.

Finally, Hin Chew was satisfied that Jim had done a passable job. He then signaled Jim to turn off the ignition, and exit into the relative freedom of the hot humid parking lot.

Nutmeg's had a modern, stark, well-lit design, but, nonetheless, the atmosphere was pleasant and intimate. There was a section of tables, in the center of the restaurant, which was bordered on one side by booths, and, on the other, by a wall of full-length windows, giving an unobstructed view of the hotel's wide second-floor interior walkway. I always liked to sit right next to the windowed wall to watch the traffic going in and out of the Hyatt's nightclub, cleverly named "Chinoiserie."

When we entered Nutmeg's, we were seated at a table with a view, right next to the windows.

Hin Chew, always the big spender in restaurants, ordered a bottle of the very best red wine Nutmeg's could muster. Just after the arrival of the prized bottle, and Hin Chew's tasting ritual, Joan entered the restaurant. She was looking very smart, dressed in black pants, topped off with a white silk blouse. Thank God, she was here, now maybe Hin Chew would be gracious enough to ease up on his brother.

No such luck. With the four of us seated, Hin Chew returned to the subject of Jim and Australia. In apparent deference to the others in the restaurant, Hin Chew muttered his invective quietly, under his breath.

"You are no match for Andrew Hewitt. You let him fuck you over, and he took charge of the business that you couldn't handle. You're so fucking drunk all the time. No wonder."

Jim made no comment. He hung his head, staring blankly at the table.

Hin Chew continued. There seemed no end. Finally, I said, "Hin Chew, can you please stop it?"

"Keep your voice down," Hin Chew whispered loudly, lowering his head down nearly to the level of the table, "can't you see? Everyone can hear you."

Joan, always circumspect and diplomatic, said, "Come on everybody, let's be happy and enjoy ourselves."

At that, Hin Chew fell silent. He stared out across the tables. After a brief pause, he looked first at Joan, and then at me, and hissed, "Bitches."

That was it! I screamed at Hin Chew, "Fuck you! How dare you call us bitches!"

Hin Chew glanced quickly around the restaurant, and then glared at me, but there was no stopping me. "You fucking bastard, leave your brother alone. You started when Jim came over to Mount Rosie, and that was two fucking hours ago. Fuck you! I'm outta here." With that, I stood up, and smashed my empty wineglass into the glass-topped table!

The restaurant fell into silence; even Hin Chew was speechless.

Jim began to cry.

They throw you out in the States, when you behave like that. In Singapore, if you are the least bit known, you can get away with such behavior. I walked to the door of the restaurant, with Joan and Jim close behind. Hin Chew immediately paid the bill, and we left—so much for a pleasant evening.

We marched silently to the parking lot, and got into the car. With me at the wheel, Joan, Jim, and I drove Hin Chew home. After dropping Hin Chew off, Joan and I took Jim for a nightcap at the American Club, which was right across the street from the Hyatt, and where Joan had parked her car.

After a brief drink, and a few more tears from Jim, Joan left to drive him back to his hotel. Unrecognizable, at least to Jim, sitting across from us, at the bar was John who had been waiting for me.

The evening wasn't a complete loss, after all.

Escape to Bali

I n September, John had to make a business trip for Citibank to California. Los Angeles was on his itinerary, and he was taking William along for a visit to his grandfather, the "movie star."

As a precautionary measure to save Stefano from the potential wrath of his girlfriend's father, John had already sent him to the States to live with friends. John and William planned to stop off in Bali for a couple of days, on their way to California. John had never been to Bali, and neither had William.

And neither had I.

School vacation was coming up, and I thought, why not join John in Bali? This would be an great opportunity for all of us to spend a couple of days on vacation, all of us being John, William, Marc, Warren, myself, and, of course, Joan.

I had already introduced John to Marc and Warren. It was prearranged, but to avoid shocking the boys, we played it as a chance encounter, done out in the open, on a busy Singapore street. My boys, especially Warren, were very wary of any males in the company, or even near, their mother, which was natural. With John, however, they seemed very much at ease.

Joan, the children and I took a different flight to Bali, than did John and William. We would all meet up and stay at the Grand Hyatt, where we would have yet another chance meeting. "Oh, fancy meeting you here?"

As planned, we bumped into John and William at the hotel. Although they were younger than William, my boys were happy to have someone who could take them to the beach. In the brief course of our stay, our children became good friends. William found good use for Marc and Warren, who served as his lookouts, ready to warn him to bury that cigarette in the sand, if John should appear.

I have traveled a lot, and seen many places, but Bali was all it is cracked up to be, and did not disappoint.

The Grand Hyatt was a beautiful and unusual hotel, with an open lobby and bar, taking advantage of the tropical air and Bali's great weather. The rooms were in low-rise Balinese buildings, set amidst lagoons, with lush gardens trailing down to the beach.

After one short week in Bali, a wonderful week of swimming, exploring, and relaxing, it was time for John and William to continue on to California. My boys, my bridesmaid, and I headed back to our lives in Singapore.

Hin Chew was waiting and ready to rumble.

No, he had not found out about John, but he would find plenty to complain about anyway.

After returning from Bali, at the request of a lady friend, I attended an evangelical dinner. On my return from the dinner, Hin Chew said he was totally against all religious groups. He threatened to throw me out of the house, if I ever had anything to do with "Bible bashers" again.

At that, he took a book from his great dilettante's library of unread books, and threw it in my direction. "Here, this is by Bertrand Russell. Read it! It condemns all forms of religion."

I made no answer, as, in a couple of days, Hin Chew would be off to Hong Kong, and I would be left in peace.

THE JEHOVAH'S WITNESS

AFTER SEVERAL weeks, John and William returned to Singapore from their trip to California.

John's father had told him he lived in a new place, a duplex townhouse, near San Vicente Boulevard, so John naturally assumed that meant West Los Angeles, or Santa Monica. Actually, John's father lived near to *North* San Vicente Boulevard, which was way off in West Hollywood. "Leaving out the 'North' was typical of my father, but we finally found it" John said.

No one ever called John's father Granddad, Gramps, or anything like that. To his family he was "Jack," and to his professional associates, he was known by his stage name, "John." William had been told, at a very young age, to call him "Jack," and never anything like "Granddad."

Now eighty, Jack was still going out every night, with one or more of his ladies, dining at Morton's, Drai's, the Bel-Air Hotel, a habitué of the very best.

When John was very young, his father, Jack, had told him, "Noby, I never really had to work, because my father was very rich. Your father isn't that rich. Sorry, you will have to work." "Noby" was John's nickname, given him at birth, and standing for "Nobody." Not very flattering, or nice, I thought.

John's trip sounded like great fun, and I suffered a tinge of jealousy, as I was not having much of a life in Singapore.

Ever since the death of my brother, I had seen little of my parents. It was no longer the same between us, as I held them at fault. Nevertheless, my father had begun to telephone me quite often to complain about my mother's involvement with her newfound religion, the Jehovah's Witnesses.

Granny had been a Jehovah's Witness, which was my mother's excuse to move her out of the house. Aunt Zena, too, was a Jehovah's

Witness, but a mild one.

My mother was seldom mild about anything, and not only had she been attending Kingdom Hall where the Jehovah's Witnesses congregate, she was out of the house in the afternoons, going from door to door, delivering pamphlets and sermonizing to the uninitiated, witnessing as they call it.

My mother had become a Jehovah's Witness only recently, and my father did not like the change.

He had good reason, as the Jehovah's Witnesses had been banned by Singapore since 1972. It was against the law, and to be a Jehovah's Witness was a crime.

Kingdom Hall was not in some sanitized church-like building, as in other countries, but was a clandestine moving target, its secret cell meetings held in various apartments around town.

I had not spoken to my mother for months, but as a favor to my father, I paid her a visit.

It was in the early evening, and my mother was sitting calmly in her bedroom, dressed in a kimono. She was brushing her Pekinese dog, which sat on her lap.

"Hello, child, I haven't seen you for a while."

"I've been busy, Mummy, school, the children."

My mother looked down at her dog, "And how are the boys?"

"Fine, Mummy. So how have you been doing? Papa says you've become a Jehovah's Witness, like Aunt Zena, and Granny," I said, coming to the point quickly, as is the way in Asia.

My mother looked up from her dog, "Your father is getting all worked up about nothing. It's his age, the old fool."

I persisted, "Yes, but Mummy, is it true? Are you really a JW?"

"It's done so much for me, Chu, I am so busy, so busy, doing good things," she said happily.

Then, in a calm otherworldly voice, my mother, always theatrical, gazed out the window, and said, "Yes, I am now a Jehovah's Witness, and have been out doing Jehovah's work, witnessing—mainly in the afternoons."

I was shocked, even though I had heard it already from my father, "So you are a JW. When did this happen?"

"Oh, child, it doesn't matter. Your Aunt Zena has been very helpful, introducing me to the congregation. Such fine people."

"But what about going out to convert others. Isn't it dangerous and illegal? I mean, where do you go?"

"The congregation assigned me to a territory. I go there with another Sister to do my witnessing. There is no such thing as danger for us."

"So where do you go? Where is your territory?" I asked.

"Selegie Road, we drive down to witness in those very old HDB apartments, you know, the old ones opposite the Selegie Shopping Complex," my mother continued serenely, almost ready to glow.

"Child, I have to tell you, I met the most wonderful Indian couple there, a young couple, just married, and the wife was already pregnant. They let us in."

"Uh huh," I said.

"Lovely couple, Chu, I gave them our Watchtower magazine, told them about Jehovah, his Godship, his purposes, and warned them that the world was coming to an end."

It was upsetting to see my mother like this.

"Mummy, I'm sorry, but how can you go and tell newlyweds, who are living in one of the poorest HDB apartment buildings, in the boondocks, that the world is coming to an end? Poor people."

"But it is, child, except for those who fit in with Jehovah's purpose of a beautified earth. They may live here on earth forever."

Ignoring her robotic remark, I continued, "You tell this young couple the world is coming to an end. You then get into your air-conditioned brand-new car, and drive back to your big house with your two maids, who wait on you, hand and foot."

My mother slowly put her Pekinese down on the floor. She looked up at me, and smiled, "Where we live doesn't matter. Someday we will all live together in harmony, rich and poor, lions and tigers, and people. All together in peace."

This was my mother talking, my glamorous, worldly, cynical, and, yes, sinful mother. I couldn't believe it.

With all her faults, I much preferred my mother to the Virgin Mabel.

MORTGAGE LENDING 101

FOR NEARLY two years, since 1990, Hin Chew had been pestering me to agree to mortgage our Mount Rosie apartment, which we owned, free and clear.

I was opposed to the idea, as aside from our car, which was in my name, my half ownership in the apartment was all that I could really call mine. If anything were to happen to Hin Chew, at least the boys and I would have something.

Hin Chew did not have a will, and carried no insurance of any kind, not even health insurance. I had no stake in any of his businesses, except for Zhongli, which was nothing but a conduit for money.

Our checking account was always overdrawn by at least S$50,000, the overdraft being secured by a deposit in some other account of Hin Chew's, which I knew nothing about.

We had a joint account at Citibank, where Hin Chew kept about US$1 million in cash, but he said that it was being used as collateral for a line of credit for X-10.

One morning, Hin Chew and I were alone in the apartment. He was pleasant and smiling with a big wide happy grin. Something was up.

He had a proposition to make.

Hin Chew explained that he needed to take a loan on the Mount Rosie apartment to provide more funds for X-10. "I have promised George Stevenson that I will come up with the money. X-10 will be a gold mine."

"Apparently not my gold mine," I answered. "The X-10 shares are all in your name alone. Didn't you tell me that Wai Lin has shares in X-10? Why don't you give me some shares of X-10?"

Hin Chew pursed his lips, shook his head, and gave a petulant, "No!"

"Well then, I see no reason for me to agree to mortgage the apartment."

At that, Hin Chew switched from cute-petulant to ugly-angry. He approached me, face-to-face, and shouted, "Fuck you! Either you do it or we divorce!"

To divorce Hin Chew was my dream, but I was still in no position to make my move. I had to get Marc safely away to Australia first, so I agreed to the mortgage.

On November 25, 1992, Hin Chew and I visited his lawyer, Ms. Chia of Drew & Napier, to sign the mortgage papers. I saw this as just another step in Hin Chew's disengaging himself from the children and me.

As we waited in the Drew & Napier conference room for Ms. Chia, I felt I was about to sign my life away. The wait was difficult, so it was a relief when Ms. Chia finally entered, documents in hand. Ms. Chia was pleasant looking, and in her mid-thirties. She was fastidiously neat, and studiously serious, in other words, very Singaporean.

We were very Singaporean, as well, Hin Chew in his shirt and tie, and I in a conservative jacket suit. All very normal, the young couple taking out a mortgage on their home.

Placing the document before us, Ms. Chia asked us to please check it over. Hin Chew picked up the contract, took a quick look, and passed it back to Ms. Chia. He must have seen it already.

"Would you like to take a look?" Ms. Chia asked me.

"No, thank you," I answered.

Ms. Chia looked at me again, and said, with emphasis, "Are you *sure* that you are in agreement with this? In fact, I would like you to initial each of the pages."

As Ms. Chia slowly turned the pages, I applied my initials, reading as we went forward.

I saw that our apartment was appraised at S$840,000 (US$510,000), and the mortgage loan amount was S$580,000 (US$352,000). I continued to read the tedious boilerplate paragraphs, carefully putting my initials on the bottom right-hand corner of each page.

Suddenly, I was struck by my name, written in large capital letters, in the middle of a short paragraph, which read:

A personal guarantee ("the Guarantee") duly executed by LEE MAY CHU ("the Guarantor") on such terms and conditions and for such amounts as may be acceptable to the bank.

I had to read the paragraph over several times for it to sink in, and sink in it did. I was the sole guarantor of the loan. I was stunned!

Hin Chew was the mortgager; he got the money, and I was the guarantor. If he ran off without paying off the mortgage, I alone would be responsible for repaying the half million dollars.

Now I understood why Ms. Chia wanted to assure herself that I knew what I was signing, and have me initial each page. She must have thought I was bonkers. I was guaranteeing loans for the Chungs.

Thoughts ran through my head. Why weren't we both just mortgagors? The apartment should have been the collateral, not me, and, if there were any need for guarantors, why not Hin Chew, or at worst the two of us?

Ms. Chia completed turning the pages for me to sign, and we came to the end of the document. It was time for me to sign on the bottom line. Sitting alone, in front of Ms. Chia, with Hin Chew present, I felt I had no choice but to sign the document.

Hin Chew had also mortgaged our membership in the Tanah Merah Country Club, pulling out over S$100,000. Finally, he asked if I would transfer my title to our car, which was in my name, to Zhongli. The car was my sole remaining asset, and I refused.

It took a week for me to regroup my thoughts and figure out what I should do about the mortgage. I couldn't let Hin Chew put me in such a position. I wasn't going to be the guarantor for his S$580,000 mortgage.

I made up my mind that the mortgage on the Mount Rosie apartment had to be revoked, even at the cost of the threatened divorce.

My decision made, I confronted Hin Chew asking him how he could have put me in such a precarious financial position. I told him I understood what he was doing, by making himself the borrower and me the guarantor.

"What are you planning to do? Drain all our assets out of Singapore, run off to Hong Kong for good, and leave me holding the bag for half a million?"

He answered evasively, "Why would I do that? You don't know anything about business. Don't you trust me?"

"No!" I said.

The fact that Hin Chew didn't lose his temper over my bringing up the mortgage convinced me that he was up to no good. This gave me the courage and impetus to hound him over the matter continuously.

The mortgage became my sole subject of conversation, and finally Hin Chew had it paid off.

Such is the power of a nagging wife!

The Call from Mrs. Waterfall

S INGAPORE IS not a religious country. Lee Kuan Yew, our leader, set the tone by telling all that he was a freethinker, a Confucianist freethinker. (How's that for a contradiction in terms?)

Therefore, Singapore has little to do with Christmas, except, of course, in the commercial sense. Since the overriding goal of Singapore, and of every Singaporean, is to make money, Christmas has become a major event. For Christmas, Singapore prides itself on being the best-decorated city, not just in Asia, but in the entire world.

So it is that a luminous Singapore, even though bathed in the heat and humidity of the primeval rain forest it has displaced, becomes very Christmassy, and enters into a long holiday season, which culminates with the arrival of Chinese New Year, in late January, or early February.

Two days after Christmas Day, 1992, I was jolted out of my holiday mood, when word reached me that Jim had been admitted to the intensive care unit of the Freemantle Hospital, in the Freemantle suburb of Perth.

His condition was serious.

Apparently, alcoholism had brought him to the point where his liver was in danger of collapse.

The news that Jim was in the intensive care unit did not seem to upset Hin Chew, who remarked, "Too bad ... Jim brought this upon himself."

In fairness to Hin Chew, none of us realized the seriousness of Jim's condition at the time. Hin Chew still hated Jim for taking over the Australian business. Of course, this was not Jim's fault, or doing, but sometimes the innocent are the easiest to blame.

Hin Chew had always maintained his very close "relationship" with Andrew Hewitt, always attempting to get Andrew to take up the cause against Jim. For Hin Chew, Jim was to have no friends and no support. For this reason, Hin Chew forbade me to go see him.

Lynn had been notified of Jim's condition, and arrived in Singapore from London on December 29. I didn't see her, as Hin Chew joined her at the airport, and they flew together to Perth where they met with S. P. and Lillian, who had already arrived.

The circumstance of Jim's illness was a lucky break for Hin Chew as it gave him the opportunity to reconcile with his father. Once again, Hin Chew was on S. P.'s team.

The next day, in the afternoon, Wai Lin came by the Mount Rosie apartment with the usual checks for me to sign for Zhongli. She told me there was no further word on Jim, and no calls from Hin Chew in Perth. I took this to be good news; Jim was probably on the mend. On Monday, January 4, the phone rang. It was Hin Chew. "Jim is getting better, so I'll be coming back this Friday."

"Has he really improved?"

"Yes, it might only be hepatitis. Lynn will be flying back to London."

"I'm so happy to hear the good news! Jim gave us all a big scare."

Hin Chew finished by giving me his flight arrival time, so the boys and I could pick him up at the airport.

No sooner had I hung up the phone, than it rang again. This time it was Wai Lin. She had just received an anonymous telephone call at the office. It was a woman's voice; she identified herself as "Mrs. Waterfall."

The caller informed Wai Lin that I was having an affair with someone named John Harding, and that I had traveled to Bali, with my children, to be with him.

Wai Lin told me she was shocked by the call, but before she could think of anything to say, the anonymous caller hung up.

Immediately after the anonymous caller hung up, Wai Lin called me. She had become very agitated and afraid; after all, she was alone in the office.

Of course, I was shocked, as well—shocked, but not completely surprised. I was known in Singapore, and the call might have come from anyone.

I told Wai Lin, "You shouldn't worry. Please calm down it's really nothing." As I spoke to Wai Lin, I was trying to tell myself the same thing—it's really nothing.

Now that John's name had been given to Wai Lin, and was out in the open, I had to do my best to keep the situation from getting out of hand. To calm Wai Lin, I said, "I know John; he's a friend of

Joan's from the American Club. I don't know why anyone should be so mean to make this telephone call."

"You'll see there is nothing to it." I paused. "John is not just a friend of Joan's; he's Swee Cheong's friend, as well. They met because Swee Cheong's son works at Citibank with John."

Swee Cheong's son actually did work at Citibank; I was weaving the fabric of my story as quickly as I could, and doing a darn good job of it, I thought.

Then I had a brainstorm, and said, "In fact, Swee Cheong, John, and I will be picking Hin Chew up at the airport when he arrives from Australia on Friday. We will all be having dinner together." Was I nuts? No, I wasn't. I had to do anything possible to defuse the situation. It was not yet time for my final battle with Hin Chew.

Wai Lin seemed to buy my explanation. She was relieved, and calmed down.

I knew Wai Lin might tell Hin Chew about the Mrs. Waterfall call, and it would have been pointless for me to ask her not to. Now, fortunately, she had my version of the truth.

Since I had played this as a crank call from "Mrs. Waterfall," a grudging bitch, I would have John prove his innocence by coming with me to the airport to pick up Hin Chew on Friday, and explain to him what had happened. I would have Swee Cheong there, as well, to show that he and John were old friends. If it worked, fine, if not, I was ready for anything.

I called John, and told him of the call to Wai Lin from "Mrs. Waterfall," and of my plan that we would pick up Hin Chew at the airport.

"You must be kidding; that's a terrible idea," John said, whispering from his office phone.

"Do you have a better idea?" I asked.

"There are no better ideas, for this situation," John answered. He paused, and then continued, "So I guess we go with it."

"Good," I answered, "I'm glad that you agree with me."

"Just one thing," John continued, "if he loses his temper with me, or with you, don't expect me to sit back and take it."

"It won't come to that, I'm sure," I said, with very little confidence.

"Maybe, maybe not. Let's see what happens."

"It's set then!" I said. "Tomorrow, before we pick up Hin Chew, I want you to have lunch with Wai Lin and me."

"Wai Lin, why?"

"It's a first step. You can convince her that you are no more than a friend, you know, you're so good with people."

"Oh, thanks for the plug. I feel so much better now. All right, I'll have lunch with you, and this Wai Lin person—she should be the easy part."

Wai Lin, John, and I met in the lobby of the Tanglin Club at high noon the next day. John had come straight from the office, as did Wai Lin.

"Wai Lin, I want you to meet my good friend, John Harding. John, this is Wai Lin."

The two shook hands graciously, and we proceeded to the Churchill Room for lunch. Only the best today for Wai Lin.

John did not disappoint. He was his usual calm, self-confident, and charming self. He did such a good job that he and Wai Lin appeared to be having a very good time. He actually appeared to be coming on to Wai Lin, the cheeky devil.

"One down, and one to go," I thought to myself.

The next morning, when I met with my 7:30 A.M. tennis group, I was actually in good spirits. What? Me worry? Not at all!

John decided that we should take his car to the airport, explaining, "That way we will all be on my territory. No way, I'm going to sit in the passenger seat while you drive, and sit in the back seat coming back from the airport. My car, my territory, and under my control."

John had a small four-door Nissan, which would be a tight fit, a very cozy ride back to town for the four of us.

On the way to the airport, Swee Cheong sat in the front next to John. I sat in the back seat. We decided that John would bring up the subject of the telephone call.

"When you tell Hin Chew about the telephone call, what are you going to say?" I asked.

"I don't have the foggiest, I'll wing it, like I did with what's-her-name."

"Wai Lin," I said.

"Yeah, her," muttered John. Then, picking up his voice, he said, "Swee Cheong, how do you feel about all this?"

"Oh, OK, I think, yes, OK," answered Swee Cheong, slowly, with an embarrassed laugh.

At the airport, we waited silently, and watched through the glass wall of windows for Hin Chew to emerge into the baggage claim area.

I asked John again, "Are you sure you haven't a game plan of what you're going to say to Hin Chew?"

John looked at me, and said strongly, "Please trust me on this."

Finally Hin Chew appeared. As usual, he spotted me and gave a cheery wave. This was the happy Hin Chew that I had seen so many times on arrival. Mr. Hyde never appeared until later.

Hin Chew did not seem to spot Swee Cheong or John, even though Swee Cheong gave a weak wave. John, who had never seen Hin Chew, was taking it all in, and broke the tension with a sarcastic, "Well, so this Hin Chew. Pudgy fellow."

Hin Chew, still bouncy, emerged from the baggage claim area. He was carrying a small suitcase.

"Hi, Hin Chew!" I said, as he came forward to give me a hug. "Hin Chew," said Swee Cheong, "it's good to see you."

"Hin Chew, I want you to meet John. John is a friend of ours," I said, putting heavy emphasis on the "ours." Hin Chew appeared a bit mystified. Who was John? They shook hands.

"I'm very sorry to hear about your brother's illness," said John. "Oh, thank you," Hin Chew replied after a brief hesitation. It must have been as though a stranger had approached him on the street to offer condolences.

Hin Chew and I walked out of the airport and into the parking lot, with Swee Cheong and John behind.

The fact that I didn't bring our car confused Hin Chew a bit more. "John drove us. This is his car." Hin Chew and John sat in front, with Swee Cheong and me in the rear.

John broke the ice with, "How was your trip?" Hin Chew answered, in a good mood, "Fine. I'm quite used to these flights. And you? What are you doing here in Singapore?"

John answered, "Citibank, I work for Citibank."

"Oh Citibank, yes, we know Citibank very well." Hin Chew sounded relieved. It was almost as though John were from Hin Chew's hometown. Citibank was familiar ground to the Chungs. How bad could John, a Citibanker, be?

With Citibank as the anchor, the conversation between Hin Chew and John flowed smoothly, and we were at the Equatorial Hotel before we knew it.

"What's here?" asked Hin Chew.

Finally I spoke, "We thought it would be nice to eat here at the Chinese restaurant," I answered.

At dinner, Swee Cheong and I had little to say. It was John's show.

Hin Chew and John were finishing up with a discussion of computers, something John knew a lot about, and something Hin Chew loved, when John broached the subject.

"You know, Hin Chew, the reason I am here ... the reason I came along, was to offer you a kind of apology."

Hin Chew, who had actually been enjoying his conversation with John, reentered his state of confusion and disorientation. "Apology? What apology?"

"Well, I don't know how to say it, Hin Chew, but someone called your office, spoke to your secretary, and said ... said, more or less, that I was, uh, involved with your wife."

Hin Chew looked at John, and said nothing. Swee Cheong and I sat waiting for who knows what; we were ready for anything.

"I don't know for sure," John continued, bravely filling the silence, "but I think the call might have been made by a lady at the American Club who saw me playing tennis with Monicka."

I thought John was clever to use my English name. Nevertheless, Hin Chew's ominous silence continued.

John plowed on, "You see, there is someone who is quite interested in me—a lady, of course ... yes, a lady, and I can't be sure, but I am pretty sure that she must have made the call."

"Are you married?" asked Hin Chew.

"Well, yes, yes I am, but my wife left me some time ago, and I live alone with my two sons here in Singapore. Not much of a life really," John said, playing innocent.

Hin Chew nodded. He appeared to be buying John's story, at least he wasn't losing his temper, and no blows had been struck.

This was progress!

In fact, Hin Chew seemed downright understanding of John's situation. I was worried, however, by a few glances Hin Chew cast my way. Still, John's performance had given me the foolish courage to add my two cents, "Yes, this woman is very interested in John, and probably didn't like my playing tennis with him. We played doubles."

Hin Chew looked at me and, getting Shakespeare almost right, said "Methinks the lady doth protest too much."

Here it comes, I thought.

But no, Hin Chew returned to his dialog with John, about technology. Swee Cheong did nothing but eat. Hin Chew finally got on the subject of X-10, telling John all about the new company. They seemed to be enjoying each other's company, which meant that John was doing his job.

The dinner ended with Hin Chew and John still talking, as Swee Cheong and I followed them out of the restaurant.

The drive home was uneventful. Hin Chew and I got out of the car, said our goodbyes, and climbed the stairs to our apartment. Swee Cheong and John went off into the night.

I was alone with Hin Chew.

Silently we got ready for bed.

Finally, Hin Chew spoke, "Fucking Lynn. She only came to see Jim for the money." With that his head hit the pillow and he was soon fast asleep.

The next day, Lynn, who was on a connecting flight to London, through Singapore, received word at the airport that Jim had suffered a serious relapse.

Lynn took the first flight she could get from Singapore back to Perth.

When I got a chance, I telephoned John, to tell him he had done a magnificent job, the evening before.

"Of course, what did you expect?"

"No you were really good, it almost looked as though Hin Chew liked you."

"Sure kid," John answered, "and did Hin Chew say, 'I think this is the beginning of a beautiful friendship?'"

DEATH BY BOTTLE

REPORTS ON Jim came in daily, and they were not good. Jim had increasing jaundice, and was becoming bloated. The right thing to do was for both of us, Hin Chew and me, to go to Perth. Hin Chew thought otherwise, deciding that neither of us would be going.

I felt strongly about going. Hin Chew was adamant, and so was I. The result was a screaming argument. Times were changing, however, and, in the midst of Hin Chew's ranting about the futility of going, I disengaged from battle, went upstairs, threw my clothes into a suitcase, and called a taxi.

In fifteen minutes, I was on my way to the airport, with no reservation, no ticket, but filled with resolve.

The only seat I could get was on a Singapore Airlines afternoon flight to Perth. It would be leaving shortly.

Singapore Airlines, claimed to be the best airline in the world; certainly it's the most expensive. For some reason, well for a moneymaking reason, Singapore Airline tickets cost twice as much at the airport than if purchased in town, a few short miles away. At the airport, they know you must be desperate, so I paid double.

From the Perth airport, I took a taxi to the Esplanade Hotel, in Freemantle, where S. P., Lillian, and Lynn were staying. None of them were there, even though it was late at night, so I knew they must be with Jim at the Freemantle Hospital.

I left my suitcase at the front desk, and took a taxi for the short ride to the hospital. The reception desk of the hospital gave me directions to Jim's room. A hospital is a forbidding place under the best of conditions, but, late at night, the antiseptic smell and the sound of my heels on the clean linoleum floor made the deserted hallways seem ominous.

They heard me approaching. I saw Lynn and S. P. emerge from a room, which had to be Jim's. They had been expecting me, as Hin Chew had telephoned to say that I was on my way.

After whispered greetings, S. P. said, "You can come in, but we must all be quiet."

Nothing could have prepared me for what I was to see.

Jim was lying on his back in the hospital bed. His head and shoulders were slightly elevated, as the bed had been cranked up a bit. His face looked normal, but I could see that his body, under the covers, was bloated. He had been slim when I last saw him in Singapore. I approached him slowly on tiptoes. There was a pulsating machine on the far side of the bed.

Jim stared blankly at the ceiling. I moved closer, and could see that Jim's skin was a sickly yellow; even the whites of his eyes were yellow. I was now at the side of his bed. Slowly, his gaze turned to me, and he managed to nod. He recognized me. Poor Jim!

I took his hand. He managed a brief smile, and I smiled back, "Hi Jim, I've come to see you." Jim said nothing, but gave me another smile. I could see that he had lost some of his teeth. How could this have ever happened, Jim, I thought. Just a short time ago, we had been together in Singapore, and you were all right. What has happened to you Jim?

Jim turned his head away. I could see he was exhausted, probably sedated. More than anything else, he needed a good night's sleep.

I gently released Jim's hand, and backed away.

Lynn touched me on the shoulder and whispered, "Jim will be going to sleep. We'll come back again in the morning, Chu." Lynn, unable to control herself, began to sob uncontrollably.

With that, we left.

I too was exhausted. It had been a long day.

Back at the hotel, I told S. P. and Lillian how sorry I was to see Jim in this state, but that I was sure he would get better. S. P. thanked me, and headed with Lillian for the elevator to go to their room.

With Lynn, I could be more open. "Lynn," I asked, "what is going on? How is Jim, really?"

"Chu, I don't know. He was getting better, and then he just began to disintegrate. They think he may have some form of hepatitis."

"I know, that's what Hin Chew told me, but what is that machine he is on," I asked.

"Dialysis, kidney dialysis. First, his liver was failing, and now his kidneys. Parents are doing everything they can, to the extent of trying to arrange for a liver transplant."

"Chu, I'm so glad you came. Parents are doing their best, I guess, but it's so horrible to be with them."

"I know, Lynn."

"I'm sure it means a lot to Jim that you came."

"Lynn, that's why I'm here."

The next day, I hoped we would be seeing a better, more alert, Jim. Instead, he was no better than the night before. His eyes were glazed, staring most of the time at the ceiling. His responses, when he did respond, were mumbled and incoherent.

Lynn had decided to leave her children, Tammy and Andrew, behind in England. She did not wish to expose them to their father, not the way he was looking. It would be too traumatizing for them. Tammy was eight years old, and Andrew, only six.

S. P. and Lillian decided, however, that the children should come, and Lynn succumbed to their wishes. Therefore, Tammy and Andrew were flown in to see their father.

Hin Chew decided not to return to Perth. He had more important things to do in Hong Kong. S. P. and Lillian thought that my children should come, as well, and I agreed.

It was important for the boys to see their Uncle Jim, for what could be the last time. I never babied our children, no baby talk, no make believe. To the extent possible, I spoke to the boys as adults. It was my job to prepare them for the real world.

With the excuse to Hin Chew of not wanting to leave the boys alone with Nanette, our new maid, I arranged for them to fly to Perth.

Marc was eleven years old at the time, and Warren nine.

When I brought them in to see Jim, I wasn't sure they would understand. In Marc's case, I was wrong. Upon seeing his Uncle Jim, Marc, my stoic little Marc cried. I was so touched, and so proud of him. Warren, ever the silent one, remained so. I could see, however, by the motion of his expressive eyes, that he understood the seriousness of the situation.

There was much speculation over the reason for Jim's illness. Some form of hepatitis was suspected, but never proven.

Lillian had a diagnosis of her own, which had come from her Buddhist monks. According to them, Jim and Lynn had been warriors in their past lives—warriors who had actually fought against each other. Their conflict, in some battle of the dim past, had not been resolved. There was no clear winner.

Now, this ancient battle was approaching its final resolution, on the bed sheets of the Freemantle Hospital. It looked as though Warrior Lynn would finally emerge victorious. It was the perfect diagnosis for Lillian; Lynn was to blame for Jim's condition.

Lillian and the monks were doing what they could to reverse the tide of battle. Lynn came to me and said, "Mother has been giving Chinese herbs to Jim, and not telling the doctor. This is mixing in with the Western medicine. This could be very bad for him."

"Do you think you should do anything about it?" I asked, trying to be as diplomatic as Lynn.

Lynn pondered for a second, "Well there is not much I can do, is there?"

"I guess not," I replied.

There was one other thing Lynn could not do much about, as Lillian didn't tell her.

While Jim lay helpless, and close to death, Lillian managed to clean out Jim's bank account, which he kept in London for Lynn and the children, just in case. This account held over S$430,000 (US$260,000) of his payoff money from S. P. for agreeing to be disinherited.

S. P. had his own theory about Jim's illness; Jim was attempting to commit suicide by drinking himself to death, because Lynn had left him. "Jim has nothing left to live for thanks to Lynn," was S. P.'s pronouncement. Again, it was all Lynn's fault,

Naturally, S. P. was leaving himself off the hook for what he had done to Jim, his disinheritance, removal from the Chungs' companies, detention in Brunei, and who knows what else. For S. P. it was easy and convenient to point the finger at Lynn.

Of course, the fact that Jim had been living in Perth with his long time mistress, Margaret, was not mentioned by S. P., nor did we know then that, when Lynn and I were out of the hospital, S. P. and

Lillian would sneak Margaret in to visit Jim. Lynn and I had no idea that Margaret was in Perth.

These clandestine visits of Margaret did not remain a secret from Lynn for long. Having been a nurse herself, Lynn quite naturally become friendly with the Australian nurses at the hospital, and finally one of them told Lynn that, when she was not there, a "young lady" was being brought in to visit Jim.

Lynn had known about Margaret for a long time. Margaret had been around for years, long before Lynn had left Jim. It had to be Margaret.

A chance meeting in the hospital elevator between Lynn and Margaret confirmed Lynn's conclusion. This meeting, fortunately, produced no sparks, as Lynn was too savvy and too smart for that. Lynn was one tough customer, which was to stand her in very good stead in her forthcoming battles with the Chungs.

Having put the blame on Lynn for the breakup of her marriage, and for Jim's decision to end his life, S. P. turned his attention to me.

For whatever reason—and S. P. always had a reason—he took the opportunity when they were alone together to speak to Marc. It was time that Marc's kindly old grandpa had a heart to heart with the boy. The facts of life, no; comforting words to bond the family together, no. Just the opposite.

S. P. told Marc that Hin Chew had never wanted to marry me, and that he had forced Hin Chew into the marriage. For a grandfather to tell such a thing to his eleven year old grandson was as evil as it was ludicrous.

Marc kept this conversation to himself for several years, so I was not aware of it at the time, but when he finally told me of the incident, my first reaction was anger. Had Marc told me at the time, I would have torn S. P. apart. I still want to tear him apart.

My second reaction when Marc told me of the conversation was, who was the catch in our marriage? I never cared about it, but in the looks department, many people including Lynn, wondered why I ever married Hin Chew. The same could be said for Hin Chew's personality versus mine. As for brains, well, he was the one into Superman comics. Money? Well, the Lees were not exactly paupers, but I was, so Hin Chew had a clear win in that department.

Still, I had gone into the marriage very much in love, and with no hidden agendas. My parents were sincerely eager to see their daughter married, as are most parents.

If S. P. had forced Hin Chew into the marriage, why did Hin Chew have to wreck my life, and his, by going through with it?

I suppose he could not say no to his father.

And what was S. P.'s motive?

At the time of our marriage, the Chungs wanted to move themselves and their operations to Singapore. Hobnobbing with the Lees and the Aws, attending charity balls, throwing money around, were all means to achieve respectability and make contacts in Singapore.

S. P. needed to establish an alibi for his move to Singapore. What better than an investment of his son in a marriage to a well-known Singaporean family, publicized by a million-dollar wedding of a thousand guests. I was part of the plan for the move to Singapore that would give S. P. a clean start, a safe haven, and a cover.

Unfortunately, S. P. failed to do his homework on my father. If he had, I'm sure he would have selected another victim to become the bride of Hin Chew.

It had been a week since I left Singapore for Perth, although it seemed much longer. Jim's condition continued to deteriorate. He was becoming less responsive, slipping in and out of a coma. There was little I could for Jim, so the boys and I left for Singapore.

Two days later, on January 26, 1993, after he had been in the hospital just one day short of a month, and with Lynn as the only person by his side, Jim died.

He was only thirty-eight.

VULTURES

No sooner had Jim died, than the vultures descended. The fight over his estate was on!

It was not enough that Lillian had cleaned out Jim's London bank account seven days before his death; there was more than that to his estate. Lillian and S. P. had more work to do.

There was another US$2 million in Jim's estate, beyond the US$260,000 already grabbed by Lillian.

Pending their divorce, Lynn had been receiving monthly maintenance payments from Jim, which with his illness, had now stopped. S. P. knew this, and offered to take over the payments to Lynn, but only as a loan.

Before agreeing to take anything from S. P., Lynn was sure that Jim had a will, and that it was probably in his safe deposit box in Perth. She decided to have it opened, as Jim's widow, it was her right to do so.

When S. P. found out that Lynn was going to open Jim's safe deposit box, he summoned her to his room in the Esplanade Hotel. In his polite, ingratiating way, S. P. asked Lynn not to do anything until Hin Chew arrived and could accompany her to open the safe deposit box.

Lynn, with admirable resolve, diplomatically explained to S. P. that she had no reason to wait. As Jim's widow, she had every right to have the safe deposit opened on her own.

Suddenly, S. P. flew into a violent rage over Lynn's "disobedience." We, the daughters-in-law, had heard of S. P.'s legendary temper, and now Lynn would be the first to witness it.

S. P. screamed at Lynn, accusing her of killing Jim by leaving him. He reached a near apoplectic state, his whole body trembling with emotion, and began knocking over chairs and lamps. Lynn fled, not hanging around to see what might happen next.

Back in the relative safety of her own room at the hotel, and seeing Tammy and Andrew asleep, Lynn realized she had to do everything possible for their future. She had come from a modest family, and made no pretense otherwise. She was a coal miner's daughter, and had been making her own living as a nurse when Jim came along.

Tammy and Andrew, however, were the children of a very rich man, and their birthright was different. Unless there was a will stating otherwise, Lynn would do her best to see that her children shared in their father's estate.

The next day, Lynn opened the safe deposit box on her own, but found no will or anything else of value.

Summoning up her courage, Lynn decided to go to Jim's Bull Creek house to see what she could find, hoping it would not be Margaret. On entering, Lynn found Jim's house was strangely sterile with an eerie neatness about it. There were packing boxes on the living room floor, containing household and kitchen items. It couldn't have been that way when Jim left for the hospital. The drawers and cupboards throughout the house had all been emptied. By the looks of the house, someone had been very busy packing up the place, well before Jim's death.

There was no will nor any other papers of consequence at Jim's house.

Someone had been there first.

S. P. and Lillian quickly sent out the word (and tickets) for the family to come to Perth for Jim's funeral.

Peter was the first to take off from Singapore. Now, divorced from Rosita, he would attend the funeral with his newly acquired second wife, Sherry Kukula.

The Chungs had kept me in the dark about Sherry. I had no idea of when or where she and Peter were married. If there had been a ceremony, I was not among those lucky enough to be invited.

However, several years before Peter had met Sherry, I had a nodding acquaintance with her, as we had several friends in common, mainly models.

Sherry was tall and attractive, first appearing on the Singapore modeling scene when she appeared on the cover of Singapore's local fashion magazine, *Her World*. Sherry's name was misleading, as she was Vietnamese, but was said to carry an American passport.

When Peter met Sherry, she had been living in Singapore for some time, and was coming out of a long relationship with the movie tycoon Shaw Vee King, my father's contemporary and longtime friend.

I guess the Chungs didn't tell me about Sherry because they were afraid I already knew too much about her from my father.

The day after Jim's death, Hin Chew returned to Singapore from Hong Kong and informed me that I was forbidden to attend Jim's funeral. Even Hin Chew's youngest brother, Paul, who had given up on studies and work, was flying to Perth for the funeral.

The next day, Hin Chew was off to join the family at the Esplanade Hotel.

The only family member not attending Jim's funeral in Perth would be me.

With everyone gathered together at the Esplanade Hotel, S. P. and Lillian held a family meeting to decide on the funeral arrangements. Lynn was not a part of the decision-making process, as her disobedience to S. P. had isolated her from the Chungs.

Without moral support, S. P. might have a better chance of getting his way with Lynn, a better chance to gain control of Jim's estate.

Fortunately for Lynn, an uninvited and unexpected guest, Rosita, showed up. Lynn might have at least some misery-loves-company support from her ex-sister-in-law.

Rosita's main motive for crashing the funeral had nothing to do with comforting Lynn. Rosita had never given up on Peter, or the Chungs. For Rosita, any contact with Peter, no matter how bad, was better than no contact at all. Besides, Rosita wanted to get a good look at Sherry.

Things were getting interesting. The explosive mix of Rosita and Sherry, Lynn and Margaret was set to ignite.

Chief Buddhist monk, Shi Ming Yi, called "Seefoo," and his assistant, Wee Bang Seng, were there to lead the chanting over Jim's body, and to invoke the powers of Buddhism. In deference to the two good Buddhist monks, I suppose they were above taking anyone's side, even though S. P. had brought them down from Singapore on first class.

Jim's coffin rested in the middle of the room at the funeral parlor.

Flanking either side of Jim's coffin was a row of chairs. Those sitting on one side of the coffin faced their fellow mourners on the other side. Several floral wreaths were scattered about the room.

The coffin was open, with Jim lying in state dressed in his favorite dark blue Hugo Boss suit, the one he had worn at Nutmegs, and his Geelong school tie. Oddly, the coffin was a bit short for Jim, and his feet with their black, newly shined shoes, were sticking out at one end.

Seated on one side of the coffin were the three Chung boys, Hin Chew, Peter, and Paul, along with Sherry, and the monks.

Conspicuously absent were S. P. and Lillian. They did not attend their son's funeral, supposedly for reasons of Chinese tradition.

On the other side of the coffin, opposing the Chung brothers, Lynn sat, between Tammy and Andrew. She wore a dark navy blue suit, and was holding her own, silent and dignified.

Rosita had taken her place on Lynn's side of the room, as did one or two others, mainly Australians. The seating arrangement looked like East versus West.

There was a faint, pungent odor in the room, coming either from the wreaths, or from the monks; this coupled with the Chung brothers facing her from across the coffin, made the atmosphere hostile and threatening for Lynn and her children.

A funeral in England would look and smell very different. Lynn's only comfort was the presence of her children.

A late entrant to the ceremony came in and sat with the Chung brothers. To Lynn's surprise, it was Margaret. Lynn gave no sign of recognition, and continued to maintain her composure.

Except for a few whispers, the room fell silent. During the ritual, Rosita, never one to avoid an inflammatory confrontation, whispered, "Lynn, my God, can you believe that they've let Margaret come … how much more are you going to take from this bitch? After all, you're the wife, not Margaret. How can you let them treat you this way?" Lynn gave a polite nod and continued to look straight ahead.

At the end of the ceremony consisting of chants from the monks, the time came for the final close-up viewing of Jim.

As Margaret approached the coffin from her side, Lynn, on the other side, stood up, and took her children by the hand. Across the divide created by the coffin and Jim, Lynn's eyes met Margaret's.

"How dare you come to my husband's funeral? Haven't you done enough damage to my marriage? Do you remember when I caught you with no clothes on with Jim in our Kensington flat?"

Margaret backed away from the coffin; the three Chung brothers quickly formed a protective circle around her.

As the monks worked their beads, Lynn continued, raising her voice, "You have done nothing but cause us pain. If you were any bloody good, Jim would not have died! You get the hell out of here."

Tammy, only eight at the time, in tears glared at Margaret, and screamed, "You killed my Daddy!"

Margaret had nothing to say. For what seemed an eternity, there was silence. Jim's funeral in Perth had ended.

After the ceremony and the unceremonious incident between his women, Jim was removed from the funeral parlor and taken to be cremated, Hugo Boss, old school tie, and all.

As soon as his ashes were cool, Jim made his final journey, with Lynn bringing his ashes back on the flight to Singapore. On the flight, Lynn, and her children, were accompanied by Lillian's good monks.

The monks sat up front in the first class section; Lynn and her children rode economy.

Hin Chew did not return to Singapore. He stayed back in Perth, lying in wait for Lynn and the children to return.

The final resting place for Jim's ashes would be at the Chow Yin Lodge, a Buddhist temple on Mountbatten Road, in an older part of Singapore, near the seamy red-light district of Geylang, where the going rate for well-used and damaged goods is a dollar a minute. The proximity of Mountbatten Road to Geylang, kept the price of land down, which was good, as Lillian had donated the funds for the temple's creation.

I attended this last remaining act of Jim's existence. Lillian, Lynn and her children were present, along with Peter and Sherry, and members of the Chung entourage. I did not see S. P. there.

The chief monk, Seefoo, dressed in a long white robe, conducted the final ritual. An assistant monk placed the urn containing Jim's ashes carefully on a table in front of Seefoo. The assistant then slowly and solemnly removed the lid from the urn, and laid out a large yellow handkerchief next to it.

With great care, Seefoo slowly removed large pieces of bone from the urn. He did this with a pair of chopsticks. I had not expected to see bones, only ashes. I suppose, for Buddhists, the crematorium flames are turned down to achieve the proper effect.

I had also never seen chopsticks being used in such a way.

Seefoo placed each bone carefully on the large yellow handkerchief. After he had finished with the bones, he put down his chopsticks, and picking the urn up, emptied its remaining contents, mainly ashes, onto the yellow handkerchief.

Dust from the ashes rose to form a thin cloud, which slowly floated about the monk, and reached out to touch each one of us.

Seefoo then tied up the four ends of the handkerchief making it into a yellow sack, which he placed in a second urn, which would remain in the temple.

That more or less did it for Jim.

ANDREW HEWITT, CATTLE RUSTLER?

AFTER THE ceremony at the Buddhist temple in Singapore, Lynn and her children returned to their room at the Boulevard Hotel, where S. P. had made reservations for them. As Lynn unlocked the door to their room at the hotel, the telephone was ringing. It was Agnes calling to say that S. P. had given orders that neither he nor his company would pay for Lynn's stay at the hotel.

Strike while the widow is weak!

Lynn was very short of funds, so she wasted no time in Singapore, returning the next day with her children to Perth to put Jim's estate in order.

Back in Perth, understanding that she had been cut off by S. P., Lynn went to the Esplanade Hotel to make sure that her bill had been paid; fortunately, S. P. had taken care of it.

All the Chungs were gone from the hotel, save one—Hin Chew.

He had been waiting for Lynn to appear. Once again, he was S. P.'s trusted number one son. It was now Hin Chew's privilege and pleasure, as number one son, to wrest control of Jim's estate away from Lynn.

Lynn's meeting in Perth with Hin Chew was one more in a chain of events, which would lead to a lawsuit between her and the Chungs.

In the lawsuit, Lynn, referring to Hin Chew as the "elder brother," gave an account of her conversation with Hin Chew in Perth in her sworn affidavit:

> My husband's elder brother met with me and told me everyone had left but he felt he owed it to my husband to offer me help if I needed it. He told me my parents-in-law were very angry with me and that if I annoyed them any further they would take any money my husband owned away from the Estate. The elder brother told me they had taken legal advice and were within their rights to do so as the monies my husband owned had been gifts from his parents.

Hin Chew did not mention to Lynn that S. P. and Lillian had given up any claim on these gifts in return for Jim's agreeing to give up his Chungco shares, and be disinherited.

Hin Chew also did not bother to tell Lynn that the US$260,000 in Jim's London bank account had been cleaned out by Lillian.

Lynn's affidavit continued:

> My husband's brother also told me that my parents-in-law wished to be sure all my husband's money went to my children and not to me. As such they wanted a trust fund set up with the assets in my husband's Estate in which one of the family would be the trustee and the beneficiaries would be my two children.

Lynn knew the Chungs.

She knew that this deal was no deal at all, not for her, and not for her children. There was no way she would let her life and the lives of her children be controlled by one of the Chungs as trustee of Jim's estate.

Alone and terrified of Hin Chew, Lynn said she would think about it. He had a threatening smirk, but held his temper.

S. P.'s next move would be to play good cop. He and Lillian were at a hotel in Melbourne, and invited Lynn and her children to come there for a visit, all expenses paid.

Lynn took the bait, she had little to lose, and flew with her children to Melbourne, a five-hour flight from Perth.

In Melbourne, S. P. greeted Lynn and the children warmly. No one could be more ingratiating than S. P. He contritely gave Lynn his personal apology for everything that had happened. So humble!

S. P. knew there had been some talk that Lynn would have to pay for the funeral expenses, but told her not to worry, as he would pay all her expenses, and he would also see that Tammy and Andrew would be all right. There were hugs all around.

Good old Ma and Pa Chung!

S. P. was buying time. He knew Lynn, and doubted that she had any intention of being cooperative; something had to be done about her.

S. P.'s next move was ingenious, and would involve, of all things, cattle rustling.

With a brilliant stroke of greed, S. P., through Anna Plains, would sue Hin Chew's good friend, Andrew Hewitt, and his company, Barrington Partners, for damages over the charge of cattle rustling—cattle and horses being stolen from the Anna Plains ranch.

The lawsuit didn't accuse Hewitt of doing the rustling himself, but of his alleged mismanagement of Anna Plains, to the extent that, "cattle and horses were unlawfully removed from the station."

Hewitt was the "principal executive officer," of the Anna Plains operation, while Jim was only a director.

Having been sued by the Chungs, Andrew Hewitt then turned around and sued Jim's estate, claiming that Jim was the true cause for the mismanagement of Anna Plains. If Andrew Hewitt lost to the Chungs, then he would have a case against Jim and could recoup his losses from Jim's estate.

While these convoluted lawsuits were pending, the assets of Jim's estate were frozen by court order. The lawsuit could drag on for years, and except for her house, Lynn was penniless.

Brilliant!

Lynn saw clearly the move S. P. was putting on her. However, Lynn's Australian probate lawyer strangely "misread" the Chungs, writing to Lynn, "The tactic of joining James' estate to the proceedings is one for which Barringtons are responsible and has nothing to do with Yokine."

Yeah, sure, except for the fact that Andrew Hewitt (Barringtons), and Hin Chew, of Yokine (the Anna Plains corporation), had been the best of friends.

In their defense against the Chungs' lawsuit, Hewitt and Barringtons named *both* Jim and Hin Chew as being responsible parties. Why then why did they turn around and sue only Jim, and not Hin Chew?

I guess Lynn's lawyer didn't want to pick up on that.

S. P. and Lillian were doing their best to become the heirs of the son they had so recently disinherited.

Whatever may have been Jim's faults, he did take good care of Lynn and the children financially. After Lynn had left him, Jim had sold his Kensington apartment to buy her a house in Birmingham. Jim put the house in Lynn's name, and it was hers, free and clear.

He had also taken a life insurance policy with Lynn as beneficiary.

At least that would tide her over until the matter of Jim's estate could be resolved.

Curiously, someone had informed the insurance company that Jim's death was by suicide, which happened to be S. P.'s theory. If Jim had died by suicide, the insurance company was off the hook and would not have to pay.

After considerable delay, and hard work, Lynn was able to establish clearly that Jim's death was not by suicide, and she was able to collect on the insurance. This was a lucky break, as aside from Jim's life insurance, Lynn had no money.

The trip had been exhausting for Lynn, Tammy, and Andrew. She and the children had been away from home for weeks, under stressful and often hostile conditions.

With Jim's estate being tied up, by the fallout from the Anna Plains lawsuit, there was nothing more that Lynn could do in Perth, so she returned to England.

There she would find out that Jim's bank account had been cleaned out by Lillian.

Lynn had a long battle ahead of her.

Papa Comes Bearing Gifts

RARELY DID my father call me, much less to ask me out to lunch. But he did. He called in the morning telling me to meet him at noon at the Shashlik Restaurant. He said he had a present for me, and that my mother would not be joining us.

Thanks to my father's early training, I am very quick to get ready, and always punctual. With my father, if you are not on time, you won't find him. "Time and tide wait for no man," was his favorite and oft repeated quote, and when I was in my teens, more than once my father drove off without me.

I admired my father's punctuality. It might have been his only virtue.

The Shashlik Restaurant is an old favorite of the graying generation of Singaporeans. The place is difficult to find, despite being on tourist-trodden Orchard Road. It's on the sixth floor of the run-down Far East Shopping Centre.

You have to know where it is to find it.

Like the shopping center in which it resides, the Shashlik Restaurant had seen better days. Its colors were dark maroon and brown, matching the borscht featured on its menu.

The headwaiter, who had been at the restaurant forever, was dressed in a tuxedo that looked as though it had been around just as long.

Like most unpretentious restaurants, the Shashlik Restaurant was comfortable and relaxing. The fashionable and the upwardly mobile were not among the restaurant's patrons. This was a place for those who arrived some time ago, and for those who might never arrive.

The food was presumed to be Russian.

I wore a brown jacket suit that day, to put on a serious front for my father. I remembered I had worn the same outfit for my second meeting with John, at the Meridien Hotel.

When I entered the restaurant, as I expected, my father was already sitting and waiting. The menu lying on the table told me that he had already ordered, as well.

My father did not stand on ceremony.

As I gave my hello, and took a seat, I noticed a large shopping bag leaning against my father's chair.

"How are you Papa. You're looking good."

My father shook his head, gave a resigned look, and said, "OK, OK, Chu. You?"

"Fine, Papa."

"And where's Hin Chew, still living in Hong Kong, ah?"

"He's in Singapore now."

"I say, terrible how that fellow Jim died. How can you drink yourself to death? I don't know. Papa drink, next day, terrible hangover already, but die? ... Eh, where's your father-in-law, S. P.?"

"He's fine, still traveling a lot," I answered.

"Wah, Chu, that bugger is always traveling; he never work, or what? After Brunei, they still got plenty of money, ah?" said my father.

"Apparently so," I answered, then changing the subject I asked, "And how is Mummy?"

"She's all right, lah," answered my father, turning silent.

I looked around the restaurant. A couple faces looked back at me, making me realize that my father and I must have looked like an aging letch and his mistress.

We ordered and ate in total silence, which was the normal way for us. Had we felt a need to fill the void with polite conversation, which we didn't, we would have found little in common to talk about, anyway. My father couldn't be his raucous self in the lone company of his daughter, at least not without a couple of drinks.

When the waiter began to clear our plates, my father began to talk.

"Ah, you know, your mother is all taken up with this Jehovah's Witness thing, all your Aunt Zena's fault. These JWs, I say man, they are no good for her"

"Papa, she was a Buddhist, and now she's a JW, why do you care about her religion?" Since my father had no real belief in anything other than a good time, why should he bother? To be a JW in Singapore was against the law, but breaking the law was not my father's present worry concerning my mother.

"You know, ah, Chu. You know, Papa is not young. Who knows,

maybe I could get sick, you know, lah?"

Well, I knew, and I didn't know, at least I didn't know where the conversation was going, so I kept quiet and played the respectful daughter.

My father looked pained. He obviously had something to say, but had a hard time getting out. A serious conversation between my father and me was something that had probably never happened. My father never had a problem telling me what I must do or not do, or having a laugh with, or at me, but a serious conversation—never.

"These JWs you know," my father leaned forward, and lowered his voice, "you know, they are against giving blood, ah."

"Yes," I said, although the fact was new to me.

"What if Papa gets sick, and needs blood, and your mother doesn't agree? Then what happens to Papa?" He leaned back, looking for my reaction.

"Well, yes ..." I said, not finishing my sentence.

"Chu, you must help Papa. Papa will give you a legal document giving you power of attorney, if Papa gets sick."

"What about Mummy?"

"She won't know ... unless Papa gets sick and needs blood. I tell you, ah, these JW people, they are terrible buggers."

I felt uncomfortable, why risk problems with my mother? What had my father ever done for me?

My father read my mind. It is an old Chinese trick, easy to perform, as Chinamen expect to get money for whatever they do, and to give money for whatever they get. Maybe not all Chinamen, but enough of them to make it a good rule to follow.

"You do this for Papa, and Papa will put you in his will. You will get half; your mother will get half. Ah?"

Now we were talking! We had finally hit upon a subject that we had in common—money. In Asia, money means more than just money. In Asia, money is the messenger of respect, of caring, even of love. This is something that is not well understood in the West, where money is more or less one-dimensional, and far less important or interesting.

For the first time in my life, my father was treating me like his daughter. It was a deal. I agreed.

The deal made, my father took up the shopping bag that had been leaning against his chair and passed it to me. "Here, this is for you, Chu."

I took the bag. In it was a beautiful Bally brown alligator tote bag, a token that our deal had been sealed. "Papa, thank you so much. It's beautiful."

Next, my father produced a large manila envelope from which he carefully withdrew some papers.

"These are for you, Chu. My lawyer has prepared them. There are two. This first one is the power of attorney, if I fall ill," said my father handing me the first document.

"You read, ah."

The document was a short two-page agreement, entitled "STATUTORY DECLARATION." It began with the usual legal recitations that my mother had "embraced the Buddhist religion" when she married my father, and that they had "been married over thirty years."

Reading on, I had to admire my father, for his willful personality. The lawyer's main contribution to the document was to correct the grammar, as my father's personality came through with each word:

In the last few years I have become increasingly perturbed over the behaviour of my wife, to wit —

(a) A few years ago she became infatuated with the movement of the JEHOVAH'S WITNESSES and her time has been increasingly given to the spreading of this religion.

(b) She has drastically changed her social habits and spends all her time with the members of the JEHOVAH'S WITNESSES.

(c) Despite every effort on my part to cater to her needs and promote a harmonious marriage she does not appreciate my efforts and exhibits no concern for me or for my welfare.

I understand that the JEHOVAH'S WITNESSES' Movement denies the giving of assistance to people who fall ill eg: they do not agree to the giving of blood transfusion or medication.

I fear for my life should I fall ill as I strongly believe that my wife may do NOTHING at all.

I would like it to be made clear that should I fall ill or become incapacitated I want my daughter LEE MAY CHU to take charge and look after all my requirements for my health.

Without comment, I looked up at my father.

"Keep it," he said, "it's your copy."

My father handed me the second document. This specified what, in addition to the alligator tote bag, I would receive for my cooperation.

This document was entitled, "THE LAST WILL AND TESTAMENT OF LEE TENG JIN," was also a simple two-page document, terse and to the point, in my father's style. It named me as the "Sole Executrix and Trustee" of his estate, Call me a philistine, call me mercenary, but I grasped immediately what this could mean to me.

I had no idea of what my father was worth, but the house at 69 Holland Road, one of the largest private residences in Singapore, had to be worth millions. Eventual security would come my way, and even without the Chungs, I would have something to pass on to my children.

True to his word, I read in the document that my father had willed his estate to my mother, and to me, "IN EQUAL SHARES."

If Mummy only knew!

MONA KOH, MAMA-SAN NUMBER 11

IN MARCH 1993, Hin Chew's cousin, Gary Chung, the son of S. P.'s brother Johnny, arrived from Canada. Gary was interested in discussing with Hin Chew the possibility of handling X-10's affairs in Canada.

Whether Gary was family or not, I had no interest in meeting him. The less of the Chung family I saw, the better.

Nevertheless, Hin Chew insisted that we take Gary out, and decided that the Ristorante Bologna at the Marina Mandarin Hotel should be the place. "He's our relative, after all."

"You mean, your relative," I answered.

In the end, I agreed to go on condition that we bring Joan along. Gary turned out to be a bore, as expected. He was married with two children, and lived in Toronto. His every sentence showed his desperation to do business with rich cousin Hin Chew. Fortunately, the dinner broke up early, on Hin Chew's initiative, as he and Gary wanted to go somewhere to "talk business."

That "talk business" somewhere, I found out, was the Lido Palace Nite Club, at the Concorde Hotel. The Lido Palace is a large cabaret-style nightclub, built along the dimensions of a movie theater.

In its large dark cavernous auditorium, instead of rows of seats, were dimly lit tiers of tables. In front, was a large stage where a lone Chinese chanteuse would wail Chinese songs nasally, while hostesses pushed the drinks, with promises to meet their marks after closing time.

Whether or not the meeting would happen depended on the hostess, her mama-san, and the mark's money. The mama-sans patrolled the club, armed with cell phones, to control and manage their hostesses. The Lido was a place mainly for Chinese *ah bengs*, the guys displaying 22-carat gold jewelry, silk suits, and other shows of money.

After the Lido, Hin Chew and Gary visited the Ginga Karaoke KTV Lounge, which was on the same floor as the Lido. At the Ginga, a much smaller place, even more intimate services were available in a mazelike warren of private rooms, each fully equipped with the latest Karaoke equipment, and sofas.

Turn up the music, pull the curtains over the window, and it's just you, the hostess, and the sofa.

Hin Chew was very lazy about leaving things lying around the house, and so I found credit card receipts for the Lido and the Ginga totaling S$990, not including cash "tips," of course.

On one of the receipts was the handwritten note, "Mona Koh, mama-san no. 11—725-3332, 727-3338, 345-3994." Three telephone numbers, no less.

I decided to give mama-san Mona Koh a call. Why not?

A lady answered.

"Hi Mona," I said, "this is Mr. Chung Hin Chew's secretary."

"Yes?" she answered flatly in a tired voice.

"Mr. Chung will be coming down from Hong Kong and would like to have his girl ready. You remember? At the Lido?"

"Lido" seemed to be the convincer. Mona's voice came to life, as she replied, "Of course, yes, yes, of course. When can we expect Mr. Chung?

"In the next couple of days, I'll call you to reconfirm. OK?"

"Oh yes, OK, you have all my numbers?"

"Yes, Mr. Chung gave me your numbers."

Mona and I said our goodbyes, politely.

I stared at the phone.

Up to that point, I never would have suspected Hin Chew of any transgressions, much less cavorting with seamy lounge hostesses. He was not exactly your red-hot lover, at least not to my knowledge. Maybe he wanted to show Cousin Gary what Singapore had to offer. I gave Hin Chew the slight benefit of the doubt, as I found it hard to believe that he was guilty of playing around.

One year later, Mona Koh was shot in the Katong Shopping Centre, in Singapore leaving her paralyzed below the waist.

The gunman was never apprehended.

I don't think Hin Chew was guilty of that one either.

My life was finally coming together the way I had hoped it would. First, there was John. We were not only very compatible and in love, but John was generous to me in every way, and I could rely on him for anything.

Equally important, both Marc and Warren got on famously with John. Did they know what was going on? Of course, they did. Was that traumatic for them? No, it was a relief for them to see me with someone like John. From their father, they felt only fear. The boys were happy when he was away. We all were.

It was time to make my move.

What triggered the moment, I don't know. John was a big factor, Hin Chew's unstable and abusive personality, my boys growing up, Jim's death, Lynn's getting screwed over by the Chungs, my father's will, even mama-san Mona Koh—they all contributed to my decision.

Although Marc was not yet safely in Australia, I made my decision to take the plunge.

Singapore is full of lawyers, most of them very expensive, and many not willing to deal with divorce or family matters, which was unseemly, counterculture, and out of line with the Chinese lifestyle.

As a favor, Swee Cheong made an appointment for me on May 4, 1993, with a lawyer friend of his, Gregory Chong.

The day before my appointment with Mr. Chong, I went to see my parents, and told them of my intention to seek a divorce. At this point, they too realized that my marriage would no longer work out.

My father's concern had nothing to do with shame or embarrassment. He was worried that I would once again become his expense, and that the boys and I might move in with him.

He gave me his approval for the divorce, but with a proviso, "OK, lah, but if you decide to move back home, I will lock the front gate by eight in the evening. You know, you must be home by then. You will also have to pay your way here."

I answered back, "Papa, I plan to stay in my own apartment. I have no need to come home." This conveyed the message my father wanted to hear. I would not be an expense, and his home would not become a battleground, or a boy's dormitory.

I knew nothing about Gregory Chong, but I did know what Singapore

Chinese men thought about divorce. For them, it was out of the question.

Why get a divorce? Mistresses were a way of life for husbands who could afford it. The chances were that Mr. Chong would recite the party line to dissuade me from anything but an accommodating reconciliation with my husband.

Gregory Chong was in his mid-forties. He worked out of a modest office in a modest building. At first thought, that might not be all bad. Chong might be easier to sway than some high-powered lawyer. Chong was a good-looking man, with graying hair, and shook my hand with an air of confidence—so far, so good. As already agreed, I gave Chong a check for S$1,000. The check was from John. I wasn't about to leave a paper trail—not just yet, anyway.

Chong listened patiently, and silently, to my painful story, and having said my piece, it was time to hear what Chong had to say. Chong leaned back in his leather chair, put on a serious face, and wisely advised me to be prudent, patient, and hopeful, and to try to save my marriage.

This was no advice at all! I explained to Chong, as politely as possible, that I had been prudent, patient, and hopeful for thirteen years, "When my mind is made up, it's made up," I said.

Chong leaned forward, and then sat back in his chair again. Finally, he came out with, "Divorce is not easy. There are very few grounds."

"I know the grounds, Mr. Chong, and in my circumstances, the grounds for my divorce should be unreasonable behavior, as defined in the Women's Charter."

Chong nodded. He was surprised that I knew anything about the law. Naturally, I did not tell him that six years prior, I had already seen another lawyer about getting a divorce. Chong's legal lecture preempted, his only out was to say, "Before you initiate any legal action for a divorce, you should notify the other party of your intentions."

"OK. I can buy that. What do we do, send my husband a letter?"

"Yes," said Chong, grudgingly, "we'll send him a letter."

I decided it would be best to send the letter to the office at Zhongli, that way Wai Lin could forward it to Hin Chew in Hong Kong. The letter was simple, it was from Chong to Hin Chew, notifying him of my intention to file for divorce, and asking him not to return to the

Mount Rosie apartment. I asked only for title to the apartment, and child support. That was all I needed and wanted.

After my meeting with Chong, I waited for the storm to arrive. Wai Lin had forwarded Chong's letter to Hong Kong, because exactly one week after my visit to Chong, the telephone rang. It was Hin Chew calling from Hong Kong.

Strangely, Hin Chew was outwardly calm, but I could tell by the tone of his voice, that he was unsettled. He did not express shock or anger. Instead, he was cooperative, and agreed, that when in Singapore, he would not stay at the Mount Rosie apartment.

He admitted his desire to spend more time in Hong Kong, and seemed relieved by the prospect of a divorce.

Were we finally talking?

This might turn out to be easy, I hoped. If we both agreed to a divorce, the matter could be resolved quickly.

It all depended on Hin Chew.

THE RECONCILIATION GAME

THE ROUTINE of Hin Chew's arrival in Singapore suddenly changed, and it seemed strange. There was no picking him up at the airport.

He did not call to announce his arrival, or call to tell where he was staying. He didn't need anything from the apartment, as most of his clothes were in Hong Kong. Somehow, I felt he was in town. Was this the silence before the storm?

On May 25, 1993, Lillian came to see me at my apartment, which meant that we were dealing with a matter of the gravest importance. Only once before had she paid me a visit, and that was to tell me that Hin Chew had been arrested in Brunei. Her visits were a harbinger of bad times.

Lillian entered the apartment, gave me a quick greeting, and made straight for the living room sofa.

She began: "Ah, May Chu, I understand you." That was news to me. This must be the understanding, reasonable Lillian, nothing like the demanding mother-in-law who forced me on my knees to beg her for forgiveness.

"Thank you, Ma," I said, courteously giving her a needed punctuation mark.

"But why must you be like that, ah?"

"Be like what?" I asked.

"You know, you have the children, this apartment. How can you want to cause all this trouble?"

"Trouble, what trouble have I caused? I think it's your son who has caused all the trouble."

"Chu, don't you think I know my son? He has always had a temper. Even I have arguments with him, even his father, Chu."

"You haven't seen the half of it, Ma. The yelling, the screaming, the physical abuse. And not only with me, but with the children, too."

As though not hearing me, Lillian continued, "You must think of the children, of this apartment, of all you have with Hin Chew."

"OK, Ma, so what do you want?"

"Nothing, all I want is for you to reconcile with Hin Chew. You must give your marriage another chance. Hin Chew has been here in Singapore for three days—waiting. Why throw everything away? Why risk your future, and your children?"

I understood a threat when I heard it, and Lillian's words were a threat—a threat to me and to my children. I knew what Lillian was capable of doing, and was not about to become a victim like Lynn.

Obviously, Hin Chew had gone back on his friendly and cooperative attitude he showed when he called me from Hong Kong, and was no longer going to agree to a divorce.

"No divorce, Chu, no good, OK?" asked Lillian, waiting for my reply.

I realized that I had moved too quickly, and could be compromising Marc's chances of going to Geelong, where he could be away from his father's bullying. Only with Marc safely away from his father could I start a divorce.

The reconciliation game was on.

To buy time, I agreed with Lillian for the proposed reconciliation. "Fine, Ma, but Hin Chew cannot continue to behave as before," I said, as though it would make a difference.

Lillian smiled. She had done her job.

Several days later, I had my final appointment with Mr. Chong to tell him that I had opted for reconciliation. Chong smiled, he was smugly satisfied over my retreat. In parting, he threw out a gratuitous piece of legal advice, saying sarcastically, "You know, your husband had every legal right to return to the matrimonial home."

Thanks Chong!

The next day was Saturday, Reconciliation Day One.

Hin Chew showed up at the Mount Rosie apartment in the afternoon. He was outwardly cordial, but was far from being a beaten man. To celebrate our reconciliation, Hin Chew had made reservations for us to have dinner that evening with the children, at the Tanah Merah Country Club.

I invited Swee Cheong to join us, as a buffer, hoping to make the evening as uneventful and forgettable as possible.

After making it through a calm dinner, Hin Chew and I dropped the boys off at the apartment, drove Swee Cheong home, and went for a drink in the lobby of the Shangri-La Hotel. It was all very civilized, so civilized, in fact, that Hin Chew told me he knew about John.

Ignoring Hin Chew's remark about John, I said, "You know, this marriage is dead. You're not happy, and I'm not happy. You've moved to Hong Kong, you have X-10, and we are literally leading separate lives …"

Hin Chew said nothing, so I continued, "All I'm asking is that we divorce amicably. You let me have the deed to the Mount Rosie apartment, and you support the children right through to the end of their college education. That's all I'm asking."

Hin Chew replied, smiling, "Sounds like a good idea. This marriage is over … but how about being man and wife for three more years?"

I was shocked at the proposal. Why three years? Was he bargaining for more time to clear out bank accounts? Three years could only be to Hin Chew's advantage.

Not yet in a position for a confrontation with Hin Chew, I said what he wanted to hear, "OK, it's over, and we lead separate lives."

The next evening, S. P. and Lillian scheduled a grand reconciliation dinner at the usual place, Lei Gardens. It was a grim affair.

It was nearly impossible for John to get away from the office, the next day he was able to meet with Swee Cheong and me for lunch at the Tanglin Club. I explained to John that Hin Chew was opposing a divorce, and needed more time to try to arrive at an amicable solution, especially if I were to get custody of the children.

I told John that we would have to cool it for a while.

The next day I resisted calling John on his cell phone until shortly after midnight. I was happy to hear that he was driving Swee Cheong home. They had just had dinner together. Good! John was lonely too!

"Lunch tomorrow?" I asked. "Sure, let's meet for lunch at the Taipan Restaurant, on Boat Quay. That's a little off the beaten track."

Cooling it hadn't lasted long. John and I had managed to stay away from each other for two whole days.

The old two-story shophouses along Boat Quay, Singapore's original sampan harbor on the Singapore River, had recently been converted into a row of trendy waterside restaurants and nightspots. With its tree-lined walkway along the Singapore River, it was a pleasant place for lunch.

During the lunch, I remember saying, "Why can't I get rid of you?" I was joking and serious at the same time, just as I was happy and worried. The stakes were high, and the outcome was uncertain.

After lunch, I went home to pick up the boys for their tennis lessons at the Tanglin Club. I sat in the stands, watched them practice, took them back home, and made it to the American Club in time for a dinner appointment with Joan.

Naturally, after dinner with Joan, I wound up with John. This time he took me to another "out of the way" place, and one of his favorites, the Ginivy country and western bar.

Ginivy is located off Orchard Road, in one of two connected buildings collectively named Orchard Towers, and known to the locals as "The Twin Towers of Sin," or as "Four Floors of Whores." By day, Orchard Towers is a normal shopping center, and quite innocent, our favorite Denny's Restaurant was located there.

Once darkness falls, however, the girls begin to appear, filtering into the dozen-odd nightspots in Orchard Towers, including Ginivy. Notwithstanding its clean and law-abiding reputation, in Singapore, everything that is forbidden is permitted. It's only a matter of price.

Ginivy was John's favorite place to take visiting Citibankers, and other business types. He had been told, in good humor, by Citibank's accounting department that it was an embarrassment to have Ginivy on his expense account.

Ginivy was dark, but not so dark that you couldn't make out the beauties strung out along the bar, and lining the walls. Most of the girls were from Thailand, "visiting" Singapore on temporary two-week tourist visas.

Two country and western bands supplied continuous non-stop music. The bands were mixed Filipino-Chinese groups, complete with whining steel guitars. They were good.

Line dancers, mainly Chinese and all paying customers, togged out in western garb, looking like so many Howdy Doodies, were gliding about the dance floor, perfectly synchronized and in unison. Asians are very precise, and make super line dancers.

Could this really be where John took Citibank people? As I followed him through the crowd, searching for a table, I was relieved to be conservatively dressed in a skirt and jacket, so I didn't look like a "working girl." Still I was embarrassed to be seen at all in such a place.

My embarrassment turned to shock, when I heard someone say my name, "May Chu!" John heard it too; even he was worried.

I turned to see a good-looking older man, with white hair. It was my father's old friend, Hans Schirmer! I had known "Uncle Hans" since I was a child.

"Uncle Hans!" I said, hugging him, "what ever are you doing here?"

"I own the place, it's mine. See? There's my wife at the cash register." True, there was a middle-aged Chinese lady at the end of the long bar, busy ringing up checks.

A nice little Mom and Pop business! I introduced Hans to John, explaining to John who Hans was, but avoided explaining anything to Hans about John.

Ginivy turned out to be a great place. It was, as John had said, a safe haven for us. Uncle Hans, a German-Chinese Eurasian, was the best of hosts, and Ginivy became a usual haunt for us.

In the meantime, things were finally happening in Joan's life. Joan was a very attractive girl. She was bright, from a good family, spoke beautiful English, had studied in Australia as an occupational therapist, and was working in one of Singapore's major hospitals. In spite of her attractiveness, and pleasant and witty personality, Joan had never met Mister Right, not until now.

Joan telephoned me, very excitedly, "May Chu, I have met this really cute guy and I think he is the one for me."

"Joan," I said, "you're sounding like a teenager."

Undaunted, she continued, "And guess what? He's an American. And guess where we met? ... In the Union Bar at the American Club, where you met John."

"Wow, I'm really happy for you, Joan, but who is he? What's his name? Where does he work? And don't leave out any details," I said, excitedly.

"His name is Chuck Neumann, he's tall, good looking, and very

American. Says he was a quarterback in college, whatever that is."

"And where does he work?"

"He's been here for some time, working for Caterpillar. He's in his forties, and divorced."

Coincidentally, I had read about Chuck some time before in *The Straits Times*. The article concerned an incident that took place in the basement nightclub at Specialists' Centre, right on Orchard Road, a favorite spot for American tourists.

As Chuck remembers it, he was talking to a security guard when someone came up from behind and hit him over the head with a full pitcher of beer. Chuck was hospitalized for three months. He got off lucky, surviving with no apparent damage.

Only a year before, in the parking lot outside the same nightclub, a Eurasian man was beaten to death by the security guards from the nightclub.

Unfortunately for Joan, Caterpillar had its rules, and Chuck's tour of duty in Singapore was ending. By the end of June, Chuck would be gone, transferred back to Peoria, Illinois. Happily, Joan would be following Chuck, but only for a brief visit.

John, too, was heading for the States, nothing permanent for him, but he would be gone on business for the better part of July.

This confluence of events presented me with a golden opportunity to catch up with John in the States, again using Joan as my cover.

I had many reasons to visit the States.

Since John and I would probably wind up there, I needed to find out all I could about the place. I wanted to check the schools, see about getting a divorce there, and get an idea of where we might live.

I told Hin Chew that Joan had asked me to go to Chicago with her. Surprisingly, he thought it was a good idea. Yes, he could take care of the boys; after all, he had our maid, Nanette, to help with them.

Hin Chew was in a good mood over the trip, probably needing the break, as much as I did. Before I left, I made sure that Hin Chew sent off the tuition check to enroll Marc for Geelong's 1994 academic year, which was scheduled to begin in January. This was a major milestone, not only for Marc, but also for me.

To prepare the boys for my absence, I took them to lunch at the

Tanglin Club, and over dessert, I broke the news, "OK, listen up, guys, I have to make a short trip to the States with Aunt Joan, but I promise you, I'll be coming back in just a couple of weeks."

Handing each boy a small piece of paper, with the dates of my departure and arrival, I continued, "When I get to the States, I'll be phoning you both immediately, and I'll be calling every day I can. I'll call in the afternoon, after you get home from school, so make sure you're around, listen for the phone to ring, and tell Nanette to be around, too. Do you understand?"

The boys nodded seriously.

"While I'm gone, stay out of your father's way." Marc and Warren looked a bit worried, but nodded again.

"Don't worry," I said, "one way or another, everything is going to turn out all right for the three of us. I will see to it." I gave each boy a hug.

It was breaking my heart that I couldn't bring them with me, but they had school, and I had my own homework to do in the States.

The boys sat in their chairs looking very sad. I couldn't leave it like this, so I said, "And I promise, that the next time I go to the States, you will both come with me."

That did it. The boys were happy. Immediately, Marc asked, "When will that be?"

"Soon," I answered.

On July 8, 1993, shortly after 6:00 A.M., Joan and I left Singapore for Chicago, on Northwest Airlines.

Things were beginning to look up, but I had to be careful, if I were going to win the reconciliation game.

THE MOVIE STAR

O N FRIDAY evening, the day after my arrival in Chicago, John flew in to join us from California, where he had been doing some incomprehensible something with the IBM Laboratories in San Jose.

John and I would be going back to Los Angeles, but first he decided to show me the little town of Lebanon in southern Illinois, where he had grown up.

We had a quick dinner with Chuck and Joan, then it was early to bed, early to rise, and into a rental car for the drive due south from Chicago to Lebanon, a distance of nearly 300 miles.

The summer's drive through the heartland of America was beautiful.

The air was warm and humid, with the changing scents of crops growing in the beautiful green countryside. I had done a lot of traveling, mostly by air, but driving gives a true sense of distance, and I was amazed at the size of America. Singapore is well under thirty miles at its longest stretch.

After several hours on the main highway, John turned off onto an arrow-straight two-lane road heading due south over gentle hills. In the distance, at the top of a long incline, a silver colored water tower appeared. It had the name "Lebanon" emblazoned on it in large black letters.

As we drove up the incline, there were houses, as the town of Lebanon began to take shape. At the top of the incline, we reached the water tower, which was perched in the midst of a small green park, complete with an octagonal roofed 1890's bandstand.

At the end of the park, John made a right turn, and I found myself on a street that leapt out of the past.

Both sides of the street were lined with shops, housed in ornate Victorian buildings, some with false fronts, others with third-floor mansard roofs. It was a street frozen in time.

"Well, here we are. This is Lebanon," said John. I remained silent, taking it all in. "It's not a very big town, around 3,000 people, I guess," he continued.

After two blocks, the buildings, and storefronts became houses again, mostly large turn-of-the-century houses, all still worthy of being part of a movie set. After several blocks, John made a second right, and we headed up a tree-lined street, flanked by period houses on each side.

Soon, we came to a college, set in a campus of green, shaded by a near forest of trees, offsetting large brick buildings.

"That's McKendree College, founded in 1828. My grandparents met there."

Directly across the street from the college was a two-story brown-shingled house. "That's it. That's the house where I lived, with my grandparents and my mother."

"How old is the house?"

"Don't know, but it was given by the college to my grandfather's uncle when he retired as McKendree's President."

"Not bad. But why would they give him a house?"

"I guess they didn't have pensions in those days. Anyway, he got the house."

"Who lives there now?"

"I have no idea. It's strange. I don't know anyone in this town, only the houses."

As we drove through the town, I couldn't have felt farther away from the Chungs and the troubles in Singapore. Before meeting John, a little over a year before, I could never have dreamt that I would be visiting a small midwestern town with an American.

That evening Lebanon celebrated its annual Fireman's Picnic. The main street was alive with people, and we were, anonymously, a part of it. We wandered about looking at the carnival booths, and had a bite to eat at the local bar. Unless you knew somebody in Lebanon, there was no place to stay. Lebanon's last hostel, the Mermaid Inn, had closed shop shortly after Charles Dickens stayed there in 1842, and was now a small museum.

With the Yellow Pages as our guide, we located a bed and breakfast in Trenton, another small town, only seven miles away. The bed and breakfast was complete with frills and flounces, as expected. After a comfortable night, we had breakfast with the owners, a retired couple, and an American couple, who had also spent the night there.

Our next stop was the St. Louis airport, only forty miles from Lebanon, where we hopped on a flight for Los Angeles where we could see how, and on what basis, the boys and I could live in America.

We checked into the Beverly Crest Hotel, a small hotel conveniently located off Wilshire Boulevard, in Beverly Hills. The hotel's restaurant, the dated, gloomy, Venetian Room was a favorite of his father's.

I had spoken to John's father over the telephone several times from Singapore. It's not an easy task to meet someone via an international telephone call, but John's father made it easy.

The first time I talked to him, wanting to be correct, I asked him how I should address him. As Mr. Harding? As Jack, as his family called him? As John, his professional name? He answered, "Just call me Jack," his family name. From then on, he was "Jack" to me. Once given an instruction, the Singaporean follows it dutifully, blindly.

We spent our first evening in Los Angeles with John's father. He had lived in a steady progression of houses of diminishing size, in keeping with his advancing years, declining resources, and dwindling family.

After selling his place in Malibu, Jack had moved to a very nice, but lesser house in the Hollywood hills above Sunset Boulevard. There, he lived with a succession of lady friends, and provided a home for John's daughter, Domitilla, during her stay in Los Angeles.

This second house had been sold, John told me, not for financial reasons, but as the only way his father could think of to get rid of his then live-in lady companion.

Jack had finally settled into a very nice two-story townhouse, south of Sunset Boulevard, not far from West Hollywood's defining bar, "Rage."

Although Jack's present circumstances were seemingly modest, John told me that his father was suffering no great hardship. He continued with his habits of a lifetime, beginning with two boiled eggs, toast, and coffee for breakfast. After a decent interval, he topped this off with his first drink of the day. Television, making phone calls, and maybe some work on his next play would follow. Sometimes, he would go out for lunch, or for a mid-afternoon ice cream.

Every night, without exception, Jack would go out to dinner, and always with one of his lady friends. Jack's outings were always to the very best, and "in" places, those frequented by movie people. His conversation was mainly about personalities, many long since dead, and his next play—not yet dead.

Jack didn't follow through immediately on his early training as an actor at the American Academy of Dramatic Arts. He chose, instead, to be a playwright.

Unfortunately, none of Jack's plays had been produced. His sole known writing effort was his collaboration, with his wife, Isobel, already extremely successful in her own right, on the screenplay of *The Kissing Bandit*, universally acknowledged to be Frank Sinatra's worst movie, ever—bar none.

With little success as a writer, and in his mid-forties, Jack decided to turn to acting. Although, at that time, everyone called him "Jack," he decided that his original name, "John Harding," was a better name for an actor. With his reel name, John Harding, Jack's career in films started with a very small part in Isobel's movie, *Love Me or Leave Me*. This was followed by a succession of equally small parts in about 30 films, many of them written by Isobel. Finally, in 1965, Jack got a featured role in *This Property is Condemned*, playing a dopey railroad conductor, who loses Natalie Wood to Robert Redford.

In addition to his activity in films, Jack had joined a theater group in Los Angeles, called the Stage Society, which produced plays in a small theater on Melrose Avenue.

As with his film career, Jack was not getting much in the way of parts at the Stage Society. He solved the problem by buying the Stage Society's theater, after which he either played the lead in, or directed, or produced everything put on by the Stage Society.

In all fairness to Jack, although he could afford financially to play the idiot, a role that he appeared to enjoy, he was extremely talented, and had some success with the Stage Society. In 1959, Dyan Cannon, before making it in films, got her start in the lead role in Jack's production of *The Firebrand*. Mala Powers appeared at the Stage Society twice, once in *Night of the Iguana*, as "Hannah Jelkes," with

Jack in the role of the aged "Nonno."

For Jack's performance as "Bill Maitland" in *Inadmissible Evidence*, movie producer Ray Stark sent him a telegram, "THE ADMISSIBLE EVIDENCE IS THAT YOU ARE JUST ONE HELLUVA ACTOR, BEST OF LUCK." Of course, it didn't hurt that Ray Stark had been Isobel's agent.

Therefore, although virtually unknown to the public, Jack was known "in the business," and with all that in mind, I stood with John in the lobby of the Beverly Crest Hotel, waiting to meet Jack.

Finally, the movie star arrived.

For a man of 81, he was in excellent shape. He had driven himself to the hotel, on his own, in his 1967 Mercedes 250SL green convertible, which he had purchased new in Germany. Jack greeted me with a big smile, "You must be May Chu!" Then I got a hug. "Noby, so good to see you!"

Jack was nothing like John. Jack spoke with a cultivated theatrical accent. His mannerisms, while masculine, bordered on the foppish, something from the Noel Coward era. He was dressed simply, in slacks, a sports jacket, and shirt with no tie.

"Dad, why don't we go to Alberto's," said John.

"Where else?" came the answer. Alberto's was Jack's favorite restaurant. He ate there several times a week.

The Mercedes was a bit of a squeeze for three people, so we decided to go in two cars. Jack and I would go in the Mercedes, and John would follow in his rental car.

The ride with Jack was harrowing. Fortunately, Alberto's was not too far away, on Melrose, and we pulled up to the curb safely, with John right behind. Valet parking took care of the cars.

Alberto's was dimly lit, with dark wood paneling, flickering candles, and maroon tablecloths, set off by a piano bar.

A tall, thin, white-haired headwaiter in a tuxedo stepped up quickly to meet us. "John, so good to see you," he said, meaning, of course, John's father. As we were ushered to the table, the pianist stuck up the chords of "The Way We Were."

"Oh, God, they're playing my theme song," said Jack as he slid slowly into the booth.

"Your theme song?" I asked, taking the bait.

Jack arched a jaded eyebrow, "It's from that dreadful movie that Ray Stark made about Isobel and me."

"Yes," John chimed in with an irreverent chuckle, "Robert Redford played Dad, and Barbra Streisand, Isobel. How could Robert Redford ever hope to play Dad?"

Jack made no response, but looked away with a bored-you'd-better-please-me face.

The crowd at Alberto's consisted exclusively of very well turned out senior citizens. Jack was the least formal of the lot, but then, I guess, he rated.

Although we had not ordered, a fifty-something waiter, in a white shirt, with a short red jacket, arrived at the table with a single drink, which he placed in front of Jack. "Good evening, Mr. Harding, your drink."

"Thanks Bob," said the star picking up the small glass and taking a long sip. I looked at my water glass, not knowing quite what to do. Take a drink, as though I too had been served, or just sit and shut up, which is what I did.

The menus arrived and we ordered. The food was steak-house Italian, and quite good. Jack took only a bite or two, and pushed the rest of the food around on his plate. He was an easy conversationalist, smooth and witty, but nothing very deep. He loved to talk about old times. John did a beautiful job of steering the conversation his father's way, with such straight-man lead-ins as, "Remember the time when …?" or "Whatever happened to …?"

"Oh God yes, Nobe, that was so embarrassing." Jack turned my way. "I had just fired our cook, a Filipino, named …"

"Eugene," John filled in.

"Well I had been very upset with MGM because they cut a line out of the Kissing Bandit. In the scene, Frank Sinatra was sneaking into Kathryn Grayson's garden. The maid came running in, and the line I wrote was, 'Your lover is coming over the garden wall.' Well, the studio thought it had a double meaning, and so they cut it out! I had this incredible argument with the producer, Joe Pasternak, and the studio. I had written the line, and was not about to compromise my standards. Can you imagine what happened?"

"No, what happened," I said responding quite professionally to Jack's queue.

"Well, they let me go. They fired me! After that, I thought, why not get unemployment? Well, I went to Santa Monica to see about getting a check, and who was in the line with me, but ..."

"Eugene," interjected John.

"Yes, Eugene, the cook I had fired the week before." And so it went ...

Dinner over, we moved to the piano bar for a final drink. The piano player was quite good, and did a great job of accompanying anyone singing anything in any key. He did so without ever looking at the keys, and while managing a cigarette.

"John, how about 'Makin' Whoopee?'" the piano player said, squinting through his cigarette smoke, and playing a couple of intro chords.

Jack gave a bemused smile, and a nod. It was showtime!

Jack sang in a casual and natural voice. He was every bit as blasé as Dean Martin, and surprisingly good. Jack's performance was rewarded by a smattering of applause, and a standing handshake from the piano player. This drew the curtain for the evening, and, his repertoire exhausted, Jack said, "Time to go."

Outside Alberto's, Jack bade us a quick goodnight as the valet parking attendant eased him into his car.

"Will he be all right?" I asked John, as we drove away from Alberto's. "He's far more aware of what's going on than he lets on. He'll be fine."

"Was it true that 'The Way We Were' was about your father and Isobel?"

"Sure. Of course, in the movie, my father was the successful one, where, in reality, it was the other way around. Dad's career consisted mainly of small walk-ons in Isobel's movies. Luckily, I was in graduate school in Italy during most of Dad's career, and was spared the embarrassment."

John had made an appointment with a lawyer for the next day. It was time to get down to work, and see what my legal status would be in the United States.

The lawyer, Mr. Miller, was a very personable fellow, and had none of the formal or judgmental aura of Singapore's lawyers. Both Miller and I sat on the floor of his office, while we talked. That's Los Angeles for you.

Miller gave me the options. Divorce would not be too difficult in California, or Nevada, but any financial settlement or child support would require personal service to be made on Hin Chew in America. True, Hin Chew made trips to America, but I had no way of knowing when and where he went, so having him served legally would be difficult, if not impossible. That ruled out divorce in America, as I wasn't about to let Hin Chew off the hook financially. I had the children to consider.

The bottom line was that I would have to divorce Hin Chew in Singapore.

For the remainder of our stay in Los Angeles, we enjoyed ourselves. John showed me all of his old haunts; we had lunch with Jack at the Beach Café at Paradise Cove, at the foot of the cliff in Malibu, where Jack and Isobel had lived. We saw quite a bit of Jack, respectfully taking him to his favorite places. He always had a lady with him, usually a charming, tall, flamboyant, and fun brunette, introduced only as "DDT" by Jack.

DDT always showed up in a different costume. At Dan Tana's, she was a matador, and at Morton's, a sailor. Only at the Bel-Air Hotel did she tone it down a bit.

During the day, we toured Rodeo Drive, and shopped at Beverly Center. In Santa Monica, we found an army surplus store, called the Supply Sergeant, something entirely new to me, and which would have been banned in Singapore. I bought some army gear for Marc and Warren. We have no militias in Singapore, but all boys like to play soldier. Throughout the trip, I had been telephoning the boys, and usually all I could get out of them, was, "We're fine, Mom." When, however, I called to tell them about the Supply Sergeant, our conversation lasted a good twenty minutes.

I saw how free and fresh the air and lifestyle was in Los Angeles. For John, it was a trip down memory lane, for me, an introduction to what might become my new home. Time would tell.

It was a great vacation and a break I really needed. After being stuck in my Singapore turret of an apartment for ten years, and after four miserable years in Brunei, I finally felt free. I was sad the vacation had to end, but John had to get back to Citibank, and I to my sons.

John flew straight from Los Angeles to Singapore. I flew back to Chicago to catch my return flight with Joan. The flight from Chicago to Singapore took over twenty hours. Joan and I were exhausted by the time our flight touched down in Singapore, and I was beginning again to feel extremely depressed about my life.

Hin Chew picked us up at the airport, and was quite pleasant, after all, we were still in reconciliation mode. "How was Chicago?" he asked. I know Joan, and I knew that she didn't want to do the talking.

"It's a great place, I love Chicago," I said.

"I guess you both had a good time?" said Hin Chew.

"You bet!" I said. Joan nodded with a barely audible "Uh huh."

Did I feel bad? Did I feel guilty? No. I knew I had done the right thing.

I also knew that I would be seeing a lot more of America.

ON THE RUN

WHEN WE arrived home from Changi airport, after dropping Joan off, the boys were waiting for me. They were overjoyed to see me. They were the only people that I had missed while I was away.

They wanted to know all about my trip. I said I would tell them tomorrow. It was late and we all should get to bed.

"Mom," Marc said, "Dad told us you weren't ever coming back."

"I don't know why he would have said such a thing. I would never leave either one of you. When did your father say that?"

"Many times."

The next day was a Wednesday. I had a bad case of jet lag and slept through the day until I was awakened by a commotion on the landing outside the bedroom door. I looked at the window, and saw that it was getting dark. I glanced at the clock. My God, it was 7:30 in the evening! I quickly put on my bathrobe and went out onto the landing.

Hin Chew was shouting. He was upset because Marc had locked the door to his bedroom.

"Hin Chew," I said, moving to put myself in front of Marc's bedroom door, "Don't you know, Marc always locks his bedroom door in the evening so that he can study in peace, otherwise Warren will go in and disturb him. When he is ready to sleep, he always unlocks the door. You should know this." I heard Marc unlocking his door, and turned to see him standing in the doorway behind me. Fear was written all over Marc's face, and he was near tears.

Hin Chew said nothing, but shoved me aside, and made a threatening move toward Marc. I struggled to keep between them, and yelled, "Be a man, take it out on one someone your own size, and leave my son alone."

Suddenly, Hin Chew turned on me. "You fucking whore, you bitch. Even a whore smiles at you when you fuck her." He slapped me.

Holding my cheek, I whispered loudly, "Please! Everyone can hear you!"

"Good."

"You bastard, if it were not for the kids, I would never have returned home."

Hin Chew yelled, "Kids did you hear that? Your mother said that if not for the two of you, she wouldn't have come home. If I knew that, I would have put a bullet through your heads!"

"Please!" I shouted.

"You three are nothing more than fucking albatrosses around my neck. If I had a fucking gun, I would kill you all!"

Warren came out of his room and ran to me. I quickly pushed the boys into Marc's bedroom and locked the door behind us.

Outside, we could hear Hin Chew banging and kicking all the upstairs room doors, running from one to another yelling at the top of his lungs for all to hear.

It was horrible, and frightened the hell out of us. That night, the boys and I stayed in Marc's room. I decided there and then that the boys, the maid, and I would move out.

This reconciliation was over.

We stayed in the room until after I heard Hin Chew leave the next morning. Before leaving the room, I called our maid, Nanette, to be sure the coast was clear.

The Garden Hotel was not far from our apartment. It is one of Singapore's less fancy, smaller hotels, and caters to Christian tour groups and conferences, which made it a good hideout. We packed our bags and left the apartment.

We were on the run. I was back in this nightmare, and a million miles away from happy times in Los Angeles.

The first evening, Swee Cheong and John joined us at the hotel for dinner. I was shaken. School was still in session, but I was afraid to send the boys out of the hotel. I had brought their schoolbooks along, so they could try to keep up with their studies, and telephoned the school making up a story for their absence.

With Swee Cheong as negotiator, Hin Chew agreed to behave if we returned home. It was also agreed that I would continue to sleep with either Marc or Warren, which I had been doing for a long time, anyway.

After two nights in the hotel, we returned home to the Mount Rosie apartment.

That day, and for the following week, Hin Chew was, once again, on his best behavior. We talked. I told him that he had to be set free since he felt coerced into this marriage, and there was no point in going on with this mental torture for all of us.

I said divorce—he said separation. We were very amicable, and talked like friends.

Hin Chew said he realized that he had wasted ten years of his life with his father. Since he did not sow his wild oats in his twenties, now, in his forties, he was entering a mid-life crisis.

I told him fine, I understood and would give him the license to do whatever he wanted. Again, Hin Chew said that he wanted to spend more time in Hong Kong.

Hin Chew and I also confirmed our agreement that Marc would go off to Geelong College for the term beginning in February, 1994, and that he would handle and guide their education, and would support them, even through graduate school, if they wanted to go that far.

I believed that Hin Chew was sincere at the time, and our only difference was in his wanting a separation, and not a divorce.

On Friday, August 6, 1993, Lynn and her children once again stopped in Singapore on their way from London to Perth, where Lynn was going to check on the status of Jim's estate.

Lynn was finally hearing rumors of S. P.'s lawsuit against Andrew Hewitt and Barringtons, over cattle rustling, and of the possibility of Andrew Hewitt's counter suit against Jim, which would block her access to Jim's estate.

It wasn't a fun trip for Lynn, but for me, it was a wonderful distraction, and a blessing to have Lynn in town. Tammy was then nine years old, and turning into a beautiful girl, and Andrew at seven was full of life and enthusiasm.

Hin Chew and I met Lynn, Andrew, and Tammy at Changi Airport in the evening. S. P. had invited Lynn to stop over in Singapore and made reservations for her to stay at the Boulevard Hotel for several days as his guest.

After the long flight from London, Lynn was exhausted. Her children, Andrew and Tammy, fell asleep in the car, as we drove them to their hotel, where we made sure they were properly checked in, even taking them up to their room.

The next evening, Hin Chew and I picked up Lynn and her children to take them to S. P.'s apartment, after which the family would have the usual ceremonial dinner at Lei Gardens.

The car was crowded, as Marc and Warren were with us. The four children were all very happy to be seeing each other again. Lynn and I rode in silence, wondering what this next encounter with the proud and prideful grandparents would bring.

To Lynn's surprise, and mine, Lillian was a no-show as, according to S. P., she was "off in Malaysia, somewhere."

The dinner, at Lei Gardens, was strained. S. P. was not in a good mood, and ate in stony silence. In deference to custom and our host, we all ate in stony silence, including Marc and Warren, who knew the drill. Even Hin Chew kept his head down, seldom glancing up from his plate. Andrew and Tammy behaved normally, and seemed to be having a good time.

I knew something was wrong, and I knew it had to do with Lynn. She knew it too.

Lei Gardens is in the Boulevard Hotel, so Lynn was only a quick elevator ride away from her room. Saying that her children were tired from the long flight, Lynn excused herself, as soon as the last dish was finished, and left with her children.

Lynn, herself, was upset with S. P., as she then knew of the US$260,000 that Lillian had taken from Jim's London bank account, seven days before his death. Lynn wasn't saying anything about it, but was planning a lawsuit of her own, against Lillian, to recover the funds.

Late the next day, Agnes called Lynn at the Boulevard Hotel. Lynn was a bit surprised to hear from Agnes, as it was Sunday.

In her lawsuit against Lillian, Lynn's affidavit gave an account of Agnes' phone call: "My father-in-law's secretary told me he had given orders for no-one in his employ or in his family to assist me or to have anything to do with me."

Immediately after speaking to Agnes, Lynn called me. She was furious; this was the second time that year that S. P. had cut her off at the Boulevard Hotel.

I answered, "Lynn, you've got to be very careful with the Chungs. You and the children can come stay with me."

"Thanks, Chu, but it's already past checkout time, so we might as well stay here tonight, and come to your place tomorrow. Don't bother to pick us up. We'll take a taxi."

"No, no, I'm perfectly willing."

"No, Chu, it'll be better for us to take a taxi."

The next day was August 9, Singapore's National Day. The entire country was in the grip of celebratory paralysis. Nevertheless, Lynn still managed to get a taxi, and came to our apartment with children and luggage in tow. Ever strong, ever resourceful, Lynn had done the right thing and had left the hotel without paying. "Let S. P. be stuck with the bill," she said on entering our Mount Rosie apartment, and placing her two suitcases by the front door. Marc was out with friends, but Warren was home. Andrew and Tammy stayed with us in the living room.

I was happy to see Lynn. Half an hour into our conversation, Hin Chew, who had not yet left the bedroom, appeared briefly on the landing at the top of the stairs, dressed only in shorts and an undershirt. He looked at us, said nothing, not even a hello for Lynn, and returned to the bedroom, slamming the door shut behind him.

I apologized to Lynn for Hin Chew's not greeting her. She nodded, and we continued our conversation.

Suddenly, we heard Hin Chew shout from the bedroom, "Where the fuck are my bathers? Nanette! Where are the bathers?" Hin Chew appeared briefly on the landing, and then turned and headed for the study, where Warren was playing a solitary game of chess.

Hin Chew swung Warren out onto the landing, by his legs. Warren stood up screaming, as Hin Chew seized him by the throat, shaking him, and yelled, "You fucking bastard, you touched my expensive chess set."

Lynn, her children, Nanette, and I watched in terror from the living room as Hin Chew suddenly released Warren, and ran down the stairs, into the living room, calling us both, "You fucking bitches. You cunts, *chee-bais*!"

He looked at me, and pointing his finger at Lynn, yelled, "She thinks she's so fucking smart. If she doesn't behave, Parents and I will fucking sacrifice her. And, if you don't listen to me, and keep siding for this cunt, I'll have you and the kids out and living in an HDB flat on twenty dollars a day. You're fucking whores and bitches!"

Hin Chew was frothing at the mouth, like a Pit Bull gone mad. Warren quickly ran downstairs. Grabbing my purse and car keys from the side table, I said, "Let's go Lynn." I took Warren by the hand, and signaled Nanette to come with us. Lynn, Tammy, and Andrew, struggling with their suitcases, followed me out the door of the apartment, and into the safety of the outside world. We ran down the stairs, as quickly as we could, terrified!

"I'm going to kill you," we heard Hin Chew shout as we reached the bottom of the stairs. We threw ourselves into the car. Lynn took the front seat next to me, while Nanette and the children piled into the back. I locked the doors, and we sped off.

We were all trembling, and the children were in tears. I felt sorry for Lynn, but knew she understood. She had met Hin Chew in England, long before I ever knew him, and seen him, on his first visit, tell her brother to "fuck off." Lynn had always disliked Hin Chew.

We decided to go to the Tanglin Club. We would be safe in public, and needed a place to calm down. We also needed a place for Lynn to stay, as her flight to Perth was still two days off. A hotel would be too expensive for the six of us, and if I could reach Marc before he went home, it would be seven.

I had never said a word about John to Lynn.

I trusted her, but there was no reason for me to take the risk. At this point, I thought, what the hell, why not call John? It was National Day, he should be off work, and we could stay at his place. I called John on my cell phone. My timing was good. He had just returned from playing tennis at the American Club.

I told him what had happened, and before I could propose anything, John said, "The guy's a nut. There's no way any of you should go back to your apartment. Bring everyone to my place, there's plenty of room."

"Chu, who are you calling on the phone," asked Lynn.

"Lynn, I wanted to tell you this for a while. I have met someone, he's an American who works here in Singapore."

"I don't understand." Lynn said, confused.

Thanks to a couple of gin and tonics, Lynn and I were beginning to relax and recover from the horrendous scene that had taken place earlier. "Lynn, there is a new man in my life," I said, taking another sip from my drink.

"Oh, Chu, you met someone, here, in Singapore? An American bloke, you say? I'm gobsmacked, Chu, when did this all happen?"

Lynn broke out into a wide smile, and we both started laughing, which seemed to be the last thing we should be doing at that moment.

"You cheeky thing, Chu! Who is he? What is he like? You didn't meet him through Pa, or the Chungs, did you?"

"Of course not! His name is John. We met at the American Club," I said.

"Oh, you have to spill the beans now, Chu. This is so romantic! Ooh, what's he like? Tell me!" said Lynn excitedly.

"Well, for starters, he's very American, the confident, silent type, and has a wry sense of humor. I can never tell when he's joking or serious."

"Oh, Chu, I'm so happy for you. You haven't lost your sense of humor, even living with that monster you married ..." Lynn paused. "My God," she continued, "does Hin Chew know?"

"They've met," I said.

"This is so refreshing to hear. Even with Hin Chew's behavior, and with Pa, Ma, and Hin Chew messing about with Jim's estate, we both still have a chance for happiness, don't we, Chu."

"We do," I said.

"So when do I get to meet John?"

"As soon as we finish our drinks, Lynn. We'll be staying with him until you leave for Perth."

Fortunately, I was able to reach Marc at his friend's place, and tell him to come straight to John's apartment. At John's we would all be safe.

Lynn and John were both survivors, and during her stay, got to know each other.

After two nights at John's, Lynn, Tammy, and Andrew left for Perth, Australia.

Neither Lynn nor I knew it at the time, but S. P. was preparing a strict and detailed accounting, down to the penny, for Jim's funeral expenses. On S. P.'s instructions, his accountants came up with a total of S\$34,280.35 spent in Singapore, and AUD\$19,581.90 (Australian Dollars) spent in Freemantle and Perth. The grand total came to the equivalent of US\$34,500. The list included such items as "FLORAL ARRANGEMENT IN MEMORY OF LATE JAMES CHUNG - S\$100," car rental expenses, and other items that Lynn knew nothing about.

Fortunately for Lynn, the monks' first class airfares were on the Chungs. She was also not asked to pay for the "HAPPY BUDDHA – FOOD TAKEAWAY FOR MONKS FUNERAL PARLOR – AUD\$177.00," or for, "TAXI FARE - ELSIE - AUD\$52.40."

S. P. sent the expense list off, not to Lynn, but to her probate lawyer in Perth. It was best to cut off Lynn's funds at the source.

Marc, Warren, and I returned to our old hideout, the Garden Hotel. It was a terrible situation. We were on the run, the children were out of school, and my life was falling apart.

The next day, I made an appointment to see Ann Tan, who was known as the leading feminist lawyer in Singapore, and a major participant in Singapore's private and governmental organizations promoting the rights of women.

I told Ann Tan what had happened, and that the children and I could not go on living this way. We needed to move back into the apartment, and to get on with life and school.

After asking me for a pre-payment of S\$3,000, which I gave her, Ann Tan took immediate action.

There was no time for a court order, so she picked up the telephone, and called Hin Chew introducing herself as my lawyer, explaining to him that the situation was damaging to the children and that, if necessary, she would proceed to obtain a court order for our protection.

After hanging up the phone, Ann Tan said, "Just let me know, and I'll get a restraining order to prevent your husband from entering the apartment."

"Good," I answered. Now, we were talking.

"Yes," continued Ann Tan, "and to proceed further for the court order, I'll need an additional retainer of S$10,000 cash, up front."

"Of course, Ann," I said, "let me get back to you on that." I was in a mild state of shock as there was no way, I could come up with S$10,000.

Fortunately, Hin Chew agreed to move out of the apartment the following day, but only temporarily, so no court order was needed, and no S$10,000 retainer was owing to Ann Tan.

Hin Chew moved out on the agreement that I move back to the apartment with the boys, and that he could return to the apartment once Marc had finished his school year at the end of November.

I agreed, and the next day Hin Chew moved to the Novotel Hotel, not far from the apartment. The boys and I moved back into the Mount Rosie apartment.

We had bought some time.

GEELONG COLLEGE

CHINESE BELIEVE that each of us is born with a certain amount of luck, an exact quantity, something like money in the bank, and like money, it can be used up.

My first lucky break was that Hin Chew had returned to Hong Kong, and X-10. With him away from Singapore, I had a feeling of freedom and optimism.

Marc had already received a United States visa for our trip with Aunt Zena back in 1986, and it would still be good for two more years. For Warren, I still needed a visa, as, after the divorce, we would be moving to America. For that, the American Consulate required an affidavit of financial support, based on Hin Chew's employment.

With Hin Chew away, I asked Wai Lin to prepare the visa forms for Warren, and the affidavit of financial support from Zhongli. Luck was on my side, as Wai Lin failed to check with Hin Chew, who would have blocked it, and Warren got his visa.

Two lucky breaks.

The one remaining obstacle for Marc to go to Geelong College was for him to pass his sixth grade Primary School Leaving Examination, Singapore's dreaded PSLE. If he passed this examination, Marc's education could continue beyond elementary school.

In the draconian Singapore public school system, Chinese is the most important and heavily weighted subject. This was a major disadvantage for Marc, as our native language, and the language spoken at home, was English. At the time, only 23 percent of Singapore families spoke English at home; we were in the minority.

Students who did not succeed in the Singapore school system by the end of the sixth grade, would be streamed to a lower level of courses, and had little chance for a university or even secondary education in Singapore. Many of these children would drop out of school, and end up working at McDonald's, Burger King, or doing doorman duty at your fancy hotel. I did not want Marc or Warren to be one of these unfortunate children.

I arranged for extra tutoring, and made it a point to be with Marc every day to help him with his studies when he came home. The pressure was on.

The hard work paid off, and, at the end of November 1993, Marc passed his exams with top grades. He received an A in every subject, except for Chinese, where his grade was a D. This was a giant step forward.

The grades were good enough for Geelong College, but the D in Chinese would cause Marc to be streamed to second-rate schools in Singapore, with no hope of being accepted to Singapore's university.

So, why didn't I send Marc to one of Singapore's private English-speaking schools, like the American School? Simple, as a Singaporean, he was bared from attending any private schools located in Singapore.

Our great leader, Lee Kuan Yew had figured out how to have a slavish docile population, saying, "If we had an English-educated middle class to begin with in 1960—querulous, arguing, writing letters to the press, nit-picking, chattering away—we would have failed."

Being only human, I telephoned Hin Chew, the naysayer, to give what was, for him, the bad news of his son's success.

Also irksome to Hin Chew was the fact that he would have to put up a National Service bond with the Singapore Government to insure Marc's return to Singapore at age 18 for Singapore's mandatory 2 ½ years of military service.

This bond, which is required for every male child from the time he is 16 ½, is expensive. It is a minimum of S$75,000, or half the parents' combined annual income, whichever is higher. For Marc the bond came to S$98,000 (US$61,000).

Nanette had come to the end of her two-year contract with us, and decided to return to her husband, a farmer, in the Philippines. For Nanette, in addition to her salary, I had to pay a monthly levy of S$300 to the Singapore Government for the privilege of hiring her, plus I had to take out a S$5,000 bond to insure that she left the country at the end of her contract.

I was sorry to lose Nanette, but I could do without a maid, and needed my organization to be lean, and my budget low. The pieces were falling into place. Warren had his visa, Hin Chew was away, and Marc was now in a position to go to Geelong.

Hin Chew did not want Marc to depart for Geelong until the last possible minute, still two months off, at the beginning of February 1994. It was the now end of November 1993 and Hin Chew could show up at the apartment at any time, arriving unannounced, as usual. I no longer trusted Hin Chew; to me his words meant nothing. I couldn't risk being stopped by Hin Chew. I had made up my mind, and said, "Pack," and the boys and I were off to Australia.

Before leaving, I typed a precautionary letter to Hin Chew, telling him we had gone off to Geelong. I left the letter in the living room, where he would find it.

I felt, then, that what I was doing was, at the same time, both total madness and the only sane course of action. I had defied Hin Chew by leaving without his permission, or knowledge. I had struck the first blow in the battle to get away from Hin Chew and his family. I knew he would retaliate.

My only ally was John. I believe that destiny brought us together, and that destiny would keep us together. John had been through a tough divorce before, and it had cost him a successful computer company that he had worked years to build.

For me, this was a first time, not only for a divorce, which would surely happen, but also to break most of the rules that I had lived under all my life.

Being Singaporean, and a Slave of Duty, my indoctrination, plus a good dose of fear, compelled me to leave a second letter for Hin Chew giving mundane and useful information regarding the new part-time maid, the keys, the telephone number of the grocery store, what I had to do in Geelong to get Marc set up in school.

At the end of the letter, I wrote, almost as a postscript, that before returning to Singapore, I would be taking the boys to Disneyland, as they needed a break.

Yes, I had decided to take a brief "detour" through Los Angeles on my way back to Singapore from Australia. The boys were on school vacation; it would give me the opportunity to have a second look at

America, and an excuse for having obtained a visa for Warren.

Yes, John would be meeting us there.

On arrival at the Melbourne airport, I rented a car for the drive to the town of Geelong, some seventy miles west of Melbourne.

Geelong is a rural seaside community. It is distinguished mainly by the presence of a Ford Motor Company plant, which provided a dwindling source of employment for its geriatric employees. Geelong had been largely untouched by the progress of the last thirty years, or, in other words, it was only about ten years behind gloomy old Melbourne. This was good, since there would be less temptation for my pubescent Marc.

We checked into the Ambassador Hotel, the very best of the very few hotels in Geelong. On entering, we were greeted by a modest lobby, a large dark pit of a restaurant, an intimate bar, and the front desk. A relaxed and pleasant man at the desk checked us in with the very minimum of formality, handed me the keys, and pointed to the elevator.

We got out of the elevator on the third floor, and walked down a curved hallway decorated with faded floral wallpaper to our room, where we found everything in perfect order—two beds, a cot for Warren, and a television set.

I was exhausted. Until I hit Geelong, I had been running on nervous energy.

We had fled from Singapore, and we had made it. Still, I could not relax completely, as Hin Chew might come bounding through the door of our room at any time. Not likely, but possible. Emotionally, I was fighting against the conditioned reflexes of fifteen years of fear.

We would be in Geelong for one very busy week getting Marc ready for school. Geelong College had sent me a complete list of what Marc needed, including school uniforms, bed sheets, blankets, towels, and pillows, right down to the toothbrush. It was as though Marc were entering Geelong College naked, monastically leaving all worldly belongings behind, which was, in fact, exactly what Marc was doing.

After a good night's sleep, I took Marc and Warren for their first visit to Geelong College. The College was as I remembered during my honeymoon visit, which now seemed eons away. It presented itself as a group of austere red brick buildings spaced at varying intervals in a field of green. Founded in 1861, Geelong College was based on "Christian principals." Attendance at Chapel was mandatory. After it's first 100 plus years as a "boys only" school, Geelong College took "the historic step" of turning co-educational.

Geelong College was as big as you could get on British-style tradition in Australia. How the Chungs came upon such a place was still a mystery to me.

Geelong College had its own store, which made it easy to order the uniforms and everything Marc needed with one swipe of the credit card. Along with my purchases, I was given a strip of labels with Marc's name repeated every inch or so. Each item had to have a label. Sewing in the labels took up the better part of the remainder of my stay in Geelong, and was great therapy.

At the end of the sewing and other preparations for Marc's entrance into Geelong College, it was on to the next step, which was to take my sons on our final holiday trip to the States.

It would be the final break before the storm.

Before the Storm

O N December 10, 1993, my work done in Geelong, I drove
to the Melbourne airport, returned our rental car, and with
the boys, took an overnight flight to Los Angeles. This time
we would be alone for a while in the States, as John had his work in
Singapore, and would not be arriving until ten days later.

Most women are uneasy about being in a foreign country on their
own. Australia was not really foreign to me, as I had spent a lot of
time there, but America was a far more daunting prospect—I was
afraid, but determined.

Aside from the vacation that we all needed, I had to look further
into the practicalities of living in the States.

On our arrival in Los Angeles, we took a taxi from the airport
to the Beverly House Hotel, a charming small hotel with a bed
and breakfast atmosphere, around the corner from the Beverly Crest
Hotel, where John and I had stayed before.

We felt no jetlag as we were swept up by the excitement of Los
Angeles. My last visit seemed years ago, even though it had been only
five short months before. The very day after our arrival, we hit Beverly
Center, where I took the boys to a movie. The following days, we
took bus tours to Disneyland and Universal Studios.

After several days of good times, I realized that hotels and children
don't mix. Since I was going to be in Los Angeles for one month, I
needed a place with a kitchen and laundry facilities. I found one, a
great place called "Oakwood Apartments," situated on Sepulveda, just
north of Venice Boulevard, not quite Beverly Hills, but a perfect place
for our stay. We took a first-floor apartment with a living room, two
small bedrooms, a kitchen, and cable television. More importantly,
just outside our apartment, there was a small swimming pool to
absorb the boys' limitless energy.

Next on my nest-building agenda was a visit to Budget Rent-A-Car,
where I rented a sporty Nissan 240SX on the theory that a small

car would be easier for me to handle. I had never driven on the right side of the road.

Singapore drives British-style, on the left, and my first trip, from Budget back to the Oakwood was white-knuckle all the way.

To complete my nest building, the boys and I made our first venture to an American supermarket. Sure, we have them in Singapore, but nothing like America. There we stood, in front of an entire wall of bread—potato bread, split top wheat bread, raisin bread, any kind of bread you could imagine.

"Mom, look at all the different kinds of bread!" exclaimed Warren.

"Quiet!" I whispered in Chinese, "Do you want everyone to think we're completely stupid? So shameful!"

We stared silently at the wall of bread. We didn't have a clue. Then, a lady brushed by us, and quickly and confidently flipped a loaf of bread into her shopping cart. What luck. I followed her example and did the same. Wonder Bread!

Silently, we wormed out way through the supermarket, up one aisle and down the next.

The shopping cart filled, we joined the line at the nearest checkout counter. Finally our turn came. I smiled at the nice looking African American lady behind the counter.

"I'm sorry ma'am, you have more than fifteen items."

"Yes?" I answered, perplexed. In Singapore, all checkouts were the same.

"Ma'am," said the nice lady, growing impatient, "this counter is for fifteen items or less."

"Oh, I'm sorry, can't you just take us anyway?" I could feel my face redden.

"Ma'am, there's people waitin."

To a humiliating chorus of grumbles behind me, I clumsily backed my heavily laden cart out of the line, as the grumblers shook their heads. The boys were silent. So shameful.

Our apartment stocked with food, we settled down to the normal pace of life. The boys spent most of their time by the pool, and my main diversion became sitting in the Oakwood's small lobby reading, and making small talk with some of the other residents.

I was amazed to find that there were quite a few college students living at the Oakwood. What surprised me was their enterprising and independent spirit. Singaporeans are conscientious and diligent, but rarely free spirits.

There were all sorts of people I had never had the opportunity to meet before—an African American limo driver, who was an aspiring actor, and every bit as good looking, charming, and deserving as Denzel Washington—a Hispanic girl behind the Oakwood desk, full of life's hopes and ambitions.

In America, there was diversity—in Singapore, uniformity.

The enthusiasm and optimism around me of those who were doing what they could to change their lives for the better gave me confidence that I too was doing the right thing. My time spent in the lobby of the Oakwood was not wasted.

On December 19, John arrived from Singapore. He took a taxi from the airport directly to the Oakwood, arriving as fresh as a daisy. A frequent flyer, he had long since conquered jetlag. "You sleep at the end of the flight traveling east, and at the beginning, going west," John explained. I found this easier said than done.

With the boys, John, and the Oakwood apartment, we had our first taste of living in Los Angeles.

John's first move was to return the Nissan 240SX to Budget for "something more practical and safe." He picked out a Chevrolet, but I insisted on a large Mercedes. We compromised on a smaller Mercedes.

It was a great vacation for us all. Fortunately for John, we had already done all the amusement parks, except for Magic Mountain, where the boys disappeared onto roller coasters, while hot coffee and junk food kept John and me from freezing.

We had our first Christmas in America, quietly, at our small Oakwood apartment,

Now that John was with us, we saw a lot of Jack, which meant more dinners out at his favorite haunts. John and I dined with Jack at the Peninsula Hotel, with Jack, and his flamboyant girl, DDT, we returned to the Bel-Air Hotel.

There, in a brief moment of folly, John and I agreed that we would meet Jack and DDT in Las Vegas for New Year's Eve. Jack and

DDT would be there as guests of Nancy and her husband. Nancy was a longtime "friend" of Jack's, going back to Isobel's time, when according to Jack, Nancy was married to a Hell's Angel.

My main worry was that Hin Chew would cut us off financially while we were away from Singapore. I could take care of myself, but it was his job to support the boys.

We picked the wrong time to drive to Las Vegas, leaving Los Angeles just in time to arrive there at the last sundown of the year. New Year's Eve was upon us. Las Vegas was crowded, a madhouse. John had made no hotel reservations, the boys were tired, and Mom was not happy.

After checking out the main hotels with no success, John succeeded in finding a room in a motel down the street from the MGM Grand. I took one look at the flimsy door to our room and said, "No way!" John continued his search—it was getting late, very late. There was no way we would make it to our dinner appointment with Jack, DDT, and friends.

John continued to look for a hotel. We drove up to the Luxor, and I watched as John disappeared into the lobby of the pyramid.

A short while later, he emerged. "I got us a room at Treasure Island."

The boys were thrilled. "Treasure Island" sounded great to them.

The next evening, we left the boys at the hotel with a babysitter, and met Jack and DDT at Nancy's, a pleasant average two-story house in a pleasant average neighborhood.

Jack and DDT were Nancy's houseguests, so it was no surprise when DDT opened the door and her arms to us. Nancy's husband was some sort of teacher or professor, a very polite fellow. Unfortunately, Nancy was out of town.

Nancy's husband had prepared dinner, and had done a good job of it. After dinner, we went to out for a drink.

Las Vegas had been a great break for all of us, but it was time to get back to business.

We left Las Vegas on January 3, 1994, which was a good time to get out of town, as Hin Chew would be arriving in Las Vegas that same day for the Consumer Electronics Show.

Our remaining days in Los Angeles were devoted to planning. We met again with Mr. Miller, the lawyer, and reconfirmed that it made no sense for me to seek a divorce in California. Without personal service on Hin Chew, which would be difficult, as his exact whereabouts were never known, there could be no child support, and no compensation for my fifteen years of married hell.

Still, we worked on our plan of moving to Los Angeles, once the divorce was over. Where would we live? How much did apartments cost? What about schools? We gathered the facts.

A week after our return from Las Vegas, on Saturday, John left for Singapore to be back at Citibank for work on Monday. The rent on the Oakwood apartment was paid until the end of the next week, so the boys and I decided to stay until then.

On January 9, the day after John's departure, at 11:00 P.M., the earthquake hit. The entire Oakwood apartment building shook. I had never experienced anything like it. It was sheer terror, and then it was over. No one knew it at the time, but this "seismic event" was a prelude to the devastating Northridge earthquake, which would occur eight days later.

My feminine instincts told me, "get out of town." That same evening I called United Airlines, and got us on the next available flight. Two days later, on January 11, we were on our way back to Singapore.

We were lucky, as Hin Chew was also flying back to Singapore that same day.

Of course, he always traveled first class on the most expensive tickets he could find, which meant Singapore Airlines.

We were safe in economy on United.

ABOVE This is a before picture of John Harding, among friends in Saudi Arabia in 1976.

BELOW This is John's after picture in 1992—many years and several pounds later, and after I had him shave off that awful mustache.

"I'm not sure who spotted whom first, but I had noticed a person whom, by his behavior, I took to be an American. He was in his late forties, or beyond, and was getting a great deal of attention from an Asian girl, who must have still been in her teens. What a fool to be pursuing a child! Wasn't he a bit old for this nymphet?"

ABOVE X-10's third anniversary party in 1992 was held at Gaddi's, a fancy French restaurant in Hong Kong's Peninsula Hotel. From left: George Stevenson, an original X-10 founder, Hin Chew, in his very shiny shantung silk suit, me, in my black spandex La Perla dress, George Stevenson's date, May, Mrs. David Miller, George Seow, and X-10's Managing Director, the Englishman, David Miller.

BOTTOM LEFT George Stevenson, a *simpatico* type, and I toast the evening at Gaddi's.

BOTTOM RIGHT On the dance floor at Gaddi's, George Stevenson was my second heaviest dancing partner of all time, the first being the Right Honorable Alexander Irvine.

"Hin Chew took one look at my dress, and freaked out. He said, 'You look like a slut in that.'"

ABOVE Joan and I on our trip to Bali in 1992. John was with us, but I
wasn't ready to provide any photographic evidence of the fact.
BOTTOM LEFT In July 1993, Joan and I flew to Chicago, where she met
up with her husband-to-be, ex-college quarterback, Chuck Neumann.
BOTTOM RIGHT By the end of my 1993 visit to Chicago, Joan and I
looked happy—John was flying in to meet me.

Before my meeting his father, Jack Harding, John prepped me with some photographs:

TOP LEFT From left: Frank Sinatra, Isobel Lennart, and Jack.

TOP RIGHT Natalie Wood and Jack getting ready for a scene in the 1966 film, *This Property is Condemned*.

MIDDLE LEFT From left: Peering out from the background is John's son-in-law, Mark Getty, with his wife, John's daughter, Domitilla, downstage, and Jack enjoying center stage.

BOTTOM LEFT Jack, with his girlfriend, "DDT," putting on his often seen Oh-God-I'm-so-bored face. Jack had obviously seen it all, and done it all—too many times. How was I going to get on with someone like this?

BOTTOM RIGHT On our first evening together in Los Angeles, John and I met up with Jack. Posing with Jack, it looked like we were getting along—and we were, thank God!

TOP RIGHT In January 1994, I enrolled Marc in Geelong College. Here I am in Geelong, Australia, with Paul Sheahan, the school's headmaster, my son, Warren, and Paul's wife. Paul had played test cricket for Australia, which was more than enough to qualify him for the position of headmaster. Where's Marc?—in the dorm, of course.

RIGHT My good friend, boutique owner, Jackie Lee (no relation) in September 1995, shown between Marc and me. Jackie helped me in a moment of need, with my divorce.

ABOVE The US$16 million dollar Holland Road houses. With my mother's action for divorce, in March, 1995, my father managed to get rid of the houses-and fast! He then fled Singapore, with his young mistress, leaving as a bankrupt, and with a warrant out for his arrest. My mother moved into public housing—the end of an era. I have not seen my father since. His whereabouts are unknown, at least to me.

ABOVE Finally divorced, and free, I visited John's sons, Stefano and William in San Mateo, California. From left: Stefano's fiancée, Cynthia, Stefano, me, and William.

BELOW John and I, together in America—happily ever after!

"My thoughts shifted to a new life in a new country. When you come to America from a country like Singapore, which is clean, antiseptic and prosperous, but still a dictatorship; the word 'Freedom' takes on a special meaning—especially if you've been on the wrong side of that dictatorship."

THE ART OF WAR

As our Boeing 747 banked for its final approach to Singapore's Changi Airport, the city's lights came into view. Cities, when viewed by night from the air, present their coldest, most distant face.

Looking out my window, I wondered what was going to happen to us in Singapore, and realized that I had no idea. There was no roadmap to guide me through the battle ahead.

It was nearly midnight, when our twenty-two hour flight from Los Angeles rolled up to the Changi Airport arrival gate. We took the long walk through passport control and out to the luggage carousel. Through the glass wall of windows separating us, in the baggage claim area, from the outside world, I spotted John. Thank goodness, he was there. We were exhausted.

On exiting the baggage claim area, with Marc and Warren, I greeted John with a formal handshake. God knows who might be watching.

It was good to be on land, and, finally, in the car with John. Time and distance made Los Angeles seem to be a far off dream.

I told John I didn't want to go back to Mount Rosie, not yet. I was pretty sure that Hin Chew would have stopped in Hong Kong, but, on the off chance that he had come directly to Singapore, it would be safer to check into a hotel. I was much too tired for a fight.

It was past 1:00 A.M. when we checked into the Shangri-La Hotel, which was a good hour for us, as the lobby was deserted, except for some happy traffic in and out of the hotel's new nightclub, Xanadu. After checking us in and seeing us to our room, John left for his apartment. He had to be at work early the next morning.

It took two days for me to summon up the courage to return to Mount Rosie. When I did, I was relieved to find the apartment empty—no Hin Chew.

I phoned the Zhongli office. I held my breath. After two rings, Wai Lin picked up the telephone. So far, so good.

"Hello, Wai Lin, May Chu here, is Hin Chew in?"

"No, he's in Hong Kong."

Good!

"Wai Lin, we're still in the States, and will be back in two weeks, on the 28th."

"I'll let Hin Chew know."

"Thanks, Wai Lin." I hung up the telephone. With luck, we could be back in Australia, and have Marc safely in Geelong without any interference from Hin Chew.

"Marc, Warren, do not unpack your suitcases. I repeat—do not unpack! We have plenty of clothes to wear right here." We were ready for a speedy getaway.

I noticed there was a letter for me on the dining room table. I opened it.

It was from Hin Chew, and read, "I hope you do not come back too late for Warren's schooling. He is already quite frivolous and does not need his mum to reinforce in him that it is OK to be casual about schooling. Look how you turn out." Hmmm ... "How flattering," I thought.

I read on, "I am going to the States on 3 Jan 94," a near miss for us in Las Vegas, as I had guessed.

"I will be back on 12 Jan." Bad news.

"I brought back S$120,000 for us to spend. I took S$20,000 to buy some new outfits with and maybe a new lap top computer. Please put aside S$10,000 for our (Marc's) trip to Geelong." Excellent news! Another confirmation that Marc would be going to Geelong. I needed reassurance.

"I suggest you put S$30,000 in our CKB a/c to reduce the overdraft. And put aside another S$10,000 for pin money. This should last for another 3 to 4 months."

"The remaining S$50,000 is for you to do whatever you want." Great news!

The letter went on with the news that Wai Lin had resigned and would be leaving, but had agreed to work on Saturdays. Hin Chew ended his letter with the ominous warning, "If you do not like the idea of her working part time and wish to fire her permanently, you will only bring matters to a head between us a lot sooner."

I had nothing to do with the hiring or firing of Wai Lin, or with Zhongli, other than signing checks when Hin Chew was away. His off-the-wall remark that I might fire Wai Lin was preposterous, and served only to give Hin Chew the excuse to finish off the letter with a warning of what lay ahead.

The note was signed "CHC."

I went upstairs to the bedroom where we kept our Chubb safe and opened it. Inside, was an envelope containing cash. I counted the money, and it came to S$100,000, as Hin Chew's letter had said.

Now I knew exactly what my position was: Marc would be secure in Geelong, I had S$100,000, and matters would come "to a head between us" sooner or later. It was only a matter of time.

The battle lines were clearly drawn.

Finally, I had a war chest. I would have to use S$30,000 to shore up our bank account, but that would still leave me with S$70,000 (US$44,000).

This was another stroke of luck. It was the first time Hin Chew had put so much money in my hands, more money than I had ever had during our marriage. I should have been happy, but I wasn't. An uneasy feeling came over me. There had to be a reason for Hin Chew to let me have so much money. There had to be a plan behind it.

Nearly every time Hin Chew entered Singapore, he brought in large amounts of cash, but this was the first time he had given any of it to me.

Usually he brought in foreign currencies, not Singapore dollars. There is nothing illegal about this, as Singapore has no exchange controls of any kind. Still, for whatever reason, Hin Chew would be careful not to exchange the cash at any one place, and never used a bank. Singapore, being a tourist location, is full of small foreign currency exchange dealers, where Hin Chew would exchange the money in small amounts.

Where did all the cash come from?

Why go to all the trouble of roaming about town to get the money converted to Singapore dollars, when any bank would do it, and at a better rate? There was no tax saving involved, as income earned outside of Singapore is not taxed. Was I curious? Yes, but it would have served no purpose to ask.

Hin Chew rarely kept to his schedules. In his letter, he said he would be back on January 12; it was now January 14. I had no idea where he was, but I knew he could come through the door at any moment. That's why I kept our bags packed and by the door.

In spite of the threat of Hin Chew's appearance, I decided to stay in Singapore as long as possible. Marc was not due at Geelong until February 1, so, to save on hotel bills, we would leave at the last possible moment.

There was also a lot that I had to do in Singapore. I had to put Warren back in school; the apartment had been left in a mess by Hin Chew and needed a good cleaning; there were bills in the mailbox to be paid; and on it went.

Evenings out with John were my only diversion, but often he could not get away from work, as he was busy closing down Citibank's computer center in Sydney, transferring the work, but not the Australian staff, to Singapore. It was all part of some sort of downsizing thing that would save millions for Citibank. It was not a popular job.

On Wednesday, January 26, 1994, the boys and I were at the dining room table enjoying a lunch of Hainanese chicken rice.

Suddenly, I heard a key turn in the front door. In came Hin Chew!

Fortunately, he was smiling, with a broad Cheshire-cat grin pasted on his face. This was better than a screaming entrance, but still not a good sign. His smiling made me nervous.

Hin Chew had caught up with us, and now what?

"Hi! I see you three are back," he said, putting down his suitcase and his briefcase, "How was America?"

After some careful responses on my part, as to where we had been, and what we had done, Hin Chew, looking at me, asked, "Well, did you get my letter?"

I nodded.

With that, Hin Chew picked up his suitcase and his briefcase, and trotted up the stairs and into to the bedroom.

He was home.

I slept on my small cot on the floor of Warren's room that night. The next morning, I remained in the room, until I heard Hin Chew leave the apartment a little after 9:00 A.M., which was early for him.

About an hour later, he called me. He was at the Zhongli office.

"I want the originals of all our documents. I want our marriage certificate, all birth certificates, the children's passports, their Singapore identity cards, your passport, and your degree from Raffles Institution, and the keys to the safe-deposit box. I know you have all these documents somewhere, and I want them today!"

Yes, I did have them—safely locked away. I had been preparing for this day for years. The documents were under my control. "What for?" I asked.

"I'm applying for Singapore Citizenship, and I have an appointment with Singapore Immigration on Tuesday, next week."

"But next Tuesday is the day Marc has to be in Geelong College. If you come with us to Australia, how do you expect to be back by Tuesday? This won't give us enough time to see that Marc is properly set up at the school. We can't leave him there without seeing him through at least his first day in school."

"I have an instruction for you. We are all going to fly down to Australia on Saturday, and we will come back on Monday. Marc will be fine."

The schedule was impossible, and it was obvious that Hin Chew had no intention of taking Marc to Australia. How stupid did he think I was? I said nothing.

Hin Chew continued, avoiding his usual obscenities, but in a voice, that by its measured and deliberate tone, was even more menacing, "You will bring me the originals of all the documents, and they must all be here, in the office, by 10:30 this morning. Do you understand?"

"Sure, no problem," I answered.

Hin Chew hung up. I put the receiver down, thought for a second, and called Ann Tan.

She had already been contacted by Hin Chew, regarding the documents, both by telephone and by fax. In addition to the documents, and the keys to the safe-deposit box, Hin Chew had requested my car keys from her.

He needed the car keys for his Singapore citizenship?

This was the end.

Hin Chew was stripping me of everything. For a moment, I became quite agitated, and then my emotion turned to anger. "Ann, what can we do?" I asked. Ann Tan had a clever legal solution. She would give him notarized copies of the requested documents and the originals of his degrees from Monash, and MIT.

"Brilliant, Ann, I'll get everything over to you as soon as possible, but I don't think I can make a 10:30 A.M. deadline. That's less than half an hour away."

Ann Tan said not to worry, she would telephone Hin Chew, and tell him that we were complying with his request, and would get everything today. She seconded my refusal to give Hin Chew the car keys, and would write Hin Chew that, "Our client has made arrangements for the car to be taken care of. She appreciates your concern."

Well worded, Ann.

I thanked Ann Tan, and was about to hang up when she said there was one more thing I should know. Hin Chew had told her he was going to cut off my credit cards. She advised him strongly not to do so; pointing out that such a move would weigh heavily against him if matters came to court, especially since children were involved.

On that note, our conversation ended.

I did not believe for a second that Hin Chew was interested in Singapore citizenship, as with its stringent regulations Singapore citizenship would only have been a burden to him.

What Hin Chew wanted was to have all the documents.

With the passports, he could prevent us from leaving Singapore. With the children's identity cards, in Singapore, he would have total control over the children.

In Singapore, your documents are your life.

I also understood clearly, then, why Hin Chew had left so much money at my disposal. It was a payoff to get me to give him the documents, but there was more to it.

I knew that Hin Chew intended the money he left for me to be my final settlement for fifteen years of married misery.

Hin Chew was carrying out his threat to reduce the children and me to poverty, making good on his threat of having us "living in an HDB apartment on twenty dollars a day." Hin Chew felt he was above the law, and, being a husband in Singapore, he was probably right.

I called John to tell him what had happened.

"That's it," John said, "Get out of that apartment right away! Go to a hotel, and get the documents to your lawyer. When you're finished, go back to the hotel and call me. I'll come over as soon as I can get off from work." The suitcases were ready and waiting; Hin Chew's smuggled money was already in my purse. Some of the documents Hin Chew needed had been right under his nose, in our little Chubb safe in the bedroom.

Out the documents came, and into one of Hin Chew's briefcases they went. In a matter of minutes, I was hauling ass out of Mount Rosie with Marc, the suitcases, and the briefcase. Warren was in school. I could pick him up later.

Marc and I went to a travel agency and purchased three round trip tickets to Melbourne. I was afraid that Hin Chew would cancel my credit cards, so I had to act fast.

Tickets in hand, my next stop was the bank, where I retrieved the remainder of the documents requested by Hin Chew from the safe deposit box. I put them into the briefcase with the other documents.

Going to another bank, across the street, I opened an account, depositing all but S$11,000 of the cash. I was now ready to see Ann Tan.

We raced through traffic, and met Ann Tan in her office. For starters, I paid her S$10,000 in cash, the retainer she had requested. It was with great reluctance that I entrusted the briefcase, with its documents, to her. Not telling her why, I insisted on having notarized copies made of our passports, before I left her office. I needed the passports for the trip to Australia.

There was no time to waste, as I was afraid that Hin Chew might try to pick up Warren at his school. Fortunately, when I arrived at the school, the morning session was just ending. In Singapore, to save on classroom space, children attend either the morning, or afternoon sessions, never both.

I was lucky to see Warren, as he was walking to the school bus. I motioned him into the car, and we sped off like the fugitives we were.

The Westin Stamford hotel in Singapore has the Guinness distinction of being the tallest hotel in the world. It's a good place for getting lost, and more importantly, not one of the hotels used by the Chungs. I decided to go there, and by the time we got to our room, we were all totally spent.

John was able to make it to the hotel after work, and we had a quick dinner in the room. I wanted to keep off the streets.

My final worry was over the car. It was in my name, and I would have been nuts to turn the keys over to Hin Chew, no matter what. I was no longer thinking of the car as transportation, but as my largest asset. My BMW 730iL was worth a lot, and I needed a place to hide it until I got back from Australia.

One of John's friends, a local IBM manager, Ajit Nair, lived in a house on the outskirts of town. John called him, saying, innocently, that I was going away for a week, and needed a place to park my car. Through John, I had met both Ajit, and his wife, so Ajit was quite willing to have us park the car in his driveway. It didn't hurt that John made the purchasing decisions for Citibank's computer center, the largest in Singapore, and perhaps, Asia.

John drove his car, and I followed him in mine, to Ajit's house. With my BMW stashed, my work was complete. I had a place for my things.

The next morning, John drove us to the airport, and Marc, Warren, and I were off for Melbourne on Qantas flight QF 10.

As before, I rented a car from Budget at the Melbourne airport, and drove to Geelong. My credit cards were still working, so I guessed that Hin Chew had followed Ann Tan's advice that it was not in his interest to cut us off completely.

Getting to Geelong was a snap, as I seemed to be making the drive on a regular basis.

We checked into the Ambassador Hotel, now as familiar and comfortable as an old shoe, and I was ready to go to work to get

Marc settled into Geelong.

For Marc, visiting the school was one thing, but living there would be a new and character-building experience. Accustomed to the disciplined ways, and demanding academics of Singapore schools, Marc would be facing an entirely new set of challenges, mainly physical, brought on by rough and tumble ways of his new Australian schoolmates. He would cope.

On February 2, 1994, the day I moved Marc into the Geelong College boys' dormitory, there was a telephone message waiting for me at the hotel. It was from Budget. I called Budget back to learn that my credit card payment for the car had been declined, and Budget needed a cash deposit, which I could make at their Geelong office.

I rushed immediately to Budget's Geelong office, where I asked the clerk to check out another one of my credit cards. It didn't work. I had him swipe a third credit card. It didn't work either. Trying to keep a smile on my face, and my chin from trembling, I had the clerk check the rest of my credit cards. None of them worked.

Hin Chew had cancelled all my credit cards!

I had barely enough for the cash deposit.

Here I was with our two sons, nearly 4,000 miles from Singapore, with no credit cards and after paying the cash deposit for the car, I was left with virtually nothing.

There was no way I could pay for the hotel bill, or for the remaining rental on the car, or for anything, except a couple of days worth of food.

Hin Chew, in cutting off the credit cards, showed no regard for his own children. He knew the boys were in Australia with me, but he didn't care about the consequences, even to his children.

This was no ordinary deadbeat dad. This was the fucking Chairman of X-10!

Hin Chew's timing was as merciless as I had expected. He was a great admirer of *The Art of War* by Sun Tzu, which is probably the only book in his library of great unread books that Hin Chew had actually read. He said he lived his life according to *The Art of War*, and idolized Sun Tzu.

The Art of War, notwithstanding its near-sacred reputation among

Chinese and Sinophiles, is a very short book. It's a fifteen-minute read. I had skimmed through it. It's filled with brilliant pieces of advice, like, "When the soldiers stand leaning on their spears, they are faint from want of food." Well, duh!

Sun Tzu's strategies were all very deterministic, made up of simple formulas and a predictable enemy—we do this, and they'll do that. Life, however, is not so simplistic, and the all-important elements of luck and chance are never considered by Sun Tzu.

The Art of War is based on the same flawed thought process as Asian martial arts, which fail to teach you the improbable—the element of luck—that while positioning yourself for a backward spinning kick to your opponent's face, a brick might just fall on your head!

So much for Sun Tzu!

Even though Hin Chew and Sun Tzu might have thought I had been defeated, maybe I had not yet used up my Chinese-allocated lifetime quota of luck.

I called John at Citibank in Singapore only to find that he had left for Australia the day before. "Where in Australia?" I asked. "I'm sorry," responded a professional Citibank secretarial voice, "we don't have a number for him in Sydney, but you might call him on his cell phone, if you have his number."

GSM cell phones are great; somehow, you just dial the number and you can get the person in any country that is set up for the system.

I dialed John's cell phone. He answered.

"Where are you?" I asked, in a state of panic.

"In Sydney, for Citibank."

"That fucking bastard Hin Chew has cancelled all my credit cards. Here I am, in Geelong, with the children, and no money. My God … what am I going to do? What about the children? What kind of father would do this to his own children?"

"Well, you expected it. The guy's a totally irresponsible prick," John said. "Don't worry, I'll catch a flight to Melbourne and be in Geelong this evening. I'll take care of the bills; you'll be fine, and so will the kids."

I didn't expect that. What luck! I still had some left!

True to his word, late in the afternoon John arrived in Geelong.

Somehow, I was surprised that he was able to find his way by car from the Melbourne airport to Geelong.

To say that I was happy and relieved to see him would have been an understatement.

John stayed with us at the Ambassador for the next two days. In spite of my difficulties, we had a wonderful time, turning a disaster into a vacation. John took Warren out to visit Australia's famed Torquay Beach to watch the surfers, and on Friday evening, we retrieved Marc from his dorm and took him out for dinner.

Sunday, I cried, as we said goodbye to Marc. It was time to drive back to the Melbourne airport to catch our flight back to Singapore.

John was with us all the way, even on the flight back home to Singapore. Having John with us in Geelong made us all feel secure and happy.

There was life after Hin Chew—the disciple of Sun Tzu.

GUERILLA WARFARE

ON THE FLIGHT back to Singapore, I thought of all the lives I had lived in Australia—my honeymoon at the Toorak apartment, the strange adventure of the Anna Plains cattle station, Hin Chew's no-show for our Perth vacation, Jim's deathbed, and finally Geelong. I never thought Australia would play such a large part in my life.

Now I was returning to Singapore, my home, but too afraid to go home. John accompanied us by taxi from the airport to the Westin Stamford hotel, where I checked in, one child lighter.

I was on the run again.

Early the next morning, I took Warren to school by taxi. At the end of his school day, I was waiting outside in a taxi to pick him up. I was taking no chances.

Late that evening, after dinner, John and I visited the Mount Rosie apartment. From the street below, we could see the apartment was dark. We took a chance and went up the stairs to the apartment.

The place was deserted, with no sign of Hin Chew's being present.

On the way out, I checked the mailbox. There were only some bills from the grocer, utilities, and the newspaperman. I stuffed them into my purse.

We left and went back to the Westin Stamford, where I wrote checks for all the unpaid bills. That's the Singapore training for you; always pay your bills as soon as you receive them.

There was no way I could return to live at Mount Rosie. Hin Chew's temper and his legal right to force his way into the apartment made it a danger.

The next night, John and I chanced one last visit to Mount Rosie. We came prepared with large black plastic trash bags to move out what we could. We filled several dozen of the bags with my clothes, the boys' clothes, toiletries, some of the boys' prized possessions, mementos, and photographs.

Like thieves in the night, we stole down the six flights of stairs, trip after trip, carrying as many of the black trash bags as we could handle. In the end, John's car was filled to the roof with our loot.

This was what my life in Singapore had come to. This was not the life I had expected.

I was a virtual outcast on my own home turf, driven into hiding by Hin Chew, an interloper, who lived not in Singapore, but Hong Kong.

I had had no support from anyone but John.

The conditions my father said he would impose, should I return to 69 Holland Road, were his way of saying no, and from the day I told my parents of my plan to divorce Hin Chew, I had not heard from them.

I was filled with resentment and anger, but I was also shaken. Any woman with children in my position of being cut off from all financial support, abandoned by my own family, and without a safe home to return to, would be afraid.

True, I had John, but there was no way I could run off with him, or live with him until the question of custody of the children was resolved.

I was reduced to desperation, and tears. This cat and mouse game with Hin Chew, struggling to get Marc safely into Geelong College, with no support from my parents, and isolation from my friends was taking its emotional toll on me. I found myself sobbing my heart out.

Crying can be a wonderful thing, especially when it comes for the very depths of your soul. It revitalized me, giving me strength, a spiritual strength, and made me a better and stronger person, tenacious and determined to forge ahead.

It is always a mistake to reduce people to the point where they have nothing to lose. Then they are out of your control. As the song goes, nothing left to lose means Freedom. I held that thought, and it picked up my spirits.

I was free to do whatever I wanted, and what I wanted was more than a divorce. I wanted revenge. No one could treat the children and me like this and get away with it.

My life, given to me by the luck of the draw, had rewarded me with a great deal of exposure to the world, more than most people could claim, and much, much more than Hin Chew, living in the protective cocoon of his father's money, would ever have.

I had been at Kong Kong's side while he opened the branches of his bank; I had been witness to my own family's intrigues, my father's dalliances, my mother's affairs, Mamak's weakness, and the final screwing over of Kong Kong by Cheng Chye, his own brother-in-law.

I had run my own magazine, been treated as a professional by I. M. Pei, made to go down on my knees before Lillian, abused by Hin Chew, and had raised my children on my own.

Even my life's negatives had become a plus, and it all added up to experience. I was my own best resource.

So what if S. P. had an unlimited supply of cash to give to his worthless and spoiled sons. So what if he was a friend of the Kuomintang, maybe still of Pehin Isa, and a friend of a friend of George Bush, through the rude CIA creep, Dan Arnold.

These people all had far more to lose than I. I would expose them all, and was now free to do so.

My thoughts returned to earth as we pulled up outside of John's apartment with our trash bags. I felt good as we hauled the bags up to his apartment, and was tired but feeling good, by the time we completed stashing the spoils in his living room.

I couldn't go on living forever with Warren in a hotel, taking him by taxi to school every day. I needed a place to stay, a place with my own kitchen and laundry facilities.

It took me only one day to find a month-to-month furnished service apartment, a place called Orchard Scotts, conveniently located one block away from Warren's school.

The apartment was a second-story walk-up with three bedrooms. It didn't come cheap; the rent was S$5,800 (US$3,600) a month, with a S$10,000 (US$6,200) security deposit.

For me, leaving Mount Rosie was a tremendous loss of face. It would have been for any Singaporean.

I was out of my comfort zone, away from my telephone, and difficult to reach. I had a cell-phone, but few people knew its number. Being out of touch was a blessing, as I didn't want anyone, not even my family, to know my current situation. It was too embarrassing.

On my first evening at my temporary Orchard Scotts service apartment, I got organized. John drove me out to Ajit Nair's house, where I collected my car. I had my wheels back.

Back at the apartment, I made a list of my tasks, the major headings were: Marc, Warren, Lawsuit, Apartment Upkeep, Check the Mailbox, Car, and Looking My Best.

Through Ann Tan, I found that Hin Chew was still in Singapore, staying again at the Novotel Hotel, and not using the apartment, doing so, he claimed, to "facilitate" my return to Mount Rosie.

Hin Chew had retained his own lawyers, the prestigious and expensive firm of Drew & Napier.

Through them, he had demanded that I return the cash I had removed from the safe, and that he be given visitation rights for Warren. His lawyers also informed us that Hin Chew was going to file for divorce, which was great news.

Hin Chew's lawyers also informed me, that, as a Director of Zhongli, I had to sign the company's audited annual report. No way! I had no idea what Hin Chew was doing with the company, and I wasn't going to be anybody's fall guy for taxes, or money laundering.

Hin Chew's request for visitation rights to Warren became a non-issue, at least temporarily, when he suddenly returned to Hong Kong. I breathed a sigh of relief, and so, I'm sure, did Warren.

Ann Tan must have been very busy, as she relegated me to one of her assistants, a pleasant girl named Catherine. Together, Catherine and I worked to put together my own set of demands, and to draft my divorce petition. For me, the most important item was to gain sole custody of the boys. Financially, I was asking for child support, and for my share of our community property.

Singapore is a community property country, but not on a fifty-fifty basis. The court determines the division of the assets, with the wife always coming out on the short end. There is no such thing as an equal partnership between man and wife in Singapore, not even under the law.

I also needed to get an interim maintenance order from the court, to force Hin Chew to pay for our living expenses until the divorce could be settled. I had no source of income, and was worried about running out of money. Expenses were mounting.

All in all, with the deposit and rent on the apartment, and the S$10,000 to Ann Tan, I had spent nearly S$40,000, and if I deposited S$30,000 into our checking account to cover some of the overdraft, I would have only about S$30,000 left, which was not enough for six month's rent at Orchard Scotts.

Hin Chew loved to do financial calculations, and I am sure he was well aware of the state of my finances, and was proud of the squeeze he was putting on me. Time was on his side, and he knew it.

Through Catherine, I made an informal request to Hin Chew's lawyers for interim maintenance to keep us going, but with no luck.

As we moved into March 1994, I was getting worried and frustrated.

Instead of filing my divorce petition and applying to the court for interim maintenance, Catherine continued to squabble with Hin Chew's lawyers, mainly over Hin Chew's demands, and not mine.

He was demanding the money back, and insisting on seeing Warren. Why did we have to cooperate in any way with Hin Chew, when he wasn't paying a single cent to maintain his children? We were getting nowhere.

Ann Tan was holding up the filing of the divorce petition because she did not think that I would be able to win a divorce against Hin Chew on the grounds of unreasonable behavior. We would have to go for adultery, and that required evidence.

I saw no way of getting Hin Chew on adultery. There was no indication, whatsoever, that he had been unfaithful. Ann Tan was adamant and insisted that I use a private detective named Andy Lek.

"Our firm uses his services for matrimonial cases, May Chu," she said, writing down a phone number on the back of one of her cards, "Here's his phone number. His office is in the OG Building." She handed me the card, "Right, just tell him that Ann Tan sent you—off you go."

Somewhat intimidated, but to keep the peace, I agreed.

Reluctantly, I phoned Andy Lek and made an appointment to see him the next day, which was Saturday, and John would be free to come along. There was no way I was going to see an unknown private investigator on my own.

I was disappointed with Ann Tan. She seemed to be more concerned with my signing documents for Hin Chew than acting in my interests, and I thought the whole adultery thing and Andy Lek was a bad idea.

I still believed that to win in court against Hin Chew, it would take more than the conventional legal approach. I realized I was dealing with a family that had no qualms about destroying their own family members.

I was not about to follow the examples of Lynn, Rosita, and Jim.

Exposing the activities of Hin Chew and his family would be my best move. Unfortunately, to do so, would take more than only my word against the Chungs. I needed hard evidence.

I decided to pay a nighttime visit to Zhongli. It wouldn't be illegal, after all wasn't I a director, and fifty-percent owner of the company?

Late Friday night, John drove me to Sime Darby Centre where Zhongli still had its office. I was dressed for the occasion with black stirrup pants, black top, black loafers, and with my hair in a ponytail.

Although John insisted on coming with me, I told him he had to wait in the car. He did so grudgingly. The last thing I needed was to give Hin Chew or Drew & Napier something new to harp on. If anything happened, I would contact John cell-phone to cell-phone.

The building, not one of the best in Singapore, was dimly lit at night, with no guard in the lobby, only in the parking lot. I took the elevator to the fourth floor. The elevator doors opened. Everything was silent and eerie.

I got out, turned left, and walked slowly down the darkened hallway, which ended with closed double doors. Opening the double doors, I continued down a narrower hallway, stopping at the last door on the left, the door to Zhongli's office. My key still worked, and I entered quickly, locking the door behind me.

The office was dark. I turned on the lights. The place was a mess now that Wai Lin worked only on Saturdays. Hin Chew needed people to pick up after him.

From my purse, I took out one of my all-purpose black trash bags.

I began by checking the desks. A red plastic binder in Wai Lin's in-box caught my eye. It was a legal file, a court order from Birmingham, England, against Lillian. Lynn was suing Lillian. That should provide some interesting reading.

I searched on. Lying on what had been my desk was Hin Chew's bill from the Novotel Hotel. In to my trash bag it went.

Next, I checked the file cabinets. Some of them were unlocked, and I went through them. I went into the back storage room, which Hin Chew used as his private hideaway. His desk was littered with papers, some of which looked like financial statements.

Instead of taking them, I decided to make photocopies, but first made a quick phone call to John to tell him that everything was OK. By the time I had finished, I had been in the Zhongli office for over an hour, and my large trash bag was half-full.

I turned off the lights and opened the door. The hallway was empty. I closed the office door slowly until its lock clicked. Making no noise, I walked down the deserted hallway with the trash bag, through the double doors and on to the elevator. There, before pushing the button for the lobby, I decided instead to take stairs to avoid the noise. Maybe I had seen too many thrillers on television.

Once out of the building, I ran to John's car, threw the half-filled trash bag into the back seat, and we were off into the night.

We went directly to the Orchard Scotts service apartment, where I dumped the contents of the trash bag onto the floor.

First, I looked at Lynn's lawsuit against Lillian. It was, as I expected, over the funds Lillian had taken from Jim's account. Lynn had secured a court order freezing Jim's funds in Lillian's account. Good for Lynn!

Next, I looked at Hin Chew's Novotel Hotel bill. There were over twenty late-night telephone calls to Hong Kong. We were into the wee hours of the morning, but if Hin Chew could call the Hong Kong number at a late hour, why couldn't I?

I dialed. The telephone, in Hong Kong, rang. "*Wayee*," Cantonese for "hello," answered a female voice, a lethargic, used, and worldly female voice.

"*Ho ma?*" how are you? I replied, in Cantonese.

"*Wayee*," came back the answer, as though waiting for me to identify myself.

"Hin Chew *yao mo oh kay?*" I said, asking for Hin Chew in my best Singaporean Cantonese.

I was answered with a click. The woman in Hong Kong had hung up on me. Guess she didn't like the sound of my Cantonese with its Singaporean accent.

"It's strange to hear you speak Chinese," said John.

"It was a woman, she sounded a bit long in the tooth, and hung up when I asked for Hin Chew."

"Maybe he isn't the innocent nerd you take him to be after all."

"Hin Chew, a womanizer—never." I answered. "Look," I continued, "here's a Singapore number that he called from the Novotel, at 11:05 in the evening. Let's try it." I said.

John did the talking, this time. "Hello? Excuse me, I'm looking for a friend of mine." There was a pause. "A blonde? Do I want a blonde?" There was another pause, as John listened, then he continued, "An escort, service? High Society? You say, High Society escort service?" asked John. "Oh good, well, thank you very much, just the same." John hung up.

"Well, guess what? That was the High Society escort service. Sounds interesting." John was enjoying the prospect of Hin Chew's calling an escort service.

On the Novotel bill, following Hin Chew's call to "High Society," was a hefty charge from the hotel's nightspot, imaginatively named "The Cheers Music Pub."

"I would say that the call to an escort service, followed by a visit to a nightspot, calls for a guilty verdict," smiled John.

I guess it did. Further research on my part, calling "High Society," as Hin Chew's secretary, revealed that he had most probably enjoyed the company of a blonde, but didn't he always tell me he didn't like Western women?

The next day, Saturday morning, March 19, 1994, John and I went to see Andy Lek. His office was located in Singapore's Chinatown, in the OG Building, an older building, of which the first several floors were shops, with offices located above.

We took the elevator to the seventh floor, and quickly found number 07-08A, Andy Lek's office.

Andy Lek's office was small, and he was alone.

Lek was Chinese, taller than average, a stocky fellow with a receding hairline, and a pencil-thin mustache. He was neatly dressed, in a short-sleeved shirt, and wore a gold Rolex on his left wrist.

After the proper introductions and pleasantries, we sat down to talk. I told Lek what I thought he would need to know about the case.

Lek explained his *modus operandi*, showed off some cameras and tape recorders, and said he could do the job. He would begin by conducting an initial surveillance in Hong Kong, which would require several days of his time. Nothing guaranteed, but for this "initial surveillance," I would have to pay him a flat fee of s$15,000 (US$9,300) up front.

I was stunned by the amount.

This put me on the spot. If I decided not to use Lek, would Ann Tan still agree to represent me? Of course not. Without a private investigator, how could Ann Tan obtain her hoped-for proof of adultery? She could put the blame on me, and that would be the end of it.

Reluctantly, I told Lek I would pay, and we agreed to meet that afternoon in the parking lot of the Garden Hotel, where I would give him the s$15,000.

That afternoon, it was drizzling rain and a perfect setting for a clandestine meeting with a private detective. Andy Lek arrived on time, driving into the parking lot in a brand-new white Mercedes 200. There was a woman in the passenger seat next to him.

He pulled up near us, and got out of the car, leaving his companion behind. I gave Lek several photographs of Hin Chew, along with Hin Chew's Hong Kong address, both at the Victoria Apartments, and at X-10.

Lek looked at the photographs, and said, "I'll be going to Hong Kong on Monday, March 21."

"Good," I answered, handing him a manila envelope bulging with the s$15,000, all in cash. He turned and walked quickly away with my money.

I felt like a gambler, betting on a long shot, as the money was running out. This was where Ann Tan, Singapore's leading feminist lawyer and activist, had taken me.

Saturday was also Wai Lin's day to be in the Zhongli office, on her new once-a-week schedule. She noticed that something was wrong. Someone had been in the office.

Being a diligent, detail-oriented, Singaporean, she made a list of everything that was amiss, down to the last paper clip.

By Monday morning, Hin Chew's lawyers, Drew & Napier, had Wai Lin's list in hand, and fired off a letter to Ann Tan, which read, "It is quite obvious that your client has entered the premises at some unspecified time during the last week."

Drew & Napier's letter then presented their evidence by enclosing Wai Lin's list of my crimes. The list, referring to Wai Lin as "TWL," is worth reading in its entirety, as it is a glimpse into the Singaporean mind:

1) Wires of TWL's Wearnes computer were disconnected;
2) Doorjamb to our client's room was overturned;
3) The chair in our client's room was placed at the working table instead of by the computer desk;
4) The keyboard slide was open;
5) Incoming documents (magazines, Keppel's newsletters received on 12 March 1994) had been removed from the centre of our client's desk and left on the top tray of our client's desk;
6) Our client's copy of documents in the green clear folder file containing Zhongli's monthly financial statement, a telephone list and a telephone manual, were missing;
7) Personal photographs of your client and another of your client with Marc which were on our client's shelf, were missing;
8) Telephone wires were unplugged from all the telephone sets in the whole office;
9) The fax machine was switched off;
10) The photocopier was used and all the paper in the tray had been removed;
11) Couple of "stretched" paper clips were found in TWL's waste-paper basket;
12) A bag containing two cans of cookies left on the desk were missing;
13) TWL's notes on a rough note-pad were missing.

Guilty as charged! Well, almost. I really didn't unplug the telephone wires, but might have, had I thought of it, and knew how to do it. I didn't take the cookies either. Honest!

Singaporeans love small details. They are trained from childhood to get lost in trivia, that way they don't think too much about the big picture. Drew & Napier might have thought a little deeper about why "all the paper in the tray had been removed" from the photocopier. The paper hadn't been "removed," it had been used to make photocopies, plenty of photocopies.

Drew & Napier finished their letter stating that my actions were "in breach" of my duties as a director, and notified us that the locks to the Zhongli office were being changed. Good to know, next time, I'll show up with a locksmith.

Hin Chew was furious by what I had done, so much so that he called me on my cell-phone.

There was music in the background, and he spoke in a drunken, singsong voice, teasing me, "You won't find any lawyer in Singapore to represent you ... and I've paid off Ann Tan."

I was too surprised by the sound of Hin Chew's voice to come up with anything better than to say, "Fuck you!" Hin Chew usually blabbed the truth when drunk, and his comment about Ann Tan had me worried.

Monday was eventful day, with Andy Lek's taking off for Hong Kong, Drew & Napier's letter, and Hin Chew's call, and, in the afternoon, I visited Ann Tan's office.

Instead of getting on with my business, Catherine continued to pressure me to sign my joint income tax return with Hin Chew, as well as the "duly audited" accounts of Zhongli.

"May Chu, you must show goodwill and cooperation. I have to send the documents back to Drew & Napier, with your signature, today."

"Catherine," I said, "I'm not signing anything. The last time I signed a document for Hin Chew, I nearly lost all claim to our Mount Rosie apartment."

I explained patiently to Catherine that Hin Chew regularly brought large amounts of cash into Singapore, which were undeclared and, perhaps, taxable. I pointed out to her that his lifestyle was completely out of line with the S$96,000 that he declared on the Singapore tax return. How could I possibly sign?

"Well, then can you sign the Zhongli audited statement?" Catherine asked.

I answered, "Is a company director, in Singapore, legally bound to sign an audited statement while being denied access to all company records, and even to the office. Absolutely not! Catherine, I have studied enough company law to know better."

Catherine made no response.

Picking up a copy of the Zhongli Balance Sheet, "audited" by Goh Boon Kok, I said, "Look, Zhongli has a negative net worth of S$125,446 (US$78,000), with S$231,632 (US$144,000) being 'owed to a director.' Catherine, neither the name of the director, nor the reason for the debt is given. I can't believe Ann Tan's legal advice. Christ!"

Catherine nodded slowly.

"Catherine, Zhongli was in the black, but now Hin Chew has removed all the money from the company, and created a debt to himself, as a director. He has taken everything out of the company, in preparation for our divorce."

Catherine looked at me blankly.

I said angrily, "And you and Ann Tan expect me to endorse his action with my signature?"

Catherine shrugged her shoulders, with a weak smile.

I smiled back, closed my purse, stood up, smiled again, and left.

The next day, March 22, 1994, Ann Tan, herself, materialized, but in the form of a letter, sent by fax.

Her letter advised, "If you do not sign the accounts as one of the directors, you would be prosecuted under the Companies Act of the Registrar of Companies. We would therefore urge you to reconsider your decision."

Ann Tan's words, "you would be prosecuted," were as inappropriate to me, her client, as they were incorrect legally.

On March 23, 1994, two days after Drew & Napier sent their letter to Ann Tan about my entering Zhongli, and Hin Chew's telephone call, I received a second letter from Ann Tan, also by fax.

I had to read the letter twice for it to sink in. It was very short. The first paragraph complained about my making changes in the draft divorce petition.

The last paragraph read, "Furthermore, we wanted to give you the Company Accounts which was sent to us but you even refused to look at it. Since we cannot seem to agree, it would be in the interest of both parties, that you engage another solicitor to act for you … Yours faithfully, Mrs Ann Tan"

Ann Tan had fired me!

So much for Ann Tan, Singapore's premier women's rights activist, and her pal, Andy Lek.

DÉJÀ VU

ANN TAN'S sudden termination of her services left me in bad shape.

I had no financial support, I couldn't return to my Mount Rosie apartment, I was locked out of the Zhongli office, I had no lawyer, and three months had been wasted with nothing being submitted to the court.

Including the original S$3,000 I had paid Ann Tan in 1993, when I fled from Mount Rosie with Lynn, I was out S$13,000, plus another S$15,000 to her man, Andy Lek, with no offer from Ann Tan to pay back a cent.

I fired off a fax to Ann Tan, telling her that I expected a refund. Equally important, Ann Tan was still holding all the documents that I had left with her, so, in the same fax, I included a list of my documents with her, and asked for their return.

The day after getting the boot from Ann Tan, I came up with the name of a new lawyer, Dennis Singham, a partner of Rodyk & Davidson, a well-known Singapore law firm. I had spotted Singham's name beforehand in an article, which I had clipped from the January 21, 1994 edition of *The Straits Times*.

Singham had represented an Australian lady, Gaye Williams, who sued her husband, Cary Williams, an American, for divorce. Singham not only won the divorce on the grounds of unreasonable behavior, but also succeeded in having the custody of Gaye Williams's two sons awarded to her. This was precisely what I had wanted Ann Tan to do for me.

In addition, Singham had won, for his client, a lump sum settlement of S$1,000,000, which, according to *The Straits Times* "was the largest amount to be awarded by the High Court." He sounded like my kind of guy.

The article went on to state, however, that on appeal, Cary Williams won a reduction of the lump sum amount to S$700,000.

Nevertheless, I was still impressed by Singham's winning custody of the children for Gaye Williams, and having been able to obtain her divorce on the grounds of unreasonable behavior.

A final plus for Singham was that he had represented a foreigner, Gaye Williams. Hopefully, this meant that he had an open mind, and could deal with someone like me.

I called Singham's office, and was able to make an appointment to see him at 10:30 the next morning, Friday.

Trying to look my best, I was wearing a conservative burgundy gabardine pants suit, with a white silk blouse.

Dennis was good-looking, short, proud, and a Singaporean of Indian origin. My first meeting with him went well. After listening patiently to my long tale of woe and lament, Dennis concluded that I did indeed have a case for divorce on the grounds of "unreasonable behavior." He agreed to represent me, and said he would inform Drew & Napier, accordingly.

Dennis asked that I bring him any papers or documents that would be helpful in the drafting of the divorce petition, saying he was confident of a speedy resolution of both the issues of child custody, and interim maintenance.

Fortunately, Dennis did not bring up the subject of a retainer, a subject I was happy to avoid with my limited funds.

As we ended our first meeting, Dennis said, "I have to tell you that I was involved in some dealings with the Chungs' company, Brunox, but that was a while back."

I appreciated his honesty, and took his work for Brunox to be a good thing, as it gave him some background on the Chungs. We shook hands goodbye, and I left.

For me, Dennis had a lot going for him. Being of Indian origin, divorce was not an anathema to him. In contrast to Ann Tan and Gregory Chong, both Chinese, he would not be a cultural ally of Hin Chew's, and, therefore, less likely to side with the enemy.

In Singapore, Dennis was a third-class citizen, the Indians coming after the Chinese and Malays. Instead of the limiting prospect of working under a Chinese boss in a local company, many Indians became lawyers, where individual efforts and brains count.

So many Indians had become lawyers that the Singapore Government, at one point, put a stop to admitting Indians to the bar. There was never any such barrier for the Chinese in Singapore's harmonious multiracial society.

I felt good that weekend. In Dennis, I was sure I had found a lawyer I could trust, and John was happy because his younger son, William, had returned to Singapore. William had spent part of his summer vacation with his sister, Domitilla, and her husband, Mark Getty, at their country house in Tuscany.

On Monday, I received a letter by courier from Ann Tan, which contained a full refund of the S$10,000 retainer I had paid her. She added up some expenses to justify her keeping my original S$3,000 payment. Well, I guess she did some work, after all, even if most of it seemed to be for Hin Chew.

Wasting no time, I gathered the documents received from Ann Tan, and drove with them straight to Rodyk & Davidson to give them to Dennis.

Although, I had not scheduled a meeting with Dennis, I found him in his office, and he invited me in. Giving him the documents, I told him that Ann Tan had just sent me a full refund of my retainer. I did this as a way of telling Dennis that I was in a position to pay him.

Instead of picking up on this, and asking me for a retainer, Dennis said he had an important matter to discuss.

"I've thought a lot about your case, and I have a recommendation."

"Yes," I said, sitting up in my chair.

"I think you should sue for divorce on the grounds of adultery."

"Why?" I asked. "I thought you said that we would be basing the divorce on unreasonable behavior."

"If we can prove adultery, the divorce could be over quickly, within six months. You would be saving not only time, but money."

"Dennis, wouldn't it be difficult to get Hin Chew on adultery?"

"Not a problem, May Chu. We can use the services of a private investigator; it would be worth it."

I began to feel uneasy. "Oh Lord, here we go again." I thought to myself.

Dennis smiled, "It's worth a try, and I have just the man, you may have heard of him, his name is W. D. Anthony."

"W. D. Anthony? No." I answered.

"Well, here's his telephone number," said Dennis, writing on a small sheet from his telephone message pad. Handing the number to me, he said, "Give him a call. I use him all the time. Tell him Dennis Singham sent you."

Déjà vu?

I made an appointment to see W. D. Anthony two days later, on Wednesday, at 5:00 in the afternoon, so John could come along with me.

As I had done with Ann Tan, I was seeing W. D. Anthony, only to keep the peace with Dennis. I hadn't yet heard a word from Andy Lek, and, here I was, off to see W. D. Anthony. I did not feel at all good about what I was doing.

Mr. Anthony, an Indian, like Singham, and a small man, was imbedded in a large office suite, complete with secretary. As we entered his office, he stood up behind his desk, and extended his hand. Affecting suave manners, Anthony began our meeting by handing each of us a bound set of photocopies of magazine articles about W. D. Anthony.

After only a short look, I put down Anthony's materials. John, being more polite, took a little longer.

Feeling conned by it all, I let John do the talking. He gave Anthony a short, and not too detailed rundown of the case. By the brevity of John's explanation, I could see that he shared my opinion of what we were doing.

Anthony listened intently. When John had finished, Anthony leaned forward in his chair, and, placing his hands on his desk, looked me in the eye, and said, "I can help you."

"Oh, good, Mr. Anthony," I said.

"I'll need a retainer, something to get me started."

"How much?" asked John.

"Just give me a retainer of S$15,000, then I can start. The first ten days will cost you S$25,000, not including expenses, air fare, etc., at your prior discretion, of course."

We were in sticker-shock. Anthony's fees were outrageous. How could any woman afford to get a divorce at such a cost? I felt sick to my stomach.

Anthony continued, "If—excuse me—*when* we achieve success in securing proof of adultery, that will be an additional S$10,000."

No sooner had Anthony uttered his last syllable than his secretary materialized with a typed quotation of the figures Anthony had just given, on his company stationary, and bearing his embossed company stamp. She handed it to John.

John took the quote, and looked at it. The grand total came to S$50,000 (US$31,000).

John thanked Anthony's secretary, stood up, thanked Anthony with a handshake, and said that we would think about it.

"Good," responded Anthony, "and for today, that will be one thousand dollars, please."

After having a brief moment with himself, John took out his checkbook and wrote Anthony a check. No sooner had Anthony taken the check from John's hand, than his secretary appeared again, this time with a stamped receipt for the S$1,000.

That was the last we ever saw of W. D. Anthony.

Sleaze? The sleaze belonged to Dennis Singham for setting me up with his friend for what would have been a wild goose chase, and a bottomless money pit.

In spite of Hin Chew's possible dalliance with the social escort from High Society—something I could still not bring myself to believe—I doubted that he had any ongoing affair for which he could be brought to the bar of justice.

What to do about Dennis Singham?

This was a reality check for me. I couldn't keep bouncing from lawyer to lawyer, so I decided to stick with Dennis, and do my best to keep him under control. Great prospects for my divorce!

I'm not one to let things wait, so as soon as were out of the clutches of W. D. Anthony, I took my cell-phone out of my purse, and called Dennis.

"Dennis," I said, "I want to thank you so much for putting me in touch with W. D. Anthony, but I am sure there is no way that Hin Chew is an adulterer. We will have to stick with 'unreasonable behavior.'"

I knew what I had just said might have finished me with Dennis, but it was a risk I had to take.

"OK, I'm cool with that," answered Dennis.

THE MISSING MILLION DOLLARS

THE WEEK after our visit with W. D. Anthony, I received a call from my other private investigator, Andy Lek. He had returned from Hong Kong, and could I pay a visit to his office? I agreed to meet him at his office the next day, at 5:30 P.M., a convenient time for John.

After the required pleasantries, Lek said, "Let me show you what I have," popping a videotape into a vintage VCR, which was sitting atop an equally dated television set behind his desk.

When the image appeared on the television screen, we were presented with a jerky hand-held video of Hin Chew walking down a Hong Kong street, carrying a small plastic bag. Pointing to the bag on the screen, Lek said, "Cup of noodles inside."

John and I watched Hin Chew walking, Hin Chew going into a store to purchase a can of something, "Pepsi," Lek explained. We watched Hin Chew sit on a street bench, eat the noodles, open the Pepsi, get up, and walk on. The camera followed him, sometimes veering off the mark so much that the cameraman's knees and feet came into view. As Hin Chew descended into the subway, we followed, watched him go through the turnstile, and that was it, the video ended.

The entire video looked as though it had been produced with Hin Chew's knowledge. He must have noticed that he was being followed by some stumblebum with a video camera. Hin Chew even looked back once or twice, probably to make sure his paparazzo was not falling too far behind.

"I gave you S$15,000, Mr. Lek, and that was it?" I asked.

"We need to do more," answered Lek, "We need to rent the apartment next to his, and bug the wall."

Did Lek think I was tripping? Did he think I was so desperate, as to have become totally daft?

We left, and not too politely.

For the next two weeks, I heard nothing from Dennis Singham. It didn't really matter because Marc was back on vacation from Geelong, and it was important to spend time with him.

It was expensive to fly Marc back to Singapore for his vacations, but I did it. Australia had not been easy for Marc, and I couldn't let him feel that he had been abandoned. There was no way I could let him be the lone boy in school, while all the others were off on vacation.

In Australia, everything was different for Marc, and nothing like Singapore. Schoolwork in Australia was not a problem, but school sports were of prime importance to Geelong College. It was for good reason that Paul Sheahan, of cricket fame, had been appointed the school's headmaster.

Nevertheless, Marc was doing very well, and had made the rowing team, which was huge at Geelong College. Unlike his father, who at Geelong College, was known for bow ties, suspenders, and chess, Marc was a big husky boy, thanks to an inheritance of thug-blood from my father.

When Marc flew back to Australia after his vacation, I was feeling very good about my decision to send him to Geelong College.

Only after Marc's return to Geelong did I pick up the threads of my divorce case. It was good to have a break from seeing Dennis. I had to take some time to get over Dennis' questionable ploy of sending me to see W. D. Anthony.

This was Singapore, where kickbacks were a way of life.

At my next meeting with Dennis, he introduced me to his assistant, a young Chinese lawyer named Koh Tien Hua.

Again, I was being shunted off to a junior, the same tactic that I had suffered at the hands of Ann Tan with Catherine.

Singapore divorce lawyers had apparently developed a standard *modus operandi* for dealing with their clients.

Tien Hua was short, shorter than Dennis. Although Chinese, Tien Hua was of a newer, yuppie and more modern breed than Catherine. He was intelligent, well educated, articulate, affable, impeccably dressed, and handled a cigarette extremely well. Tien Hua cast a dashing, albeit diminutive figure.

Tien Hua had already prepared himself for the meeting by reading Ann Tan's draft of my divorce petition.

"I am appalled at this petition. It would have been thrown out of court," he opined, in a voice a bit deep for his size. Comforting words, but could Tien Hua do any better?

Very quickly, within several days, Tien Hua came up with his version of the divorce petition, and called telling me he was ready for a read-through. That evening, John and I met with Tien Hua in the Rodyk & Davidson conference room.

Tien Hua's draft petition was good, very good, and the grounds were "unreasonable behavior." Finally, we were getting somewhere.

Two days later, Tien Hua's opus was filed in court, and my divorce was underway. We were moving. Finally!

At the end of April 1994, John was off on a ten-day trip to Saudi Arabia for Citibank. Having lived nine years in Saudi Arabia, and with a mastery of things Arabic, including the language, John was invaluable as Citibank's "emissary" to Citibank's subsidiary, the Saudi American Bank, in Riyadh.

John had taken the trip on short notice, and the only routing available was to Karachi on Singapore Airlines, where he would have to transfer to Saudia, Saudi Arabia's national airline, for the final leg to Riyadh.

Saudia's non-alcoholic flights were always packed with workers and maids. On arrival in Riyadh, the length of John's line to passport control was better measured in hours than in distance. It was evening, and the Saudi passport control officers were off to prayers.

An experienced traveler, John left the line, found a cozy corner on the marble floor, and stretched out for a nap, using his laptop case as a pillow. John knew how to make use of technology.

Back in Singapore, I battled on alone.

The mounting pressure by Drew & Napier to let Hin Chew see Warren forced me to agree to a meeting between the two. Dennis advised me that it was the wise thing to do, even though Hin Chew had paid nothing for the children's support or for mine for four months.

We set the visitation date for Saturday, April 30, at noon, in a neutral and public location, the coffee shop of the Shangri-La Hotel.

Naturally, I was afraid that Hin Chew might try to spirit Warren away. With John out of town, I prevailed upon Tien Hua to accompany me to the Shangri-La Hotel. During Hin Chew's meeting with Warren, I planned that we would wait outside the coffee shop, standing guard, all five feet four of Tien Hua, and 125 pounds of me. Some guards!

I needed more help, and was lucky enough to reach John by telephone, in Saudi Arabia. Yes, he could catch a flight in time to arrive in Singapore shortly before 9:00 A.M. Then he could pick us up for the drive to the Shangri-La Hotel.

Saturday morning, John arrived at Orchard Scotts, as planned. Together, we went to fetch Tien Hua.

Some might think that a snazzy young lawyer working for a prestigious Singapore law firm would have a car of his own, but he didn't. On his monthly salary of S$2,000 (US$1,200), even though it put him in the top 30 percent of Singapore's wage earners, there was no way Tien Hua could afford a modest stick shift Toyota Corolla 1.3, which, new, would cost at least S$67,000 (US$42,000).

In Singapore, before buying a car, you must first purchase a Certificate of Entitlement (COE) from the government, allowing you to purchase the car. At that time, the COE for a small new 1,600 cc car cost S$46,000 (US$29,000).

A used car? Not a chance. If you didn't junk your car after ten years, by selling it back to the government for a predetermined price, you would be subject to a prohibitive tax. There are very few old cars on the road in Singapore.

Tien Hua could not afford an apartment of his own on his salary, and still lived with his mother. Nevertheless, when we picked him up, Tien Hua was bouncy and optimistic. If he persisted, some day with luck, he could become a partner of the firm, and would be earning from twenty to fifty times his current salary. Top Singapore lawyers can make a million or more annually.

We were at the Shangri-La Hotel by 11:00 in the morning, with plenty of time to position ourselves for Hin Chew's arrival.

We sat Warren in a chair near the entrance, where Hin Chew could spot him easily. Tien Hua and I went up to the hotel's mezzanine, and took seats overlooking the lobby. John was strategically placed on a sofa in the back of the lobby, his face hidden behind a newspaper.

Thinking back, the scene was comical, at the time, however, there was a great deal of tension, not only for the adults involved, but, more importantly, for Warren, who had to go one-on-one with his father.

We waited.

Hin Chew arrived, late as usual, by about fifteen minutes. He sailed into the lobby as if floating on a cork. How could I have had anything to do with him, I wondered. Hin Chew hesitated for a moment, bouncing on his toes … spotted Warren and made straight for him.

From the mezzanine, we could see the two of them disappear down the escalator to the coffee shop. Seconds later, John followed; his job was to cover the other exits from the coffee shop.

It was an awkward situation for Hin Chew, as he was not used to being with his children, much less talking to them, so, mercifully for everyone, their lunch was over in less than an hour, and Warren was free to go.

I was relieved to see Hin Chew and Warren coming up the escalator. Once back in the lobby, Hin Chew, fluttering his fingers, gave a dainty wave to Warren, and bobbed out of the hotel.

Nearly in tears, I rushed down the mezzanine stairs to Warren, who I found to be unimpressed by the whole affair.

"What happened? What did you talk about? Did he ask you about school, or Marc?" I said, excitedly.

"We didn't talk much. He asked me about money."

"Money?" I asked.

"He said 'Does Mummy have any money?'"

"Yes, and you told him …"

"I told him you had no money."

"Good! And what did he say?"

"He said, yes, you did."

I didn't burden Warren with any more questions, but I could tell that Hin Chew had used the visit to give Warren the third degree.

The next week Hin Chew, having been served with my Divorce Petition, filed his first affidavit with the court requesting access to Warren for the weekends.

The battle was on, and it involved more than one front.

John advised me that, since Hin Chew had removed the funds from Zhongli, it might be a good idea to check on any other bank accounts I knew about.

Always, well almost always, the obedient Asian wife, I had never looked into any of Hin Chew's financial affairs. It was not my place. Like his father, Hin Chew had money stashed all over the place, so I had no idea of what he had, or where he kept it.

Aside from our overdrawn account in Chung Khiaw Bank, I knew we had a joint account at The Citibank Private Bank, a subsidiary of Citibank.

The Citibank Private Bank required a minimum balance of US$1 million, and, in return, offered meeting rooms with Persian carpets, free coffee, and first-class service.

On May 9, 1994, I called The Citibank Private Bank and asked to speak to our account representative, Diana Quek. I was told that "Ms. Quek" was out of the office.

Immediately, I sent a fax to Citibank requesting a statement of our joint account, after all, my signature was on file, and I had equal authority with Hin Chew over the account.

After a delay of two days, on May 11, Diana Quek responded to me by fax, requesting a "Letter of Authorization" before Citibank could furnish me with any statements.

Why the delay? Diana Quek knew damn well who I was. We had met several times and she knew the account was operated on a single signatory basis, which empowered me to give instructions independently of Hin Chew. There was no reason for any delay, and no need for any letter of authorization.

Nevertheless, as requested, I sent the requested letter of authorization that same day, May 11.

After five more days of receiving no reply from Diana Quek, I hand-carried a second authorization letter to the bank, and handed it personally to Diana's boss, Paul Kwek. It was now May 16, 1994.

I could get better service from any normal bank account, with no minimum balance, through a teller machine with a debit card, than I was getting from The Citibank Private Bank.

It was not until May 19, ten days after my first request, that I finally received a hand-delivered letter from the bank, it was not from Diana Quek, but from a Mr. Ong, and contained the statements for our account from January through April 1994.

Ong's letter stated, "You may notice that the quality of these statements is not up to our usual high standard due to the fact that these copies were reproduced from microfilm and faxed across from our Hong Kong Branch."

The statements for January, through March were fax copies of fax copies. They were not only smudged, but parts of them looked fudged.

From the barely legible statement for March 1994, as well as I could make out, the funds were still in the account. Strangely, the April statement was crystal clear and clean, and showed that the funds were gone, and the balance was zero.

Hin Chew had cleaned out the account. He had taken out US$1.2 million in cash, leaving a balance of zero.

Over one million dollars gone! But when?

I was furious, and fired off a letter to Paul Kwek's boss, Nanoo Pamnani, giving him a timeline of Citibank's delays, stating, "I was of the understanding that Citibank is technologically and globally advanced, with information available at the 'press of a button.'" I was even ready to blame John for this. Didn't he work at Citibank? Wasn't he in charge of the data center?

"No," John explained calmly, "The Citibank Private Bank has a completely different management structure, and computer setup."

"Why?" I asked.

"Has to do with management, and done probably to protect the Citibank Private Bank clients. If I had any money to launder, The Citibank Private Bank would be my guy."

"Great bank for the Chungs," I replied.

Several days later, in answer to my letter to Nanoo Pamnani, I received a letter, not from Mr. Pamnani, but from Citibank's Singapore lawyers, the firm of Khattar Wong & Partners.

Khattar Wong's letter, which began ostentatiously with "We act for Citibank," informed me that our joint account had been closed on April 8, 1994. Interesting, as Citibank's "statement" gave *April 26* as the date the account was supposedly closed. Khattar Wong's letter ended with the admonition, "Please cease writing any further letters to our client."

Huh? I shouldn't ever write another letter to Citibank? Is Citibank about to get a gag order, so I can't request any more statements? Can't they take the heat? Get real, Khattar Wong, even in Singapore we have the freedom to write letters to whomever we want.

The war of words with Citibank, and Khattar Wong, no longer mattered. The establishment and Hin Chew had won, and the bottom line was that Hin Chew had successfully removed his liquid assets from Singapore.

The only assets remaining in Singapore were the Mount Rosie apartment, and my BMW 730iL.

What was the reason for Diana Quek's inexplicable and unjustifiable delays? Why was I stonewalled by The Citibank Private Bank, and why did they go to the expense of hiring lawyers to deter me?

My conclusion was that Hin Chew, lazy as usual, had not thought to transfer the funds out of our joint account, until after he had been served with my Divorce Petition, on April 29, 1994, at which time he was legally bound to leave the funds in the joint account.

Hin Chew and the Chungs being prime customers, The Citibank Private Bank had decided to fudge the date that Hin Chew cleaned out the account, to cover up the fact that he did so after having been served with the Divorce Petition.

That's only my theory, but it fits. With their computers, and red-carpet treatment for their million-dollar customers, no sane person could believe that Citibank could not have come up with clean clear statements in a flash.

Did I blame Diana Quek, Paul Kwek, or Nanoo Pamnani? Not at all. Knowing Citibank, I'm sure they had no choice.

I wouldn't have dared withdraw the funds myself. I knew better. As a woman, in Singapore, I would have faced the possibility of criminal charges for theft. Under our law, most of the matrimonial assets are deemed to belong to the husband.

I knew there was nothing I could do about the missing million dollars.

SOLE CUSTODY

Now that Hin Chew had put his bank accounts beyond my reach, he went to work to gain custody of the children.

May 23, 1994, was set as the date for the temporary custody hearing in the Singapore High Court, with Justice Lai Kew Chai presiding.

Hin Chew knew that, for me, the most important part of my divorce was not money, but custody of the children. I could always work, so we wouldn't starve. Naturally, I would do my best to get a fair settlement for my children and myself, but money wasn't my main goal.

Custody was everything for me. There was no way I could accept losing the children. If Hin Chew won only visitation rights, the boys would be truly lost.

Hin Chew could have afforded to settle matters amicably, and consented to an equitable divorce. That, however, was not his style. Although he knew the marriage was over, he was driven by hatred for the children and me, and greed to block the divorce by any means possible.

Tying up the children was his first move.

Hin Chew filed an affidavit with the court requesting to have Warren for weekends, picking him up on Friday, and returning him to me on Sunday evening.

Strangely, Hin Chew's affidavit made no mention whatsoever of Marc.

In the midst of my troubles with Citibank, I was able to put together a short affidavit of my own. I had time only to hit the highlights of my case—Hin Chew's incarceration in Brunei, his temper tantrums, his foul language, the example of his treatment of Lynn, his cutting off of our credit cards, the High Society escort service, and his lady friend in Hong Kong.

Just before the hearing, in rebuttal, Hin Chew filed a second affidavit containing a number of statements, many of which would have been comical, had there not been so much at stake.

In his second affidavit, Hin Chew, objecting to my use of the word, "incarcerated," stated, "This is a blatant lie. My passport was impounded for a year by the authorities in Brunei pending investigation into allegations of corruption."

I had never been able to come up with any legal proof of Hin Chew's incarceration, detention, or whatever he wanted to call it, in Brunei. Now, by Hin Chew's own sworn statement, I had the proof. Thanks, Hin Chew.

By that admission alone, Hin Chew, at the very least, would put Justice Lai on a high state of alert. In Singapore, you had to be squeaky clean—at least for the public record. On to the subject of his temper tantrums, and the children, Hin Chew declared, "I have *never* caned my children without reason and if I cane them, it is only to discipline them." I wished Justice Lai could have seen Hin Chew's collection of canes in our kitchen.

On his use of foul language, Hin Chew continued, "By virtue of my overseas education, I have grown accustomed to using expletives. Although I will admit that it is not the best environment in which to bring up the children, the truth is that this has been the environment that we are all accustomed to." Good stuff, huh?

Hin Chew's affidavit then went into a rambling three-page discourse on Lynn of all people.

It began with his remarks relating to the incident when he lost his temper in front of Lynn over not being able to find his "bathers," or swimming trunks: "When my sons retreat from our attempts to discipline them, they in fact run away sniggering as the whole episode is like a game to them. The incident where I had become angry with my sons when I could not find my swimming trunks is such an incident. I may have scolded my boys over the issue, but I did not hit Warren or Marc over the issue."

Only a game? Getting angry with your sons because you could not find your swimming trunks? Hin Chew had just scored two more very good points for my side, and corroborated the incident, which took place in front of Lynn.

True, Hin Chew did not hit Warren, only seized him by the throat, and gave him a good shaking. True, he didn't hit Marc either, as Marc was at a friend's house at the time.

Having brought Lynn into the picture, Hin Chew used her in a bizarre attempt to build his case against me, stating, "Unable to cope emotionally, James took to drinking very heavily and later died of liver failure. It is obvious to me that the petitioner is hoping that history will repeat itself so she is conducting herself on the same basis as Lynn."

Translated into English, what Hin Chew was saying was that, by behaving like Lynn, I would drive him to drink and to death by liver failure, à la Jim.

Justice Lai must have been scratching his head at this point.

Once on the subject of Lynn, Hin Chew veered completely off course, attacking her viciously: "I told Lynn that if James had been mentally stronger, he would not have died but would have gone through with the divorce. If that were the case, Lynn would not have ended up with James' estate, the bulk of which were gifts from my parents in any case. As it turned out, it was Lynn and not James's current girlfriend who had won the battle for James' estate."

Hin Chew failed to mention that Jim's estate had yet to be settled, and still couldn't get over the prospect of Lynn's inheriting Jim's estate—better it should have gone to Jim's mistress, Margaret, rather than to Lynn and her children.

Hin Chew went on to state that he tried to "structure a plan" for Jim's estate, but that, "As it turned out, it was all for naught. Lynn was only using me to advance her own cause. After agreeing to my proposals, she subsequently obtained a different solicitor in England, and ultimately reneged all her promises to me."

At this point Justice Lai, if he were still reading the affidavit, must have checked the cover page to make sure he was on the right case.

Hin Chew's diatribe against Lynn ended with the sentence, "While overly long, and ultimately irrelevant, the above passages serve to show my mood and frame of mind after meeting my sister-in-law again."

It had taken three pages for Hin Chew to explain that Lynn's presence, and her influence over me, had caused him to lose his temper, and scold Warren over the missing swimming trunks.

Captain Queeg, of Caine Mutiny fame, couldn't have turned out a nuttier affidavit.

I could tell that Hin Chew had dictated this affidavit to his lawyers in the heat of emotion, as its tone and grammatical errors were typical of him.

His lawyers must have been aghast at his ramblings, advising him against most of his remarks, but Hin Chew saw no reason to listen to them. He was richer than they, and he was paying.

Could it get any better for me? Yes, indeed!

Hin Chew next launched into his defense for his telephone call to the escort service, High Society: "I was in a black and despondent mood. In fact my business partners, fearing that I would give in to despair, visited me during this period for several days from Hong Kong and the States. It may well be that one of them or the other did phone the escort services that night. We had been drinking ..."

Hin Chew's being despondent, drunk and even suicidal—which is what giving into despair is all about—must have made a great impression on Justice Lai.

Finally, Hin Chew admitted the indiscretion with his lady friend in Hong Kong with the mawkish statement, "This 'lady friend' is indeed a friend, but just that, and no more. She provided a sympathetic shoulder for me to cry on. I was going through a period of self pity."

Great stuff! Wouldn't any judge love to award custody of children to a guy like that? I couldn't have hoped for a more idiotic affidavit from Hin Chew, had I written it myself.

On a serious note, a new and interesting fact emerged from Hin Chew's second affidavit. He explained that his frequent absences from Singapore were due to business trips to Hong Kong, Texas, and the Bahamas.

The Bahamas?

Hin Chew had told me about Hong Kong and Texas, but never mentioned the Bahamas. What was the Chairman of x-10 doing in the Bahamas? I filed that one away for future reference.

No matter how stupid your adversary may be, the judicial process can be like Russian roulette. Strange things can happen, and despite Hin Chew's wonky affidavit, I was worried.

Justice Lai's decision on temporary custody would most likely signify the final outcome, as it was doubtful, that, down the legal road, his decision would be overturned.

The dreaded day for the hearing came upon us on May 23, 1994, as scheduled.

All parties were present and assembled in Justice Lai's courtroom, a large dark wood paneled room, with a high ceiling, and thick red curtains covering the windows of the far wall. Hin Chew and his lawyer, a young lady, sat down on the wooden benches at the far side of the room. Dennis Singham, Warren, and I took our places, near the entrance to the courtroom, as far from Hin Chew as possible.

Apart from a few hushed echoes, the courtroom was silent as we waited anxiously for Justice Lai.

After a good ten minutes, a door to the right of the judge's bench opened. It was the door to Justice Lai's chambers. A clerk emerged. Walking into the courtroom, the clerk broke the silence, asking, "Is Mr. Singham, here?"

Dennis stood up.

"Could you please follow me?" said the clerk.

Dennis followed, and they disappeared into Justice Lai's chambers.

After no more than a minute, Dennis emerged from the judge's chambers, and came quickly to us. "Justice Lai wants to see Warren in his chambers, alone."

Dennis took Warren's hand, and led him quickly through the door, and into Justice Lai's chambers. Leaving Warren there, Dennis returned immediately to the courtroom.

Taking his seat, Dennis whispered to me, "This is most unusual, without precedent, I would say. Justice Lai never questions children."

"What does it mean?" I asked.

"We'll have to see," whispered Dennis, shaking his head.

After a full half hour, the clerk came out, and invited us all into Justice Lai's chambers. Justice Lai, a good looking man in his prime, with immaculate patent leather hair, was seated behind a large desk, which rested about four inches above floor level, on a raised dais. Warren stood by his side.

Silently, we took our places on the wooden chairs facing Justice Lai. I sat in the chair on the far right, with Dennis to my left.

To the left of Dennis, sat Hin Chew's lawyer. She gave her name as Christina Dorett. Hin Chew could not have been happy with her.

Not only was she not a man, she was not even Chinese. Like me, she was of mixed blood, but with a strong Indian tint.

Hin Chew sat next to her, slumped down in his chair. I could tell he was not happy.

After giving us all the once-over, Justice Lai shuffled through the papers on his desk, and wasting little time, said, "I do not interview children. That is usually the work of the child psychologist, however, I have decided to treat this hearing differently, because of the unusual nature of the case."

With barely a pause, Justice Lai looked at Hin Chew, and asked, "Mr. Chung?"

"Yes," Hin Chew moved to the edge of his chair.

"Mr. Chung, what day is today?"

Hin Chew's eyes shifted. He answered meekly, "It's the twenty-third of May, your Honor."

"Yes, Mr. Chung, and what day is this?"

"Well, yes, your Honor, it's the twenty-third of May. It's ... Monday."

"Is that all, Mr. Chung? The twenty-third of May, Monday?"

Hin Chew could only nod to Justice Lai, and then he began to smile—the Asian expression of embarrassment—and play nervously with his hair.

"Nothing else, Mr. Chung?" Justice Lai asked in a strong voice.

"No."

"Mr. Chung, you appear to have forgotten that today, the twenty-third of May, is, in fact, the birthday of your son Marc."

Hin Chew said nothing.

Justice Lai continued, "Mr. Chung, your behavior towards your children, and your wife, is a total disgrace. I myself have two sons, and I dearly cherish and love them."

Turning to me, Justice Lai continued, "Madam Lee, Warren is a very intelligent boy. You have done a good job, and have my sincere admiration and sympathy."

Game over!

After various thrusts and parries by the lawyers, Justice Lai rendered his decision. He awarded me sole custody of the children. Hin Chew would be allowed to see the children for a brief period every Saturday, and only in a public place.

Victory!

The credit for the win was all Warren's. In chambers, he had told Justice Lai what life was like with Hin Chew, and had set the trap by telling Justice Lai that today was Marc's birthday, and that his father would not know.

As Dennis, Warren, and I were leaving the courthouse, we could hear Hin Chew screaming at poor Christina Dorett in the street, for all to hear.

Keep up the good work, Hin Chew!

COUNTERATTACK

THE SATURDAY following the custody hearing, Warren and his father met for their second tense and silent lunch at the Shangri-La Hotel.

As before, Tien Hua, and I sat and waited out of sight on the mezzanine floor, while John roamed about. Happily, for all concerned, the lunch was over in less than an hour. This became the usual routine for the weekends when Hin Chew was in town.

I was now in for the long haul. Divorce, with all the financial issues to be settled, would take a long time. Could I hold out? Hin Chew was paying nothing to support the children or me, and I was waiting for my court hearing for interim maintenance.

John was traveling more and more for Citibank. He would be off to San Francisco, New York, Malaysia, Indonesia, and Saudi Arabia. When in Singapore, his workload, always high, increased to the point where he would often be at work until midnight. Usually I would drop by his office around ten in the evening to keep him company, and to discuss the day's events.

In July, Hin Chew initiated a counterattack. He had replaced Christina Dorett with a new lawyer from Drew & Napier, Tan Cheng Han, a man, Chinese, and an expert in matrimonial law. Armed with Tan Cheng Han, Hin Chew began a war of attrition, bombarding our side with letters, affidavits, and petitions.

Hin Chew knew that each one of these items would add to my legal fees. Maybe he could destroy me financially. So far, Dennis had not sent me any bills for his services, nor asked for a retainer. I kept my fingers crossed.

The first thrust of Hin Chew's counterattack began on July 16, 1994 when I was served with his "Answer and Cross Petition" in response to my Divorce Petition. Now, Hin Chew was counter-suing me for divorce on the basis that John was living with me at Orchard Scotts.

Had I wanted to live with John, I would have moved into his

apartment, saving me the S$5,800 monthly rent I was paying for Orchard Scotts. However, it would have been stupid to compromise myself by living with John. The embarrassment alone of not being in my Mount Rosie apartment kept me from contacting my friends, and there was no way I was going to make things worse.

John lived with William, and I lived with Warren.

Hin Chew took the additional bold step of having his Cross Petition served on John, right in his office at Citibank. This was calculated to embarrass John with the bank, or, even better, get him fired.

In his Cross Petition, Hin Chew raised an issue that I had considered settled. Again, he asked for "joint custody and care and control of the children." He knew my weak point, and apparently, I was back to square one regarding my custody of the children. This was extremely discouraging, as I realized that, at any time, my sole custody award of the children might be only as good as my next court hearing.

Hin Chew's Cross Petition requested that I be awarded monthly maintenance of S$4,000 (US$2,500), and that I pay my own legal costs. There was no mention by Hin Chew of the Mount Rosie apartment, or matrimonial property. That was it.

On the S$4,000 a month, it would take me a year or two to pay only my legal bills. Unlike Tien Hua, I didn't have the option of living with my parents, and even if I brought Marc back from Australia, and moved into an HDB apartment, I saw no way I could make it on Hin Chew's offer. I'm sure Hin Chew would have agreed with me on that.

Hin Chew's Cross Petition continued with his usual immature ramblings.

He admitted making threats to me, but "without any intention of carrying them out" (thanks for telling me now). He stated that I "liked to dress provocatively" (guilty as charged), and accused me of being "extremely jealous of the neighbors karaoke set" (huh?).

I "was usually the aggressor in the bedroom" (wha?), and I drove recklessly as I knew that would "unnerve" Hin Chew "tremendously" (why didn't the wimp learn to drive?). I "ate at unusual hours" (how true!).

Great stuff, especially if you have a sense of humor. If there was any justice left in the Singapore legal system, I might have a chance.

However, there was nothing comical about what Hin Chew was

doing. His requests to the court were a threat, and, regardless of how ridiculous his allegations were, I had to answer them, further adding to my legal costs.

Dennis had delegated all of the dog work of the case to Tien Hua, including the writing of affidavits. A top product of Singapore's Chinese-oriented educational system, Tien Hua was handicapped in Singapore's legal system, which used only the King's English. Singapore may have not planned that one out too well. As a result, Tien Hua wasn't exactly "writing smart" in English. John was, and so, who better to write the affidavits than John?

No workload, however great, seems to daunt John or to be beyond his workaholic capabilities. This was both his strength and his weakness.

As required, we answered Hin Chew's Cross Petition. John wrote a paragraph-by-paragraph rebuttal of Hin Chew's accusations, stressing the important point that I lived alone with Warren.

My affidavit came to forty-two double-spaced pages, which, with me by his side, was written by John, who delivered the finished product to Tien Hua on a computer diskette.

Tien Hua had little left to do, other than insert a bit of legalese, and on August 1, 1994, this new affidavit was served on Hin Chew's lawyers.

Three days later, giving us little rest, Hin Chew's lawyers fired off yet another affidavit.

This time Hin Chew increased his proposal for my interim maintenance and child support to S$6,298 (US$4,200), but claimed this would leave him only S$3,000 (US$2,000) a month to live on, based on his S$12,000 monthly salary from Zhongli. He explained, "I am able to subsist on this amount only because I am presently living in my mother's apartment rent-free."

Was I dealing with a pauper? Was Hin Chew no better off that Tien Hua? Well, not at all.

Hin Chew was living in one of several million-dollar apartments Lillian owned at The Waterside, Singapore's best new beachfront apartment complex. Hin Chew's apartment was on the twenty-first floor, and had a beautiful view of the sea.

In his new affidavit, Hin Chew made no mention of his earnings from

X-10, his company-paid US$5,500 a month apartment in Hong Kong, or of the sources of the cash he was bundling back to Singapore.

He also attempted to mislead the court by declaring he owned 75 percent of Chungco Bermuda, which came to 9,000 shares at a "par value of US$1.00 each," implying a value of US$9,000. Hin Chew did state that Chungco Bermuda owned 50 percent of X-10, but it was doubtful that any Singapore judge would know that X-10 was a well-known brand name in the United States.

The affidavit ended with a copy of a letter from Diana Quek of Citibank, giving a summary of his assets in Citibank. The US$1.2 million had been transferred to a Citibank account located in the safe tax-free haven of the island of Jersey.

Another of Hin Chew's accounts, this one at Citibank in Hong Kong, held S$353,572.72 (US$235,000), which he had lifted from Zhongli, as he was afraid that I "would withdraw and spend it."

Thanks, Hin Chew, for keeping the money safe for the kids and me.

In Hin Chew's new affidavit, there was an interesting omission. It made absolutely no mention of John. What happened?

Hin Chew had failed to do his homework on John.

After filing the Cross Petition, he discovered that John had worked at Inland Revenue at the grade of a Senior Deputy Assistant Commissioner. At that point, Hin Chew decided to back off from provoking John; the Chungs didn't want to offend anyone even remotely connected with Inland Revenue—who does?

Since Hin Chew, in his affidavit, chose not to reveal the full extent of his assets, I decided it was time to pay another visit to Zhongli. It was early in the evening on Friday, August 12, 1994, and, as before, John drove me to Sime Darby Centre, where again he waited in the car.

For some reason, this time I wasn't afraid as I walked down the long hallway and through the double doors on my way to the Zhongli office. Trying my key in the lock, I found it didn't work. I took my cell-phone out of my purse, called a locksmith, and returned to the parking lot to wait in the car with John. After about 45 minutes, the locksmith showed up, and opened the door to the office for me. To return the favor to Hin Chew, I had the fellow change the locks. Now Hin Chew would be locked out.

The Zhongli office was in disarray. There were packing boxes all about, some filled, some partially filled. I could see that Hin Chew was preparing to move out.

Written on the office whiteboard were the instructions:

(1) TRANSFER DATA FR TWL'S COMPUTER
(2) CLEAR ALL IRRELEVANT PROG/& DATA FR BOTH COMPUTERS
(3) COLLATE ALL DATA/MATERIAL FOR BOTH CPUS
(4) SELL BOTH CPUS!!
(5) SUBSCRIPTION CHANGE OF ADDRESS.

I always carry a small camera with me, so I took photographs of the whiteboard and the office as possible evidence.

The desks in the front office and most of the filing cabinets had been cleaned out. Not finding anything in the outer office, I went into Hin Chew's storeroom hideaway, where only the furniture remained. The wastebasket was full, and I dumped it out onto the floor.

Sifting through the mess, I came up with some X-10 financial statements, and other documents, which I put into the oversized purse I always carry.

As I left the office, it irked me to think that I had no knowledge of what was going on with Zhongli, and yet Hin Chew still expected me endorse his annual report with my signature. Still unafraid, I took the elevator down. The long struggle was changing me, maybe not for the better, but for the stronger. If anyone caught me, well, fuck them. I was only doing my fiduciary duties as a director.

In the lobby, I found that my key to Zhongli's mailbox still worked. Inside was a large envelope from Deloitte Touche Tohmatsu, an accounting firm, addressed simply to Zhongli. I stuffed it into my purse. Leaving the other letters, mostly bills, in the mailbox, I locked it, and walked out of the building.

Back at the Orchard Scotts apartment with John, once again, I laid my spoils from Zhongli on the living room floor.

I opened the envelope from Deloitte Touche Tohmatsu. It was a bound report. The title page read "x-10 Ltd., Financial Statements for the Year Ended June 30, 1993." This was x-10's audited financial report for 1993.

Hin Chew had told me that x-10 was in receivership when he bought the company, which was true, but had left me with the impression that the company was still struggling.

The Deloitte report painted a far different picture.

According to Deloitte's report, x-10's sales for the year ending June 30, 1993 totaled us$25 million dollars with a profit of us$3 million. In addition to the profit, there was a "consultancy fee paid to a shareholder" of us$944,974.

Who else could the fortunate "shareholder" have been other than Hin Chew? He was the Chairman of the Board, and the major shareholder, having told me he owned 86 percent of x-10.

Hin Chew was making millions. What a liar!

Among the documents I had taken from Zhongli was x-10's report for the month of September 1993, which stated, "The operating profit of us$860,000 was the highest ever achieved in x-10's history. With other income of us$205,000, net profit for the month hit a staggering us$1.065 million."

x-10's profits had hit a level of a million a month, and that was nearly a year before.

And here I was, supporting the children, with nothing coming in. From the report, I saw that Wai Lin owned 1.5 percent of Chungco Bermuda. That did it! I threw the report across the room.

I wasn't just angry, I was afraid. In Singapore, money is everything. If Hin Chew had that kind of money, in Singapore he had power. The only power I had was willpower, but what was that worth?

Luckily, John was with me. He never seemed to be discouraged by anything. He's not reckless, or carefree; he just has a very good nervous system.

I asked John to look at the x-10 reports to see if my untrained eye had it right.

"Yes," he said, "x-10 is making millions, and they are very clever about it. They sell a lot to Radio Shack."

"What do you mean?"

"Well, X-10 has a number of subsidiaries, X-10 Canada, Pico in Scotland, and X-10 USA."

"Yes," I nodded. "That's how the Chungs operate—a lot of corporations."

"Let me speak as a former taxman," John said, "most of X-10's profits are made in the US, but only about 2 percent of their sales are funneled through X-10 USA. They circumvent X-10 USA and sell just about everything direct from Hong Kong."

John looked up from the report, "X-10 Ltd Hong Kong makes a profit, while X-10 USA generates a loss, and so they avoid paying US taxes. Pretty good."

"You mean, instead of buying from X-10 USA, their American clients purchase direct from Hong Kong?" I asked.

"Looks like it. See," John put his finger on the report, "last year Radio Shack started buying direct from Hong Kong, instead of going through X-10 USA."

"Isn't that illegal?" I asked.

"Well, it doesn't look kosher to me."

"Couldn't I turn them in?"

John didn't look up from the report. "Hey, get this! They charge four times the rate of expenses to X-10 USA than they do to X-10 in Hong Kong."

I grabbed John's shoulder. "Listen, couldn't I turn them in for this?"

"Don't you have enough to do, just with the divorce?"

The next day, Hin Chew made an official report to the Singapore police that Zhongli had been broken into, and that he "suspected" that I was the culprit. Thanks, Hin Chew.

At about the same time as Hin Chew was reporting me to the police, I was driving to Tien Hua's office to give him Deloitte's financial report on X-10, along with other X-10 reports.

After I had explained the reports to Tien Hua, using John's words, and giving him some time to look them over, I said, "Tien Hua, I want you to let Hin Chew's lawyers know that we have these documents. Fax copies to them."

"But we'll be tipping our hand. I must advise you against letting them know," said Tien Hua, emphatically.

"Just do it!" I answered.

Within days, Hin Chew filed a new affidavit disclosing the true status of his ownership in X-10, enclosing the Deloitte report as its main exhibit.

In addition, Hin Chew's new affidavit confessed to some other "oversights," including his ownership of the Toorak apartment in Australia, and his S$180,000 (US$120,000) membership in Singapore's posh Tanah Merah Country Club.

A pauper no longer!

I had flushed out Hin Chew's X-10 assets.

It surprised me that Hin Chew was able to submit contradictory sworn affidavits and get away with it. This would become Hin Chew's practice throughout the case, reinventing his version of the truth as he went along.

How he got away with this, I do not know.

Lying in a sworn affidavit is perjury, a serious crime under Singapore law. How can there be any justice done when there is no enforcement of truth in sworn statements before the Singapore court?

Every time I caught Hin Chew lying in his affidavit, all he had to do was to come up with a new affidavit, admitting the lie. Was this justice? Were the judges inept? Were they corrupt? Or was *truth* not a highly valued commodity in Singapore?

Most Chinese proverbs are about being clever, but you'll have to search hard to find one about being truthful.

Flushing out Hin Chew's assets was all to the good, but my funds were running low, and I desperately needed a court hearing for interim maintenance as soon as possible. I hoped also to get a personal protection order, so I could move back into the Mount Rosie apartment.

Fortunately, the court finally gave us a date for the hearing; it would be on August 31, 1994.

That day, as I was happily getting ready for the hearing, the telephone rang. It was Tien Hua.

"Tien Hua, I will meet you at your office a full hour before we are due in court."

There was a pause.

"Dennis has decided to postpone the hearing," replied Tien Hua.

"What?" I couldn't believe what I had heard. "Let me speak to Dennis."

"He isn't here"

"Where the fuck is he?"

In measured tones, Tien Hua replied calmly, "Dennis is in Malaysia."

"Why didn't he tell me? Don't I deserve to know what is going on?"

"Well, Dennis decided that it would be best to try to negotiate with Hin Chew, instead of going into court. The other side seems willing." Tien Hua answered.

"Tien Hua, I had clearly told Dennis that there would be no negotiations. There is no way to get Hin Chew to negotiate—I know him, Dennis doesn't. We would be wasting time. What am I supposed to live on, while we negotiate? How could Dennis shaft me like this?"

There was silence on the other end of the line.

I slammed down the telephone.

We would have to schedule another court hearing for interim maintenance.

I went back to my cooking, cleaning, and paying of the bills.

Hin Chew, the deadbeat Dad, still had his Saturday visitation rights, always for a quick lunch and always at the Shangri-La Hotel. John, Tien Hua, and I, or just John and Tien Hua would take Warren to the hotel, and wait in the lobby.

Sometimes, it was too painful for me to go.

I continued to live in relative isolation. I hadn't heard a peep from my parents. Zena was still sticking by her Jehovah's Witness's principles, and considering me a sinner and a member of the army of Satan, had told me not to call her.

No matter what my circumstances were, I didn't deserve such treatment. Aside from anger, I felt emotional pain and hurt over being abandoned by my own family at the time when I needed them most.

Finally, we were given a new date for the interim maintenance hearing of October 10, 1994.

I had lost a lot of confidence in Dennis. I had more or less forgiven him for setting me up with W. D. Anthony. We all have to earn a living, but when Dennis failed to show up for my first maintenance hearing, I became very disillusioned with him. The Chungs had a way of getting you on their side. It was called money.

In addition, I found out that Dennis's father-in-law, a Singapore police officer, had been murdered in Brunei, while conducting an investigation. He was found dead, floating in a hotel swimming pool. Although this had happened some time before, and I doubted that it had anything to do with Dennis or with Brunox, I didn't like the way the stars were lining up.

As luck would have it, while John and I were having an evening drink at the Tavern bar at the Tanglin Club, we ran into my on-again-off-again modeling friend, the tall good-looking blonde, Mandy Fairfield.

Mandy's husband, an Englishman, had lost his cushy expatriate job, his fancy company-paid British-built colonial bungalow, his friends, and finally lost Mandy herself.

Mandy had found someone new, a good-looking gray-haired American, with the romantic name of Cary.

The four of us engaged in the usual mindless pleasantries, until we found common ground on the subject of divorce.

Cary said his wife had divorced him in Singapore, and won a large settlement, but that he, Cary, had appealed, and cut her to a mere S$700,000, "not enough to live on in Singapore for very long," he laughed.

Naturally, this caught my interest. "How did you manage to win on appeal?" I asked.

Cary answered that he had paid his ex-wife's lawyer, "bribed him with S$50,000," to appeal unsuccessfully, and see to it that her settlement was reduced in the bargain.

I took Cary's remarks for drunken bravado.

"Who was your wife's lawyer?" I asked.

"Dennis Singham," came the answer.

Hairs stood on end. Then it came to me. This was the case I had read about in *The Straits Times*. This was the basis on which

I had chosen Dennis!

Back home, I retrieved the article from my diary. It was the same case. Cary's wife was named Gaye Williams, and yes, her settlement had been reduced *as a result* of Dennis Singham's appeal on her behalf.

Even though I had no proof of any wrongdoing by Dennis, this was the final blow. I had lost all faith in him. I knew I had to do something to keep him on the straight and narrow. I could not afford to have a second hearing cancelled.

My remedy for this was typically Singaporean.

Singaporeans are tattletales. It's a police-state thing. The rulers of Singapore are much too bright to have a traditional old-fashioned goose-stepping police state. Instead of tanks in the streets, we have a sophisticated, modern government, who gets the job done working behind the external face of benevolence—no tanks needed.

Whenever one of us spots another one of us diverging from the accepted norm, our natural bent is to inform the proper authority of the transgression. In simple terms, we love to make police reports over anything—a grievance with a neighbor, failure to flush a public toilet (you get fined for that), or even an unclean stretch of sidewalk is enough.

Hin Chew, himself, enjoyed making police reports, such as reporting his wife, a director of Zhongli, for daring to enter Zhongli's office.

The Singapore police entertain all reports eagerly, duly giving a copy of the report to the complainant with an official reference number. The rulers of Singapore thrive on information, and do nothing to discourage even the most irrelevant tattletale.

To keep Dennis in line, I decided go one better than a normal police report.

On October 15, 1994, I wrote a letter to Singapore's top cop, Minister of Home Affairs, Professor S. Jayakumar. Of course, I did not expect Professor Jayakumar to take any kind of action. He had more important things to do, like keeping Singapore safe from the activities of Hong Kong Triads, and Jehovah's Witnesses.

My letter stated, for the record, that I was in the process of divorcing my husband, Chung Hin Chew, and then went into some length about Hin Chew's problems with the Brunei authorities. I gave, as my reason for writing the letter, that there should be "no misrepresentations," that I had anything to do with the Chungs' activities in Singapore, or their problems in Brunei.

Having set the record straight with Professor Jayakumar, I sent Dennis a copy of my letter, showing that I raised the stakes for him, should he fall under the spell of the Chungs.

Dennis answered me a terse letter, stating that my letter to Professor Jayakumar "could be construed against you in the worst possible light," and that "We therefore strongly advise and urge you to refrain and to cease from writing to persons or institutions not a party to your divorce or any other persons whatsoever."

So, Dennis didn't like my writing to Professor Jayakumar. Good! With an appropriate cover letter, I enclosed a copy of the letter from Dennis and sent it off to the Professor, as well.

I then called Tien Hua to tell him what I had done with Dennis's letter, and that Professor Jayakumar should enjoy reading it.

"What ...?" said Tien Hua.

Mission accomplished.

Several days before the hearing, I received yet another affidavit from Hin Chew. He needed to patch up some "inconsistencies" in his previous affidavit.

Yes, Hin Chew admitted, his expenditures had greatly exceeded his income, but that was easily explained by the fact that he "made a large amount of money between 1984 to 1986 investing in shares," stating, "This belongs to me."

I guess Hin Chew was a day trader during his incarceration in Brunei.

Since Singapore has no capital gains tax, no one has to keep any records of their stock market activity. Money can easily be laundered using the excuse that it came from the stock market.

Hin Chew had told me that his father paid him a million dollars to lie to the Brunei authorities, and I suppose, if Hin Chew wasn't lying to me, that could have been the explanation for part of Hin Chew's wealth.

Hin Chew foolishly admitted again in his affidavit that he had a "short-term arrangement only" with his lady friend in Hong Kong, but blamed me for harassing her so much that "this friend no longer wishes to associate with me." Good! I was happy to be guilty as charged.

Finally, and most importantly, Hin Chew claimed that Chungco

Bermuda owned 50 percent of X-10, and the other 50 percent was owned by a corporation named Lido Limited.

Who owned Lido? Hin Chew was not saying.

Hin Chew claimed he owned 75 percent of Chungco Bermuda, which through Chungco Bermuda's 50 percent stake in X-10 gave him a 37 ½ percent interest in X-10.

Several days later, Hin Chew's lawyers followed up with a letter admitting additional "unintentional omissions" in Hin Chew's affidavits, including a large amount of cash in the Central Provident Fund, Singapore's form of social security, and yet another bank account. Hin Chew's money was popping up from all over the place.

The October 10, 1994 for hearing for maintenance was before Justice Rajah, a Singaporean of Indian origin. This was unexpected good luck. I knew that an Indian judge, a third-class citizen in Singapore, would have a better understanding of my case.

I was right. Spousal maintenance orders in Singapore are usually for a pittance, but Justice Rajah awarded me S$9,000 or the equivalent of slightly over six thousand US Dollars per month. At the time, it was the second highest support order ever granted in Singapore.

My sole custody of the children was reconfirmed, and Justice Rajah gave me a personal protection order to restrain Hin Chew so that I could return to the Mount Rosie apartment.

After nine months out in the cold, with no home, no family, and not a cent of support from Hin Chew, I could finally go home to my Mount Rosie apartment, and prepare for my next battle.

CHRISTMAS AT MOUNT ROSIE

WITH MY PERSONAL protection order, giving us safety from Hin Chew, at least physically, it was time to get out of the expensive Orchard Scotts apartment and back into Mount Rosie.

Immediately after the hearing, I went to the Mount Rosie apartment. It was a total mess.

Empty beer cans littered the dining room table, the living room floor, and the master bedroom. Rotting food festered in the kitchen, and old newspapers were littered about—all Hin Chew's doing.

The telephone was dead; the bill had not been paid. Luckily, the electricity was still on, otherwise the apartment would have baked in Singapore's heat.

I arranged for movers to come the next day to pack up Hin Chew's belongings. The packing took an entire day, and when it was finished, the total amount of Hin Chew's junk came to over 100 good-sized packing boxes. I saw to it that everything that should be packed was packed, including old newspapers, trash, empty beer cans, and rotting food. Off the boxes went to Hin Chew's fashionable Waterside apartment.

Next, I brought in the exterminators, and following them, a crew of cleaners. It took one whole day, and well into the evening for the crew to clean the apartment, but in the end, the place was looking good.

While the cleaners were at work, I sorted through the mail that had piled up. There were no personal letters at all, nothing from my parents, Mamak, Zena, or any of my dear relatives, only flyers for the wastebasket, and bills to be paid—piles of bills, utility bills, building maintenance, property tax, and the television license tax.

Thanks Hin Chew.

Mount Rosie had not been painted from the day we moved in, eleven years before. The walls had yellowed, and going up the stairs, was a smudged line of gray left by years of children's handprints.

John suggested that I paint the entire interior white, and replace the old scarred cheap brown interior doors with new white doors with brass fittings to give the place a modern up-to-date look. He also said I should remove the plastic covers from the sofa and the lampshades, something Hin Chew had forbidden me to do.

The entire renovation process took the better part of two weeks, but at the end, it was worth it. I had the old sofa set in the living room reupholstered in ivory white, and the dark brown floor moldings painted black to match the staircase railings.

The Mount Rosie apartment was now light and airy, with new paint, sheer see-through white draperies, and new light beige carpeting in the bedrooms. The place looked entirely different. To purge the apartment of Hin Chew's presence, I had his old California king-sized bed in the master bedroom thrown out, and replaced it with a new queen-sized model.

Long live the Queen!

Next, I decided to get rid of the overdraft on our joint checking account at Chung Khiaw Bank. I never liked the idea of an overdrawn checking account, even though it was backed by a fixed deposit—of how much, I had no idea.

I called the bank to find out about the fixed deposit—something I never dared do in the far off days with Hin Chew. The news was good. The fixed deposit was S$75,000, and the checking account was about S$59,000 in the hole. I closed the fixed deposit, and transferred it into the checking account, giving me a positive balance of S$16,000 (US$11,000), which I immediately yanked from the bank. Cash in my hand! I never thought I could have done such a thing.

I felt wonderful, and so at peace with myself back in my Mount Rosie apartment, and once again able to face the world with confidence. Most important of all, my sons would be coming home to a "brand new" apartment, exorcised of all the memories of the fear and abuse we had suffered under Hin Chew.

This was a new beginning for all of us.

The first person I telephoned was Swee Cheong. We had not been in touch during my exile from Mount Rosie, and it was good to talk to him.

Swee Cheong had news, "May Chu, did you know your mother has left her house, and left your father?"

I was shocked.

"Swee Cheong, how do you know this?"

"May Chu, I have seen your mother, since she left."

"What is she going to do?"

"Divorce! She is going to get a divorce from your father. She will lose everything, May Chu, everything."

Swee Cheong was truly concerned for my mother.

"Where is she staying, Swee Cheong?"

"I cannot say for sure, but she says she is being put up by some of her JW friends."

"You mean the Jehovah's Witnesses?"

"I can't talk to her freely. She is always surrounded by four or five of her JW friends. They watch her like a hawk, May Chu. This is terrible. You know, May Chu, as a Jehovah's Witness, she can be arrested. The Singapore government takes this very seriously. Your mother is playing with fire." Swee Cheong said.

"Did she tell you why she left my father," I asked.

"Yes, she said, as a Jehovah's Witness, she could not live under the same roof, because your father is a Buddhist, and a sinner. She says he has a new girlfriend from China, named Jin Yan."

There were many more downsides to living with my father than his Buddhism, which he did not take seriously at all, and for all his faults, my father did not abuse or mistreat my mother. He never yelled at her, or hit her. True, he was a philanderer, but he was no Hin Chew.

My poor mother, her timing was off by at least twenty years. She should have done this in her thirties when she was in full bloom, and still had a chance for a life.

I saw Zena's hand in this.

She was a Jehovah's Witness, had always been jealous of my mother, and had most likely convinced her to leave my father.

Sadly, there was nothing I could do. I didn't know how or where to contact my mother. It was our family's season for divorces.

I invited Swee Cheong out to dinner with John that evening. We were getting back to old times.

I was in a great mood again, upbeat, happy and optimistic, back to my true self.

Marc was home from Geelong for Christmas vacation, and John thought that, with three boys around, the Mount Rosie apartment should have a Christmas tree.

We never had a Christmas tree. Christmas trees were something we saw only in the movies, but not part of our tradition. Naturally, I had bought the children presents for Christmas.

There are Christmas trees for sale in Singapore, and John bought a large one. He strapped it to the top of his car, and brought it to the Mount Rosie apartment, with Christmas ornaments and lights left over from his past lives. It was a real tree, and filled the Mount Rosie apartment with the scent of pine.

Brought up by his maternal grandparents, in the small Illinois town, Christmas was important to John, and decorating the Christmas tree was a tradition, a ritual, and a science.

Marc, Warren, William and I watched respectfully as John showed precisely how trimming the tree should be done.

"First, you start with the lights." We watched silently as John strung the lights around the tree with care and precision, weaving the strand of lights in and out over the branches as he slowly circled the tree.

Next came the ornaments. Happily, John invited us to participate.

Last came the tinsel. I had seen how this was done in some movie, probably starring Doris Day. I eagerly grabbed a bunch of tinsel and threw it at the tree.

"No! No! What are you doing? Not like that! Not like that at all!" admonished John. "Each strand of tinsel must be placed on the tree individually, with only one short end touching the branch. It makes all the difference."

It also took all the time, as we, the assistants, applied the tinsel, under the watchful eye of John. No tinsel throwing allowed.

I must admit that the finished product looked great. I quickly ran upstairs, and brought down the presents I had bought for the boys, William, and John. Taking my queue, everyone did the same, bringing their presents to the tree. At the end, under the warm glow of the Christmas tree lights, there lay a tempting bed of presents.

"Can we open them?" asked Warren.

"Not until Christmas morning," said John, "back in Lebanon, we never opened the presents until Christmas morning."

None of us had the expertise to prepare Christmas dinner. No problem, the experts were at the nearby Marco Polo Hotel. John had put in the order and would pick up the dinner on Christmas Day.

The day before Christmas fell on Saturday, Hin Chew's visitation day. John and I took Marc and Warren to the Shangri-La Hotel where Tien Hua was waiting to meet us.

Tien Hua, John, and I went to the mezzanine floor for a drink. The hotel was beautifully decorated in the best Christmas spirit, making us forget that we were in the midst of a wet humid rainforest. We were in the best of Christmas moods.

Suddenly, in the lobby below, I saw Marc and Warren run through the lobby. As quickly as we could get ourselves together, John, Tien Hua and I followed. We caught up with the boys in the parking lot.

"What happened?" I asked.

Marc, breathing heavily said, "Dad kept going on about all the money he had, and that we would never get it."

"So?" I said, "He always goes on like that."

"Yes, but this time I told him he was nothing but a loser. He really began to get mad, so Warren and I ran away."

Marc was entering the teens, and teenagers answer back, especially if they have lived overseas.

"Mom," said Warren, "Dad didn't have any Christmas presents for us."

My desire had been to protect the boys from their father, not to alienate them. Apparently, Hin Chew wasn't worried what the boys thought of him. As long as he got his way, nothing else mattered to Hin Chew. That was his way with everybody.

The next day was Christmas, and, on his way to Mount Rosie, John picked up his traditional Christmas dinner order at the Marco Polo Hotel. Most of the customers were Singaporeans and also had no idea of how to prepare a Christmas dinner, but felt that it was the thing to do.

With Christmas dinner, and the opening of the presents, the boys, William, John, and I enjoyed our Singapore Yuletide by our tree.

We were getting to be a family.

On Friday, December 30, 1994, Hin Chew's lawyers sent a letter by fax to Dennis, informing me that Hin Chew would not be attending the next day's meeting with the boys.

Since that Christmas Eve meeting, Marc and Warren have not seen nor heard from their father again.

PANDORA'S SILVER TRUNK

IN JANUARY 1995, Marc returned from his Christmas vacation to Geelong and I carried on with my life in Mount Rosie. There was little that I could do to speed up the divorce. Even though the wheels of justice were grinding exceedingly slow, life went on.

It was Sunday evening, John was in the office, Warren was asleep upstairs, and it was laundry night.

Our washer and dryer were on the back terrace of the apartment, behind the kitchen. The back terrace was a large room with a window-like opening on one side, covered only by a protective grill. This was our laundry area, and it was open to the outside so that the clothes could be hung up to dry.

I had used clotheslines for drying, as very few Singaporeans used or knew about dryers.

Several years before, I had been visiting one of my neighbors at Mount Rosie, an American lady, when I saw this large machine in her back terrace, next to the washer. "What's this?" I asked.

She replied that it was a dryer.

"What's it for?" I asked, not understanding.

"It's for drying clothes," she said politely.

"Why would you need a clothes dryer when we have the sun here, and you can just hang up your laundry up to dry?" I laughed.

The woman sighed and didn't bother to explain.

Of course John, being American, had a dryer too, and it was only when he showed me that the clothes came out nearly ironed, and not like the stiff boards from the laundry line, that I caught on.

All alone for laundry night, dressed in shorts, a tank top, sandals, and with my hair in a ponytail, I carried a huge load of laundry onto the back terrace, wondering how Warren could go through so many clothes. The back terrace was dark, with only the moon shining through the grill, but enough light for me to see what I was doing.

Both my washer and dryer were old-style front loaders, so I had to stoop down to heft Warren's laundry into the washer, and as I did, my eye caught a glint of something.

It was coming from the crawl space under the grilled terrace opening. I put the clothes into the machine, got up, and switched on the lights, a double fluorescent tube in the ceiling. There was nothing pretty about the back terrace.

The crawl space ran the length of the terrace, about ten feet wide, was about two feet high, and three feet deep, a place where few women would dare to go. I always thought the crawl space was the perfect hideout for an intruder. It gave me the chills.

I got down on my hands and knees to look into the crawl space. Far in the back, I could see something like a metallic or silver box. Cautiously, I reached into the crawl space, and finding a handle, pulled the thing out. It was a medium-sized silver trunk, covered with dust. Picking up a rag, I cleaned it up, and dragged it into the living room. I never liked the back terrace. It was ugly, isolated, and creepy. Anyone could be watching you from the outside.

The silver trunk was locked. I went into the kitchen to get a knife, and returned, sitting down on the floor to pick the lock.

Using the knife, and with a little work, I was able to force the lock open. Slowly I raised the lid of the trunk, almost afraid of what I might find.

This was the beginning of my Pandorian experience.

Fishing through the trunk, I found a small white envelope. It was addressed to Hin Chew in Brunei, and had a return address of P. O. Box 29, Jakarta, Indonesia. Inside was a letter, the stationery decorated with the imprint of a cute little teddy bear. Dated Jakarta, June 28, 1983, the letter began with "Dearest Hin Chew," and was followed by a short handwritten poem:

I don't tell you
Quite as often as I should
How very dear you are to me.
How thoughtful and how good
But hopefully you understand

And know at least in part
How many loving thoughts
Of you I keep within my heart.

The letter was signed, "With all my love, Vei Vei."

I was in a state of disbelief. The letter was written at the very time that Warren was conceived. I could feel my face redden, my eyes fill with tears, and my stomach turn.

I took a second letter out of the trunk. It was also from Vei Vei, with a postmark of July 21, 1983. This letter was in the same soppy style as the poem. The phrases from its ungrammatical drivel read:

Does it excite you to be a good friend of mine as I should think so … Cause I know 'just not easy to meet you.' …

I'm trying not to, I'm scared to go on but the feeling so strong. It's not your fault and it's not mine, we did the best we could …

You stole my heart from me, now I know just how much I have lost . . .

Ow! What's been happening to me. Tell me what to do please?

Much Love,
Vei Vei

As maudlin and stupid as the letters were, as tawdry as this Vei Vei person seemed, I was devastated. Tears streamed down my cheeks. I realized much, if not all, of the abuse the boys and I had suffered all these years from Hin Chew was purposeful.

I thought back to the summer of that year, and remembered that Hin Chew and I were in the process of moving from Brunei to Singapore. Hin Chew was doing a lot of traveling then, giving him the opportunity to meet with Vei Vei, while leaving me, his pregnant wife to roost in Singapore.

Hin Chew wasn't the innocent, ill-tempered nerd I had always taken him to be. He wanted a life away from us, and he had a life away from us. The ugly truth was staring me in the face.

I called John immediately. He was still at the office.

"Didn't I tell you so? How can you think the guy was twiddling his thumbs when he was away from you most of the time? I'm sorry, but what did you expect?"

That was not what I wanted to hear. What I wanted was sympathy, which I knew was crazy to expect, but I still wanted it.

I was angry and furious over Hin Chew's betrayal.

The fact that it had taken place so long ago, and at a time when I was eager to escape from Hin Chew, had nothing to do with it. He had sinned! I had been a woman scorned.

With what little rationality was left in me, at that moment, I was also shaken by my error in judgment, for failing to know the person I was with.

My voyage of discovery continued into the night, as more documents popped up.

There was the original handwritten memo from Agnes to Hin Chew regarding his October 1985 meeting with Dan Arnold and China Resources in Hong Kong. Why save the original of an old memo from Agnes? Was Hin Chew keeping this for some sort of leverage over Dan Arnold, George Bush's trusted CIA buddy? That would be a dangerous game.

The silver trunk also held the originals of letters and minutes of the 1984 meetings relating to the Chungs' problems with Brunei. Previously, I had seen only photocopies, but now I had the originals of the Brunei documents and the memo about the Dan Arnold meeting in Hong Kong in my possession.

I reread the old letter, written on November 3, 1984, from Peter to Hin Chew, advising, "You should stress your innocence and if it was a misunderstanding, you would be grateful if No. 4 in his wisdom can put things right again," and the cautionary handwritten post script, "Please make own notes & destroy this note."

I could only guess why Hin Chew had held onto the originals of the Brunei documents. He wanted to have a hold over his father, just in case.

The Brunei documents brought me back to what was now only a bad dream of the past.

I remembered the code names used: "Carl" was Hin Chew, "No. 4," Prince Jefri, with "No. 2" being his brother, Prince Mohamed. "City" was Citibank, and "Hardy" was the Citibank employee in New York responsible for exchanging the gold bars, "the bricks," to the "Madame Yeo," Lillian.

I read again the checklist coming out of the two-day November 14, November 15 meetings, where one of the items read, "Check if the States has an extradition treaty with Brunei."

Then I read the minutes of the November 17 meeting which stated that, "The man said that Carl's life is in danger," S. P. being "The man," and "Carl" being Hin Chew. I remembered how upsetting that was to me, at the time. This was followed by S. P.'s admonition to Hin Chew, "Your position is too young to shout at the other people." And finally, S. P.'s humiliating statement, "I am very shamed to do this to my family."

It was too much emotionally for me to read on, so I put everything back into the silver trunk. I would organize it all in the morning.

On standing up, I noticed a small brown piece of paper on the floor. I picked it up. It was a check dated September 18, 1978, made out to Hin Chew. It was from S. P., and had never been cashed. The check was drawn on Credit Suisse in Geneva, bearing S. P.'s account number 162 289. Even that was saved by Hin Chew.

I didn't sleep well that night, and lying awake, my emotional decision to become the Chungs' worst nightmare now found a basis in logic—in my logic, at least.

I knew already that the only way to get through my divorce without being ruined was to resort to guerilla warfare. I had no faith in the Singapore legal system, and no trust in Dennis. He had disappeared from the case, leaving me with Tien Hua, a bright junior, but years away from establishing a reputation that might carry weight with a Singapore judge.

The main weapons of guerilla warfare at my disposal were the Brunei documents, and my knowledge of the Chungs' businesses.

There were also the letters from Vei Vei. These were more of an embarrassment than a threat to Hin Chew, but would serve to show him that our field of battle would not be limited to the courtroom.

The next day I drove to Rodyk & Davidson to give Tien Hua photocopies of some of the key Brunei documents, along with copies of Vei Vei's love letters. I asked Tien Hua to write a letter, informing the other side that we had the original Brunei documents, and to give out some of the code names to prove our claim.

The next day, Hin Chew's lawyers, Drew & Napier, wrote back "Kindly explain the reference to "Donald Duck, Mickey Mouse, No. 4 or No. 2 in your said letter." Either they were in the dark, or just pretending.

That was not much of a response to my explosive revelations, but maybe I was beginning to get someone's attention. Late in the evening, I visited John at his office and showed him Drew & Napier's "Donald Duck" letter.

It had been a busy day for John, as by the time I entered his office, he had his sleeves rolled up, and his tie was loosened.

John read the letter, and thought for a moment, then looked at me and said, "Sure, if you can expose the Chungs to the Singapore government, or if this Mafia family you've got yourself into feel they are losing too much face, they may soften up, and let you go."

"What are you saying to me? You don't sound overly optimistic," I said.

"All right … listen, why not try to get something new—something they don't know you have?"

"What would that be?"

"Why don't you see what they are up to in America?"

"Like with Dan Arnold?"

John rubbed his face and eyes, shook his head, and said, "No, no, I wouldn't go there. I'll check out X-10 in the States and the people involved. It shouldn't be too difficult. Banks do this all the time. You know, credit checks."

"OK," I nodded. "Can you help me?"

"Don't I always?" John smiled.

"Will you check for me?" I asked.

"Sure, but it will take a little time—a month, or so," said John.

John did check, and it would prove worth the wait …

The Scam of 69 Holland Road

O N APRIL 29, 1995, I received the good news from Tien Hua that the final hearing for my divorce would take place in about four weeks. The long wait was finally ending.

Tien Hua said he needed to get together with me to finalize my request for a financial settlement. I told him to come to the American Club at 7:30 that evening, and to look for me in the Union Bar, where I would also be meeting John. It was Saturday, and the three of us could have a leisurely meeting over drinks and dinner.

When Tien Hua entered the bar, he was in a good mood. He bounced across the barroom, hopped up onto a stool next to us, and placed his new cell-phone conspicuously on the bar. As a joke, I warned Tien Hua that we were sitting only several feet away from the historic spot where John and I had first met nearly three years before. Poor Tien Hua, he didn't quite know whether to accept my remark with a smile or reverence. He did a bit of both.

After a brief drink, the three of us headed upstairs to the Presidential Room for dinner.

Tien Hua appeared optimistic over my prospects at the impending hearing, and as soon as the waiter had taken our orders, got down to business.

He had drawn up a rough estimate of Hin Chew's net worth, based on assets we could prove in court. It came to about S$7 million, or close to US$5 million.

This did not include the value of X-10, Hin Chew's largest asset, which, conservatively estimated, would have brought Hin Chew's net worth to S$14 million (US$10 million). We had no idea of what Hin Chew was being paid as Chairman of X-10, and knew nothing about the source of endless stream of cash Hin Chew was bringing into Singapore.

Based on what we could prove, Tien Hua suggested that I ask for the Mount Rosie apartment, plus a lump sum settlement. By law, I could be entitled to as much as half of Hin Chew's assets, but Tien

Hua said that was only what we would ask for; what we would get would be far less. That was the practice.

I didn't care. Originally, all I had wanted was the apartment, and child support. More than that, I had wanted to be free of Hin Chew, so I told Tien Hua not to ask for any specific settlement amount, we would leave it for the court to decide.

Tien Hua, who like most Singaporeans, was very much into details, was unhappy that I wasn't specific in my request. Fortunately his protest was interrupted by something of greater interest to him—dinner.

Singaporeans aren't into making pleasant dinner conversation when there is food on the table. Instead, we eat. Tien Hua was digging into his food in the way that most Singaporeans do, and so was I. John likes to say it's a hangover from past poverty, jokingly calling it "ancestral hunger." If true, Tien Hua was living proof, as he consumed a full prime-cut bone-in roast beef dinner and everything else in sight, including two baskets of bread. It was only after his desert of apple pie à la mode, an American Club specialty, that Tien Hua finally came up for air.

John smiled, and patting Tien Hua on the back said, "You OK, Tien Hua? Enjoy the food?"

"Yes, John, thank you," said Tien Hua wiping his mouth and checking his French cuffs for stains. That done, he bent far to his left side to reach into his now tight pants pocket for something. Struggling, he came out with a folded piece of paper.

"Good work, Tien Hua," said John.

"Yes, John, thank you," said Tien Hua unfolding the piece of paper. Then, looking at me, he said, "Your husband's lawyers have requested that you give him all the Chinese antiques still in your possession. Some of the pieces are very expensive. Here's the list."

He handed me the piece of paper. I took a quick look and handed it back.

"Aren't there any antiques on the list that you want to keep?" asked Tien Hua.

"Tien Hua, I want to forget all those reminders. I don't want to get wrapped up in details. Hin Chew loves details, loves his Chinese antiques, and has the time and money to drag this case on forever. Let's keep it simple. Give him all the antiques. Anyway, they were all taken from graves. Let him have the bad luck that goes with them."

"OK, I know what you mean. Unlucky," said Tien Hua.

"By the way, Tien Hua, did Hin Chew ask for anything else?"
I asked.

"No," answered Tien Hua.

"He didn't happen to ask for a silver trunk, did he?"

Tien Hua looked surprised. "A silver trunk? Certainly not! Anybody
would have remembered something like that. No, Hin Chew's list
is quite complete," Tien Hua took another look at the list, "No,
no silver trunk."

"Good," I said, as John stood up and helped me with my chair, as
a signal that dinner was over.

"Oh," said Tien Hua, pushing himself out of his chair, "I forgot
to tell you. A couple of weeks ago, on my way to work, I passed
your father's house, May Chu, and there was a large moving van
from K. C. Dat Movers parked outside."

The next morning, Sunday, John and I drove out to my parents'
residence at 69 Holland Road to check on it.

I hadn't seen my old home for some time, and was shaken by its
unkempt look. Singapore is carved out of a tropical rain forest, and
nature is always ready to reclaim what has been wrested from her. The
jungle was quickly reclaiming 69 Holland Road.

The front gate and most of the front wall to the property were
covered with a new growth of vines. As we pulled up in front of the
house, I noticed a piece of paper affixed to the front gate.

We were cautious as we got out of the car. My father could be
inside the house, or out anywhere on the grounds. We had no idea
of what to expect.

I removed the piece of paper from the front gate. It had been
stuck on with scotch tape.

It was a Warrant of Arrest for my father! A Warrant of Arrest! My
first thought was typical for a Singaporean—so shameful! I wondered
if anyone else knew; if anyone had seen it.

I read the warrant to John.

"You have failed to appear in court on April 26, 1995. A warrant of arrest has therefore been issued by the Subordinate Courts of Singapore. You are therefore wanted by the Police and liable to be arrested at your home, place of work, any checkpoints or wherever there is information as to your whereabouts."

The warrant stated that my father had "failed to comply with" a court order to pay my mother S$2,700 (US$1,800) monthly interim maintenance (not much, I thought, considering what my father was worth).

The warrant gave my father until May 2 at "10:00 AM SHARP!" to turn himself in.

My father had always been an embarrassment to me, but now, this!

"Well," John said, "At least he isn't wanted for murder."

"What's the difference?" I answered.

I pushed open the front gate. It was not locked.

We entered slowly and walked over the vines covering the walkway, up several steps to the front door landing.

A wooden chair was placed outside the front door, and several pairs of shoes were scattered about the landing. Someone appeared to be living in the house.

On the doorknob was a dirty plastic bag. It was stuffed with mail, which I dumped out onto the landing.

There were unpaid telephone bills, cancellation notices for non-payment of gas and electricity, credit card bills, income tax forms, notices of registered letters, and a letter to Jin Yan, my father's mistress, from her brother in China.

The letter was in Chinese, and the only item of interest was "Although Singapore is said to be a good place, it's still not as good as your own home."

Finally, there was a notice that the Singapore government was going to knock down the front wall guarding the 69 Holland Road to widen Holland Road, making it into a freeway.

I had never received any support or understanding from my parents, but their existence gave me the childish hope that some day I might. Now, with the disappearance of both my mother and my father, I felt I was truly on my own.

John is good at getting to the bottom of things, and his connections at Singapore's Inland Revenue Authority were a great help. Within days, he had uncovered what had happened to 69 Holland Road.

I knew that Uncle Jimmy had wanted to sell his house, numbered 67 Holland Road, for years, but couldn't without my father's permission, ostensibly because the houses were connected. Uncle Jimmy lived in Australia, and his house was vacant.

My father, on the other hand, had never wanted to sell 69 Holland Road. His brother's desire to sell 67 Holland Road meant nothing to my father.

According to the Singapore property tax records obtained by John, my father owned half of Uncle Jimmy's 67 Holland Road house. Neither Aunt Judy nor my mother had any ownership in either property.

My father and Uncle Jimmy had kept their options open.

However, with my mother's action for divorce, my father's situation had changed, he too wanted to get rid of the houses—and fast.

It is not easy to sell such a large and expensive property in a short amount of time. It could take months. My father was desperate, and had to find a solution, any solution.

My father went to the law firm of Helen Yeo & Partners to see what he could do. Helen Yeo was well connected. She was married to squeaky-clean Yeo Cheow Tong, then Singapore's Minister for Trade and Industry, and now Minister of Communications and Information Technology.

My father made the right choice in Helen Yeo.

A shell game was set up to transfer the properties out of my father's hands and away from my mother as quickly as possible.

The Holland Road properties would be "sold" to a newly formed corporation, Goldplus Investments Pte Ltd, conveniently owned by two junior lawyers in Helen Yeo's employ, Alvin Chia and Janet Tan.

Goldplus was what Singapore calls a "two-dollar corporation," meaning that it was set up with two shares of stock, costing one dollar each. Alvin and Janet owned one share each, two dollars in total.

On April 3, 1995, 69 Holland Road was transferred to Goldplus for S$4,800,000, and 67 Holland Road for S$5,020,000, a grand total of S$9,820,000 (US$6,700,000)—at least for the record.

Pretty good! They acquired the 67 and 69 Holland Road houses for two bucks.

So how did Goldplus, with a total paid up capital of only S$2, manage to purchase such expensive properties? Easy, with the properties in hand, Goldplus took out two loans from the Overseas Chinese Banking Corporation totaling S$23,600,000 (US$16,000,000).

The two large Holland Road houses were located on an acre of land in the best part of Singapore, so it was not surprising that they should be able to fetch a mortgage of S$23 million. The houses were worth even more than that.

If the two houses were worth in excess of S$23 million, then why did my father and Uncle Jimmy sell them for so little?

I don't think they did. My father and Uncle Jimmy were just parking the houses in Goldplus, safe from any claim by my mother, until they could find a legitimate buyer.

Normally such transactions are blocked when a divorce is in progress. There was also the matter of the warrant of arrest out for my father for non-payment of interim maintenance.

How was my father able to sell the Holland Road properties with all these legal problems?

It pays to have lawyers in high places.

Still, my mother's lawyer easily could have blocked my father's sale of the houses, and although I had not seen nor heard from my mother for a year, I took it upon myself to help her as best I could.

Ever the dutiful daughter, I had Tien Hua track down the law firm my mother was using. It turned out to be J. S. Yeh & Co, a modest law firm located in a very modest building in the most modest part of Chinatown.

I wrote to Yeh telling him about the transfer of the Holland Road properties to Goldplus, enclosing copies of the documents showing the sale of the houses.

I went so far as to give Yeh the home addresses of Helen Yeo's two lawyers, Goldplus owners, Janet Tan and Alvin Chia. I laid it all out for Yeh, and told him to block the sale of 67 and 69 Holland Road.

Even though the properties had already been sold, in Singapore it takes months to complete the transfer. All Yeh had to do was file a caveat with the court, and the sale of the Holland Road properties would be blocked; he had plenty of time to act.

That was the best I could do, but it was all to no avail. Through Goldplus, my father and Uncle Jimmy managed to complete the sale of the houses. My fugitive father and Uncle Jimmy must have escaped with something better than US$16 million between them.

My father was able to sell his property at an all time high. Singapore was pricing itself out of the market, and becoming unable to compete with Asia's new dragon, China. Singapore's property values and currency were to begin a slide that could force Singapore to skid back into being a part of Malaysia. Lee Kuan Yew himself admitted this possibility.

Why Yeh never blocked my father's sale of the Holland Road properties, I do not know.

I added Yeh to my Hall of Fame of Singapore Lawyers, which also included Dennis Singham, Ann Tan, and Helen Yeo.

Did I overlook the junior lawyers Koh Tien Hua, Janet Tan, and Alvin Chia? No, they were in my Hall of Stooges.

Eventually, the court awarded my mother a settlement of S$1,445,456.30 (US$1,000,000) against my father. Having fled from Singapore, he never paid, and in 1996, my mother, on a motion to the court, had my father declared a bankrupt.

Just like the warrant for my father's arrest, I found the resulting bankruptcy notice affixed to the usual place on the front gate of 69 Holland Road. So shameful.

My father, the Tiger Balm King grandson, was a bankrupt, a fugitive from the law, and on the run.

And my mother?

Singapore is full of women like her. They appear to be well off, they attend charity functions, and fashion shows. Their photographs appear regularly in the *Singapore Tatler* showing them dressed in the latest haute couture, the preferred fashion houses being Versace, Armani, and Escada. Bejeweled, and with watches by Cartier, Patek Philippe, or Bulgari, they arrive at their functions, chauffeur-driven in a Mercedes-Benz, BMW, or like Lillian, in a Rolls-Royce.

In reality, these glittering society matrons are no better than aging concubines.

On a whim, perhaps for a new harem girl, their husbands can

transfer everything out of Singapore or into surrogate corporations, even during a divorce, deserting their wives and children, leaving them with nothing—abandoned and penniless to disappear into lives of despair, embarrassment, and shame.

In Singapore, it happens all the time.

Hin Chew did it with our joint and Zhongli Citibank accounts. My father did it with his houses. That's the way the Singapore government wants it. It's a long-standing Third World tradition in countries where women have no rights. Singapore, with its claim of being a First World country, holds up its Women's Charter as an example of its progressive attitude toward women, but, when you see that "brothel" is that document's lead-in definition, you get a different picture. In Singapore, you have to look beneath the surface to find the truth.

Where is my fugitive father?

The rumor amongst his cronies in Singapore is that he fled with his money to Brazil, where he lives happily ever after in a villa in Rio de Janeiro, with his mistress Jin Yan, two cars, and a yacht.

I think I know my father better.

Brazil would be too far from his comfort zone. Jackie Lee has had it too easy and lacks the guts for such a change. He's probably living somewhere in Sydney, close by brother Jimmy Lee.

I've asked Mamak many times to tell me where my father is.

She claims she doesn't know.

Do I believe her? Of course not!

FISHING VESSELS TO THE RESCUE

TIEN HUA informed me that he had the date for my divorce trial; it was set to begin on June 5, and end on June 9, 1995. I was puzzled and upset by the four-day duration of the trial. Four days would make sense for a murder trial, but this was a simple divorce. Four days of grilling on the witness stand could bare your soul, and break your bank.

"Why does the trial have to be four days long? Is this case so complicated?" I asked Tien Hua.

"That's what the other side wanted, and that is what the judge gave them," replied Tien Hua flatly as he ground his cigarette into the ashtray.

"Isn't that going to cost me a lot of money? How much do you think it could cost, Tien Hua?" I asked.

Tien Hua looked up from the ashtray, brushing off his jacket. "If you win, it shouldn't cost anything. The winner is entitled to costs."

"All costs, including your fees?"

"Yes," answered Tien Hua, checking his watch.

"That's if I win, and what if I don't? It's a long trial and with some tight-ass puritanical Singapore judge, it seems like a hell of a risk."

"I think we have a pretty good case," said Tien Hua, lighting another cigarette.

"What will happen to my maintenance? Will my maintenance continue after the trial? And why do they call it a trial? Can't it be just called a hearing? Goddamn it Tien Hua! Getting any information from you is like squeezing blood from a rock." I said.

I was in a state of near panic. By any standards, Hin Chew had been abusive. The grounds for divorce on unreasonable behavior would be clear to anyone, any human being, but to a Singapore judge?

How high did the threshold of pain have to be for me to be granted a divorce? My guerilla warfare tactics had not worked. The Brunei documents, and Vei Vei—my extracurricular weapons—did not have the firepower to defeat the Chungs. I was in total despair.

Not even John's steady optimism could lift my spirits. I knew I would not get a fair trial.

This was Asia, and I was a woman. Hin Chew was home free. He wouldn't even have to bribe the judge.

It's always darkest before the dawn.

John's investigation had confirmed the disturbing facts about S. P.'s longtime friend, Dan Arnold.

After leaving the CIA in 1979 to work on the Bush presidential campaign, Dan Arnold returned to Thailand in a "private capacity."

In 1982, before the U.S. Senate Select Committee on POW/MIA Affairs, Dan Arnold was mentioned as an arms trafficker, and linked to the CIA drug trade in Southeast Asia.

Dan Arnold's name had appeared in several newspaper articles and books, linking him to the drug trade, but, unfortunately, he never got the notoriety he deserved. Like his buddy, S. P. Chung, Dan Arnold was, and remains, an unknown quantity to the general public.

Although the information on Dan Arnold served to confirm my suspicions about S. P., it was not something that John said would be wise to reveal in a Singapore court.

On Saturday, May 6, 1995, John came up with something new, something more concrete and provable. He was able to confirm that Peter Lesser, the President of X-10 USA, had taken out a number of loans, three of which listed "fishing vessels" as collateral.

We had received news of the fishing vessels several weeks before, but now we had documentary confirmation. I was very excited by the news of the "fishing vessels."

Recently, my suspicions about the Chungs' activities had been reinforced by a fax I found in the Zhongli office. The fax was from X-10's Hong Kong office, dated February 26, 1993; it was addressed to a person named "V----e" at Leviton, one of X-10's major clients.

After some innocent looking quotes for X-10 devices in the first paragraph, the second paragraph of the fax made the puzzling statement, "We are pushing ahead with solving this problem. I can now confirm that we will have a solution, most probably aqueous for shipments after May 1."

Huh? I couldn't see what an "aqueous" solution had to do with the shipment of electronic goods. There is nothing "aqueous" about X-10 devices. If the shipment were by sea, why not say it in so many words? I am sure that everyone was innocent, and that there must have been an easy explanation for the terminology used in X-10's fax. I just haven't heard it yet.

It was time to talk to my lawyer, Tien Hua. Dennis Singham had completely disappeared from my case. On Monday morning, May 8, 1995, I called Tien Hua at his office and told him the news about the fishing vessels.

"Tien Hua, Hin Chew and X-10 may have fishing vessels—you know what can go with fishing vessels ..."

"Fishing vessels, I see," said Tien Hua, flatly.

"Aren't you excited about this information, Tien Hua?"

Tien Hua did not seem to share my excitement over the news, and asked me for a day to think about how best to use this information.

I never like delays, but one day wouldn't make a difference, so to keep the peace, I let Tien Hua have his way. However, I cautioned Tien Hua, saying, "Don't tell anyone about my discovery of the fishing vessels, not Dennis, not anyone. No one is to know but us, until we've talked. Do you understand?"

"Of course, May Chu," Tien Hua answered.

We terminated our conversation, and I could hear Tien Hua exhaling smoke as he hung up the phone.

On Tuesday, May 9, 1995, in the morning, I called Tien Hua again to tell him what I wanted done. I had made up my mind.

We would send Drew & Napier a letter about the fishing vessels. I had already faxed Tien Hua a draft copy of the letter, so his task was very easy. He should be able to get it out in no time.

On Wednesday, May 10, 1995, it was a national holiday in Singapore, *Hari Raya Haji*, so I called Tien Hua at home.

"Tien Hua, so sorry to call you at home, I know it's lunchtime, but did you get my fishing vessels' letter off to Drew & Napier?"

Completely dodging my question, Tien Hua asked, in a matter

of fact way, "Do you know what routes the fishing vessels take, and where they are parked?"

"Tien Hua, you're asking me strange questions. I'm asking you to send a simple letter to Hin Chew's lawyers to inform them of my knowledge of the fishing vessels, and you're asking me these questions?"

Suddenly, I had a very bad feeling about Tien Hua.

I repeated my question, "Well, Tien Hua, did you send the letter?"

"I'm still studying it," was Tien Hua's excuse.

"Tien Hua, what are you on about? It's a very simple letter. I can't believe you're not sending it out. Please get it out tomorrow."

With that, I was careful to end the conversation with a very polite "Goodbye." I was in a sweat and my heart was pounding when I hung up the phone.

Tien Hua's strange questions concerning the routes and locations of the fishing vessels had to be questions that he had been prompted to ask. Someone was coaching him.

He might have asked me questions about ownership and value of the fishing vessels, to see if they could somehow be treated as matrimonial assets. That would have been reasonable.

My take was that Tien Hua had betrayed me and had already told Drew & Napier about the fishing vessels. With Tien Hua as their modem, Drew & Napier, or someone on their side, was trying to find out how much I knew.

Thursday, May 11, 1995, Singapore got back to work, and it was a busy day for me. There was a maid coming to clean the apartment, and I had to go into town to run errands, collect some clothes, and be back in time for Warren's tutor to arrive in the afternoon.

Lawsuit or no lawsuit, life had to go on.

All day, as I ran about doing my errands, I stewed about Tien Hua, and mulled over the apparent change in his attitude toward me.

Tien Hua had become uncooperative, unenthusiastic, unwilling, and untrustworthy. I was having a very tough time pushing him to get the letter to Drew & Napier about the fishing vessels.

I had learned from experience that, when people are not cooperative, they are not interested, or worse they have their own personal agendas.

I decided to set a trap for Tien Hua.

I sent him a fax, which read, "Where are the Fishing Vessels 'parked?' Which routes do these Fishing Vessels take? As of today, I have the INFORMATION pertaining to your QUERY."

Of course, I had no idea where the fishing vessels were "parked," as Tien Hua put it, or where they might be going, but why not spook everybody as much as possible. I had nothing to lose.

My fax went off May 11, 1995 at 5:39 P.M. Disgusted with Tien Hua, I didn't phone him that evening. I was tired of bugging the little twerp.

To get my mind off worrying about the impending trial, I went out with John for what was intended to be a relaxing dinner at Dan Ryan's Chicago Grill, a place for Singapore "Cheers" wannabes. During dinner, however, I could not get myself off the subjects of the fishing vessels, Tien Hua, betrayal, and the looming four-day divorce trial.

Finally, John began to put things into perspective, saying, "So what? Who gives a damn if Tien Hua told Drew & Napier or even told Hin Chew directly."

"But Tien Hua betrayed me," I said, angrily.

John pointed his finger at me, "You've got it! That's where the damage is. You've got a lawyer you can't trust."

I started to say something, but John cut in with a sudden thought, "Look at it this way. Tien Hua tells the other side about the fishing vessels, we agree on that, OK?"

"Yes," I nodded.

"But little Tien Hua stalls on sending the letter to Drew & Napier, and why?"

"Yes, and why?" I asked, puzzled.

"Because the other side has told Tien Hua not to send the letter, at least not yet. They don't want any hard evidence that they know about the fishing vessels."

"So they can't be incriminated?" I added.

"No," said John, "they're holding that letter up until they know how to answer your move on the fishing vessels."

"Why would they do that?" I asked.

"That way, if they decide to do something, based on the fishing vessels, they can say 'what fishing vessels, we didn't know about any fishing vessels?' and still look clean."

"You mean, the fishing vessels have them thinking."

"My guess is that you've got them in crisis mode."

"What do you think they'll do," I asked.

"If we're onto something with the fishing vessels, or even going in some direction they don't like, they'll make a move."

"What kind of a move?

"We'll see, most likely a good move for us. Want some dessert?"

"You're so so smart, aren't you?" I said, leaning forward and smiling.

"Hey, that's me. I even get paid for it by Citibank."

Back at the Mount Rosie apartment that evening, in spite of John's confident attitude, I again had trouble falling asleep. Nothing seemed to be working in my favor. I could be on the road to destruction. If the judge ruled that Hin Chew was a kind and loving husband, I could be stuck with the bum forever.

I awoke several times the next morning, but each time went back to sleep. Worry and despair does that.

The next morning, Friday morning, May 12, 1995, the phone rang at 10:45 A.M., waking me up for the final time that day. I picked it up, and whispered, "Hello."

"May Chu? It's Tien Hua. Did you get my fax?" "Yes, maybe—just a minute."

Not quite myself, after too much sleep, I got out of bed, opened the curtains to let some light in, and went over to the fax machine.

There was a letter. It was from Drew & Napier, dated Thursday, May 11, 1995, and addressed *not* to me, but to The Registrar of the Supreme Court of Singapore. After an opening paragraph filled with the usual legal recitals, the second paragraph read:

> We are writing to inform your Honour that our client no longer wishes to contest the Petition. Our client is prepared to withdraw his Answer and Cross-Petition (without admission to the allegations raised in the Petition) and allow the Petition to proceed on an uncontested basis.

I'm not a morning person, especially without a cup of black coffee, so I went back to sit on the bed, and reread the letter.

Then, picking up the phone, I said, "Tien Hua?"

"Yes."

"Tien Hua, what does this letter mean? Does this mean that Hin Chew has given up?" I asked.

"Yes, it means that Hin Chew has dropped all opposition to the divorce. No more four-day trial."

I HAD WON!!!

Justice Delayed

I N AN AMERICAN divorce, the financial settlement comes before the granting of the actual divorce. In Singapore, it comes *after*. You must first get your divorce, and then return to court for a final hearing to fight over the financial settlement.

Until this final hearing, called the *ancillaries*, the divorcée is in limbo. The woman, divorced and out in the cold, has no idea of what her financial future will be. Very few women, especially those with children, are willing to take the risk.

Singapore's purpose for this strange order of events is not only to deter women from getting a divorce, but also to insure that the men remain in control of the money.

The matrimonial assets are divided not on a fifty-fifty basis, but in accordance with the Women's Charter, by "the contributions made by each of the parties to the marriage to the welfare of the family."

My contribution for cleaning, cooking, and running the home, established my worth at a maid's salary of S$350 (US$200) a month.

Hin Chew's contribution to our welfare includes the cash he spirited into Singapore, his millions from X-10, the principal and interest on the US$1.2 million he grabbed from our Citibank joint account, plus whatever other sources of income he might have.

Hin Chew would be way ahead of me when it came time for the judge to divvy up our assets.

Later on that same Friday, Tien Hua faxed me a copy of a letter he had just received from Drew & Napier. The key paragraph in Drew & Napier's letter read:

> Please be informed that the Respondent shall be withdrawing his answer and cross petition and that he shall not be contesting the divorce. He has however decided to contest the ancillaries and he would want the ancillaries heard on 5 June 1995.

Well, there you go, Hin Chew, "the Respondent," who had made a major climb-down only the day before, was having second thoughts about the money part, and had decided to fight my request for a final settlement, rather than negotiate. The hearing for this was set for June 5, 1995, our original court date.

No sooner had I read the fax, than the phone rang. As expected, it was Tien Hua, calling to tell me that Hin Chew wanted the ancillaries to be heard, and to remind me that my financial affidavit for the June 5 hearing had to be filed with the court by May 22.

John helped me grind out another affidavit, in time for me to deliver the draft copy to Tien Hua on May 22, in time for the deadline.

The next day, May 23, another letter slithered through the fax machine. Again, it was from Tien Hua, notifying me that the date for the court hearing had been "refixed" to July 27, 1995. Tien Hua's fax included a copy of the letter of the Registrar of the Supreme Court, attesting to the change, which stated:

> Please note that the Petition is refixed for hearing on Thursday 27 July 1995 at 10:00 a.m. The hearing dates from Monday 5 to Thursday 8 June 1995 are thus vacated.

Looking closely at the letter, I could see that the date of the Registrar's letter had been partially erased. I could make out, however, that the letter was dated May 20; today was May 23. Why the delay?

I immediately phoned Tien Hua—no hello from me this time.

"Tien Hua, what the hell is going on? Our court date has been delayed two months. Who changes these dates without my knowledge or agreement?"

"Oh, May Chu, the June 5 was only a request date, nothing fixed."

"If the June 5 date wasn't fixed, as you say, then why does the letter from the court say it has been refixed? How do you refix a date that has not been fixed, Tien Hua? Huh?"

There was silence on Tien Hua's end, punctuated by a muffled cough.

With frozen words, I continued, "Do you know what I think, Tien Hua? I think, just as you leaked the news of the fishing vessels to Drew & Napier, you leaked my financial affidavit to them. Are you there?"

"Yes."

"Now that Hin Chew has had the opportunity to see my financial affidavit, Drew & Napier has asked for more time to figure out what to do."

Silence was Tien Hua's answer.

"I notice that someone attempted to erase the date on the letter of the Registrar."

"May Chu, we received that letter only today."

"Oh really? You should have done a better job erasing the date. You say today, but I can see the date as May 20, three days ago."

Silence.

"Look, I know that Drew & Napier could not have rescheduled the hearing to July 27 without your consenting to it. The same goes for the four-day trial. How could you have given them your consent, without getting my agreement? Fuck you!"

I slammed down the phone.

There was nothing for me to do but be patient until the July 27 court date for the financial hearing rolled around. I was furious over the delay, but at this stage of the game, there was little that I could do. With at least my divorce assured, I decided to rejoin the world of the living for a while. I would relax and be happy.

Nearly three weeks later, on July 5, Tien Hua called me at 8:45 in the evening, opening with a happy, "May Chu, it's me, Tien Hua, how have you been?"

"Well, right now I'm mopping the floor with Pine-Sol, is how I am," I answered.

There was a brief pause on Tien Hua's end, as he searched for some deeper meaning in my statement. Finally, the best he could do was repeat, "How have you been?"

"Fine, Tien Hua. I haven't heard from you in over a month." I said.

"You may want to modify your June 5 affidavit, the one we didn't use, for the July 27 hearing. It's up to you."

"Yes, when do you need it?" I asked.

"The affidavit has to be filed on July 24, so if you could get it to me a week before—would that be OK with you?"

My, but weren't we being so polite with each other.

"Of course, Tien Hua," I said.

We said very cordial goodbyes, and I was happy for small mercies. At least my lawyer and I were no longer estranged. As little as I trusted Tien Hua, which was not at all, I did need a lawyer to carry on, and Tien Hua was as bad as any.

My brief vacation from divorce matters had refreshed me. I was back to my old battling self, and decided to beef up my financial affidavit with more facts. Since Hin Chew was trying to do me in, it would now be for all the marbles, as much as I could get. I was no longer content to let the court decide on its own. I was determined to shoot my wad, and my gunslinger in residence was John.

This time, I decided to beef up the financial affidavit for the July 27 hearing with audited financial reports of the Chungs' Singapore companies, as Hin Chew had been involved in all of them.

Singapore corporations are required to file their annual reports with the Singapore Registrar of Companies. Once on file, copies of these reports are available from the government for a very modest charge. With little difficulty, therefore, we were able to obtain microfilm copies of the annual reports for all the Chung companies in Singapore, at least all the ones we knew about.

The annual reports were very informative. They showed that there was a lot of money flowing through the Chung companies, all of it generating a very healthy loss.

The Chungs' companies in Singapore had total accumulated losses of US$12 million, on sales of US$43 million. How did the Chungs finance such losses?

The Chung companies' annual reports showed a flood of money coming in under the category of "Extraordinary Cash Inflows." These "inflows," often in the millions, were described in the annual reports as coming from "Dealing Securities," "Amount owing from related party corporations," and "Amount due to a director waived."

Hin Chew had been a director of all of these companies, and a shareholder of most. He was a major player in the Chungs' corporate shell game. By exposing this information, I hoped to show that the

Chungs and Hin Chew had unrevealed sources of money.

Obviously, Singapore is a great place to set up a corporation. Since only S$2.00 of paid up capital is required you are free to do pretty much as you please. Singapore has no tax treaty with the United States, so the IRS will never know.

Finally, in my affidavit, I addressed the major assets that I could prove belonged to Hin Chew. The most valuable of these, by far, was Hin Chew's crown jewel, X-10 in Hong Kong.

According to the Deloitte, Touche Tohmatsu's audited financial statement for X-10 for 1993, the latest information I had, the company had an annual profit of US$3 million, of which more than US$1 million would be Hin Chew's share, based on his admitted 37 ½ percent ownership in X-10.

On July 17, 1995, I delivered my Big Mama financial affidavit, with a pile of exhibits to Tien Hua. This was one week in advance of its due date, which would give Tien Hua plenty of time to check it over, and have the necessary copies made.

On Monday, July 24, the financial affidavit had to be signed by me, delivered to the Court, and to Hin Chew's lawyers.

That morning, I dropped by Astonii, a boutique owned by a lady friend of mine, coincidentally named Jackie Lee. For no particular reason, I asked Jackie if she would like to keep me company while I went to my lawyers to sign some documents. She needed a break and came along.

Jackie and I arrived at Rodyk & Davidson at 2:00 P.M., in time for me to sign my affidavit and have it witnessed. Routine stuff.

The receptionist politely ushered us into the conference room, and after a brief wait, Tien Hua entered.

He didn't sit down, but stood in the doorway, and gave me a stupid, "Yes?"

"Tien Hua, I'd like you to meet Jackie Lee, a friend of mine."

Tien Hua shook hands with her, and then looked at me blankly.

"I'm here to sign my affidavit," I said.

"Oh, I thought it was tomorrow. You're right; it's today! I'm not sure I have it all ready," Tien Hua said, sheepishly.

"Bring out what you have, and let's see," I said.

Tien Hua returned shortly with a bunch of papers held loosely in his hand, not more than twenty pages altogether.

"Where are all the exhibits, all the exhibits I gave you on the Chungs' companies," I said, standing up.

I marched over to Tien Hua, and snatching the papers from his hand, said, "Let's see what you've got."

I looked. It was only the affidavit. "Tien Hua, this is only the financial affidavit. No exhibits! Where are my exhibits? Where are the Chung company financial reports? Where's the stuff on Brunei? Without the exhibits, we are giving the judge nothing more than *words*, hearsay."

"I am not sure you really want to submit all the exhibits. That would be a huge amount of stuff to photocopy and bind," blinked Tien Hua.

"Tien Hua, I think you are well aware of the fact that without the exhibits, the evidence, the judge will not give any weight to this affidavit. Is that what you want? Tien Hua, maybe you want to protect the Chungs?"

Tien Hua said nothing.

I raised my voice, "Are you on Hin Chew's payroll, Tien Hua? You have been sabotaging this case all along! You even double crossed me when you told the Chungs about the fishing vessels, when I expressly told you *not* to!"

I moved a step closer to Tien Hua, "And why in the fuck did Dennis Singham disappear from the scene? Is this case too hot for Dennis to handle?

I didn't know then, but that very day, Dennis was off in the Kuala Lumpur Shangri-La Hotel screwing, literally fucking, another one of his clients, a lady named Angela—she too was using Dennis for her divorce.

I knew I was hitting hard, really freaking out.

I stared at Tien Hua, paused, lowered my voice, and said facetiously, "Are you going to take the rap for Dennis? I guess as a two-thousand dollar a month junior you're expendable." Tien Hua still said nothing. Jackie, my boutique-owner friend, who had remained seated, stood up, but didn't say a word.

I screamed, "Tien Hua, where the fuck are the exhibits that I brought to you? I want my fucking exhibits!" I took another step closer to him. This was about to get physical!

Hastily, Tien Hua spoke, "May Chu, I have them in my office."

"And you haven't made copies? How are we going to file on time? My God! How can you fucking do this to me?" I said.

Tien Hua backed up facing me and put one hand on the conference room doorknob.

As angry as I was, I still needed the jerk, so, doing my best to get my voice back to normal, I said "Let's get the photocopying machine going, Tien Hua bring me all the exhibits." I turned to Jackie, who appeared to be in a state of near-shock, "Can you help me?"

"Sure, May Chu" Jackie smiled.

"Tien Hua, give me one girl to help." I said.

Tien Hua did so as he had no choice.

We finished the job at 6:00 P.M., barely in time to get the entire financial affidavit, with all its exhibits, notarized, and filed.

On my way out, I shook hands with Tien Hua, and said, "I'm so glad we had a chance to clear the air, now I know whom I am dealing with—and so do you."

Shortly after I had turned my financial affidavit in to Tien Hua, with Deloitte's audited financial statement for X-10 for 1993, Drew & Napier sent us a copy of Deloitte's audited financial statement for X-10 for 1994.

While my affidavit was based on the older 1993 X-10 figures, Deloitte's new report for 1994 showed that X-10's profit had more than doubled, jumping to US$8 million. It also showed a US$1.8 million "Consultancy fee paid to a shareholder."

Hin Chew's admitted share of the 1994 X-10 profits was US$3 million. That, plus the US$1.8 million consultancy fee, plus what X-10 was paying to Zhongli, brought Hin Chew's take to over US$5 million for the year.

Hin Chew was rolling in money, and he was rubbing it in my face.

The 1994 X-10 annual report, which itself was one year out of date, had been withheld from me by Hin Chew just long enough to make it too late for me to include in my financial affidavit.

There was no way for me to undo the damage.

I decided that John should come to the July 27 hearing.

If necessary, he would be able to explain to Tien Hua or anyone else, issues that might arise regarding the financial side of things.

I had no idea whether Hin Chew would attend the hearing, but at this point, it didn't matter. Effectively, I was divorced, the judge had only to lower his gavel for me to get the piece of paper certifying the fact.

July 27, 1995, the fateful day of the hearing was upon us. I was ready very early that morning, simply dressed in a white buttoned-up jacket, black skirt, and black low-heel shoes. John drove. We went first to pick up Tien Hua at his office. There wasn't much to say to him at this point other than hello, so we made the short drive to the courthouse in silence.

We arrived in the courtroom a good fifteen minutes ahead of the appointed time of 10:00 A.M. I always like to arrive early, and, as we entered the courtroom, I was relieved to see that we were the first to arrive.

The courtroom was a large dark wood paneled cavernous place, much like Justice Lai's, but a more dated version. There was a raised bench for the judge, and in front of it, and to his right, was the witness stand, fenced in on three sides, and raised, with three steps leading up to it.

The witness stand looked like those I had seen in the movies, old black and white movies, where it was more likely to be occupied by an Edwardian-era ax murderer than a soon-to-be divorcee.

Behind the area for the witness stand were two large wooden tables, with several chairs scattered about. On the back wall of the courtroom, and facing the judge, were several rows of dark brown wooden bleachers.

Tien Hua put his briefcase down on the table farthest from the entrance to the courtroom, and told us to take a seat on the bleachers behind him. John and I took our places.

The silence of the courtroom was broken by footsteps, as two people entered.

It was Hin Chew and his lawyer, Tan Cheng Han. Hin Chew walked in with head held high, avoiding any glance in our direction. Tan Cheng Han followed, clutching his papers to his chest. Reaching the vacant table nearest the entrance, where he put his papers down, Tan Cheng Han motioned Hin Chew to the bleachers.

Tan Cheng Han then moved over to shake hands with Tien Hua.

Were they shaking hands as fighters, or as friends? I wondered.

Finally, the Judge, Amarjeet Singh, entered the courtroom from his chambers. He was a tall lean man with a serious demeanor. Amarjeet Singh was well-known in Singapore. Previously, as a lawyer, he specialized in criminal law. Recently, Judge Singh had added to his reputation by playing a key role in the caning of the American schoolboy, Michael Fay.

A number of cars had been vandalized in Singapore, and, one morning, Judge Singh found that his wife's car had been spray painted with some red paint. Judge Singh had the police organize an ambush which netted the son of a Thai diplomat and a boy from Hong Kong. The diplomat's son went free, but seven hours of interrogation with the other boy linked Michael Fay to the incidents of vandalism. Even though Fay had not been caught in the act, he decided, after days of questioning by the police, that it was better to admit his guilt and plea bargain.

Just like Nick Leeson, the rogue trader who bankrupted Baring Securities, was to learn several years later, you don't plea bargain with Singapore. Fay was sentenced to four months in jail, a S$2,200 fine—and six strokes of the cane. Out of deference to President Clinton, the Singapore Cabinet respectfully reduced Fay's sentence to four strokes.

You didn't mess with Judge Singh. Was he presiding simply to hear my unimportant case, or had he been brought in by the Singapore government to check on the Chungs' activities? Far-fetched? Not in a police state.

Still, I was pleased with this luck of the draw, since Judge Singh was not Chinese. Moreover, his wife was a well-known women's rights activist, a real one, not like my ex-Judas, Ann Tan.

With the entrance of Judge Singh, we all stood up, and remained standing until he motioned us to sit.

There was no bailiff, no court reporter, only Judge Singh.

Taking his seat, Judge Singh looked about the room and asked the parties to identify themselves. Tan Cheng Han did so in a precise and prissy voice. Tien Hua identified himself in a very subdued and respectful tone. His voice was barely audible.

Judge Singh summarized the purpose of the hearing, which was the finalization of the divorce, and the determination of the financial matters, the ancillaries.

He then looked at Tien Hua, and said, "Will you please have the Plaintiff take the stand?"

"Your honor!" interrupted Tan Cheng Han, "I would like to bring up a matter regarding the Petitioner's affidavit."

Judge Singh, taken aback by the interruption, looked at Tan Cheng Han and said simply, "Yes?"

Tan Cheng Han continued, "Your Honor, the Petitioner's affidavit contains exhibits which are irrelevant to these proceedings, and may be damaging to my client. I respectfully request that certain of the exhibits in the Petitioner's affidavit be deleted."

Judge Singh took one of the four bound volumes that made up exhibits to the affidavit, and looked it over calmly, turning the pages slowly. Having finished, he took another one of the volumes and did the same. Then he wrote something down on a notepad. I looked at Tien Hua. He wasn't moving. No one was moving.

I knew that Tan Cheng Han must have wanted the exhibits relating to the Chungs' money-losing companies, the Brunei documents, and the fishing vessels, thrown out.

Judge Singh finished writing down his notes, looked at Tan Cheng Han, and said simply, "Request denied. The exhibits will be kept, and they shall be made part of the record."

Tan Cheng Han began to object, but was cut short by Judge Singh who said sternly, "Sit down and keep quiet! The exhibits will be kept as evidence."

Judge Singh then directed himself to me, "Will the Petitioner take the stand please."

I climbed down the short row of bleachers, and made my way up the steps to the witness stand, where I was sworn in by Judge Singh.

There was very little courtroom drama. Judge Singh merely wanted my sworn testimony that I was seeking a divorce, and that what I had submitted in my affidavit was true. In less than a minute, I stepped down, and returned to my seat next to John.

Next came the discussion of the financial settlement. Tien Hua opened by challenging the facts contained in Hin Chew's affidavit, saying that Hin Chew had presented most of the figures without proof.

Specifically, Hin Chew had submitted no proof that he owned only 37 ½ percent of X-10, as he claimed. Previously Hin Chew had told me that he owned 86 percent of X-10, and had written so in a letter to his Bermuda offices.

Judge Singh agreed that sufficient proof of Hin Chew's assets had not been given, and ordered him to produce audited financial statements bearing the "chop," or stamp of a certified accountant, to verify his assets, and his percentage ownership in X-10.

Unfortunately, to give Hin Chew time to have this done, would call for the scheduling of another hearing, but an informal one, in chambers.

In closing, Judge Singh ruled that I would continue to have "sole custody and control" of the children (absolutely no visitation for Hin Chew), my occupancy of the Mount Rosie apartment would continue, and my interim maintenance would continue until a final decision could be rendered concerning the financial settlement.

Judge Singh finished by granting me an interlocutory decree of divorce, which would become final after a three-month waiting period.

The hearing was over.

Well, not quite. Tan Cheng Han stood up, stooped forward, and, looking a bit like a praying mantis, turned his head to look at John. Then turning to Judge Singh, Tan Cheng Han literally screeched, "Your Honor, we demand to know who is the Caucasian man, seated next to the Petitioner."

Tien Hua quickly retorted, "Your Honor, the gentleman in question has no relevance to this case."

Now it was my turn to speak up. "Your Honor, I would be only too happy to inform Your Honor who the Caucasian gentleman is."

Judge Singh nodded.

Without saying a word, I returned to the witness stand, where I continued, "Your Honor, the gentleman seated next to me is John Harding. He was formerly with Inland Revenue, and is here to advise me on financial and tax matters, especially regarding the Chung companies"

Glancing at John, Judge Singh was a bit confused. Inland Revenue was populated exclusively with Chinese at the top, Malays in junior positions, and Indians cleaning the hallways and toilets. Where did this Caucasian fit in?

"The Singapore Inland Revenue Department?" asked Judge Singh.

"Yes, your Honor, the Singapore Inland Revenue Department."

Judge Singh nodded with the look of a man who had seen it all, and excused me from the witness stand. He took a minute to write down his final notes, and then lowering his gavel, said "Dismissed."

Even though Judge Singh had ordered Hin Chew to present audited statements of his financial position to the court, I was not satisfied with the hearing. It had really accomplished nothing, at least not for me. I would have expected at least some discussion on the financial merits of my claim.

Tien Hua had failed to press the issue, and Judge Singh had failed to do anything other go though the formality of declaring me divorced, and ordering up yet another hearing.

There was no court reporter, no record of a transcript or of Judge Singh's orders for Hin Chew to produce audited financial statements to support his claims, there was no record of anything, only Judge Singh's scribbled notes.

The hearing seemed very amateur to me, amateur on the part of the lawyers, and Judge Singh as well.

During the period leading up to the hearing, I had been watching the O. J. Simpson trial on television. I am sure, that if Alan Dershowitz were my lawyer, he would not have been sitting on his ass like Tien Hua, while Judge Singh allowed the hearing to drift aimlessly to nowhere.

Unfortunately, I wasn't in America.

During the wait for the next hearing, Hin Chew and his gang would have time to plot, plan, and do God knows what. I *knew* that something was amiss.

There was more to what was going on than just a simple case of justice delayed.

JUSTICE DENIED

THE HEARING in chambers over the financial settlement was fixed for the end of August, then refixed for the end of September, and finally re-refixed for October 24, 1995.

Did I have any control over what was happening? None.

With time on my hands, I returned to my usual routine of taking care of the apartment, helping Warren with his homework and driving him to the Tanglin Club for his tennis lessons, I didn't want Warren to turn into the wimpish nerd role model of the Singapore school system.

John slogged on with his long hours at Citibank, his daily grind broken only by our late-night dinners and evenings together, and by a couple of sets of tennis on the weekend.

Outwardly, our lives appeared normal, routine, and settled.

In truth, as soon as the divorce was over, John and I planned to escape to America. That was where my children would have the best chance to survive and succeed.

Only John and I knew the plan.

We would tell no one, not even the boys, until after we had arrived safely on American soil. My fear was that Hin Chew would ask for a court order requiring that the boys remain in Singapore.

Late in September 1995, I received Hin Chew's affidavit for the forthcoming court hearing on our financial settlement.

The affidavit described my conduct in the proceedings as being "unreasonable and vexatious." I took that as a compliment, meaning that I was doing a good job. Hin Chew charged that I was using the "proceedings for an ulterior motive." You bet! Hin Chew and the Chungs deserved to be exposed.

Protesting a bit too much, Hin Chew claimed that his withdrawing from the case had nothing to do with the issue of "fishing vessels." He produced, as an exhibit, a letter in which Peter Lesser denied that he owned any "fishing vessels." Perhaps Peter Lesser was telling the truth, but I had never maintained that Peter Lesser *owned* any fishing vessels; only that he used them for *collateral*. The fishing vessels could have belonged to anybody, to Hin Chew, or even to S. P. Chung.

On the financial side, Hin Chew listed only the items that I already knew about, declaring his net worth to be S$5.8 million (US$4 million), about half my current estimate of close to US$10 million.

Where was the discrepancy? Hin Chew had based the value of his X-10 holdings on a very low estimate based on the company's 1989 financial position which was six years out of date, when the company was still in receivership.

X-10 was so bad off that Hin Chew swore that, "No dividends have ever been paid to its shareholders."

This was an outright lie, as on September 15, 1993, two years before, Hin Chew had sent a check to S. P., writing:

> We are pleased to enclose herewith a bank draft for the sum of US$75,000 (United States Dollars Seventy Five Thousand Only) being Chungco (Bermuda)'s maiden dividend. Our investment in X-10 Ltd is now bearing fruit and we thank you for your patience and faith in the company.

Therefore, as early as 1993, X-10 had already paid a healthy dividend to Chungco (Bermuda). Hin Chew's false statement on this subject of X-10's dividends is a good example of his impunity, or better, immunity, with the Singapore court.

In the face of Hin Chew's lies, I still had to keep on trying, for what it was worth. Once again, John turned out a masterpiece of an affidavit. It was short, but said it all.

I was now able to include, as an exhibit, Deloitte's 1994 audited financial statement for X-10.

The Deloitte report showed that X-10's sales for 1994 had risen to $44 million, with an after-tax profit of US$8 million. The 1994 X-10 balance sheet showed the shareholders' funds to be worth US$9.6 million.

If Hin Chew owned only 37 ½ percent of X-10, as he maintained, in 1994, his shares were worth US$3.6 million, based on Deloitte's financial statement.

That was book value. The possible market value of Hin Chew's X-10 shares could be much higher. Based on his admitted 37 ½ percent ownership, Hin Chew's share of X-10's US$8 million profit for 1994 came to US$3 million. At a very low price-earnings ratio of five, Hin Chew's shares, at market value, would be worth US$15 million.

Heaven knows what Hin Chew would be worth if he could take X-10 public on the NASDAQ, where X-10's price-earnings ratio could have been 20, or better. That's US$60 million, and up for Hin Chew.

When Hin Chew and I were still on speaking terms, he told me there would be "too much scrutiny" if the company went public. Still, "going public on the NASDAQ," was Hin Chew's dream, and he was working on it.

It had nothing to do with my settlement, but the Deloitte report revealed that, in spite of its profit of US$8 million, X-10 and its subsidiaries, including X-10 USA, the American subsidiary in New Jersey, paid only US$2,350 in corporate taxes. The Deloitte 1994 report stated, "No provision for taxation has been made in the Company's financial statements as, in the opinion of the directors, the Company's income is not subject to taxation in any jurisdictions in which it operates."

How can this be when the bulk of X-10's sales came from the United States? Easy, incorporate X-10 in Bermuda, and sell to the United States direct from Hong Kong, circumventing X-10's United States subsidiary, X-10 (USA) Inc.

John, with his experience as a taxman, said the IRS calls such activity "transfer pricing."

"It's what the IRS put Gucci's Chairman, Aldo Gucci in jail for, at the ripe old age of seventy-seven. I know the IRS agent who got him, Charles Landry. I met Landry in Rome, a blondish guy, medium height. Coincidentally, Landry works in Singapore, now," explained John.

If after getting your money out of the States, you happen to have some tax due in Hong Kong, you can always use the gimmick of a "Consultancy fee paid to a shareholder" to reduce even that. If that shareholder is protected by a tax haven like Bermuda, you are home free with no taxes to pay.

Deloitte's 1994 report did, in fact, show that US$1,824,203 was paid to a shareholder. Who did that go to, if not Hin Chew?

Why pay taxes? Only salaried guys like John had to pay taxes.

In his affidavit, Hin Chew divulged no compensation from X-10. Was Hin Chew, the Chairman of X-10, working for free?

Shortly after my lockout from Zhongli, the company's fortunes changed. Zhongli received a tax-free windfall of S$242,425 (US$166,000) from the "Gain on sale of investment."

What investment? Zhongli's financial statements did not say. Did Hin Chew sell one of Zhongli's old typewriters to another Chung company for the S$242,425, or did he simply deposit cash into Zhongli and enter it in the books as "Gain on sale of investment?"

This ploy of financial windfalls from the sale of an investment was used *many* times by the Chungs to infuse their companies with funds without having to specify from where those funds came. The Chungs financial statements are filled with "Gain on sale of investment," "Dealing Securities," "Amount owing from related party corporations," and "Amount due to a director waived."

Where did all the money come from to support the large losses in the Chung companies?

Hin Chew claimed, in his affidavit, that the large amounts of cash he brought into Singapore were from his "Hong Kong bank accounts." I pointed out in my affidavit that Hin Chew had never disclosed any Hong Kong bank accounts, and where did *their* cash come from?

Finally, I reminded the court that Hin Chew's affidavit did not comply with Judge Amarjeet Singh's court order to produce audited financial statements.

Hin Chew's affidavit consisted only of Hin Chew's words to support Hin Chew's claims.

How could he get away with this?

On October 24, 1995 the hearing in the judge's chambers was scheduled for 10:00 A.M. Tien Hua said, since the hearing was informal, there was no need for me to attend. I agreed with Tien Hua, assuming that Judge Singh would simply hand over his decision, and the matter would be closed.

Minutes before the hearing, Tien Hua telephoned me from the courthouse to tell me that Judge Singh had disappeared from the scene.

The hearing would instead be presided over by Choo Han Teck, a new judge appointed to the court only several months before, on April 1, 1995. Choo Han Teck was not a Justice, but only a Judicial Commissioner, a lawyer who serves as a judge on a contract basis. Choo Han Teck was known to be an inexperienced political appointee who spoke with such difficulty that he appeared to have a speech impediment.

Why, after having two of Singapore's top judges, Lai Kew Chai and Amarjeet Singh, assigned to my case—apparent overkill for a matrimonial action—was my hearing being relegated to the new and inexperienced Choo Han Teck?

The disappearance of Judge Singh from the case was suspicious. Had I outlived my usefulness to the Singapore judiciary? Had they gathered all the information they needed about the Chungs? Was I being thrown to the dogs, or was this the normal procedure? I could only guess at the answers.

Only several months before, in July 1995, Choo Han Teck had received a great deal of notoriety in the Singapore press over a case involving oral sex. *The Straits Times* published an article under the byline, "Did you know … That oral sex, even between consenting adults, is an offense?"

The article cited the recent case of a twenty-six year old man, not Chinese of course, who was jailed for six months and fined S$2,000 by Choo Han Teck for being on the receiving end, so to speak, of a blowjob.

The facilitating lady involved was not mentioned in the article. She probably plea-bargained for a lesser charge, something like "voyeurism."

The Straits Times had interviewed no less than six learned Singapore lawyers, all experts on the subject of oral sex—at least from a legal point of view—who concurred that this particular offender had been extremely lucky to have received so lenient a sentence from Choo Han Teck.

According to Section 377 of the Singapore Penal Code, oral sex can "be punished with imprisonment for life," plus a fine.

Who says Singapore Judges are strict? Why, if he wanted to, Choo Han

Teck could have put the blowee away for life, and fined him, to boot.

That such a crime could be discussed seriously on the pages of *The Straits Times*, says a lot about the quality of the Singapore judicial system.

The Singapore judicial system is all about government control, and very little about the rule of law. The appointment of Yong Pung How, a banker, to the position of Singapore's Chief Justice proves the point.

Yong Pung How, a classmate of Lee Kuan Yew's at Cambridge, claimed to have worked briefly, in Malaysia, for his Daddy's law firm, Shook, Lin & Bok. However, in 1964, Yong Pung How was appointed Chairman of Malaysia-Singapore Airlines, the predecessor to Singapore International Airlines, and had no further involvement in the practice of law.

In 1969, the well-connected Yong Pung How switched careers to become a banker.

In 1989 Yong Pung How, then chairman of Singapore's largest bank, the Overseas Chinese Banking Corporation, was approached by his crony, Prime Minister Lee Kuan Yew, who asked him to become Singapore's Chief Justice.

Lee Kuan Yew alone appointed Singapore's Judges, no advice nor consent was needed from the Singapore Government.

In Lee Kuan Yew's own words concerning his appointment of Yong Pung How, "If he agreed, he would first have to be a Supreme Court judge for a year, to get himself back into the law before he took up the appointment as chief justice."

Yong Pung How did agree, and after a year of on-the-bench training as a judge, became Chief Justice on September 28, 1990.

As Singapore's Chief Justice, Yong Pung How holds a position, which is the equivalent of all nine United States Supreme Court Justices, rolled into one. He and he alone is the ultimate court of appeal in Singapore, where there is *no* such thing as a dissenting opinion.

Yong Pung How's total compensation of well over US$1 million a year is greater than that of all nine United States Supreme Court Justices combined, and then some. If you do the work of nine people, you should be paid for it.

Such is the quality and standard of the Singapore judiciary.

The last thing I wanted was to have a Chinese male decide my fate, but what to do? I sat in my apartment with John and waited by the telephone for Tien Hua to call with the outcome of the hearing.

The telephone rang.

It was Tien Hua, "We are still in the hearing. I have one question, what is a price-earnings ratio?"

I told Tien Hua what a price-earnings ratio meant, and reminded him to use it to put a price tag on x-10.

Tien Hua answered, "I have to get back to the hearing, they are offering you 26 ½ percent of the matrimonial assets, and we are countering with 35 percent. I'll talk to you later." With that, he hung up.

It didn't take long for the phone to ring again. It was Tien Hua again.

"Yes, Tien Hua, what's happening?" I asked anxiously.

"May Chu, it's over. We were shafted. You got a raw deal and should seriously consider filing an appeal."

"What happened? What did Choo Han Teck say?"

"Judge Choo pretty much agreed with Hin Chew's own unsupported estimate of his declared assets. Choo didn't even ask for proof ..."

I interrupted. "Was Hin Chew there."

"Yes," answered Tien Hua, "he was, but he didn't speak—just sat in the corner reading a book."

Tien Hua continued, "The Court awarded you only 20 percent of the matrimonial assets."

"Tien Hua, only a couple of minutes ago you told me they were offering 26 ½ percent, and you were countering with 35 percent. What happened?"

"Well, yes," said Tien Hua, avoiding my question, "Choo figured that 20 percent would be the equivalent of your getting the apartment and s$600,000 (US$411,000). He ruled also that your monthly maintenance checks be stopped."

"And for the children, child support?" I asked.

"Nothing. Choo said he wasn't inclined to go into child support today. You will have to re-apply to the Court for another hearing on that."

"So we lost. Great, Tien Hua! Great! I paused to collect myself, "OK, OK, and when do I get the money and the apartment, Tien Hua."

"It takes a while, a couple of months. You'll get your settlement after the court determines no appeal has been filed, but May Chu, I really have to advise you to appeal."

"And how long would *that* take?" I asked.

"It could take several years," answered Tien Hua, playing it straight.

"No kidding, but since Choo Han Teck stopped my monthly maintenance he put me in a position where I couldn't afford to wait. I'm sure he did it on purpose, didn't he, Tien Hua?"

"Judge Choo ..." began Tien Hua.

Interrupting, again, I raised my voice, "So Choo Han Teck expects us to live on nothing, while waiting for Hin Chew to come up with the settlement, or waiting for an appeal? Did you point that out to fucking Choo Han Teck?"

"I'm sure Judge Choo took everything into account," said Tien Hua, raising his voice to match mine.

"And, Tien Hua, did you ask if Hin Chew received a salary for being the Chairman of X-10?"

"No."

"Wonderful, Tien Hua, and did you ask about Hin Chew's Hong Kong bank accounts, where he claims he gets the cash from to bring into Singapore?"

"No," said Tien Hua, becoming impatient.

"Didn't this Choo Han Teck ask about Hin Chew's salary or his Hong Kong bank accounts? Isn't it the judge's responsibility to get to the bottom of things?"

After a pause on Tien Hua's end, he avoided my question again, saying, "We'll have to analyze what happened."

"I'll analyze it for you right now, Tien Hua. Choo Han Teck sat on his ass, and swallowed every piece of crap that Hin Chew's lawyers fed him, while you did nothing!"

There was silence on Tien Hua's end.

"And, what about my membership to the Tanglin Club?"

"Gone."

I was about to slam down the phone, when Tien Hua quickly added, "And, yes, by the way, there was no order as to legal costs."

"What? What did you say, Tien Hua? I thought that since Hin Chew withdrew his opposition to the divorce that he would have to pay all the legal costs, including mine. That's only normal. He forced me to incur the costs. That's the law, isn't it, Tien Hua?"

"Yes, but there can be exceptions," Tien Hua answered meekly.

"You did not ask for legal costs for me, Tien Hua?"

"No, I didn't."

"Hin Chew withdrew his opposition to the divorce, and I have to bear my own legal costs?"

I slammed down the telephone.

John, hearing my side of the conversation, understood what had happened. "Look, at least you may get something, and this Choo guy didn't take the kids away, did he?"

"You're right," I answered.

"So relax, cheer up. This Mickey Mouse lawsuit is finally over, and we can get on with our lives. You don't need a penny from this guy to survive."

"You have no idea what I went through with Hin Chew—and now he's getting away with this?" I said.

"Listen, who gives a damn about Banana Republic judges, crooked lawyers, and the fucking Chungs." John gave me a reassuring hug and a kiss, "You've achieved your goals. You have custody of the boys, and are finally out of the Chung Mafia. That's all that matters. Cheer up."

My award, s$600,000, seemed a lot as a lump sum, but not much when it had to last you a lifetime of payments for children, education, taxes, medical expenses, and just plain living.

At Singapore's low interest rates of 3 percent, the s$600,000 would earn me s$18,000 (US$12,000) a year, less than one percent of Hin Chew's US$3 million share of X-10's profits for 1994.

If I lived off the interest, my settlement boiled down to my getting s$50 (US$34) a day, before taxes. Hin Chew had come pretty close to making good on his previous threat, "I'll have you and the kids out and living in an HDB apartment on twenty dollars a day."

According to court rules, Hin Chew had two months in which to pay me the settlement amount and turn over his share in the Mount Rosie apartment.

Choo should not have stopped the interim maintenance until I received the settlement. Until Hin Chew paid, if he paid, there would be nothing coming in to support the children and me. There was no way I could keep Marc in Geelong College.

Even my membership at the Tanglin Club was gone, and belonged exclusively to Hin Chew.

Marc would understand, but how do you explain to Warren, an eleven year old, that his tennis lessons had stopped, and we could no longer go to the Tanglin Club. How could Warren explain that to his friends?

Choo Han Teck's court order for the division of our assets had left open some loose ends for Hin Chew to exploit. Since Judge Choo said nothing about our car, and even though it was in my name, Hin Chew was demanding that I turn the keys over to him.

Judge Choo had also said nothing about the furniture in the Mount Rosic apartment, and Hin Chew continued to insist that I turn over all of our Chinese antiques to him; otherwise, he would not sign the apartment over to me, nor would he pay the court-ordered settlement.

To compound my problems, Tien Hua continued to pressure me to file an appeal, as the filing deadline would soon pass. All I had to do was to give him a check for S$7,000, and he would get started.

I saw an appeal only as a way to lose everything, and to be stuck in Singapore for years with no money while the process dragged on.

No way! I was determined to get out of town as soon as possible, and rushed a letter off to Tien Hua, pointing out that he and Dennis had failed me completely, and telling him that I did not have the funds to fight for an appeal.

Dennis's answer to my letter was an invoice for his "services." He charged me S$125,471.52 (US$88,700)—a cost I never should have had to pay.

No problem with paying, Tien Hua told me, Dennis would take it out of my settlement, which he was empowered to collect.

It didn't end there. Hin Chew's lawyers managed to schedule another court hearing for February 26, 1996, for "clarification" of Judge Choo's settlement order. This was getting to be a never-ending story, but I wasn't about to stick around.

It was time to get out of Dodge.

ESCAPE FROM PARADISE

DECEMBER 22, 1995, the last day for Hin Chew to make good on the court-ordered financial settlement, came and went with no word from his lawyers, or mine.

Since receiving the exorbitant invoice from Dennis, I had heard nothing from my own lawyers, other than a letter from Tien Hua giving me a list of antiques to be delivered to Hin Chew, and the notice of the hearing requested by Hin Chew's lawyers in February 1996, still two months away.

No one was going to alter my plans.

Marc was back in Singapore, on vacation from Geelong, and John had scheduled his own vacation from Citibank for the end of December.

We made reservations on United Airlines to fly to Los Angeles on December 28, 1995. That was when we were going to leave for good.

Aside from the suitcases we were taking with us on the flight, everything would stay in the Mount Rosie apartment, as is. When John returned to Singapore, he would pack up our belongings and ship them to the States. With that done, he would resign from Citibank, and rejoin us in the States.

I told Marc and Warren that John and I would be taking them to Disneyland after Christmas. Naturally, they were thrilled. The Disneyland story gave a purpose for our trip, and a believable story for all to swallow.

To cover up the fact that Marc would not be returning to Geelong College, I paid his tuition for the next school term, scheduled to start in February 1996.

After that, I had US$15,000 dollars remaining for our new life in the States, but I had John, and he would take care of us. So, settlement, or no settlement, we were going.

It was a rush making the final arrangements for the trip. I typed out a complete list of instructions for John on what should be shipped to the States from the Mount Rosie apartment, and what should be sold. The Chinese paintings and the two large Burmese tapestries, called *kalagasas*, I wanted. After all, I was part Burmese, and I needed something to remember me by.

Organizing the shipment and getting it off would be no small task for John, as we were leaving virtually everything behind.

Finally, John had the odious task of making sure that Hin Chew's precious Chinese antiques were returned to him, but that would take place only if my settlement came through. Otherwise, the antiques, which were already packed and with a storage company, would remain entombed in the warehouse.

As my last act with Dennis, I wrote him a letter telling him that his fee was high by a factor of at least four, and if he didn't reduce it, I would bring him to court. It was not an idle threat.

In all the rush, we had very little time to go through the rites of Christmas, no tree, minimal presents, and no Christmas dinner at home. Instead, John and I took the boys and William out for dinner to Dan Ryan's for what would be my last meal, maybe ever, in a Singapore restaurant.

After dinner, we dropped the boys off, and John drove me to the Mount Vernon Crematorium, where the ashes of my brother Sam lay in their small niche. I said goodbye to Sam, and told him he would always be in my thoughts—my poor brother, he had no chance for a life.

The day before taking off for Los Angeles was devoted to the final small details of organizing our getaway. At noon, I went to the bank to retrieve our birth certificates, documents, my jewelry, and other items from our safe deposit box. The jewelry consisted of things from my parents, much more from my grandparents, a couple of items from S. P. and Lillian, and some pieces from Hin Chew, usually given in return for maltreatment.

Each piece of jewelry had a story, and each object brought forth a memory of a person—Kong Kong, Mamak, my father, my mother, or one of my life's milestones—the day Kong Kong died, my ill-fated engagement and wedding—all memories, and most of them no longer any good to me. Like my old photographs, my memories were now tainted by a life I had not expected. Having loaded my documents, jewelry and other distillations of a past life into my carry-on bag, I closed the safe deposit box for the last time and returned the keys to the waiting attendant.

The rest of the day was devoted to packing. I did my best to travel light, but there were birth certificates, vaccination records, and school transcripts to pack. I managed to get everything into three suitcases.

At 5:00 A.M. on the morning of December 28, 1995, William drove us through the darkness to Changi Airport. Until John returned, he would stay back in Singapore.

I was happy that we were escaping, but sad at leaving Singapore, which, whatever its faults, held a lifetime of memories for me. My final thoughts were of Lynn, Rosita, and myself, the three daughters-in-law who gave the Chungs a new generation of seven grandchildren. Each one of us was a victim who had suffered at the hands of the Chungs. In the early days of our marriages, young wives that we were, we had no idea what was in store for us.

Leaving Singapore, United Airlines is the only way to go. United has far less bureaucracy than Singapore Airlines and the United people at the check-in counter are far more lenient with the weigh-ins. The metronomes at Singapore Airlines never know when to bend the rules.

In no time, we were checked in and wandering about the airport transit lounge, buying magazines and books to see us through the twenty-two hour flight to Los Angeles.

My mood lifted as we boarded the airplane.

My thoughts shifted to a new life in a new country. When you come to America from a country like Singapore, which is clean, antiseptic and prosperous, but still a dictatorship, the word "Freedom" takes on a special meaning, especially if you've been on the wrong side of that dictatorship.

In the airplane, Warren, Marc, and I had three seats all together. Across the aisle was John. Our flight taxied onto the runway, gathered speed, and lifted into the sky. We were off, and Singapore slowly disappeared beneath the clouds.

We had made our escape from paradise.

FOIA: The Freedom of Information Act

Two and a half years later, in 1998, I found out that Hin Chew's old company, Chungco Technology, run by Peter Chung, had become a contractor to the United States Navy in Singapore.

How on earth, or in hell, did a family like the Chungs land a sensitive contract with the United States Navy?

To exercise my newfound freedom in America, I made use of the Freedom of Information Act (FOIA) to find out, or rather I had John do it. He's a bona-fide American citizen.

John's FOIA request went all the way from the Department of Defense in Washington to the United States Naval base in Singapore. Impressive!

I was even more impressed when we received an international telephone call from Singapore. Calling John was a most cooperative operative at the Singapore Naval Base, a very friendly American-born Chinese fellow, named Gilbert Chong.

Gilbert Chong told John that he had spoken *personally* to Peter Chung (knowing the Chungs, I was not sure I liked that). Nevertheless, Mr. Chong gave John his assurance that the Freedom of Information Act information regarding the Chungs' contract with the United States Navy would be mailed shortly.

"Oh, and would it be OK if the Chungs withheld their client list? They've requested that." Gilbert Chong asked.

"Why sure," said John.

Mr. Chong, ever helpful, then sent a follow-up letter, both by email and by post, on September 11, 1998. It read:

> This refers to your Freedom of Information Act request sent to the Directorate for Freedom of Information and Security Review dated June 12, 1998 in which you sought information relating to Chungco Technologies Pte Ltd, which request was forwarded to this Command. This also confirms your telephone conversation with the undersigned

on the above date wherein you were advised that we require more time to process your request.

This Command anticipates a response can be mailed to you by September 25, 1998. It is my understanding that you are agreeable to an informal extension of the statutory time limits while we continue to process your request.

Sincerely,
GILBERT H. CHONG
Freedom of Information Act Coordinator

On November 9, 1998, not having received a letter from Chong, John sent him a follow-up email saying, "In your e-mail to me of September 10, 1998 (below) you stated that a response can be mailed to me by September 25, 1998. If so, I would have expected to receive the report by now."

Emails are great. You can tell if they are received or not, at least John can, and this one to Chong was received.

Several years have now passed, and still no word from Gilbert H. Chong or anyone else regarding John's Freedom of Information Act request.

Welcome to the Chungs, United States Navy!

THE **IPO** OF **X-10 WIRELESS TECHNOLOGY, INC.**

H IN CHEW's company, X-10 Ltd., and its maze of subsidiaries has been successful. How successful we can't tell, since X-10 Ltd, the parent company, is still a privately held corporation operating out of Hong Kong.

In spite of his success, Hin Chew had not achieved his dream of "going public on the NASDAQ," as he was still hindered by the problem of "too much scrutiny."

To go public on the NASDAQ, you have to bare your soul to the United States Security and Exchange Commission (SEC). That was the problem. However, Hin Chew had been wrestling with the problem, and had come up with a brilliant solution. He would go public with a surrogate corporation, and hide behind a front man, one of his "stupid *ang mohs*," or whites.

Hin Chew chose George Stevenson for his front.

In 1999, Hin Chew started a new venture, a division X-10 USA Inc., to sell X-10 products over the Internet. He set up offices for his new venture in Seattle, Washington.

A second Microsoft? Not quite—Hin Chew's new venture was losing money from the start.

In July 1999, Hin Chew spun the new venture off from X-10 USA Inc., incorporating it under the catchy name of X-10 Wireless Technology, Inc. Unfortunately, the new venture continued to lose money, and X-10 Ltd had to pour millions into it just to keep it going.

For the nine months ending in September 2000, the company, X-10 Wireless, lost US$8 million on sales of US$21 million, losing 38¢ for each dollar of sales. The accumulated losses of X-10 Wireless amounted to US$17.6 million.

X-10 Wireless was looking like just another dot.com disaster.

That's a lot of money to lose, even for Hin Chew, but he had the answer—go public! Turn this lemon into an IPO! Let the U. S. investor pick up the tab.

Working quickly, by November 27, 2000, X-10 Wireless had filed with the SEC for an initial public offering of 5 million shares to be priced at US$15, to suck in US$75 million from the U. S. investors.

The SEC permitted X-10 Wireless to reserve the ticker symbol, "XTEN," for its NASDAQ listing.

Hin Chew was on his way.

Here comes the clever part. It's all in the X-10 Wireless Prospectus, duly filed with the SEC.

After the IPO, the "existing stockholders," Hin Chew and company, will own 20 million shares of XTEN, for which they paid only US$20 thousand, and the U. S. investors will own 5 million shares, for which they will pay US$75 million.

That puts a market value on X-10 Wireless of US$376 million, of which US$301 million will belong to Hin Chew and company.

Not bad for a money loser.

Does anyone other than your trusted stockbroker, ever bother to read a prospectus? Does the SEC ever read a prospectus—or do they just print what is fed to them?

The SEC is all about disclosure. It's their job to warn you. The SEC-approved prospectus is like the old warning on an iodine bottle, "POISON, DO NOT DRINK." If you drink, the SEC is off the hook, because they warned you, didn't they?

If you've never taken the time to wallow through a prospectus, I've done it for you, making my summary short, painless, and, hopefully, a fun read.

You are about to learn a lot, and it could save you some money. You, too, might learn how to get your own IPO going, just like Hin Chew.

The X-10 Wireless Technology Inc. prospectus identifies Hin Chew as a director, stating, "Since 1989, Mr. Chung has served as chairman of our affiliate, X-10 Ltd. Mr. Chung currently serves as chairman of Zhongli Investment Pte Ltd., his privately held investment company based in Singapore."

Very impressive, this guy's the Chairman of Zhongli! We know what Zhongli is all about, but did the SEC look into what Hin Chew's detention in Brunei was all about, and his relationship with the CIA guy, Dan Arnold? Are those facts included in the X-10 Wireless prospectus? Of course not.

The prospectus reveals that good old George Stevenson has been the CEO of X-10 Wireless since its inception in 1999. Despite Stevenson's being the CEO of X-10 Wireless, the prospectus tells us that he is not employed by the company, but receives an "annual management service fee paid by X-10 Ltd," which for 1999 came to US$264,000.

The CEO of X-10 Wireless is not employed by X-10 Wireless, but by another company? Good thinking, Hin Chew, we're learning.

The prospectus warns, "Mr. Stevenson's and Mr. Chung's positions at X-10 Ltd. could create real or apparent conflicts of interest ..." I bet!

It continues to get better.

The prospectus goes on to show that X-10 Wireless is more of a captive of X-10 Ltd., than I was of Hin Chew during our marriage.

It discloses, "We depend on X-10 Ltd., X-10 (USA) and other affiliates of X-10 Ltd. to provide substantially all of our manufacturing and fulfillment services, to sell and distribute products to retailers and other resellers and to provide product development services." In other words, X-10 Ltd. does "substantially all" the work of X-10 Wireless, manufacturing, warehousing, selling, distribution, research and development—the works.

So what does X-10 Wireless do? Does it do anything? Does it only run the Seattle office?

No way!

Hin Chew wants it all. A company called "Orca Monitoring Services" will run the office.

Who the hell is Orca? Why it's a company owned by X-10 Ltd., of course.

The prospectus tells us that X-10 Wireless has an "Administrative Services Agreement with Orca Monitoring Services, a wholly owned subsidiary of X-10 Ltd., under which Orca provides to us telephone reception services, customer service and technical support after our normal business hours, as well as general office administration and support."

The final instruction, in its directions on how to find its offices, X-10 Wireless states "Enter lobby for Orca Monitoring Services and ask for X-10 WTI [X-10 Wireless]." Sounds like Hin Chew doesn't even want to put the X-10 Wireless name on the office door.

All the normal functions of X-10 Wireless, from manufacturing and selling its products, to answering the company telephone, have been signed away with binding contracts to X-10 Ltd, and its subsidiaries.

X-10 Wireless has been bound hand and foot by Hin Chew, the control freak.

So, after having everything done for it by X-10 Ltd., and its subsidiaries, what's left for X-10 Wireless to do?

Get US$75 million from the U. S. investors—that's what.

If X-10 Wireless does well, good for Hin Chew. If it doesn't do well, good for Hin Chew. The money can always be siphoned out of America, using the Chungs' old ploys like "consultancy fee paid to a shareholder," and "management fees charged to related party corporations."

Should any trouble arise out of this confusing corporate shell game—no problem, X-10 Wireless states in its prospectus that it will "indemnify" and "secure insurance" for its directors "for certain expenses, including attorneys' fees, judgments, fines and settlement amounts incurred."

Good idea, Hin Chew, and the protection is all at company expense, and tax-deductible, too.

Hin Chew has found a way to go public in America, without exposing the mysteries of X-10 Ltd, of himself, or of the Chungs.

Welcome to the Chungs, America!

WHERE ARE THEY NOW?

Mamak

Living happily in Singapore.

The Deadbeat Dad

Hin Chew has not been in touch with his children since December 24, 1994, nor has he paid a cent for their support. I didn't have the chance to apply to the court for child support, but you don't need a court order, a piece of paper, to tell you to support your children.

I support my children, and so did John—all without a piece of paper telling us we had to do it.

In 1997, Hin Chew donated US$150,000 to MIT's Ocean Engineering Laboratory. In the words of MIT, "This is being funded in part by one of our alumni, Mr. Hin Chew Chung. The only stipulation made by the donor was that the funds be used for education and preferably to provide space where students will be allowed to work together."

How laudable! The Deadbeat Dad wheedled his way back into MIT's good graces by helping other people's children, while not paying a cent for his own.

Jackie Lee

My father is still a fugitive. The warrant is still out for his arrest, and he remains on Singapore's official list of undischarged bankrupts—a bankrupt with millions in the bank.

His address is unknown, at least to me.

Maybelle Lee

I invited my mother to come live with us in America. She declined, saying she preferred to stay in Singapore, alone with her two small dogs.

Still a Jehovah's Witness, she lives alone in an HDB apartment, public housing, on the outskirts of Singapore, and makes ends meet by giving English lessons.

Lynn

Lynn is living quietly and raising her two children in England. Recently, while visiting Cyprus, with her children, Lynn was shocked to see Peter Chung walking down the street. Lynn, Tammy, and Andrew saw Peter *first*, and made sure he didn't see them.

Lynn and her children have yet to receive the money from Jim's estate—they've been waiting since 1993.

Rosita

Still living in Melbourne with her children, but in an apartment now, as Peter pulled the mortgage on her house.

Rosita wrote me in December 2000, regarding Lynn's sighting of Peter Chung in Cyprus, "What a bombshell! What on earth would Peter Chung be doing in Cyprus? Somehow the two don't go together, especially seeing that he is so paranoid about safety and security. But then again, this man has been doing some really weird stuff lately and I know he is up to no good."

Sounds like Peter is following in Daddy's footsteps.

S. P. Chung

The Straits Times reported, on February 1, 1994, that S. P. sold the Anna Plains cattle station, together with 14,600 Brahman cattle, 197 horses, and a small airplane.

Long live Jock Chung!

S. P.'s rehabilitation became complete when the Singapore National Arts Council awarded him a Year 2000 Associate of the Arts Award for giving at least S$50,000 to the Nanyang Academy of Fine Arts. Lillian also made a donation, and got her very own award.

Ma and Pa Chung have become philanthropists, just like their boy, Hin Chew.

Dan Arnold

Dan Arnold is a Board Member of Jefferson Waterman International, a lobbying firm, which does good things for Burma.

The Washington Post, on February 28, 1998, reported, "For a fee of nearly a half-million dollars, for example, a Burmese company that U.S. officials say is close to the military leadership last year hired a former assistant secretary of state for narcotics control, Ann Wrobleski, and her lobbying firm, Jefferson Waterman International, to communicate the company's 'positions and interests,' according to the contract."

Dennis Singham

John, through his government contacts in Singapore, was able to locate a new lawyer for me, a fellow who turned out to be both competent and honest. To give his name, would do him a disservice. With this new lawyer, I sued Dennis over his fee and had it reduced by S$31,000 (US$19,000).

Recently, Dennis surfaced in *The Straits Times*. He was caught, and confessed his guilt of "improper conduct" over his sexual relationship back in 1995 with his client, Angela. The charges against Dennis showed he was shacking up with Angela in Kuala Lumpur, Malaysia, the day I was beating up Tien Hua for not having my affidavit ready.

On November 24, 2000, Dennis was hauled into the court of Chief Justice Yong Pung How for sentencing. The Chief Justice suspended Dennis from the practice of law for three years and charged him with costs for the case.

The Straits Times reported that Dennis had paid Angela S$200,000 (US$141,000), supposedly for breaking off the affair, but it sounds more like hush money to me.

In closing, *The Straits Times* referred to Dennis as a "serial womanizer." Maybe there is a God, after all.

Tien Hua Koh

Tien Hua has left Rodyk & Davidson, but has found his niche, specializing in matrimonial cases. He has become, in fact, Singapore's answer to Dr. Laura.

The Straits Times, on June 4, 2000, in an article entitled, *Breaking Up Is Easy To Do*, quotes Tien Hua extensively, "'Sometimes, fact is stranger than fiction,' said Mr. Tien Hua Koh, a lawyer who has handled many divorces. 'Young couples sometimes rush into marriage and don't think of the consequences.'"

Yes, Mr. Koh, sometimes fact is stranger than fiction, especially when you're on the case.

Joan Lai

Living happily with her American husband, and their son Michael, in, of all places, Peoria, Illinois.

"If it plays in Peoria, it will play anywhere."

Swee Cheong Lim

Swee Cheong's wife died in 1998, and he now lives with his youngest son and his son's wife in Singapore, and tells me he's writing lyrics for an American rock group. A cancer survivor since 1981, he is preparing a new edition of his book, *Dawn Breaks Upon the Darkest Hour*.

The Children

None of them are really children anymore.

Marc is in college; Warren is in high school. Both Marc and Warren have had their passports cancelled by the Singapore Embassy in Washington, for failure to post bonds of US$50,000 each to buy the privilege of deferring their two and a half year military service in Singapore.

Stefano and William are computer jocks in Silicon Valley, and Domitilla lives in London with her husband and their three sons.